THE FLETCHER JONES FOUNDATION
HUMANITIES IMPRINT

The Fletcher Jones Foundation has endowed this imprint to foster innovative and enduring scholarship in the humanities.

The publisher gratefully acknowledges the generous support of the Fletcher Jones Foundation Humanities Endowment Fund of the University of California Press Foundation.

The Country of Football

SPORT IN WORLD HISTORY

Edited by Susan Brownell, Robert Edelman, Wayne Wilson, and Christopher Young

This University of California Press series explores the story of modern sport from its recognized beginnings in the nineteenth century to the current day. The books present to a wide readership the best new scholarship connecting sport with broad trends in global history. The series delves into sport's intriguing relationship with political and social power, while also capturing the enthusiasm for the subject that makes it so powerful.

The Country of Football

SOCCER AND THE MAKING OF MODERN BRAZIL

Roger Kittleson

UNIVERSITY OF CALIFORNIA PRESS

BERKELEY LOS ANGELES LONDON

University of California Press, one of the most distinguished university presses in the United States, enriches lives around the world by advancing scholarship in the humanities, social sciences, and natural sciences. Its activities are supported by the UC Press Foundation and by philanthropic contributions from individuals and institutions. For more information, visit www.ucpress.edu.

University of California Press
Berkeley and Los Angeles, California

University of California Press, Ltd.
London, England

Library of Congress Cataloging-in-Publication Data

Kittleson, Roger Alan.
  The country of football : soccer and the making of modern Brazil / Roger Kittleson.
      pages   cm.—(Sport in world history; 2)
  Includes bibliographical references and index.
  ISBN 978-0-520-27908-7 (hardback) — ISBN 978-0-520-27909-4 (pbk) — ISBN 978-0-520-95825-8 (ebook)
    1. Soccer—Brazil—History.   2. Soccer players—Brazil—History.
3. Brazil—Social life and customs.   I. Title.
  GV944.B7K57   2014
  796.3340981—dc23

                                                     2013046594

Manufactured in the United States of America
23   22   21   20   19   18   17   16   15   14
10   9   8   7   6   5   4   3   2   1

In keeping with a commitment to support environmentally responsible and sustainable printing practices, UC Press has printed this book on Natures Natural, a fiber that contains 30% post-consumer waste and meets the minimum requirements of ANSI/NISO Z39.48–1992 (R 1997) (*Permanence of Paper*).

For Zayde

CONTENTS

ILLUSTRATIONS

ACKNOWLEDGMENTS

The idea of writing about *futebol* first occurred to me when I was starting my career as a historian of Brazil. In the two decades it has taken for that initial idea to become this book, I have relied on more people than I can mention here. No assistance or offer of help, however, has gone unappreciated, so let me begin with a general thanks to all those who have contributed to my formation as a Brazilianist.

Most of my professional life has been spent at Williams College, and the debts I have incurred there are many and deep. Three separate deans of the faculty—Tom Kohut, Bill Wagner, and Peter Murphy—have overseen the structural and financial backing Williams has given my research. Peter, along with college president Adam Falk, stepped in to allow me the time and space necessary to finish the book, and I am especially grateful to them for this vital support. I have been fortunate to work with extraordinary colleagues in the History Department and the Latina/o Studies Program, who have not only challenged me to sharpen my analysis but have also served as models of engaged teachers and scholars. Tom Kohut has most consistently pushed me to clarify my project, while Magnus Bernhardsson has shared information and articles on soccer from the Middle East and other regions. Eiko Maruko Siniawer, meanwhile, has been a wonderfully effective department chair in the last phase of this project. My Latina/o Studies colleagues, particularly Carmen Whalen and Mérida Rúa, have helped me to think about historical processes in more complex, transnational ways. Like friends in History and other units at Williams, they have also been sources of much-needed humor and moral support. I am grateful as well to the students from my sports history courses for the thoughtful questions and analyses that forced me to consider new perspectives on soccer in Latin America and around the world.

Everywhere I carried out research for this book, I benefited from the knowledge and efforts of research librarians and archivists. In São Paulo the staff of the Arquivo do Estado, the Biblioteca Municipal, and the Museu do Futebol lent their expertise on repeated occasions. Their counterparts at the Arquivo Nacional, the Biblioteca Nacional, and the Museu da Imagem e do Som in Rio de Janeiro did likewise in the latter stages of my project. I found more than I had dared hope in the United States, with the able assistance of research specialists at the Charles E. Young Research Library and the Southern Regional Research Facility at UCLA, the American Folk Life Reading Room and the general collection of the Library of Congress, the Yale University Library, and the Brown University Library. Closer to home, Alison O'Grady and her Interlibrary Loan team in Sawyer Library at Williams seemed to perform miracles when I most needed them.

Friends old and new also gave me crucial support during the research process. In São Paulo, Carlos Jorge Vogel helped me find my way in the megalopolis and shared many entertaining meals. Kika Vogel Sangiorgi made vital connections for me, as well as driving me through the city's intimidating traffic. Wagner Correa shared his own experiences as a soccer player and coach and introduced me to other *boleiros*. In Rio, Arno Vogel introduced me to a very different city with his acute ethnographic eye and regaled me with fantastic stories of soccer. More recently, Cesar Oliveira welcomed me into his home and showed his fabulous Arthur Friedenreich collection to me. He has such warmth and commitment to the study of *futebol* that he would have done this even if I were not a Botafogo supporter. José Inácio Werneck, whose *Jornal do Brasil* columns I had long enjoyed, became a generous source of information and contacts after I discovered that we had both migrated to central Connecticut. Other friends, colleagues, and mentors whose kindness and guidance helped me through the long journey of research and writing include Anne Hanley, Brenda Elsey, Devyn Spence Benson, Felicity Skidmore, Jeff Lesser, Jerry Dávila, Jim Green, Joe Chambers, Joel Wolfe, the late John Monteiro, Karl Monsma, Linda Saharczewski, Maria Helena Machado, Megan Konieczny, Paulo Roberto Staudt Moreira, Peter Beattie, Silvia Maria Fávero Arend, Stefanie Chambers, Sueann Caulfield, and Tom Skidmore.

Sueann was among those who gave me feedback on the manuscript itself. She and Bryan McCann both read an early chapter and gave me excellent suggestions on the project as a whole. Joel Wolfe took on the arduous task of reading the entire manuscript, bringing to bear his profound knowledge of modernity and popular culture in Brazil. His comments were at once conceptually challenging and concretely practical, a rare combination indeed. My thanks also go to the two readers who gave their careful attention to the manuscript for the Press; their corrections and recommendations were invaluable. Many others gave me input on the early and partial versions of my research presented in lectures and conference papers. Among those whose interest and insight meant the most are Betsy Lasch-Quinn, Brian Bunk, Bryan McCann, Celso Castilho, Cesar Augusto Barcellos Guazelli, Cláudia Mauch, Claudia Wasserman, Eric Galm, Joel Wolfe, Josh Nadell, Karin Rosemblatt, Norman Kutcher, Regina Célia Lima Xavier, Silvia Petersen, Todd Diacon, and Zach Morgan.

None of this work, though, would have evolved into a book without the wise counsel of my editors. Executive Editor Niels Hooper helped me define a track and keep to it. From proposal through production, he used his experience and sagacity to lead me past obstacles, all with the deadline of the 2014 World Cup looming. Kim Hogeland made the book happen with her eagle eye and endless good will, while Rose Vekony guided me on the last logistical march to publication. But it is the four series editors—Bob Edelman, Chris Young, Susan Brownell, and Wayne Wilson—who deserve my deepest professional gratitude. They brought me into their exciting new series as it was taking shape and gave me excellent and timely advice over the past two years. Chris has been my most frequent contact of the four, and his good humor and graciousness have cheered and inspired me. All four championed and challenged me, encouraging me to take intellectual chances. Their guidance improved the book in many ways, and their collaborative efforts put the lie to all clichés about the work of committees.

My family has always been my most powerful source of support. My parents, Jean and Russell Kittleson, introduced my brothers and me to Brazil early on. Although it has been a long while since we were all there together, their endless encouragement has seen me through wonderful times and rough patches alike. Zayde and Edwin Child and Phoebe Antrim have expressed their enthusiasm in many exciting discussions in many beautiful settings. My son, August, has lately become a "wall" in the center of his soccer team's defense, and he is always the joy of his parents' lives. Sharing a life with Zayde Antrim and benefitting from her supple mind and loving heart is a blessing that brings happiness to all the mundane and magnificent details of our days and years together.

Serious Play

Nothing is cheaper as an education than sports, and nothing
more political in this country than soccer.

SÓCRATES

Shortly after his appointment as manager of the Seleção (Brazil's national
soccer team) in August 2010, Mano Menezes proclaimed that his mission was
to make Brazil a "protagonist" once again on the world stage. As encouraging
as this was, most observers were even more pleased when he said he would
accomplish this by embracing the true national style. After all, he explained,
"The world is playing soccer closer to the Brazilian way than we are."[1] Coming
as the country was beginning its preparations to host the 2014 World Cup,
the pressure to win in a convincingly Brazilian manner was intense. In this
context, his pledge was a deft first touch.

Mano's words conjured up the familiar image of Brazil as "the country of
football" (*o país do futebol*). This is not, of course, a universally accepted position. Other nations covet the special status that Brazil holds in the global
game, and their fans have often made compelling cases for the supremacy of
the teams they support. Such challenges have not, however, seriously dam-
aged Brazil's reputation as the source of the best soccer in the world. It has
long been a common trope for sports journalists around the world to use
phrases like "a bit of Brazilian flair" to describe any skillful pass or dribble.
Such stereotypes draw on Brazil's unmatched record of international success.
The only country to have participated in every single World Cup tournament, Brazil was the first to win three times and added two more victories in
1994 and 2002. Perhaps more central to celebrations of Brazilian soccer,
though, is the country's fame as the birthplace of *craques* (stars, from the
English "crack" players), whose supposedly innate skills allow them to perform in a unique, fluid way. In other words, Brazil reigns as the country of
football because of the championships it has won and the exuberance and
creativity its players have displayed in their victories.

Being the country of football clearly comes with almost impossibly high expectations. Memories of the Brazil sides that managed to delight spectators while conquering titles—especially the World Cup winners of 1958, 1962, and, above all, 1970—bring joy to fans but also impose incredible burdens on all those who dare to serve on the Seleção. It is not enough for the national team to beat its adversaries; it must overwhelm them with sheer talent.[2] Anything short of this ideal carries a hint of defeat. Understandably, most versions of the national team have failed in one way or another. Some played well before losing to Italian, Uruguayan, French, or—worst of all—Argentine foes; others defeated all comers, taking the grandest of trophies but doing so without displaying creativity; the poorest sides delivered neither titles nor entertaining soccer. These last teams went down in the history of *futebol* as not only weak but also profoundly un-Brazilian.

Soccer, like samba and Carnaval, has proved "excellent terrain" for the cultivation of a national identity.[3] All of these iconic cultural practices have both reflected and contributed to processes of national definition singling out Afro-Brazilianness as an essential element of *brasilidade* (Brazilianness). Unlike samba and Carnaval, though, soccer has pitted representatives of Brazil against those of rival nations. This is, in fact, one of the traits that make soccer particularly useful in the formulation of a collective sense of what it means to be Brazilian. Played everyday and almost everywhere, the sport's highest competitions take place at regular intervals in mega-events that draw enormous, global audiences. The specific actions that make up World Cup matches have no intrinsic meaning, but the context of tournaments in which national teams clash before billions of viewers makes them ripe for epic narration. With so much symbolically (not to mention financially) at stake, an errant pass might easily become a mistake that lets the nation down, while a last-minute goal might become the salvation of national honor.[4] At the same time, however, soccer enjoys an apparent cultural innocence. It is just a game and thus does not seem a serious subject, which helps explain why something so ubiquitous as to be part of "the obvious" in Brazil has remained relatively understudied until recently.[5] The triviality of soccer also means that people feel free to talk about politically dangerous issues in apparently apolitical ways. A lot of soccer talk, of course, amounts to little more than *conversa fiada* (chitchat), but even simple jousting over the performance of clubs and players can touch on complex problems confronting members of communities across the country. Everyday conversations about soccer, with their casual consideration of serious issues, are one way that

Brazilians think about the nation—and by extension their place in it—in the face of persistent social, economic, and political uncertainties.[6]

The deceptive lightness of soccer talk first struck me at the start of the 1990s, when I was living in Rio de Janeiro and Porto Alegre. I knew Brazil well, having grown up with strong family connections to the country and having traveled through much of it. The importance of soccer was not lost on me. I had seen city streets painted in the national colors of yellow and green during a World Cup, had witnessed the passion (and learned some useful curses) at soccer games in São Paulo, and had made a pilgrimage to Maracanã Stadium in Rio. In 1982, on the occasion of my twentieth birthday, my brother Gary and I had the great privilege of meeting Pelé at his apartment, an encounter that left me utterly starstruck. No details of the conversation survive in my memory, only the impression of this famous man's incredibly friendly and down-to-earth manner. It was not soccer, however, that led me back to Brazil in 1990. By that time I was a fledgling Brazilianist studying the politics of daily life, but my research focused on a period before soccer's ascension in Brazil. Although this work made me familiar with generations of scholarship about race formation in the country, I was still surprised by the blatantly racialized complaints about the Seleção from 1990 to 1992.

It was shocking to hear how openly journalists argued that Brazilian soccer was deteriorating because it had too few Afro-Brazilian players or bemoaned the destruction of empty lots (*várzeas*) where poor kids had learned to play in pickup games. Prominent figures across the media made explicit connections between Afro-Brazilianness and national culture; exponents of these views were demanding that the nation rely on the largely Afro-Brazilian *povo* (people or common folk) and its allegedly inherent abilities. At the same time, however, those hailed as the source of authentic *futebol* were often treated as criminals—or at least potential criminals—by the government and the press, particularly in the early 1990s, years of escalating violence on the streets of Rio and other cities.[7] The explicitness of that racial commentary stuck with me as a reminder to listen critically to even the most banal discussions of soccer.

RACE AND THE TROPICAL-MODERN

The overriding reason that expressions of overt racism were acceptable in Brazil, acquaintances in the United States and Brazil have told me over the years, is that the country does not have a racist culture, certainly not a U.S.-style one. Without real racism, the logic goes, references to racial markers cannot be as offensive as they would be in a society riven by racially based conflict. This is a longstanding argument against critics of race relations in Brazil; the allegation is that historians and other observers merely transpose understandings of race from one country to another, seeing tension or even hatred where none exists.[8] Of course, Afro-Brazilian activists and Brazilian scholars have denounced racial discrimination in their nation since the nineteenth century. Some of the most influential critiques came out of Unesco-funded studies in the 1950s and '60s, but before and since that wave of scholarship individuals and groups have protested the image of racial harmony that became a pillar of national identity.[9] Scholars working in various disciplines since the 1950s have established that the country's notions of race have in fact sanctioned prejudice and discrimination throughout the history of independent Brazil. Race relations may feel cordial and exhibit flexibility—with certain contexts displaying harder racism than others—but overall racial hierarchies permeate society.[10]

Soccer appeared in the country at a time of uncertainty, when the connections between race and Brazil's modernity were taking on new shapes. One of the cultural influences that flowed outward from England to both its formal colonies and its informal empire in the late nineteenth and early twentieth centuries, the game appeared as Brazil was negotiating its very late abolition of slavery (1888) and experiencing the growth of cities, incipient industrialization, and wider contacts with the vibrant economies of the North Atlantic.[11] The range of transitions affecting the country in these years brought into high relief key questions that would trouble Brazilian politicians, artists, intellectuals—anyone trying to define the nation. Almost all of these thinkers accepted Europe as a model of modern civilization; the question, though, was how European they could make Brazil. Some efforts suggested a will to Europeanize, most notably through programs that promoted the arrival of millions of German, Italian, Portuguese, Spanish, and other immigrants, as well as through urban reforms aimed at reshaping Rio into the Paris of South America. By the first decades of the twentieth century, however, many voices in Brazil argued for the need to pursue a more organically Brazilian modernity, one that would include more of the population and perhaps forge the common folk into a proper people instead of a primitive mass undeserving of an active role in national affairs. This new Brazilian Brazil would be both tropical and modern.[12]

At no point, however, did a static tropical-modern *brasilidade* appear. Modernity is always and everywhere a moving target, of course, and the pursuit of a modernity appropriate to Brazil took different shapes across the long historical sweep from the late nineteenth to the early twenty-first century.[13] In each period, though, the question of modernity generated frustrations and tensions. Embracing a tropical modernity meant recognizing a distance between Brazil and the Europe that local elites had romanticized; at its base, it required conceding that Brazil had to find its own path. It also implied an approximation to the people that many of these same elites thought distasteful and perhaps dangerous. This dual process, as Roberto Ventura and Florencia Garramuño have framed it, obliged Brazilians to exoticize themselves.[14] However exciting it may have been, the exotic was a frightening foundation for a nation. After all, it was by definition a negative construction; Brazilian culture was exotic insofar as it was not normal and European. Although they did not throw off European models entirely, Brazilian thinkers sought a primordial basis for their own nation, something that would allow them to define Brazilian identity as separate from, but just as potent as, the European countries that dominated the early twentieth-century world (or as much of it as interested these American elites). This quest for a "usable past" paralleled the actions of European nationalists, and the artistic and intellectual approaches the Brazilians adopted drew on European forms. In the end, Brazilian elites found themselves in the uncomfortable position of celebrating people and practices they habitually considered primitive, in order to construct a unified, modern nation capable of competing against European powers.[15]

SOCCER IN MODERN BRAZIL

Soccer was one of the areas in which the formation of a tropical-modern *brasilidade* occurred, and thus the stresses and conflicts that marked the wider history of Brazil in the "long twentieth century" also defined the history of *futebol*. This is not to say that "the knowledge of Brazil comes through soccer"; soccer is just one possible path toward such understanding.[16] At the same time, however, soccer is one of the practices that "make Brazil, Brazil."[17] In part this means that soccer metaphors have factored into discussions over the meaning of *brasilidade* for more than a century and that arguments about soccer have reflected broader political and social trends. Much less frequently, the sport also became the site of more active interventions in national debates, with players, journalists, and officials from the world of soccer participating in political and social movements *as* football figures.

The project of constructing tropical modernity came together over the first half of the twentieth century. This was a period in which soccer became a cultural world unto itself, with more people playing it around the country, growing attendance at the ever-larger stadiums that were built, and the emergence of a language of *futebol* not only in casual conversation but also in the printed press and later on the radio. This expansion engendered anxieties among those who had considered "foot-ball" the exclusive domain of white, privileged men. By the 1930s and '40s, however, the game had become part of popular culture. As such, it became subject to analysis by journalists and scholars who formulated notions of a distinctive national style; the centralizing government of the time embraced the vision of a Brazilian soccer that grew out of and integrated the people. It was in these decades that the national style was born, not so much on the soccer field as in the discussions of what went on there.

Conceptions of *brasilidade* in soccer depended on theories that Brazil had a mixed-race culture. Africans and Amerindians as well as Europeans had made telling "contributions" to many areas of Brazilian civilization, in the patronizing formulations of thinkers like the sociologist Gilberto Freyre. Authentic *brasilidade,* though, lay not in any of the individual peoples who had met in this vast American territory, but rather in the mixture they had produced. In this sense, the national culture was by definition *mestiço* (mixed Amerindian-European) or mulatto (mixed African-European). The style of soccer that developed in the country reflected this miscegenation, with Freyre and most other proponents of this approach emphasizing the African underpinnings of the Brazilian game. Not only Afro-Brazilians but all Brazilians had become culturally mulatto, in this line of analysis. Freyre argued that *futebol* resembled a sensual dance, a similarity that derived from "the influence . . . of Brazilians of African blood, or those who are markedly African in their culture: they are the ones who tend to reduce everything to dance."[18] Not all the influential descriptions of the national style shared Freyre's explicit fascination with race, but those depicting *futebol* as "the consummate expression of the Brazilian people" or of Brazil as "the country of football with samba in its veins" also conveyed racial meanings.[19]

In theory, the concept of a mulatto football was highly inclusionary. All Brazilians, wherever their predecessors had come from, were effectively *mes-*

tiço or mulatto and thus shared in the creation of the national style.[20] This was also a notably homogenizing notion, since it asserted that authentic *brasilidade* had only come into being through blending; a mixed-race culture, on the soccer pitch and more widely, made few allowances for the preservation of distinct, subnational identities. This meant in practice that assertions of separate Afro-Brazilian experiences and visions for the nation, for example, could be labeled antinational insofar as they refused to accept the ideal of a new Brazilian civilization that subsumed distinct races.[21]

This integrative ideal was never free of internal divisions, and evidence of the persistent differences and mistrust among Brazilians surfaced in the 1950s. The trauma of losing at home in the final game of the 1950 World Cup led to a flare-up of antiblack sentiments in some corners. Tensions continued beneath the surface in the subsequent golden age of Brazilian soccer, when the country won three out of four World Cups. The champions of 1958, 1962, and 1970 were not all *mestiço* or Afro-Brazilians, but they played in a way that seemed proof of the triumphant *mulatismo* (mulatto-ism) of Brazilian soccer. Moreover, they projected a physical image of tropical-modern progress on the field, with the *preto* (black) midfielder Didi leading the 1958 team, the *mestiço* Garrincha taking over in 1962, and Pelé, also *preto*, looming above all others throughout these years. Whiter players, from Bellini to Rivellino and Tostão, also played key roles and seemed to prove that even light-skinned Brazilians were mulatto in some essential way. Blackness—or brownness—remained a vital sign, however, of the overall mixture.[22]

The qualities associated with blackness were at once the source of great pride and grave doubts. The mental liveliness and the physical plasticity that were allegedly innate to Afro-Brazilians were fundamental to the *jogo bonito* (beautiful game). These traits made possible the improvisation and creativity that Garrincha, Pelé, and other *craques* employed to bedevil opponents. The proper attitude was also necessary, however, for Brazilians to perform artistically; they had to display an innocent love of the game (*alegria*) while also drawing on the guile of the lower-class trickster (*malandro*). In short, the beautiful game depended on a range of attributes that featured in stereotypes of the mixed-race *povo*. Such primitive, instinctive, and childlike qualities, though, provoked anxieties among many of the officials and thinkers preoccupied with achieving tropical modernity. Particularly in a period of grand nationalist development, first under democratic administrations in the late 1950s and early '60s and then under dictatorship (1964–85), the men in charge of soccer came to worry that some guidance and control from above was necessary to harness the abilities of the *povo*. Evident in the preparations for the 1958 World Cup, initiatives to control the natural gifts of the masses grew by the 1970s into a full-blown reorganization of soccer culture in Brazil. With scientific training and tactics adapted from European football, reformers sought to impose a mature rationality onto players they considered worryingly backward.

Thus the tensions inherent in tropical modernity exploded in the 1970s and '80s. Instead of a quick victory for a new vision of Brazilian modernity, one based more firmly on the restraint or possible removal of the tropical and primitive, what followed was a battle between *futebol-força* (strength soccer) on one side and *futebol-arte* (art soccer) on the other. Advocates of *futebol-arte* harkened back to the glories that past heroes had brought the country and expressed confidence that new heroes would inevitably be revealed. Their *futebol-força* opponents, by contrast, argued that soccer and the world in general had changed so dramatically that Brazil, once more, was playing catch-up. Each side had its turns in power. Neither, though, showed itself capable of reestablishing Brazil's dominance in the global game. The best showings at the level of the Seleção came through *arte,* though only in the tragically beautiful defeats in the 1982 and 1986 World Cups. The clubs Flamengo and Corinthians, both teams of the masses, linked *futebol-arte* to democracy in the early 1980s, in the process providing the country's greatest footballing triumphs in these years and demonstrating that the game could enter broad political movements in direct and vigorous ways.

The dispute never disappeared completely but fell to a low simmer by the 1990s. On the field, Brazilian teams moved toward safe, pragmatic styles, with defense and counterattacking as their guiding precepts. Two more World Cup victories by the Seleção bolstered the old image of the country of football, but its connection to the nation grew more complex. The beautiful game based on the capabilities of the *povo* has survived largely as an abstraction. Coaches like Mano Menezes continue to pledge fealty to it, and journalists and fans from around the world recall the peaks it has reached; its most vibrant expressions, though, have occurred in the world of marketing. Brazil reached a welcome—if not complete—stability in the mid-1990s, after nearly a decade of political, economic, and social crises that marred the transition from dictatorship to democracy. Coming in the midst of the rise of the new globalism, this achievement allowed the country to attain an unprecedented status as one of the emerging powers in the new world economy. Along with this global position have come the diversification and intensification of cultural as well as financial links on an international scale. The country of football has survived but on different terms. From the mid-1990s on, Brazil became above all a brand that multinational corporations as well as Brazilian politicians and companies promoted and sought to exploit. The unified image of the mixed-race nation became in large part a marketing tool. At the same time, the plurality of Brazilian national identity became more pronounced; the country moved toward multiethnic visions of *brasilidade*.[23]

FORGING A FUTURE WITHOUT NOSTALGIA?

My focus in this book is on how people thought about soccer and, through it, about the nation. Most of the conversations that Brazilians have had about the sport during its transformation from the imported "foot-ball" into Brazilian *futebol* and then into "brand Brazil," of course, went unrecorded, perhaps even unremembered by those who participated in them. Much soccer talk, however, made it into lasting print, audio, video, and electronic formats. Guided and at times goaded by generations of scholarship on Brazilian soccer, I have plumbed newspapers, magazines, memoirs, government publications, popular poetry and music, interviews, films and videos, and blogs and other internet sites for debates about soccer and the modernization of Brazil. The story I have put together from these various materials traces the sport's trajectory as a central cultural feature of modern Brazil.

In its most basic form, this story follows a distinct arc. Soccer expanded throughout the population, gained recognition as the national sport and thus the reflection of authentic Brazilian culture. In this process Brazil emerged as the country of football by the late 1950s, shored up its claim to this title by winning major tournaments and creating a unique style of play, and held on even as exhibitions on the field made the description seem at best a facile romanticism, at worst an unscrupulous marketing ploy. Each segment of this arc, though, was marked by deep cultural work, as Brazilians argued over who should be permitted in official leagues and on the national team and what sort of soccer those selected (hence, Seleção, or "selection") should play. These discussions touched at least implicitly and metaphorically on the composition and modernizing potential of the people and the nation.

In order to present the changing debates over soccer and nation, each of my chapters focuses on individual *craques,* presenting their experiences in the contexts of the dominant discourses of their era. The first chapter examines three early Afro-Brazilian greats—Arthur Friedenreich, Domingos da Guia, and Leônidas da Silva—as key figures in the invention of both a Brazilian national style of play and an ideal of tropical modernity. At the core of the second chapter are three heroes of the golden age (1958–70): Didi, Garrincha, and Pelé. The stories of their successes on the field and the scrutiny they came under off the field played out against debates about how the nation could achieve the maturity necessary to become a true world power. Doubts about the reliability of the common folk as the foundation of modernization appeared in this era but came to define the 1970s and '80s. These two decades are the subjects of chapters three and four, in which the frustrations and triumphs of Ademir da Guia, Reinaldo, and Paulo Cézar Caju in the 1970s and of Zico and Sócrates in the 1980s tied into wide-ranging debates about the place of the mixed-race *povo* in the nation during a dictatorship and the gradual move to democracy. The final chapter looks at the fate of the country of football and its tropical-modern project in the age of new globalism, when intense transnational flows of capital and information forced reformulations of local and national identities. Here Romário, Ronaldo, and Ronaldinho Gaúcho are joined by Ricardo Teixeira, the "boss of bosses" in *futebol* administration, in the analysis of the mutation of the beautiful, artful Brazilian style within the ever more commercialized and international business of soccer.

Set against the grand debates of their day, the careers of these stars illustrate the repeated reinvention—and not the progressive dissolution—of an ideal of *brasilidade*. The vision of a mixed-race civilization that gave rise to a sumptuous style of soccer has persisted into the twenty-first century, even as it verges on the anachronistic.[24] Contradictions, however, have always been present in depictions of the *jogo bonito* and *futebol-arte,* as well as of "the country of football." Implicit on all of these, after all, is the assertion that race and other social relations are fluid and cordial in Brazil, since the national game has given, as Roberto DaMatta has written, a "potent lesson in democracy."[25] Certainly *futebol* has been a space of relatively soft social relations, in which racism especially has generally taken milder forms than in other contexts. Moreover, as supporters of their clubs and the Seleção, Brazilians have been able to forge at least temporary and contextual bonds across lines of power that divide them in their everyday lives.[26] At the same time, though, the gap between what *futebol* promises and the lived reality of hierarchy and social injustice was never lost on Brazilians—certainly not those on the receiving end of discrimination.[27]

The history of Brazilian soccer has included not only exceptional players and teams, but also an evolving sense of exceptionalism. Soccer has served as a realm in which Brazilians have negotiated their way toward a collective sense of a distinct and integrated nationality. The ascent of "mulatto football" in the 1930s and '40s, along with the various reconfigurations of the national style that emerged in later periods, provided a language through which different people could imagine themselves part of a tropical-modern future for Brazil. Only in this unrealized future, though, could soccer, or Brazilian culture in general, deliver unqualified equality and democracy. This is not to suggest that warm recollections of authentic *futebol* be thrown out, just that they be tempered with a critical assessment of the conflicts and the inequalities that characterized its construction.[28]

ONE

A National Game

FUTEBOL MADE POPULAR, PROFESSIONAL,
AND AFRO-BRAZILIAN

May the Leônidases and the Domingoses
Fix on the stranger's retina
The miraculous reality
That is Brazilian man

GILKA MACHADO, 1934

On 13 June 1950, choruses of the joyously silly song "Touradas de Madri" (Bullfights of Madrid) reverberated around the concrete bowl of Rio's Maracanã Stadium. With the beat—"pá-rá-rá-tim-bum-bum-bum"—seeming to match the rhythm of the home side's passing, more than 150,000 spectators gloried in the Seleção's 6–1 demolition of the Spanish national team.[1] Three days later, a crowd approaching 200,000 people—proudly but exaggeratedly trumpeted as 10 percent of the city's population—gathered with every expectation that the celebration would continue on in the final game against Uruguay. The climate of anticipation extended onto nearby streets, where samba schools stood ready to burst into a special Carnaval of victory.[2] This time, though, the match ended in the host's defeat and a stifling silence. While FIFA (Fédération Internationale de Football Association) officials quickly ushered the victorious Uruguayans through the presentation of the Jules Rimet Trophy, Brazilians sat stunned, some crying, many just staring, and one allegedly dying of shock-induced heart failure.[3] Fans in the stands and others hearing the news elsewhere shared the feeling that Brazil's star midfielder Zizinho expressed with one of his characteristically pithy phrases: "The world collapsed on me."[4] Pelé, then a nine-year-old who idolized "Mestre Ziza" (Master Ziza, as Zizinho was often called), later recalled that he, too, had "participated in that immense sadness." Sitting in front of the family's large box radio with his father in Bauru, São Paulo, he had the impression that the defeat was "the end of a war, with Brazil the loser and many people killed."[5]

The event known as the Maracanazo—the word is often left in Spanish, a linguistic concession to Uruguay's triumph—came as devastating shock. Hosting the World Cup had promised a home-field advantage as well as the opportunity to demonstrate the country's ascent to the realm of modern nations. Planners intended the site of the final, Maracanã, to be the world's largest stadium and thus a monument to Brazilian progress. In fact, the construction of Maracanã had not been complete when the tournament began. Over the course of the Cup, though, both the stadium and the nationalism focused inside it took their final forms. The Seleção bulled its way through the competition, with a 2–2 tie against Switzerland the only cause of consternation. This worry gave way to an overwhelming patriotic euphoria that made it inconceivable, as Brazil coach Flávio Costa put it, that this team, containing the greatest players in the world, might lose in "Maracanã, our field, our land."[6] As soon as Alcides Ghiggia scored Uruguay's second and winning goal, however, all of the ecstasy simply evaporated. In its place came not only disappointment but also real trauma. The defeat was an injury, a São Paulo newspaper predicted at the time, certain to leave "permanent scars."[7]

What was worse, the wound festered before it could close. Fans, journalists, and officials all cast about for a satisfactory explanation of the "tragedy of 1950" and the blow to national prestige that it had dealt. Many Brazilians, after all, considered their country an emerging power after its participation in the Allied cause during World War II and its subsequent return to democracy. Descriptions of the World Cup final as a mere footballing accident—one of the illogical events that can always happen in sports—provided no solace.[8] Too much had been riding on the country's success in this tournament; more serious explanations were necessary. In the end, the prevailing argument placed the blame on three Afro-Brazilian members of the national team—Bigode, Juvenal, and particularly Barbosa—and the qualities they supposedly embodied. Superficially, the singling out of these players was natural; Bigode and Juvenal were defenders who lost track of Ghiggia, while Barbosa was the goalkeeper who lunged the wrong way and let in the fateful goal. It was, however, unclear that they had in fact erred; the debate over whether Barbosa had committed a *frango* ("chicken," slang for a goalkeeping blunder) rages to this day. For his part, the goalie complained in 2000 that in a country where the maximum jail sentence is thirty years, he had suffered a half-century of punishment for a crime he had not committed.[9] The rest of the Seleção—including Danilo, who lost the ball before both of Uruguay's scores—got off more easily, though they were all tainted by the loss.[10] For many of their compatriots, though, what mattered was that the team—and particularly Barbosa, Bigode and Juvenal—had revealed an immaturity, an unmanliness that marked the mixed-race *povo* (people, or common folk) from which they had come. Apparently without irony, the editors of a 1950 sports almanac opined that "when things got black [*pretas,* here meaning 'tough']" in the final match, Brazil lacked the "virile game" to win.[11]

Losing this World Cup thus offered proof to many observers that Brazil and its people still had a long way to go before joining the ranks of global powers. The nation remained "the country of the future" (*o país do futuro*), a tag that reminded Brazilians that they had not yet made good on their nation's promise. The "tragedy of 1950" brought forth the more pessimistic element in Brazilian nationalism—in particular, the disdain that many in the upper classes felt toward the poor majority. This efflorescence of negativity highlighted two defining features of *futebol* in first half of the twentieth century. First off, soccer had not only become the national sport, but a key part of national culture. As the condemnations of the vanquished 1950 squad suggest, the Seleção had come to serve, in Nelson Rodrigues's famous phrase, as "the fatherland in cleats." Based on this symbolism, the performance of Brazilian teams in international soccer competitions provided a ready measure of the nation's standing vis à vis other countries. Regional rivalries—with Uruguay and especially Argentina—piqued Brazilian interest, but contests with European sides held special significance. From the very start of soccer's history in the country, Europe—not just specific teams or countries but an imagined, united Europe—represented an ideal of modern civilization that Brazil should strive to attain or, if somehow possible, overcome. Even those who rejected this goal found themselves having to frame their projects for the nation in reaction to it, so hegemonic was the appeal of European modernity.

Discussions of the Seleção's defeat in 1950 also reflected the transformations soccer had undergone since its introduction to Brazil in the late nineteenth century. The sport had risen from modest beginnings as a novel diversion to become one of the most common leisure activities of people of all classes. This popularization culminated in its acceptance as a reflection of the national spirit, but this status came only through decades of conflict. By the time that sociologist Gilberto Freyre offered his description of a distinctively Brazilian "mulatto foot-ball" in 1938, much of the revolution had passed: battles had been fought along lines of race and class, gender and region, and if a clear victory was hard to discern, a general compromise had emerged.[12]

Soccer had experienced its democratization—meaning the inclusion of men from outside the white elite in the organized game. This did not, however, eliminate social hierarchies; racial tensions in particular roiled under the surface, bursting out in circumstances more mundane than the Maracanazo. Still, the struggles of members of the *povo* and the reactions they elicited from those in power helped forge a redefinition of who could properly participate not only in *futebol* but also the nation. Soccer's expansion, in other words, formed part of the consolidation of a modern Brazil that brought a greater swath of the population together in an uneasily integrated national identity.

This revamped Brazilianness welcomed the contributions of Afro-Brazilians to the national style of soccer and, more generally, to the country's history and culture. From Arthur Friedenreich in the 1910s and '20s to Domingos da Guia and Leônidas da Silva in the 1930s and '40s, Afro-Brazilians became icons of their country's manner of playing soccer and heroes in its efforts to triumph in the global arena. The lionization of such stars was part of the creation of a tropical modern Brazil, a process underway by the 1920s and in full bloom by the 1940s. In politics and the arts, as in sports, leading figures put forward ideas for the revitalization of the country, plans designed to make Brazil as modern as old Europe but in its own way. Most often, such initiatives sought to identify the real Brazil and proposed the best means of building on the strengths—and correcting the weaknesses—thus uncovered. The criticism of three Afrodescendant footballers (Barbosa, Bigode, and Juvenal) in 1950 serves as a vital reminder of the internal fault lines in the nation's dominant myths about itself. Tropical modernism, for all its recognition of the Afro-Brazilianness of Brazil, was never free of racism and other ignoble judgments.

"VOILÀ, LE FRIEDENREICH": KINGS AND PAUPERS IN THE NEW GAME

Arthur Friedenreich is not a name redolent of a tropical Brazil or the *jogo bonito* (beautiful game), at least not to the uninitiated. One of his nicknames—El Tigre—comes a bit closer, though of course it is in Spanish and not Portuguese and thus misses the mark as well. In fact, though, Friedenreich (also known simply as "Fried") was an Afro-Brazilian forward whose performance over a long career on the field, as a player from 1910 to 1935 and as a referee for many years thereafter, made him one of the first great stars of Brazilian soccer. Indeed, when the Club Atlético Paulistano made the first European excursion by a Brazilian club in 1925, it was Fried whom fans recognized at the port in Cherbourg. As the Brazilian players passed from their ship toward the train that would carry them to Paris, one fashionably dressed young man with a sports magazine tucked under his arm pointed excitedly toward the lanky striker and exclaimed simply, "Voilà, le Friedenreich."[13]

The 1925 journey of Paulistano created excitement and curiosity in France and turned into a tremendous success for the prestige of Brazilian soccer.[14] On a stopover in Rio, Fried declared that he and his teammates would do "all that we can on behalf of Brazil." The Europeans might, he added slyly, not only witness Brazilians' ball handling skills but also perhaps even pick up a few tricks.[15] Paulistano lived up to Fried's bold words. Powered by his eleven goals, the club won eight of its ten matches in Portugal, France, and Switzerland and generated great interest in Europe and pride at home.[16] Their two losses came at the hands of small clubs, but their victories included two defeats of the French national side—the first a 7–2 pasting—and one of the Swiss national team. When news of the first great win over the French team reached Rio, crowds took the streets in celebration.[17] In Paris, the triumphs over France were enough to inspire the newspaper *Le Journal* to dub the Paulistano team "les rois du football" (the kings of soccer). The "clean" and "efficient" game of the Paulistanos earned plaudits even in more measured newspaper accounts, with the "dribblings" of Fried and his attacking companion Araken standing out.[18] Such displays of skill on the trip foreshadowed the glorification of a fluid, specifically Brazilian style that European as well as Brazilian observers would note in the 1938 World Cup. That Cup came too late for Fried; he had retired in 1933. Nevertheless, the trajectory of his career, with the Paulistano excursion coming in his peak, captured many of the stresses that accompanied the expansion of soccer in Brazil, from the early domination of elite white men to the increasing participation of men of color and of the lower classes and on to the full professionalization of the sport. El Tigre, a mulatto with an ambivalent attitude toward his race, a dapper sportsman who exhibited the manners of an elite gentleman but played for pay in the years of false amateurism, lived out many of the conflicts and contradictions of this transitional period.

Fried was born just two years before the mythical introduction of soccer to Brazil by Charles Miller, who also bore a European name that belied his Brazilian nationality. The son of a Scottish engineer and a Brazilian mother,

Miller had gone to study in England, where he gained proficiency in "Association Football," as it was properly known. Turning out for school, county, and club sides—most notably, St. Mary's, which later became Southampton FC—he had performed well enough to attract praise in newspapers, one of which described him as a "sharp left winger."[19] More impressively, his play garnered an invitation to fill in for the short-handed Corinthians when the famed English side visited Southampton. In both cricket and soccer, Corinthians held to the highest standards of a pure, gentlemanly, and amateur ethic; they rejected the notion of material gains through sports. The aim, in the sporting ethos they epitomized, was to play in a fair and rugged style that reflected the values of the old English aristocracy. They traveled widely, including trips to Brazil and other South American countries, serving as white-uniformed ambassadors of high amateurism.[20] Miller only briefly appeared for Corinthians, but he carried with him their spirit   along with an English soccer ball, some boots, and a book of official rules—on his journey home. Soon, other men followed similar paths. Oscar Cox, for instance, finished his studies in his father's home country, Switzerland, and brought his experience with soccer, along with proper equipment, back to his home in Rio. Cox's schoolmate in Switzerland and fellow Carioca (Rio native), Antônio Casemiro da Costa, joined Miller as one of the major figures in the organization of the sport in São Paulo.[21]

In truth, when men like Miller, Cox, and Costa unloaded their bags, the game had a small but scattered presence in Brazil. Foreign sailors and railroad workers had mounted casual matches before onlookers bemused by the odd, foreign kicking game. Various secondary schools, including the noble Colégio D. Pedro II, had been instructing their students in ball games, including soccer as well as the cruder *bate bolão* ("hit the big ball"), which involved smashing a ball against a wall, since about the time of the regularization of Association Football in England in 1863.[22] Young, cosmopolitan men like Miller and Cox proved energetic promoters of the game among their peers, however; they may not have delivered the game to Brazil, but they certainly worked hard to solidify its place as an acceptable leisure activity for the country's upper class.[23] In this sense, the legends that grew up around them—Miller has long been designated the father of Brazilian soccer—had some basis in fact. They were, after all, pioneering figures who pushed the game in São Paulo, Rio, and other cities; they also represented a set of values—particularly fair play and amateur spirit—that many in the local elite found appealing.[24]

By the first decade of the twentieth century, young and moneyed men had founded soccer clubs or set up soccer teams within existing social organizations in cities across Brazil. Miller presented the game to fellow members of the São Paulo Athletic Club, which consisted overwhelmingly of high-ranking British functionaries of English companies. Although the club showed greater enthusiasm for cricket than soccer, Miller managed to put together football matches in early 1895. Within seven years, São Paulo gained more elite clubs, including a team assembled by the students of the Colégio Mackenzie in 1898. German immigrant Hans Nobiling goaded Mackenzie into a game against a side—the Hans Nobiling Team—that he assembled out of acquaintances. Soon after that March 1899 game Nobiling invited these and other players to form a new club, which he wanted to name Germania, after the side he had played for before moving to Brazil. Coming from a wide range of ethnic backgrounds, however, the players opted to call themselves Sport Club Internacional, to reflect "the internationalism of the young men present at the meeting."[25] Nobiling left and, with fellow Germans and German-Brazilians, created SC Germânia a month later.[26] By the time that the Club Atlético Paulistano—Friedenreich's future side—took the field in 1901, a handful of clubs had been formed, all dominated by resident foreigners or European immigrants. Together, these elite societies made up the Liga Paulista de Futebol (Paulista Soccer League) and initiated regular competition in 1902.

Rio did not lag behind São Paulo for long. As a major port, the largest city in Brazil, and the national capital, Rio was a center of trade and political life. Its native elites eagerly affected European tastes in many realms, from literature to fashion to architecture.[27] Together with men from the city's relatively well-established colonies of European residents, the Carioca upper class experimented with soccer. Oscar Cox had introduced the game to the Payssandu Cricket Club and the Rio Cricket and Athletic Association but departed to organize a more soccer-oriented club, the famously elitist Fluminense, in 1902.[28] After losing an informal match that pitted Brazilians against Englishmen on the grounds of Payssandu, several students, sons of some of the city's most distinguished families, established Botafogo as a "foot-ball club of purely Brazilian origin."[29] More major clubs appeared by 1905, when the city received its own local league, the Liga Metropolitana de Football (LMF, Metropolitan Soccer League). Although the formation of the Rio league followed similar events in São Paulo (as well as Salvador), the Cariocas proved formidable rivals for their Paulista peers. Indeed, it was the advent of competition between Rio and São Paulo that gave added impetus to Rio's consolidation of league soccer.[30]

Parallel processes were occurring across the country. The northeastern city of Recife had its own version of Miller in Guilherme de Aquino Fonseca, who had picked up the game while studying at Cambridge University. Still farther north, São Luís do Maranhão benefited from the return of Joaquim Moreira Alves dos Santos, called "Nhôzinho," from Liverpool.[31] Elsewhere, though, clubs emerged through the efforts of enterprising Europeans and their Brazilian acquaintances.[32] In 1897, for instance, two businessmen, one German and the other English, put together a club in the southern port city of Rio Grande. Like other pioneering entities, Sport Club Rio Grande lacked rivals, so its members mostly scrimmaged among themselves or took on sides they assembled out of visiting sailors. They also traveled to nearby cities, not only looking for a game but also trying to spark the formation of competitors in the region. Their efforts paid off in the 1903 creation of two clubs dominated early on by German immigrants—Grêmio Foot Ball Porto Alegrense and Fuss-ball Porto Alegre—and others, like Sport Club Internacional, started by Brazilian and Italian-Brazilian men soon thereafter.[33]

Although soccer benefited from a large-scale rise of sports, which invaded the leisure time of Brazilian elites as never before, it also suffered the criticisms that this frenzy of activity provoked. Physical exertion had not been part of upper-class ideals in the country until the latter half of the nineteenth century. Such sports as existed among the elite tended to provide opportunities for socializing rather than demand participation. Horse racing (o turfe) was chief among these, moving from irregular events on beaches or in other open spaces to dedicated and closed tracks by the 1860s. The principal allure of the sport lay in its reputation as "the predominant taste of all civilized societies," in poet Olavo Bilac's phrase. Although the first Jockey Club in Rio failed in the 1850s, a second was inaugurated by Brazil's Emperor Dom Pedro in 1869. Together with Rio's three other tracks, the Jockey drew large publics by the close of the century and even inspired fans—male and female—to incorporate images of horses and racing equipment into their attire and sporting slang into everyday conversation.[34]

By the first decades of the twentieth century, however, horse racing lost some of its audience to other pastimes that were attracting attention. Cricket had its adherents in the English colonies of major cities. Miller's own São Paulo Athletic Club had been established as a cricket association; the names of other societies in Rio, the Payssandu Cricket Club and the Rio Cricket and Athletic Club, make clear their shared interest in the game. Newspaper advertising in the 1890s and early 1900s suggests, however, that Brazil's refined youth were experimenting with a wide range of sports; stores offered equipment for soccer, tennis, golf, baseball, roller-skating, gymnastics, fencing, and bicycling, among other activities.[35] All of these represented the new and the cosmopolitan; their rising popularity in Europe and the United States was central to this allure. Some of them, moreover, had an extra appeal in the use of technology and the physical velocity that they entailed. Bicycling and roller-skating stood out in this regard, though automobile driving (and racing) would soon overtake both in Brazil.[36]

It was rowing, however, that reigned as the "king of sports." Not only in coastal cities like Rio, but in inland cities like São Paulo as well, rowing emerged by the end of the nineteenth century as the dominant sport of the well-off. Its advantages were many. Modern because of its association with European elites, it was also accepted as the epitome of vigorous exercise. Rowers developed muscles and exhibited them in their uniforms. At the same time, the sport remained socially exclusive—in spite of the large crowds that watched regattas from shore—and seemed to bolster both individual discipline and social order. The ideal rower showed both vigor and politesse, as is clear in the description of the national champion of 1903 in the pages of *A Canoagem*. Arthur Amendoa, the magazine attested, was of "fine stature, [with the] fine complexion of an athlete, well-muscled, endowed with a very good spirit and courteous in his manners."[37] If rowing was "the sport for men," it thus produced a particular sort of man, one unafraid of showing off his modern physique. As a chronicler of the day noted, "Throughout the city, young men, ... flaunt large pectorals and thin waists and sinewy legs and a Herculean musculature in their arms."[38]

There was in fact a great deal of overlap between practitioners of soccer and other sports. Charles Miller, to take one example, won renown not only on the soccer pitch but also on the cricket field and cycling track. Even those who organized different sports often cooperated with each other, as when the governing bodies of rowing and soccer tried to avoid scheduling conflicts between the two sports in Rio in 1911.[39] Moreover, the same areas of the city were often used for multiple sporting events. Many of the early soccer matches in São Paulo, for instance, took place at the Velodrome, which the patriarch of one of the city's most prominent families had built at the behest of his cycling-mad son.[40] Finally, even those clubs that had specialized in one sport came to sponsor many more. Some of the largest soccer clubs in Rio, for instance, maintained a commitment to rowing, not to mention including the word "regatta" in their full names, reflecting their initial interest in the sport or, in the case of Botafogo (de Futebol e Regatas), their later merger with rowing groups.[41]

The simplicity of soccer and its particular pleasures, however, soon gave it a leg up. Rowing remained an activity "for the privileged, for higher beings," who could gain acceptance into the sport's social circles and afford the equipment needed to compete in regattas. In soccer, by contrast, anyone could play with just a ball and a bit of open space; official, leather balls and measured and lined fields with fixed goals were highly appreciated luxuries, but not strictly necessary, for those wanting to practice "the English game." With its running and tackling, soccer offered robust exercise, along with opportunities to display the ability to pass, dribble, and shoot.[42] The application of these skills could impel a team to victory, while also affording individuals a chance to stand out. Not only matches between elite clubs but also pick-up games (*peladas*) proliferated in cities and towns from north to south. Brazil had succumbed to a footballing fever by the 1910s.

The rapid expansion of the game put in doubt the social exclusivity that had been a hallmark of the so-called big soccer (*futebol grande*) of the elite clubs. Most of the famous clubs served as redoubts of masculine elitism, their members hewing as close to possible to their ideal of English gentlemen. They referred to themselves as "sportsmen," using the English; indeed, they preferred English terms for all elements of the game.[43] Luso-English mutations popped up; a ball could be "shootado" (close to the Portuguese *chutado*) instead of "shot," but the linguistic evolution proceeded slowly and unevenly.[44] More marked were the wealth and social status of the leaders of clubs like Fluminense. To become a member of Fluminense, Mário Filho reported, "a player had to live the same life" as Oscar Cox and his peers, "all established men, heads of firms, high ranking employees of the great [business] houses, sons of rich fathers, educated in Europe, accustomed to spending."[45] In this regard, Fluminense was no different from other clubs such as CA Paulistano or São Paulo AC; only men of "good family" and ample resources could enter.[46] For those able to become members, these clubs became another venue for their exclusive socializing. When they traveled to take part in São Paulo–Rio matches or when they fêted visiting teams from England or South Africa, for instance, they wore formal clothes—"smokings," or dinner jackets, were required. This pattern held throughout the country; regional elites enjoyed their class standing at sporting as well as more conventional social events.[47]

Nonetheless, social diversity was present from the very advent of organized soccer in Brazil. After all, featured among the clubs of the well-off were several tied to specific ethnic communities and identities. Englishness was at the heart of São Paulo AC, the Rio Cricket and Athletic Club, and many others around the country, but German, Portuguese, Spanish, Syrian, and Italian residents and immigrants set up their own clubs as well in the first decade and a half of official soccer. São Paulo, for instance, had AC Germânia among its earliest clubs, while Portuguesa de Desportos, Hespanha Foot Ball Club, Sport Club Sirio, and Palestra Itália joined it by the second half of the 1910s. Many such ethnic clubs used relatively relaxed criteria in evaluating prospective members, which only made sense in light of the small numbers that made up ethnic communities in some Brazilian cities. Palestra Itália, for example, counted small business owners, artisans, and workers among its *sócios* (members). In addition, ethnic categories like "German" and "Italian" brought together immigrants of different regional, linguistic, and religious identities.[48] Clubs like Rio Grande in the south and Internacional in São Paulo drew on various immigrant communities, while other clubs strove to be distinctly "national"—that is, made up of the Brazilian-born, as reaction against the early dominance of "foreign" organizers.[49]

The mainstream press generally ignored the unofficial, "small soccer" (*futebol pequeno*) practiced by poor white and Afro-Brazilian men. When the big newspapers took notice, they often associated working-class soccer with criminality. This was especially true of informal games in open lots (*várzeas*) in and around cities.[50] Groups of working-class players appeared in newspapers as *maltas* (mobs), a term that had been used derogatorily to refer to gangs using the Brazilian martial art capoeira in late nineteenth-century street battles.[51] More commonly, those who played outside elite clubs came to be called *varzeanos;* and *varzeanos,* in the minds of elite observers, amounted to nothing more than vagrants.[52] Labeling players vagrants did not mean that they were literally without employment or domicile; rather, it implied that they acted in a disorderly manner and failed to show proper respect for their social betters. These alleged qualities made small soccer seem "loose and insupportable," as one Bahian newspaper wrote, more a matter for police attention than a serious sporting practice.[53]

However offensive their efforts may have been to their social betters, workers and Afro-Brazilians threw themselves into the game, setting up their own clubs and leagues.[54] To a great extent, soccer became part of the lively associative life of the lower classes in cities at this time. Religious and lay societies of varying types had always been present in the country; now, with the end of slavery, rising immigration, and urbanization, the number and variety of such organizations multiplied. Members of the *povo* found not only entertainment in these groups, but also communal belonging and, often, positive political identities. Some leaders initially doubted the value of soccer; anarchists and anarcho-syndicalist organizers, for instance, argued that soccer wasted time, money, and energy that would be better spent confronting employers.[55] Over time, anarchists joined with communists and socialists in supporting this "bourgeois" sport as a tool for promoting "proletarian solidarity." Less ideologically driven organizations, moreover, adopted soccer as a useful leisure activity.[56]

The sport of soccer, it is important to emphasize, did not naturally trickle down from elites to members of the *povo*. Rather, men and women turned it into a means for the assertion of identities—of class, ethnicity, race, neighborhood. Looking back from the late 1940s, Mário Filho wrote, a player went "where his people were. And when his people had no club, the thing to do was to found one."[57] Clubs sprang up in working-class neighborhoods, often in the suburbs that surrounded the more upper-class city centers. The overwhelming sense was that urban Brazil was becoming "one vast soccer field."[58] Some of these new teams took on names that signaled their self-conscious class orientations, like Operários (Workers) FC of Campinas and Primeiro de Maio (May First) FC of Rio.[59] More commonly, though, clubs resulted from the initiative of men living and working in a particular part of the city. Sport Club Corinthians Paulista, for instance, may have adopted the title of the elegant British amateur club, but it started as just one of many *bairro* (neighborhood) teams. Meetings in the barbershop of Salvador Bataglia, in the largely Italian *bairro* of Bom Retiro, produced plans for the new sporting club; its first headquarters were located in Afonso Desidério's bar and bakery nearby. It took a few years, however, for the club to establish itself as a distinct entity; it shared many members with another Bom Retiro team called Botafogo. Among the players who took the field for Corinthians and Botafogo were a tailor, a factory worker, a house painter, a taxi driver, and a carpenter. Later one of the great teams of the masses, Corinthians slowly separated from Botafogo and climbed into the upper division of elite-controlled big soccer in the city. It did not do so, however, as an explicit political gesture; its members simply wanted to compete with the best teams.[60]

Afro-Brazilian proponents of soccer shared these desires. Nuclei of Afro-Brazilians in working-class neighborhoods produced their own teams. In

Porto Alegre, for instance, ex-slaves and other Afrodescendants had congregated in small residential areas in the Navegantes *bairro* and in the Colônia Africana (African colony) on the fringes of the downtown. From their homes, men made their way to the Campo do Bom Fim and other spaces to play soccer. When the city government granted SC Internacional a new lot on which to build a stadium, Afro-Brazilians took over the team's old field. By 1920 they had also organized their own clubs in the Liga das Canelas Pretas (Black Shins League), very much outside the jurisdiction of Porto Alegre's first and second divisions.[61] Afro-Brazilian clubs in São Paulo—such as Diamantino FC, Perdizes FC, and Aliança FC—suffered a similar fate.[62] The governing bodies of big soccer in Porto Alegre and São Paulo, like their counterparts elsewhere, shunned Afro-Brazilian teams and players.

In response to this exclusion, Afro-Brazilian sportsmen treated soccer as one more area in which to assert their value and their rights; soccer became part of alternative "black worlds" within cities like São Paulo and Salvador.[63] Forming clubs thus became a way of demonstrating pride in Afro-Brazilian culture and a strategy for "improving the race." Both Pelotas, Rio Grande do Sul, and Campinas, São Paulo, had Afro-Brazilian clubs named after the mulatto hero of abolitionism, José do Patrocínio.[64] The black press in São Paulo hailed the performance of Afro-Brazilian clubs, particularly the Associação Athlética São Geraldo (founded in 1910) and the Club Cravos Vermelhos (Red Cloves Club, founded 1916, which later became the Club Atlético Brasil). Journalists at Afro-Brazilian papers praised the on-field success of these clubs but expressed even greater satisfaction in the dedication and discipline that Afro-Brazilian players demonstrated. Much like their counterparts in the white elite, Afro-Brazilians believed sports to be ennobling and healthy; as members of a subordinate group, they simply demanded the opportunity to get the full benefits of rowing, swimming, and soccer. Players from São Geraldo and other clubs, in this sense, were offered up as proof that Afro-Brazilians had both sporting ability and social respectability—that they, and the communities from which they came, deserved full membership in the nation.[65]

Perhaps the greatest challenge to the elite clubs, however, came from factory teams—teams organized by the owners and managers of the growing number of manufacturing firms. Such clubs were concentrated, unavoidably, where industrialization first took off: Rio, São Paulo, and to a lesser extent, smaller cities like Sorocaba in the interior of São Paulo state. The most influential factory team by far was Bangu AC, or, as it was formally known, the

Bangu Athletic Club.[66] Soon enough, the club was known simply as Bangu, after its location in the hinterlands of Rio de Janeiro. In 1892 Companhia Progresso Industrial do Brasil, a Brazilian firm, had built a textile factory in the town of Bangu, bringing in English and Scottish technicians and administrators to help oversee production.[67] In 1903 these British functionaries, together with Brazilian colleagues, proposed the creation of a sports club, which would field a soccer team the following year. Perhaps encouraged by their relative isolation—Bangu felt distant from Rio, though a rail line provided a handy link—the club directors soon included regular workers in the team. The squad that took the field in 1904 against Rio Cricket counted five Englishmen, three Italians, one Portuguese, and a single Brazilian. It was this last member, Francisco Carregal, who stood out, less because of his being Brazilian and more because he was "one hundred percent *preto* [black]."[68] Bangu was not the only factory team in the Rio area with players "of color"; the textile center at Andaraí, in the city of Rio itself, had Afro-Brazilians in its factory and on its squad as well.[69] Bangu's case was more provocative, however, since the status of its directors allowed for its entrance into the rarefied heights of elite football in Rio.

The prospect of facing Carregal and other Afro-Brazilians who later joined Bangu caused distress among those who strove to preserve the sport's exclusivity. Indeed, shortly after the League reorganized itself in 1907 (as the Liga Metropolitana de Sports Athléticos, Metropolitan League of Athletic Sports), it issued a bold decree: "the directorship of the league . . . resolved by unanimous vote that persons of color will not be registered as amateurs in this league."[70] Bangu officials immediately withdrew from the league's competition, with the club's secretary declaring that he was "very happy to have left such an association."[71] This rejection of a race bar found mixed support outside Bangu. One official from Botafogo offered a particularly interesting justification for the exclusion of Afro-Brazilians. Given that political parties had broadly accepted "the principle of equality, without distinction of color or belief," he said, social and sports clubs needed to maintain the right to social and racial distinctions.[72]

Indeed, democracy was a troublesome matter for the distinguished members of elite clubs. Most of them at least tacitly accepted the formal democracy of the First Republic (1889–1930), but this was a highly restricted system that reflected the hierarchies of the age. In keeping with this orientation, they conceived of official soccer as a haven of upper-class privilege and aristocratic values. In the face of pressures from the rapid diffusion of soccer throughout society, this position made them conservative, perhaps even reactionary. At the same time, they were defending a version of modernity; their big soccer was modern in its cosmopolitanism and its links to new understandings of the body.

The spread of popular soccer, though, threatened two defining traits of the elite game: whiteness and amateurism. The paladins of official soccer often derided the illegal payment of players as "brown professionalism" (*profissionalismo marrom*); players willing to stoop to such practices, it was implied, could not be proper sportsmen and thus were not fully "white." Some champions of the old ideals continued to long for the "purity" of the amateur game even after the federal government approved professionalism in 1933 and clung to their doubts about the value of Afro-Brazilians in competitive soccer even after large clubs and the national team had come to depend on Afro-Brazilian stars.

It was in the early years of conflicts over race and professionalism that Arthur Friedenreich entered the scene in São Paulo. His father, Oscar, had moved to the Paulista capital in the late 1880s after a business failure in his hometown, the German-Brazilian city of Blumenau in the southern state of Santa Catarina. Although he set himself up nicely in São Paulo, buying a respectable home and making himself an active member of the tightly knit German and German-Brazilian community, he made a highly unconventional choice in his marriage. He fell in love with and then wed Matilde, a beautiful dark-skinned Afro-Brazilian woman who had been born into slavery.[73] As uncommon as such formal unions were among the elite, the marriage did not result in the exclusion of either Oscar or his mulatto son from decent society. Oscar entered the Club Germânia and soon brought Arthur along with him. Arthur played soccer voraciously as a child on the streets of his neighborhood, the Bairro da Luz, as so many *craques* (stars, from the English "crack" players) would do in subsequent decades. When he began to play at Germânia in 1909, he took the style of the *pelada* with him, showing improvisation and quickness with the ball. An older player, the German immigrant Hermann Friese, helped the frail-looking boy refine his shot and other skills—although Friese was known for his more brutish style of play. The result was that Fried became an exceptionally savvy as well as technical player.[74] Noted theater critic Décio Almeida remembered the "elegance" with which Fried sent "low shots into the corner of the goal," and his ability to keep dribbling forward, "almost without pausing the ball."[75] In part because Germânia favored more robust attackers—the young Arthur was lanky—he followed his footballing ambitions to another club, Ypiranga, which had just

FIGURE 1. Arthur Friedenreich in a playful moment. Collection of Cesar Oliveira/LivrosdeFutebol
.com, Rio de Janeiro.

won qualification for the São Paulo first division.[76] He went on to star at other clubs, from the short-lived Mackenzie and Payssandu sides to CA Paulistano, which enjoyed great notoriety before also passing out of existence, to São Paulo AC and Flamengo.

As his club career was just taking off, Fried was also integrated into the new national team. In 1914 he made his mark on the first Brazil squad, which took on the visiting English club Exeter City. Soon thereafter, he played for his country in the inaugural game of the Copa Roca, a regular competition between Brazil and Argentina that former Argentine president Julio Roca had proposed the previous year.[77] On both occasions, Fried distinguished himself by his skilled play and his valor, especially in the Exeter game, when he continued on after an adversary knocked out two of his teeth with a malicious high kick.[78] It was the 1919 victory, however, that proved a sea change. Coming into the tournament, many Brazilians considered their soccer inferior not only to the European game but also to that of Argentina and Uruguay. With Fried leading the forward line, though, the Seleção achieved a "relatively easy victory over a powerful Argentine team."[79] The final was a more torturous affair, involving numerous brutal fouls. Ultimately, though, a sharp shot in extra time by Fried produced the winning goal, setting off thunderous applause in the crowd.[80] Journalists matched the spectators' enthusiasm; an editorial in *Vida Sportiva,* for instance, framed the victory as a sign of Brazil's ascent: "The new Brazilian generation that is developing on the field of play, that is acquiring the combative qualities necessary for the great collisions of life, must inevitably transmit to their descendants the same qualities of resistance, the same attributes of energy, the same strength of will, the same desire to fight and to win that they have acquired in sporting tournaments."[81] Moreover, the nickname El Tigre, bestowed formally by the Uruguayan captain with a certificate that hailed him as "the most perfect center forward of the South American championship," fell into common usage. In a final salute, a jewelry shop, Casa Oscar Machado, exhibited Fried's boots in its front window in Rio's downtown.[82]

It was not only Fried's technique but also his *raça*—literally, "race," but figuratively, fighting spirit—that had so impressed the Uruguayans. Race in the more common sense, however, was an increasingly tricky issue for Fried. He carefully groomed his public image, "whitening" himself as best he could.[83] He never went as far as the player Carlos Alberto, who in 1914 felt compelled to apply rice powder to his face when appearing for Fluminense. The ploy fooled no one, making Carlos Alberto the butt of jokes and providing a nickname—Pó-de-arroz (rice powder)—that rivals still use to refer to Fluminense and its supporters.[84] Fried focused on the clothes he wore and the manners he used, which reflected his efforts to look and act like the white elites around him. His biggest challenge was hiding the marks of his racial identity, his curly hair and the mother who had presumably passed it on to him. Throughout his life, he took care of the latter concern by appearing in public with his father but not with his mother. Matilde was a notable absence even in the detailed personal records he kept, while Oscar avidly attended their son's games.[85] The problem of his "bad" hair, meanwhile, arose in every match; the frenetic energy of the sport always threatened to mess up his slicked-down styling, which he intended to be "non-black" but which others found as artificial-looking as a wig.[86] Fried stuck with his efforts, though, never embracing his position as the first great Afro-Brazilian star; he seemed content with his place as a *moreno* (a vague term meaning dark, but which could apply to olive-skinned whites as well as light-skinned people of mixed race) member of noble clubs and the national side. In his 1947 book *O negro no futebol brasileiro* (The Black Man in Brazilian Soccer) journalist Mário Filho traced the conquest of the sport by Afro-Brazilians but counted Fried as a "mulatto who wanted to pass for white."[87]

However conflicted he may have been about his racial identity, Fried was a strong and at times provocative figure. He had no problem playing alongside men who identified as Afro-Brazilians or putting himself in positions of prominence on clubs and the national team. His role as a leader of the Seleção of 1919 transformed him into a positive symbol of racial integration.[88] When, for instance, directors of Rio's big clubs opted not to play a goalkeeper because of his dark skin—because he was "not a little bit lighter"—the newspaper *O Imparcial* jibed at them by asking, " . . . and who knows if that player is not going to be another Friedenreich?"[89] Moreover, El Tigre became one of the more notorious beneficiaries of the "false amateurism" that came to dominate the game in the 1910s and '20s. As tournaments grew in size and competitiveness, clubs began to pay players, in direct defiance of laws that continued to mandate amateurism. Fried, though never making himself a public spokesman for professionalization, clearly believed that players should be paid for their services, and he accepted under-the-table bonuses (*bichos*) throughout his career. When the 1919 Sul Americano had to be postponed because of the influenza epidemic, the Brazilian Sports Confederation asked players to return the expense money that had been disbursed. Along with two of his colleagues, Fried responded in letters that were published in the press, offering the straightforward explanation that he could not send the advance back, since he had "employed the money in the way he found necessary."[90] This mild, if curt, message was one of the most aggressive stands Fried took in public. Keeping to himself, however, he made clear by his actions that he supported professionalism and opposed amateur ideals as "duplicities of our football."[91]

Fried, then, presented a complex sort of pioneering spirit. To see him as truly innovative, we must view him against the backdrop of the resistance by individual players and elite clubs to the inclusion of Afro-Brazilians and professionals. Fried's teammate in the 1919 Sul Americano, goalkeeper Marcos Carneiro de Mendonça, provides an instructive comparison here. Mendonça was the other great Brazilian hero in 1919 and had been the main star of the 1914 Copa Roca; after Brazil's victory in 1914, fans had carried him off the field on their shoulders, in a spontaneous exhibition of joy.[92] Despite these and the other glories he won on the field, he retired from the game shortly after the 1919 Sul Americano, making only a few club appearances afterward. The first goalkeeper of note in Brazil, he embodied the ethos of big football.[93] An "aristocrat in everything," as one contemporary noted, Marcos came from a wealthy family that moved from Minas Gerais to Rio 1901. Childhood illnesses weakened him but did not dull his interest in soccer. At only fifteen years old, he was drafted into his older brother's team to fill in for a missing player. Soon he established himself as a promising goalie, "with an excellent, quick eye, positioning himself perfectly and with secure and firm hands."[94]

Marcos always played for the love of the game, the competition it provided, and the fine skills it encouraged him to develop.[95] He stopped playing out of principle; the game he had so enjoyed was transforming into a sport of which he disapproved. Rather than playing for pay, he had in fact "paid to play"—since he paid monthly dues to his clubs, which provided only a ball and a soccer field. That changed, he argued, sometime after World War I, when clubs felt pressured to attract a large, ticket-buying public.[96] The "other interests" that came into soccer in this period ruined things for Mendonça. Neither the players who sought illegal salaries nor the massive and at times ill-behaved crowds attending matches shared Mendonça's background, manners, and expectations. The game had, in a sense, moved away from amateurs like him.[97] At the height of his glory—after his "impeccable" performance in the 1919 final, which included what he himself deemed "the most important and most incredible defense" of his life—Mendonça chose to quit the game he loved but could no longer respect.[98]

NATIONALIZING THE DIVINE AND THE BRILLIANT: DOMINGOS DA GUIA, LEÔNIDAS DA SILVA, AND THE BRAZILIAN STYLE

Despite the ragged state of its administration, Brazilian soccer gained acceptance as part of the "national vocation" in the 1930s.[99] Key to this development was the emergence of a national style by the end of the decade. The creation of a Brazilian *futebol* involved the identification of supposedly distinctive and inherent traits; these qualities added up to a peculiar Brazilian "gift" (*dom*) for playing skillful soccer. Those who shaped this notion of a Brazilian style highlighted the central role that Afro-Brazilians had played in its development. In other words, the 1930s and '40s saw *futebol* become not only national but Afro-Brazilian. This tendency only intensified as the increasingly dictatorial government of Getúlio Vargas adopted soccer, along with the Afro-Brazilian identified practices of samba and Carnaval, as material for its nationalist propaganda.[100] The consolidation of this style certainly did not resolve the conflicts that marked Brazilian society or even soccer itself—the reactions to the Maracanazo, after all, demonstrated the unresolved nature of racial tensions in 1950. Through conflictive and selective processes, a style was invented that provided a framework for a fragile but lasting sense of *brasilidade* (Brazilianness) that could appeal to much of the national population and, in its mature forms, earn the admiration of foreign observers as well.

Identified early on as "the British game," soccer nevertheless spawned a sense of Brazilian distinctiveness at the start of the twentieth century. Games against foreign opponents fostered the sense that Brazilians—even European residents of Brazil—were beginning to play in their own fashion. Brazilian teams strove to prove themselves against clubs from England, South Africa, Portugal, Argentina, and Uruguay.[101]

The tours of these visitors tended to be ragtag affairs. Before Exeter City played the Brazilian national team in 1914, it first took on a squad of Englishmen who lived in Rio and then a Carioca side that drew from a wider range of the local upper classes. It was only through a last-minute compromise between the São Paulo and Rio leagues that the first-ever "Brazil" team—really just a Paulista-Carioca selection—came together to confront (and defeat) the English club.[102] The victory over Exeter, however hastily organized, brought forth expressions of national pride. "Brazil defeated England on the field of play," proclaimed one newspaper, while others gloried not only in the performance of individual players but also in the "instinct of patriotism" that had inspired team members and spectators alike.[103] The downside of this connection between the nation and national team appeared when the Seleção failed to deliver victory. In the first Campeonato Sul Americano (South American Championship), held in 1916, for example, the national team drew against Chile and Argentina and lost to Uruguay. In spite of such results, soccer officials and journalists continued to praise the country's participation in international competitions. Columnist Paulo Barreto went so far as to call soccer "the shaper of American unity," a force that would simultaneously encourage friendly relations between countries and raise the level of civilization in each.[104] Afrânio Peixoto went even further, praising not only the potential but also the existing benefits of the game for the nation; by teaching "discipline and order," he wrote, soccer "was reforming, if not remaking the character of Brazil."[105] Not all agreed with Peixoto's highly favorable view, of course; many well-known writers worried that the game might actually weaken the national spirit.[106] The most tenacious critics continued their attacks into the 1930s, but many more toned down their rhetoric as soccer's potential to integrate social sectors under the banner of nationalism became apparent.

Brazil's victory in the 1919 Sul Americano was crucial in this regard, especially given the dramatic circumstances of the final game. Friedenreich's late goal—well after the point at which the second overtime should have ended—sent observers into rapture about the country's development of its soccer. Journalist Américo R. Netto praised not only the victory but also the "innovation" that Seleção players had shown, asserting that "Brazilians have in this way earned the honor and the glory of having created ... a new system of playing 'Association [football]' and thanks to which we have already conquered the title of South American champions and can, without vanity, attempt that of world champions."[107] Accounts of the time describe jubilation on the street as proof of "the conquest that soccer had definitively made over the popular heart."[108] In the glow of victory, officials from the Brazilian Sports Confederation (CBD, Confederação Brasileira de Desportos) and the government cemented an agreement to bring the Sul Americano back to Rio in 1922 and insert soccer into the celebrations of the centennial of the country's independence.[109] Although Brazil repeated as champion, circumstances undercut the propagandistic value of the accomplishment. The tournament was marred by controversies over refereeing, with two games abandoned by teams who refused to put up with what they saw as incompetence and bias. After Uruguay traveled home, only two teams remained; Brazil, with three ties and only one victory to its credit, defeated Paraguay easily. The chaos of the soccer competition proved a blight on the centenary celebrations, suggesting to some disenchanted observers that "sympathy and relations are not made though kicks."[110]

Broader problems hampered the performance of the national team in other instances during the 1920s and '30s. Racism, in often blatant form, had a profound impact. A series of incidents in the early 1920s showed that Brazilian authorities harbored serious reservations about including Afro-Brazilian players in any team representing the nation. When the city of Rio prepared to receive an official visit of King Alberto of Belgium in 1920, officials tried to present the most modern and civilized image of Brazil they could. This meant not only clearing prostitutes and other indecorous poor folk from areas the king was to visit, but also excluding Afro-Brazilians from the team that put on an exhibition of the Brazilian style of soccer for this "Sporting King."[111] Very soon, however, such exclusion became a heated topic in the Carioca press. On its way back from the 1920 Sul Americano, the Brazilian squad stopped for a few days in Buenos Aires. There, they agreed to a friendly match with their hosts, who had just beaten them in the final in Chile. To the dismay of the players and especially Seleção officials, the local press and public launched a series of racist critiques of Brazilian players and of Brazil itself. Brazilian journalists and politicians met the racist vitriol with disgust but also with some embarrassment.[112]

When the time came to assemble the Seleção for the next Sul Americano, to be held in Argentina, authorities balked at the idea of sending mulattoes and *pretos* as part of the Seleção. They did not want to give their rivals any more reason to call Brazilians *macaquitos* (little monkeys).[113] Two congressmen proposed that Afro-Brazilian players be banned outright, a position that set off furious debates. In the end, a rumor appeared that the country's president, Epitácio Pessoa, had intervened personally, ordering the CBD to enlist only white players, "the best of our footballing elite—that is, young men from the best families, with the lightest skin, with straight hair." He also supposedly argued that this would reduce racial friction within Brazil, since the defeat of a team of Afro-Brazilians might provoke the resentment of their white compatriots.[114] Assuming this report to be true, players and union leaders protested, but to no avail. It was an all-white Seleção that lost in that year's Sul Americano, 1–0, to Argentina.[115]

Another internal tension, the highly charged rivalry between São Paulo and Rio, hurt Brazil's chances at the 1930 and 1934 World Cups. The two cities had vied for soccer supremacy in regular matches since 1901. Political antagonisms increased through the 1920s, boiling over in São Paulo's 1932 revolt against the centralizing Vargas regime. Arthur Friedenreich, El Tigre, took an active role as a sergeant in the Paulista rebel army with hundreds of "sportsmen" under his command.[116] More often, soccer players were pawns in officials' struggles to dominate the Seleção.[117] This infighting kept some of the country's best talents off the national team simply because they played in the wrong city. Given that the 1930 World Cup was the first ever held and that it took place in Uruguay, already two-time Olympic soccer champion, officials wanted to assemble a powerful Seleção. The Rio-based CBD called up fifteen players from São Paulo; the CBD refused, however, to include any Paulistas on the coaching staff. In retaliation, the governing body of Paulista soccer barred its players from taking part. In the end, only one Paulista, Araken Patusca, defied his regional authorities and played in Uruguay; the rest of the team consisted of Rio players, many of them mulatto and *preto*. Although at least one of these Afro-Brazilians, Fausto, emerged as a star, the Seleção put in a poor performance, losing in the opener to Italy. A victory against Bolivia in the second game was not enough to get Brazil through the first stage.[118]

The Seleção made an even more fleeting appearance at the 1934 World Cup, being eliminated in the very first match by a strong Spain. This time, the dispute over professionalism reinforced the regionalist antagonism. The Rio-based CBD, clinging to amateurism, decided to build the national team around players from Botafogo, one of the few clubs still paying lip service to the antiprofessional position. The CBD also managed to convince a few players, most notably Leônidas da Silva, to switch sides. To do so, though, the CBD had to abandon its ethical stance and pay players to join the Seleção. Still, most of those who seemed willing to accept CBD money backed out under pressure from club directors.[119] In the end, the Seleção traveled to the Cup in Italy on the cheap and took part in nine exhibitions after falling short in the main competition. All in all, as Leônidas recalled three decade later, "It was a disastrous campaign, in spite of a few victories. Like gypsies, we traveled by train and bus, due to a shortage of funds, uncomfortable and badly fed .... We seemed a band of exiles running from one side to another. In this climate there could be no discipline either, for everything was done using that in which we Brazilians are masters: improvisation."[120]

However demoralizing the 1934 experience had been, it contained the key elements that paved the way for the construction of the national style in the years that followed. Two of these factors—government guidance and the performance of stars like Leônidas—are evident, if in early and relatively ineffective manifestations, in the 1934 World Cup delegation. The third shows up only in Leônidas's description of Brazilian improvisation. The 1930s would witness the celebration of Afro-Brazilian "contributions" to the nation's history and identity. Expressions of this reevaluation of "the Afro-Brazilian" included the identification of traits, such as the ability to improvise in difficult circumstances, that came to be defined as inherently Afro-Brazilian. The growth of state support for soccer, together with the examples that Afro-Brazilian icons supposedly provided, fed into this redefinition of Brazil and its *futebol* as not just the site but also the product of a tropical modern civilization.

It is easy to understand the motives for the embrace of soccer by Getúlio Vargas and his allies, who had come into power in 1930. *Futebol* had become the most widely practiced and discussed sport in the country, after all, and these men hoped to bring unity in a turbulent period. Moreover, the nationalism that had permeated soccer culture only grew with the expansion of international tournaments; particularly with the advent of the World Cup, footballing competition between countries presented a tempting opportunity for propagandists of any stripe. As the Vargas regime hardened from its early status as a "provisional government" to the heavy-handed, centralizing, and nationalistic dictatorship of the Estado Novo (1937–45), its leaders became increasingly convinced of soccer's value as an instrument of national integration. "The sporting passion," Vargas told a confidant, "has the miraculous power" to unite even the far right and the far left wing in politics, "or at least to dampen their ideological incompatibilities." What was necessary—what he intended to do—was "to coordinate and discipline those forces that invigorate the unity of national consciousness."[121]

Unlike presidents before and after him, Vargas did not care for soccer. In the end, though, his appreciation of the potential influence of soccer and other sports made his lack of sporting passion irrelevant. He and his fellow "revolutionaries" of 1930 saw themselves as remaking the national body, which they understood as in part reshaping the actual bodies of Brazilians.

Like the European fascists whom Vargas and many of his advisors admired, the government promoted physical education to stimulate vigor. To this end, they mounted carefully choreographed demonstrations of exercise. Often, these displays were part of grand civic celebrations such as Labor Day and were eventually held in great soccer stadiums, especially São Januário in Rio and Pacaembu in São Paulo. These instructive, mass rituals were accompanied by the creation of administrative structures.[122] In 1933, for instance, the government founded the Army Physical Education School (Escola de Educação Física do Exército) in Rio, which supplanted a Provisional Course in Physical Education that the School of Infantry Sergeants (Escola de Sargentos de Infantaria) had offered since 1929.[123]

Vargas also carefully chose those who would oversee the state-led development of sports and soccer in particular. He appointed his daughter Alzira Vargas to serve as the symbolic position of *madrinha* (godmother) for the Seleção of 1938.[124] Luiz Aranha, the president of the CBD who brokered compromises between Rio and São Paulo on professionalism, was the brother of one of his closest allies.[125] Another of the original "revolutionaries" of 1930, the journalist Lourival Fontes, took over the central propaganda department of the government in 1934, increasing his power with the reorganization of his agency under the Estado Novo.[126] It was Fontes who made perhaps the clearest statement of the government's stance on sports. On his way to the 1934 World Cup, he proclaimed, "Only the supreme authority of the State, considering that sports are the discipline that forms citizens . . . will be able to intervene in the coordination, discipline, structuring, and the technical orientation of Brazilian sports, in all their aspects."[127]

After the fiasco of the 1934 World Cup, the government set about trying to instill greater patriotism and to provide better funding for the country's next try. A campaign to sell stamps bearing the motto "Supporting the *scratch* [national team] is the duty of all Brazilians" raised money to support the team. Vargas provided significant backing, and some of the governors he had appointed to administer the states contributed additional funds.[128] Finally, in 1941, the regime effected an across-the-board restructuring of Brazilian sports. Decree-law 3.199 created confederations for six branches of sports, with corresponding federations in each state; together, these entities fell under the control of the National Sports Council (CND, Conselho Nacional de Desportos), which was in turn part of the Ministry of Education and Health. The function of the CND was to rationalize and centralize sports, while also promulgating their practice throughout the country.[129]

These broad initiatives would support "the perfection of the race" and thus solidify Brazil's place as a rising world power.[130]

All of these strenuous attempts to turn sports into an instrument of national administration depended on much more than a new organization for their success. The regime needed to reach citizens through publicity. In part it fostered the diffusion of news about the sport by making print and radio journalists part of official delegations to major tournaments. Thus, newspaper and radio reporters traveled with the team to the 1938 World Cup. The effusive narration of Gagliano Neto made him almost as famous as the players; his voice seemed to be everywhere, as a reporter back in Rio noted. "Thanks to the radio," wrote Alberto Byington Júnior, "the Brazilian public follows play by play, minute by minute, all of the unfolding of the anticipated combat, described with confidence and enthusiasm in the voice of the Brazilian commentator."[131] Working under the gaze of regime censors, reporters stressed the unity that devotion to the Seleção forged: "Not a single discordant voice was raised," claimed one paper on the eve of the competition.[132] Differences between immigrant groups vanished while the national team played "For the first time," Rio's *Gazeta* declared, "soccer, which has been the reason for international grudges, united in one bloc the [foreign] colonies living here and Brazilians."[133] Similar processes of unification were reported in São Paulo, where those generally seen as foreigners now became Brazilian through the game.[134] Both newspapers and government officials, moreover, expressed certainty that the Seleção presented a positive image of the nation to the world. The squad's display, one reporter gushed, moved not only Brazilian fans but also the "millions of Europeans who followed the team." Soccer showed itself, he concluded, a tremendous "element of propaganda in the exterior."[135] The powerful Minister of Education, Gustavo Capanema, drove home the government's message in a telegram to the national coach: "The victory today has one meaning: everything for Brazil."[136]

To be effective, calls for uniting behind the nation must give some sense of what this entity represents. Government propaganda about the Seleção remained, however, rather short on details. With regard to soccer, Monica Pimenta Velloso's general observation held true: "The State showed itself more interested in converting culture into an instrument of indoctrination than properly speaking of research and reflection."[137] Official messages about soccer tended to emphasize the "courage, discipline, joy, and patriotism" that members of the national team allegedly exhibited.[138] Still, from 1938 on, the Seleção's performance took on tremendous symbolic weight, as a sense of

Brazilianness grew and became linked not only to *futebol* in general but to the national team in particular. Government officials were savvy enough to pick up on this vision of *brasilidade,* but it did not originate with them; they concentrated, as ever, on messages encouraging bravery and decorum.[139] Rather, this idea of Brazil emerged from the efforts of scholars and journalists as they reproduced for audiences at home the magnificent feats of Brazilian *craques.*

Of the many stars of the 1930s and '40s, perhaps the two who acquired the most iconic status were Domingos da Guia and Leônidas da Silva. Born within two years of each other, one in a suburb of Rio and the other in the city proper, these men confronted similar obstacles as dark-skinned Afro-Brazilians who wanted to making a living in soccer. Both, though, persevered not only to shine on club and national sides but also to become central symbols of the new *brasilidade.*

Despite all they shared, the two were as different as the positions they played. Domingos da Guia was a central defender, a *beque,* but one who displayed more intelligence and grace than force when shutting down opponents.[140] Indeed, observers often commented on how "serene" he looked.[141] He watched the patterns of a match develop, stepping in to intercept a pass or tackle an attacker at precisely timed moments. This high-risk style left spectators anxious, uncertain if he would manage to get a foot in just when he needed to; he seemed to play "in slow motion," while all around him whirled in a frenzy.[142] Domingos, though, remained calm even when an adversary got past him; he tracked back and recovered the ball, as Zizinho recalled.[143] Once in possession of the ball, he did not just clear it, but brought it up the field himself. One subtle move in the 1931 Copa Rio Branco, when he faked as if to head back to his own goal but then cut back sharply, inspired a spectator to gasp, "Divine mulatto!"[144]

His command of the game made him a star, but the structures of soccer set up barriers even to so impressive a player. He was born in 1911 to a poor family not long removed from slavery; his paternal grandfather had been a captive in the interior of the state of Rio. Domingos grew up in a large family in Bangu, where he followed his brothers into the factory and, eventually, into soccer. He played from an early age on the street that ran next to the church and, by happy coincidence, continued past the Bangu soccer field.[145] Because the factory team was literally the only club in town, it took a while for Domingos to make it onto the first squad. His brother Luiz Antônio had been revered as a skilled and disciplined player—their father later said that

Domingos was "small coffee" (*café pequeno,* not much) compared to Luiz Antônio—and in 1929, when the full team needed a replacement for an injured defender, he recommended Domingos.[146] The teenager had been a center midfielder on the junior squad, a position he liked because it gave him a full view of the field. He brought that vision—and what he had learned from using it—to defense.[147]

Quickly establishing himself as a talented starter, he felt the frustrations of the amateur regime of the era. He knew soccer was, as he said after retiring, "his path in life," but at first he had to follow it through the paternalistic system of bonuses or, as he liked to call them, "tips" (*gorjetas*). While other players were content to receive their money back in the factory, he sought his directly from Bangu's owner. Although the amount was not bad, he later said, it depended on the results, so that a loss or tie paid little or nothing.[148] Moreover, he felt frustration at the limits that racism imposed; he knew that at the time he could not go to Fluminense or Botafogo, since they would not hire players as dark as him. These norms hampered not only his freedom of movement but also his ability to seek the best tips. Still, he transferred to Vasco, which had begun to sign mulattoes and *pretos,* and managed to earn a decent wage, even when regulations kept him on the second team.[149] Later, he joined a handful of other Brazilians who moved to Uruguay's professionalized soccer. The thought of leaving his homeland made him hesitate, but in the end a steady, legal salary swayed him, and he joined the club Nacional. His career zigzagged geographically from that point on. After a year at Nacional, he received an offer to return to Vasco. His Uruguayan club tried to hold him to the contract that he had just extended, but he pushed through his move to Rio.[150] There, as at Nacional, his team was champion. The following year, at Boca Juniors of Buenos Aires, he won still another competition, making him—to his great pride—champion in three countries, something that not even Pelé could match.[151]

He played out his career in Brazil, a key piece of one of the great Flamengo sides of all time. The formerly all-white and amateur club had resolved to achieve not only victories but also a mass following; signing Afro-Brazilians like Domingos, along with his brothers Otto and Ladislau, was part of this double strategy.[152] Domingos had, as these developments suggested, survived the racist amateur era and, in a moderate way, even prospered as he did so. That achievement notwithstanding, in the waning years of his playing career, he experienced precisely the lack of autonomy that he had always resisted. Abruptly, and without seeking his approval, Flamengo sent him to Corinthians of São Paulo. He felt, he later said, that he had been sold "like cattle."[153] At this late point in his career, however, he could do little but go, although as he told an interviewer in 1945, he remained "as Carioca as the best samba."[154] Three years later, after agreeing to lower his wage demands, he moved back to Bangu and soon retired.

Despite his stoic appearance on the soccer pitch, he had always been a strong and outspoken player, and these traits carried on after his playing days. He fearlessly shared his strong opinions about sensitive issues in interviews and in a series of articles in the paper *Última Hora* in 1957. With the provocative title "The Tragedy of Brazilian Soccer," these latter pieces carried his denunciations of racism by coaches, referees, and *cartolas* ("top hats," slang for club and confederation directors) not only against players but also against the only prominent Afro-Brazilian coach of the day, Gentil Cardoso, whom he considered deserving of a chance to manage the Seleção.[155] He also lashed out at the pass system, by which clubs kept the rights to players even after their contracts expired; Domingos labeled this little more than "slavery."[156] The practice of maintaining a closed camp before games and during tournaments—called *concentração*—he found to be a "prison."[157] After his triumphs on and off the field as a player, then, he continued to battle the structures of the national game that had hurt him and, as he said emphatically, remained threats to the autonomy of players into the 1950s.[158]

If Domingos impressed fans and rivals, Leônidas da Silva dazzled them. Dubbed the Black Diamond (*Diamante Negro*) and Rubber Man (*Homem-Borracha*) for his fluid and highly athletic game, Leônidas was as much an icon as Domingos but more of a celebrity than the defender ever was. So great was his fame that news of his move from Flamengo to São Paulo in 1942 momentarily displaced reports of World War II as the lead story in many Brazilian newspapers.[159] Advertisers used his name and image to sell all sorts of products, from toothpaste to cigarettes and refrigerators to hair pomade; Black Diamond chocolate candy is still sold today. Recognizing the value of his fame, especially his reputation as the inventor of the overhead or bicycle kick, he hired a journalist to handle his marketing deals.[160] Most impressively, though, this unmistakably Afro-Brazilian man—even Domingos said that Leônidas was *"preto-preto,"* doubly black—achieved not only fame but also great symbolic value.[161] It was Leônidas as much as anyone who inspired the formulations of Brazilian soccer as essentially Afro-Brazilian; he served as a foundational image of tropical modern *futebol* and provided a standard against which future stars were measured.[162]

Leônidas grew up in the city of Rio, playing on the streets and beaches just as Domingos was doing out in the open spaces of Bangu. Like his colleague, Leônidas dreamed of turning soccer into his profession. "The ball," he later said, "was one of my passions and the great ideal that inspired me was converting myself into a complete *craque*."[163] Living in the city, he had more varied chances than did Domingos; the two shared, however, the will to move in search of higher and more reliable wages. This meant that Leônidas engineered his own transfer to Uruguay in the years before professionalism in Brazil, as well as between clubs in Rio and São Paulo. Indeed, Carioca though he was, he was as great a star in São Paulo as in his home city.

His stardom grew out of his fantastically technical and improvisational style of play. It did not hurt, of course, that he played as a center forward, the most consistently glorious position in the game. It was the brilliance he displayed there, though, that led others to label him "the Black Diamond." He began to develop his skills as a soccer-mad kid in a suburb near Praia Formosa, where his parents had moved when they could no longer afford to live in the São Cristóvão neighborhood. After the death of his father deepened the family's poverty, a stroke of good fortune befell his mother. Friendly neighbors took them in, employing his mother as maid but also helping to raise little Léo. He was, from the start, a handful, infamous for breaking windows in the neighborhood, despite his mother's attempts to rein him in. Playing against the older and bigger kids from the next street over, Léo and his friends learned to pass quickly and to read the ball's caroms off walls.[164] By the age of twelve or so, he was determined to become a proper footballer. His *pai de criação*—informal adoptive father—decided, however, that he needed to learn to work hard, no matter what he ended up doing, so he arranged a job for the boy at the Canadian-owned electric utility, known as Light. He was not interested in the work, as his boss later said: "Leônidas never did anything except think about soccer. He was a fanatic!"[165] He did excel on the company's soccer team, though, and soon on another local squad, Havanesa Futebol Clube, which was also technically amateur but paid bonuses to keep hold of its better players. Leônidas proved himself worthy of the *bichos* he received, but his ambition drove him on, eventually taking him to the Sírio e Libanês club and then, after this club shut down, to the club Bonsucesso.

Still a small fry in Rio soccer, Bonsucesso tried to compete with richer teams by bringing in Afro-Brazilian aces. Under the guidance of coach Gentil Cardoso, whose demanding practices caused Léo to bridle at times, the team climbed up to seventh place in the city—an accomplishment that brought media attention to the club's young attacker. Bigger clubs wanted him, particularly América. He had, however, heard stories from his coach and others about how badly the club treated its Afro-Brazilian players, and he did not want to spend a year in the reserves (as Domingos did at Vasco). Abruptly he pulled out of an initial deal with América.[166] *Cartolas* from the big club retaliated by blocking Leônidas from a spot on the Rio and national teams, while fans showered him with racist epithets such as *negro sujo* (dirty black) and *preto sem vergonha* (shameless black). In one match a group invaded the field shouting, "Lynch him, lynch him."[167] He escaped the physical threat and the political opposition, becoming one of the first players from a suburban team to represent Rio against São Paulo. Still only 18, he was supposed to be a reserve but ended up playing and scoring. After Rio won in the third and deciding game, Arthur Friedenreich, by then near the end of his career, sought out Leônidas, giving him a handshake that seemed, in retrospect, a passing of the baton from the first great attacker to his successor.[168]

From Bonsucesso, Leônidas moved to the professional soccer of Uruguay. Playing for Peñarol, his achievements paled in comparison to those of Domingos, at least in part because of knee problems. He was, therefore, even more eager than his compatriot to return to Brazil, staying a year at Vasco, two at Botafogo, and six at Flamengo. He ended his career in São Paulo, for São Paulo FC, becoming an idol there as he had been at Flamengo.[169] Indeed, although he could not match Domingos's titles in three countries, he helped Botafogo to two Rio championships and Flamengo to three more, and São Paulo to five Paulista titles. He also made his mark on the Seleção, first in the 1932 Copa Rio Branco competition against Uruguay and then in the 1934 and 1938 World Cups. The 1932 squad brought new life to the Brazil team. Given the rebellion that São Paulo was waging and the CBD's inability to marshal established stars even in Rio, this Seleção was made up mostly of young and Afro-Brazilian men, including Domingos and Leônidas. Against a veteran Uruguayan team looking to avenge a loss the previous year, the unknown Brazilians exceeded all expectations. Léo not only played brilliantly but also performed the overhead kick for which he became famous. An astounded Mário Filho described the phenomenon: "With his back to the goal Leônidas gave a leap backward, ended upside down, legs upward, pedaled in the air, reached the ball with the tip of his boot, extended a pass more than fifty meters to Valter. What was most shocking was that, without seeing where he was passing, Leônidas had delivered the ball, with mathematical precision, at Valter's feet."[170] The moment when he captured the

FIGURE 2. Leônidas da Silva in 1983, with photo of himself performing a bicycle kick in the 1948 Sao Paulo state tournament. Gil Passarolli/Folhapress.

attention of a wider sporting world, though, came in the 1938 World Cup in France. There he became the center of attention for his aggressive, skillful attacking. Brazil's loss in the final appeared in press reports as largely due to the injury that kept Leônidas out of the game; his absence underlined his value to the team.

His behavior on the Seleção's return trip to Brazil, however, reminded officials of another side of this great player. He was willful, at times rebellious, and did not shy away from using his fame to get away with behavior for which lesser players would have been punished. While still at Bonsucesso, he became "the player who most filled the sporting headlines" of the time, one Rio newspaper noted, but also involved himself in improper "facts" and "adventures." Behind these vague but suggestive terms lay late nights out dancing or frequenting elegant cafés and bars.[171] As he rose to larger clubs, he indulged these tastes more frequently. Looking back three decades later, he confessed that his "Bohemian" nights—borne out of homesickness, he claimed—"nearly ruined" him during his year at Peñarol. Along with Fausto and Domingos, he left Flamengo's team hotel to "take advantage of their popularity" in Salvador, going to a "cabaret" and getting in a fight there.[172] He had from the start shied away from what he considered excessive training and never changed this attitude. He also was not afraid of protecting himself aggressively during games, in ways that sometimes exceeded what rivals and referees would tolerate. In 1932 he found himself subject to a police fine for his "inconvenient behavior" in a Rio league match.[173]

Still more serious in the eyes of the sporting administration was his behavior toward club officials. Nearly a decade after his troubles with América, for instance, he refused to make token appearances for Flamengo in exhibitions after he had injured his knee. Already in dire financial straits, the club stood to lose money if he did not take part in exhibitions, but he held his line; the club's doctors had agreed that he needed surgery.[174] After club directors grew so angry that they arranged for his arrest, he fought back with legal action. Despite his powerful arguments against the servitude that he was being forced into, he ultimately spent eight months in jail for failing to obey his bosses. Still he maintained his independent streak, using his prison time, spent at a military camp, to recuperate from his knee operation.[175]

He was not the only strong-willed and gifted Afro-Brazilian forward of the day; he had formed lethal attacks with some of the others, like Fausto and Waldemar de Brito. Leônidas stood out, however, for his uncanny ability to get into positions to score. His dribbling skills were not as "voluptuous" as those of his colleague Tim, as Décio de Almeida Prado later wrote, but he knew how to hold on to the ball and was a master of the one-touch pass. More than anything, though, he forced his opponents into mistakes through *malandragem* (roguery) and *malícia* (cunning), or simply beat them with impossible-seeming moves that led many to label him a *malabarista* (acrobat or magician).[176] In all of this, he exhibited an overall athletic ability that left fans rubbing their eyes in disbelief.[177]

Although the Seleção, with Leônidas leading the forward line and Domingos securing the defense, fell short in their semifinal match at the 1938 World Cup, the praise they received in the European press was heady stuff. Indeed, the reactions to the feats of Leônidas and his teammates produced a "first epiphany," a moment in which Brazilians, more consciously than ever before, identified with the national team and, at the same time, set out to define the features that made Brazilian soccer distinct.[178] The breathtaking technique that players like Domingos and Leônidas exhibited on the field became infused with meaning in daily conversations and in newspaper stories, books, and other more formal contexts. Consciously or not, the people discussing "their" players and "their" team ended up proposing new notions of who they were themselves; they recreated *brasilidade*.

The most influential formulations of this *brasilidade* appeared in the 1930s and found reinforcement in the 1940s and '50s. A simple newspaper article by a provincial scholar, Gilberto Freyre, served as a touchstone here. Scion of a traditional family in the northeastern state of Pernambuco, Freyre had studied sociology in the United States. Both his work with Franz Boas and his experiences of a different system of racial identities attuned him to the particular manifestations of race in Brazil. A prolific writer, he produced a series of canonical works on Brazilian history and society, beginning in the 1930s.[179] It was, however, a short piece that he published in reaction to the 1938 World Cup that proved an inspiration to many others.[180] Appearing under the title "Foot-ball mulato" (Mulatto Soccer) in a paper in Recife, Pernambuco's capital, his analysis projected onto soccer his understanding of the Brazilian national character.[181] This article turned out to be his earliest major statement on a theme he went on to develop throughout his long life.[182]

Above all, Freyre gloried in the fluid brilliance of the Brazilian stars who had so impressed the world that June. He saw them as the natural emanation of the national character. This character, in turn, he defined as deriving from *mulatismo* (mulatto-ism), by which he meant not so much the miscegenation that had taken place in the centuries since the Portuguese arrived on South American shores, but more a "psycho-social expression" that contrasted with "European Aryanism."[183] In fact, he went so far as to assert that "psychologically, to be Brazilian is to be mulatto." In soccer this meant playing in an exuberant, free, improvisational style; Brazilian soccer, in Freyre's eyes, was a veritable "Dionysian dance." Always, Europe remained an instructive Other: "Our style of playing soccer seems to contrast with that of the Europeans because of a combination of qualities of surprise, of guile, cunning, lightness, and at the same time of individual spontaneity . . . ," all of which, he claimed, expressed *mulatismo*. If Brazilians were Dionysian, then Europeans were Apollonian. Moreover, he applauded Brazilian officials for abandoning the "anti-Brazilian" policy of sending out teams of white players; by fielding a truly Brazilian team, they revealed to the world how "the Brazilian mulatto de-Europeanized soccer, giving it the curves . . . the grace of dance." Mulatto football was, ultimately, an art, not the sterile science that Europeans had made their soccer.[184]

As startling as Freyre's claims were, they built on existing ideas. His use of terms like *mulatismo* and Aryanism suggests that he worked very much within the framework of scientific racism that had developed in Europe and the United States in the nineteenth and early twentieth centuries. The key proponents of this pseudo-science warned that miscegenation would bring the superior white race down by mixing it with the inferior African race. The spin-off of this modern racism, the eugenics movement, sought to "improve the race" by selective breeding. Although some of his compatriots applied the vicious taxonomies of this racism to Brazil rather directly, denouncing the supposed psychological instability or intellectual limits of Afro-Brazilians, Freyre joined the ranks of those who saw value in what Africans and Afro-Brazilians had brought to Brazilian culture. Indeed, although he was certainly not the first to present this perspective, he was a leading voice in the depiction of racial mixing as foundational to Brazilian "civilization."[185] More to the point here, he helped shape the discussion of soccer by linking it to miscegenation.

At the onset of the 1930s, Brazilians spoke about the dribbles of Domingos or the "disconcerting mobility" of Leônidas, but without putting together a full image of a Brazilian—much less a heavily Afro-Brazilian—national style.[186] In this regard Freyre proved an innovator. As he developed his ideas, the centrality of Leônidas to his conception of the Dionysian quality of Brazilian soccer became apparent, as did the limits that Freyre thought this style of play should respect. In the preface he wrote for Mário Filho's *O negro no futebol brasileiro* (The Black Man in Brazilian Soccer) and in two 1955 magazine articles, he singled out Leônidas as an ideal type, the epitome of the "danced" style that Brazilians had created. Again working with some broad psychological assumptions, he wrote in 1947, "With so much of what is most primitive, most youthful, most elemental sublimated in our culture, it was natural that soccer in Brazil, as it burgeoned into a national institution, would also ennoble the Black, the descendant of Blacks, the mulatto, the *cafuzo* [a mixed Amerindian-African identity], the *mestiço* [a general mixed-race identity]."[187] Some might worry that the "Leônidas's" of Brazil might fall into selfish individualism in international competitions marked by the "predominance of Anglo-Saxon patterns." Fortunately, though, *mulatismo* meant not "pure anarchy" but rather a "constant interaction between the collective effort of the group and the exploits, the initiatives, the very improvisations of individuals who, acting in this way, distinguish themselves as heroes..."[188]

Freyre formed part of a web of intellectuals and artists in Rio who treated elements of popular culture—not only soccer but also musical genres like samba—as the bases of authentic Brazilian culture. In conversations at bars and bookshops as well as in more formal academic settings, his ideas found a receptive audience.[189] His influence appeared, for instance, in the description of the 1932 Copa Rio Branco that his fellow Pernambucan, José Lins do Rego, published in 1943. Speaking of the relative unknowns who comprised this Seleção, Lins do Rego wrote, "The young men who triumphed in Montevideo were a portrait of our racial democracy, in which Paulinho, son of an important family, united with the black Leônidas, the mulatto Oscarino, the white Martim. All done in the Brazilian way."[190] This formulation stops short of Freyre's; Lins do Rego celebrates the happy coexistence of men of various races on the team and in the nation, but he does not go so far as to posit a distinctive style that arises from racial mixture itself.[191] In 1949, commenting on Leônidas late in his career, though, he takes this step. Seeing the forward sustaining his glorious talents after so many other *craques* have faded, Lins do Rego presents him as "a case for scholars of Brazilian miscegenation." Once more, he is less overt than Freyre, but he connects racial mixture to style.[192]

The most influential force in the sports world, though, was Mário Rodrigues Filho, the energetic journalist who often met with Lins do Rego and Freyre at the José Olympio bookstore.[193] Although it is certainly an exaggeration that Mário Filho (as he was and is known) invented sports journalism or the Afro-Brazilian player, as has been asserted, he was a key figure in establishing norms that later journalists followed in their depiction of *futebol*. The son of a fiery newspaperman (Mário Rodrigues) and brother of a famed playwright and sports columnist (Nelson Rodrigues), Mário produced a body of work that is still a "primordial source" for soccer and race studies.[194] He approached sports with deadly seriousness, writing his column on a Fla-Flu (Flamengo-Fluminense derby match) "as if he were writing a chapter of world history."[195] This sense of purpose led him to run the major sports daily of the era, the *Jornal dos Sports,* and to publish passionate essays in that and other papers, magazines, and collections. He also applied himself to the creation of several soccer competitions and threw his support behind the construction of Rio's Municipal Stadium—Maracanã—at the end of the 1940s. In recognition of his contributions to Brazilian soccer, Maracanã was renamed Journalist Mário Filho Stadium after his death.

Of all his intellectual achievements, it was his 1947 book, *O negro no futebol brasileiro,* which most clearly presented his master narrative of the growth and democratization of soccer. For this author, soccer became Brazilian by virtue of its domination by Afro-Brazilian players. The very chapter titles of his classic text suggest as much. After opening with "Roots of Nostalgia," he moves the reader through the phases of the sport's popularization, culminating in phases he labels "The Revolt of the Black," and "The Social Ascent of the Black."[196] Having covered the sport for several newspapers since the 1920s, he included a wealth of anecdotes in this book to back up his narrative of the Afro-Brazilianization of soccer. Many of his tales have become common sense—that is, so widely accepted that their veracity is taken for granted.[197]

At the time, though, Mário Filho was presenting a provocative argument that built on Freyre's ideas. Freyre's influence is obvious throughout *O negro,* but perhaps nowhere more than in the discussion of Leônidas and Domingos, which relies explicitly on the contrast between the Dionysian and the Apollonian. Citing Freyre, he agrees that Afro-Brazilians had given Brazilian soccer its distinctive style, which he also likens to the *ginga* (swing) and rhythm of samba. He also sees Leônidas as the outstanding embodiment of this Dionysian element. Domingos served as an instructive comparison, his Appollonian air making him appear a teacher giving lessons during the game. Public reaction to Leônidas was so strong, he ventured, "Perhaps because what Leônidas did was more Brazilian [than what Domingos did], it was in the blood of our whites, mulattoes, and *pretos*. Like samba. Play a samba, wherever it may be, we will be swinging our bodies." Unlike Freyre, though, Mário Filho made room for Domingos in the realm of Brazil's tropical soccer. Domingos seemed like an Englishman on the outside—"cold, unshakeable"—but inside he had the rhythms that allowed him to dribble through opponents, leaving them holding their heads in shame. Even a Brazilian who tried to come off as Apollonian, then, could not hide the "Dionysian dance" that marked his culture and shone through in his soccer.[198]

Soccer thus became national and Afro-Brazilian by the 1930s and '40s not only because, as Nicolau Sevcenko notes, the sport "had been adopted with enormous enthusiasm by popular groups who, with a basis in their rhythmic and recreational traditions, related to the dexterous use of the feet and movements of the body and waist, constructed their own version of the British sport, closer to diversion and Carnaval than to aggression, tactical discipline, and objectivity."[199] What mattered even more were the meanings attached to the version of soccer that Brazilians created. These meanings wound together to form a sense of a peculiarly Brazilian *futebol* that reflected a national culture that, in turn, derived from the combination of African, Amerindian, and European cultures. This highly beneficial miscegenation led to a *mulatismo* that could impel not only the national soccer team but also the nation itself to glory.

At first glance this vision would seem a promising development for Afro-Brazilians and other groups wanting a place in the modern nation. After all, the *brasilidade* that emerged in the 1930s and '40s was, in theory, highly inclusive. Not only did it count Afro-Brazilians as well as whites in the nation, but it accorded the former a place of special significance: they appear as the source of the tropical qualities that defined Brazil's unique powers. Defined in this way—as embodiments of authentic Brazilianness—Afro-Brazilians could hardly be excluded from full membership in Brazil. Freyre, Mário Filho, and other voices of the period served up a vision of Brazil that included people from different racial identities within an overarching national identity, all represented by the men who suited up for the national team. The sense of Brazil as not only multiracial in origin but also racially democratic proved to have a wide and lasting appeal. Freyre was among its most renowned champions, but it long remained a dominant way of understanding Brazil, for many if not most Brazilians.

This way of thinking about soccer fit in with the centralizing and nationalist aims of the Vargas government. In a May Day speech in 1938, Vargas proclaimed, "A country is not just the conglomeration of individuals in a territory; it is, principally, a unity of race, a unity of language, a unity of national thinking."[200] Embracing soccer served as a means of fostering this unity, as well as attempting to control it. As also occurred with samba and Carnaval, the Vargas regime championed a particular version of soccer—which turned out to be the one that Freyre, Lins do Rego, and Mário Filho had described. This choice meant that certain elements and mythic formulations received official sanction.[201] In the footballing realm, the idea of the *craque,* the star with innate gifts for dribbling, for subtle feints, for joyful and artful trickery—in short, for all of the allegedly Afro-Brazilian abilities that Freyre and Mário Filho had highlighted—became enshrined. Brazilians played with a *ginga* that other peoples did not possess; without the *ginga, futebol* was just the same football that Europeans clomped and bashed their way through.[202]

Despite its predominance and its government support, the new ideal did not, however, come close to guaranteeing fair treatment, much less full and equal citizenship, in practice. The very terms of proposed inclusion posed one problem in this regard, since they reflected paternalism as well as racial anxiety. This side of the celebration of the Brazilian style emerges when we look at the types of traits that made up *mulatismo.* Mostly, these were corporal qualities—a swing, a rhythm, a knack for improvisation and unpredictability. Others had to do with primal emotions, such as the joy that the archetypal Afro-Brazilian player derived from exhibiting his instinctive skills. All of these, though, add up to at best an impulsive, primitive, and exotic genius, not a sophisticated, higher degree of rationality. Notions like Freyre's *mulatismo* might have served as a critique of the scientific modernization that "the European" had developed, and they certainly countered the more brutal theories of racism in the first half of the century.[203] They did not, however, unconditionally embrace Afro-Brazilians—even stereotypes of Afro-Brazilians—as a sound foundation for modernization. Doubts about the true value of Afro-Brazilian traits endured for decades. If Brazilians were born with wonderfully creative but still primitive abilities, would they need cultivation and discipline to go beyond the realm of animal instinct? Anxiety over such matters should not be surprising; after all, the elevation of the mostly poor and Afro-Brazilian masses had to cause discomfort in the whiter and more powerful upper classes, even if many of these elites cheered on Domingos, Leônidas, and other great mulattoes and *pretos* who represented Brazil on the national team.

The new, more positive vision of Afro-Brazilianness had very definite limits in a more directly practical sense as well. Mário Filho might assert that "a request from Leônidas to Getúlio [Vargas] was a command."[204] Afro-Brazilian stars like Leônidas might receive increasing wages and endorsement deals during their playing days; they might inspire passion among millions of fans. These were, however, individual and ephemeral gains. The racial democratization of soccer did not translate into lasting social and political victories for the vast majority of Afro-Brazilians, whose lives went on much as they had been.[205] Indeed, even in the realm of soccer itself, Afro-Brazilians suffered racist abuse in the period when Freyre and his colleagues were asserting a mulatto national culture. The episode in which supporters of the club América called for Leônidas to be lynched was a particularly grisly example. Most discrimination worked in less harrowing, but still degrading ways. Well into the 1950s, for instance, Afro-Brazilian players were expected to use the side entrance when going to practice for Fluminense and were treated dismissively off the field by officials at many clubs.[206] During matches, too, not only referees but also white players tried to humiliate Afro-Brazilians, as Domingos da Guia recalled in 1957. The Afro-Brazilian player, he said, "comes to be seen, not as a human being, equal to the rest, but as 'the Black,' 'the *preto*,' or, even, 'the boy'." This abuse, as Domingos insisted, "injured" but at the same time inspired players to "magnetize the multitude with . . . virtuosity"—to fight back as best you could in the game. He agreed with Mário Filho about Afro-Brazilians' special abilities, saying of the midfielder Didi, "If he had been white he wouldn't have been so perfect and so precise a stylist." Domingos, however, attributed the "characteristically racial" virtues of *craques* like Didi or Leônidas to the difficulties that they had confronted because of their race, not to inborn qualities they possessed. They had to learn to play better than whites just to have a place on the team, and even then endured injustice.[207]

CONCLUSION: TROPICALISM PAST TRAUMA

To any soccer fan today, the image of Brazilian soccer that took shape by the 1940s will seem familiar. The language that Freyre, Mário Filho, and less renowned observers adopted remains common in descriptions of Brazilian soccer and players.[208] The skills and instincts that Brazilians are said to display—qualities, the stereotypes tell us, that just cannot be taught—remain central to ideas about the country's distinctive style of play.

In the 1940s and into the '50s, however, these notions were still fresh creations. Experience had taught Afro-Brazilians and their compatriots that reality did not match the racial inclusion and equality that the vision of an inherently mixed-race or mulatto Brazilian soccer—and by extension, Brazilian culture and nation—seemed to promise. Still, the idea of this soccer was a cruelly captivating dream, and the heroic status that a *preto-preto* like Leônidas gained through it was something that delivered vicarious pleasure, perhaps even hope of more than merely symbolic citizenship.[209] Soccer had recently become part of the basis of the powerful, state-driven nationalism that the Vargas government fostered, and this added to the sense that, whatever daily life was like, change might somehow be on the way.[210]

The appeal of the newly minted national style was such that it survived the trauma of the Maracanazo in 1950, as well as the rough defeat to a famous Hungary side in the "Battle of Bern" at the 1954 World Cup. Indeed, the ideal of this style not only persisted but flourished from the late 1950s to 1970, the period in which Brazil became the first nation to accumulate three World Cup titles. Proponents such as Nelson Rodrigues and João Saldanha refined the prevailing notion of the Brazilian game, turning it into the concept of *futebol-arte* (art soccer). New iconic players, most notably Garrincha and Pelé, offered up glorious and triumphant performances of this art that seemed to prove the superiority and the authenticity of their Brazil. Even during the affirmation of this tropical, mulatto national style, though, tensions and doubt lingered. Not nearly as visible or as vociferously defended as *futebol-arte,* worries about basing the nation's modernization on people and traits that still read (to some) as exotic and primitive surfaced at times. The golden age of Brazilian *futebol* was thus marked not only by extravagant displays of artistic soccer but also by increased and invasive vigilance of the men who embodied the nation. If, as Mário Filho argued, mulattoes and *pretos* had conquered the national sport, they came under increased scrutiny in the wake of their victory.

TWO

When It Was Good to be Brazilian

TROPICAL MODERNITY AFFIRMED, 1958–70

It was good to be Brazilian because Brazilian superiority had been one of intelligence, talent, genius. It was invention, imagination, instantaneousness. It was creative power . . .

It was good to be Brazilian because I knew that the Brazilian could make of anything what he had made of soccer.

MÁRIO FILHO

The Seleção's conquest of its first World Cup turned 1958 into "the year the world discovered Brazil."[1] But which Brazil did this happy hyperbole imply? Most observers were content to see it as merely the source of a soccer that dominated through sheer skill and audacity. This footballing Brazil arrived in the Swedish summer of 1958 and endured through a Chilean winter in 1962 and a depressing English summer in 1966, before reaching its peak during a sweltering Mexican July in 1970. It came in the shape of footballing geniuses, not only Pelé—the King and the most famous of all—but also Garrincha, who was named after a little bird he loved to hunt around the factory town where he grew up. It also included Didi, whose erect posture and thoughtful passing gave him the air of an imperial magistrate. It took the form of an encyclopedia—the fullback Nilton Santos, whose knowledge of the game led commentators to call him "the Encyclopedia of Soccer"—and a hurricane—the attacker Jairzinho, "o Furacão," who scored in every game of the 1970 World Cup—and a range of other stars with their own distinctive skills and quirks.

In the end, of course, this golden age passed, leaving behind especially strong nostalgia among Brazilian fans and lovers of soccer almost everywhere. (As trite as the claim may sound, the Portuguese word *saudade* captures this longing more immediately than anything English has to offer.) Images of the young Pelé bouncing home a header in 1958, of Garrincha taking over in the absence of the King and confounding line after line of defenders in 1962, of the 1970 Seleção working the ball up the field, with almost every player touching it before Pelé laid it out gently for the marauding Carlos Alberto to slam into Italy's goal and win the 1970 World Cup ... these fed the sense that, as the writer Nick Hornby later observed, Brazil "had revealed a kind of Platonic ideal that nobody, not even the Brazilians, would ever be able to find again."[2]

This was, however, far from a socially or politically innocent ideal. Seen in deeper focus, the soccer that Brazilian teams performed in these years emerges as the product of long struggles over the definition of a modern *brasilidade*. Brazilians—especially those of the upper and middle segments of society—had been obsessed with modernity since the late nineteenth century, chasing after it in a pursuit complicated by the term's changing definitions and by their own feelings toward the *povo,* the masses of the Brazilian people. By the middle of the twentieth century, Brazilians had forged a dominant national identity that rested on the depiction of their nation as a rising, modernizing power—and as a "race" (*raça*) that drew its strength from the poor, mostly Afro-Brazilian majority of its people. The country that had equated Europe with civilization now asserted itself as the center of a tropical modernity that could compete with, and vanquish, the great powers of a differently modern Europe.

"Tropical," here, carried inescapable racial connotations; the Brazilian modernity of the 1950s to the 1970s was generally an African-descended identity. The roots of this identity lay in the 1930s and '40s, in notions of a mixed-race culture. In sporting terms, this meant the concept of a Brazilian "mulatto football," which grew from its early formulations in the work of Gilberto Freyre and Mário Filho into a distinctively Brazilian *futebol-arte*. The racialization of the national style caused great unease in the country's ruling groups. Historical processes may have led to the celebration of characteristics associated with Afro-Brazilians, but they could not make the white and wealthy embrace the brown and poor unreservedly. It was one thing to romanticize discrete qualities as reflecting the vitality of the people; this may have given a certain symbolic capital to the actual members of the *povo,* but it provided them with little, if anything, else. It would, however, have been quite another matter altogether to forget about social hierarchies, including racial ones, that kept the allegedly primitive and dangerous members of the lower classes in their place.[3] The racialized tropical, after all, was never far from the primitive.

The prevailing national identity thus contained two contradictory attitudes—one celebrating the *povo* (generally taken to be Afro-Brazilian) as the source of a potent national culture, and another fighting against any real empowerment of groups outside the elite. Tensions between the more fluid and democratic on the one hand, and the more strictly hierarchical on the other, charged social relations with a peculiar electricity. The balance between the two logics, moreover, shifted in different social contexts, so that Brazilian culture came to encompass both "softer" and "harder" realms of racial and other discrimination. Alliances that crossed lines of race or class were common in some areas but nearly unthinkable in others.[4]

Soccer remained, by and large, a realm in which more inclusive visions held sway; *futebol* was an area of comparatively "soft" race relations. Domingos da Guia noted this in 1957, writing that the unfortunate fact of racial prejudice in soccer was usually "disguised, attenuated."[5] The triumphs of Brazilian teams in the period from 1958 to 1970 only supported this impression. Led by dark-skinned Afro-Brazilian men like Didi and Pelé, but also by *mestiços* like Garrincha and whiter players like Gérson and Tostão, the Seleção seemed to perform the country's supposed racial democracy. What is more, their success suggested that Brazil and its people had reached a level of maturity that could produce continued progress.

Since the World Cup of 1938, when Leônidas da Silva and his colleagues had displayed a glittering style, Brazilians yearned for a victory that would mark their arrival as a fully developed protagonist. World War II had forced them to wait for such an affirmation, since the disruption of the war years turned the 1940s into "the decade without a [World] Cup."[6] Optimism swelled into euphoria when Brazil hosted the first postwar Cup. Dealt a mighty blow by Brazil's defeat in the Maracanazo, faith in the national team was staggered further by another defeat four years later, to a Hungary side that almost won the 1954 World Cup even without its star, Ferenc Puskás. After this physically brutal but hardly dishonorable defeat to the "Golden Magyars," the Seleção underwent a promising reformation. Still, on the eve of the next World Cup, Brazilian supporters experienced a flare-up of both wild nationalism (*ufanismo*) and disbelief (*descrença*).[7] As Nelson Rodrigues, playwright, journalist, and enthusiastic supporter of the *escrete* (from the English "scratch," slang for the national side) wrote in the weeks before the first kickoff, many Brazilians shared a sense that the national team "implicates all of us and each of us," since it serves as "a projection of our defects and our [good] qualities." Like so many of his compatriots, he believed the country had the talent to win the title but worried that a chronic shortage of self-confidence—what he labeled the "mongrel complex" (*complexo de vira-latas*)—held his compatriots back.[8] When the title came, Rodrigues's voice was only one in the national chorus that hailed the World Cup victory as proof that they—through their team—had finally grown up enough to become a "winning nation" (*país vencedor*).[9]

Soccer was not the only realm in which optimism reigned in the 1950s and '60s. This was a period of bold movements in the arts, with the new sounds of bossa nova capturing worldwide attention while films like Anselmo Duarte's *Pagador de promessas* (The Payer of Promises) and the politically aggressive Cinema Novo work of Glauber Rocha won notice and prizes at international festivals.[10] More than any other achievement, though, the 1960 inauguration of Brasília, with its sculptural architecture, provided an iconic representation of the heroic nationalism of these years. Part of President Juscelino Kubitschek's program to deliver "fifty years of progress in five" through state-led development, the expeditious construction of this "capital of hope" promised to open up the interior of the country and cleanse politics of its unhealthy old patterns.[11] Neither the political nor the economic health of the country proved as inspirational, however, with the twin problems of chronic inflation and trade imbalances leading to massive strikes and contributing to the deterioration of formal democracy.[12] The military, which had overseen the reinstatement of an electoral regime in 1945, joined with conservative civilian forces to impose a dictatorship in 1964, stamping out a lively and varied expansion of social, cultural, and political organizing across the country.[13]

The success of the Seleção focused nationalism even after the advent of the military regime, but it did not end disputes about either the Brazilian national team or Brazil itself. Actions by those in charge of the national game retained vestigial doubts about the capacity—physical but primarily psychological—of players as members of the *povo*. Officials remained on guard, selecting only those players they deemed suitable agents of modernization and then monitoring these players to ensure they performed appropriately on and off the field.[14] The cerebral Didi, the capricious Garrincha, and the perfect Pelé all entered into the pantheon of Brazilian and world greats. Garrincha and Pelé in particular came to be seen as the embodiment of the best that Brazilian *futebol*—and the Brazilian people—had to offer. All of them, however, came under scrutiny for their behavior and, indeed, their bodies; the way that they acted as Afro-Brazilian or *mestiço* men was a special focus of critical attention. The expansion of the media—and the media-consuming public—was one explanation for this sharper gaze.[15] The long drive toward modernity, though, provided another, inescapable cause of this phenomenon. Brazilian officials, intellectuals, and fans continued to worry about their ability to compete with other nations, especially those of Europe. Their anxieties, moreover, often led them to target the character of the players who seemed to symbolize the nation as "the fatherland in cleats."[16]

ORCHESTRATING VICTORY: DIDI AND PREPARATIONS FOR THE 1958 WORLD CUP

Before 1958 only the most provocative commentators argued that victory would come from the excellence of its players alone. Such assertions were more typical of a later period, after Brazil had become two-time World Cup champions. In the 1950s, many of those who hailed the talents of Didi, Garrincha, and the young Pelé were also pushing for a rational organization of the national team.[17] A more comprehensive approach to planning for World Cups followed the trauma of 1950 and the "hangover" of 1954 and found support not only in the upper echelons of the national soccer confederation (CBD, Confederação Brasileira de Desportos) but also among former players. Barbosa, principal scapegoat after the Maracanazo, declared, for instance, that Brazil's organization for international competitions remained "precarious" in January 1958.[18] Indeed, the country had minimal integration of its domestic game; irregularly held championships that pitted state seleções against each other were the closest thing Brazil had to a truly national league. This inter-state competition, moreover, often served as a means by which players could be scouted and bought by clubs in Rio and São Paulo.[19] Although the national Seleção enjoyed some successes in these years, the CBD did not always manage to assemble a full Brazil squad to meet its international commitments, sending the Rio Grande do Sul state seleção to the 1956 Pan American Championship and a Bahian side to dispute the O'Higgins Trophy in Chile in 1957.[20] By that time, however, a unifying plan had been put together under João Havelange, former Olympic swimmer and water polo player and now vice president of the CBD, and Paulo Machado de Carvalho, director of soccer at Sao Paulo FC and later supervisor of the delegation to the World Cup. The two had been formulating their ideas since the previous September, when Havelange was casting about for ways to win the World Cup for Brazil and the upcoming election for CBD president for himself.[21] Both set themselves to a wide-ranging analysis of the problems that their players confronted. Havelange later recalled his father's astute observations after the two watched Argentina beat Brazil in the Copa Roca in the 1920s; the Brazilian players, Havelange summarized, "were full but not well fed." He pointed sentimentally to this lesson about proper preparation as the basis for his desire to transform the Brazilian "artist" into a true "athlete."[22] Carvalho, given carte blanche by Havelange, enlisted the services of São Paulo–based journalists, meeting regularly with them to sift through ideas drawn from their own experience and from the medical research of the day.[23] Their program aimed to eliminate the "errors and improvisation" that had characterized Brazil's preparations for previous World Cups and replace them with a meticulous scheme "based in study and planning."[24]

In a sense, the Paulo Machado de Carvalho Plan, in versions that Havelange quietly distributed to CBD members in late 1957 and early 1958, offered a systematized response to feelings that soccer officials and other observers had harbored since 1950.[25] The Seleção had bounced back from the Maracanazo to defeat Uruguay in the Pan American Championship of 1952 and then again in the South American Championship of 1953, showing the "fiber, heart, and class" that had deserted them in the 1950 World Cup final.[26] The trauma of the Maracanazo remained, however, and with it some of the disdain toward the *povo* that had emerged in the wake of this historic failure. The head of the delegation to the 1954 World Cup asserted that the team's loss in this tournament derived from the poor cultural development of Brazil's players and its people, who lived at the level of basic instincts, lacking real knowledge of "common rules of education and hygiene."[27] Even those who would have taken offense at such remarks agreed that some specialized assistance was necessary for Seleção members to achieve the confidence to win a major trophy. Nelson Rodrigues, for instance, argued that the nation had not recovered from the Maracanazo, leaving its players "emotionally defeated" before they even took the field. A coach, who was "not a psychologist, not a psychoanalyst, not even a priest," would not suffice; medical professionals had to be called into service.[28] For others this was primarily a racial matter; these officials hoped to present the whitest possible Seleção in 1958 and thus save the country from the vacillations to which Afro-Brazilian and mixed-race players were allegedly prone. Whether Havelange and Carvalho used racial terms in private remains unknown, but certainly their plan aimed at selecting the individuals who would have not only the physical skills but also the psychological strength and sophistication to handle the complicated challenges of a World Cup.[29]

The Havelange and Carvalho initiative shared the energetic, forward-looking orientation of the Kubitschek government's push for accelerated development, the "fifty years of development in five" plan of 1956 to 1961. Like Kubitschek, these soccer administrators found it necessary to engage in prickly politics, since club directors, CBD colleagues, and the press questioned their aims and methods. They also faced moments of internal dissent and even crisis. Although they maintained their overall focus on the modernization of the Seleção through top-down management, they at times fell into conflict over the choice of the personnel who would help them achieve this goal.[30] With Vicente Feola in place as head coach, Havelange had to convince club directors to free up players to join the Seleção and had to find funding to implement the ambitious Carvalho Plan. The first was fairly simple; the problem in this regard was controlling *cartolas* (club and confederation directors) who insisted that their players were more deserving of a spot than others. (The president of Corinthians, for example, protested the absence of Luizinho on the Seleção, saying he was "a thousand times better" than Pelé.[31]) To address the second matter, Havelange used personal connections to appeal directly to Kubitschek. He received the guarantee of sufficient funds to carry out the training they wanted and to make the trip to Europe. A share of ticket revenue from exhibitions in Italy had to be factored in, but in the end he achieved the financing of the World Cup campaign.[32]

While Havelange was finalizing these deals, his partners had already been at work implementing their far-reaching plan. Physician Hilton Gosling, who had long served at the clubs Bangu and Fluminense and had completed a specialization in sports medicine in 1949, had been in contact with Carvalho since 1957.[33] The thoroughness with which he scouted locations for training centers in Brazil and a headquarters in Sweden—a task that had been left to sort out after arrival at previous Cups—impressed Brazilian as well as foreign observers.[34] In addition to the usual members, the technical staff included a sociologist licensed to administer psychological tests (a "psychotechnologist"), João Carvalhaes; a dentist, Mario Trigo Loureiro; and even a manicurist, Geada.[35] By April 1958 the technical and coaching staff set about choosing the members of the team. Club politics intruded inevitably, though Havelange reduced their effects by careful actions, agreeing to hold an exhibition against Corinthians in São Paulo, apparently as compensation for not calling up Luizinho to the squad, and going out of their way to show no favoritism toward either side of the Rio–São Paulo rivalry.[36]

More vital to their efforts were other criteria: they demanded players who would remain disciplined on and off the pitch, who showed the toughness and maturity to perform under pressure. Toward this end they conducted a

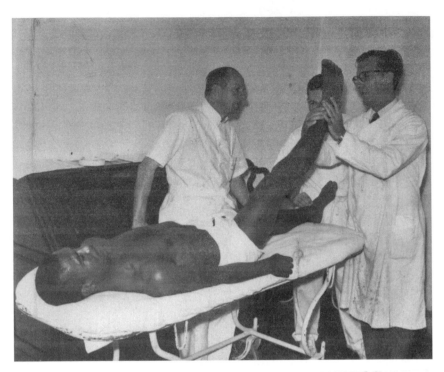

FIGURE 3. Didi undergoing a medical examination before the 1958 World Cup. Coleção *Correio da Manhã*, Arquivo Nacional.

"gigantic" series of exams over several days, subjecting players to thorough physical and psychological tests.[37] The results reflected the humble origins of the thirty-three players brought in, only twenty-two of whom could make the final roster. For example, few, if any, of the players had ever seen a dentist before. So bad was the state of their teeth that Dr. Trigo and his colleagues performed dozens of extractions—seven from the left back Oreco alone—as well as hundreds of other procedures.[38] Gosling and the other physicians, meanwhile, encountered the joint and muscle problems they expected, but also had to address gall bladder, circulatory and other issues. Minor surgeries corrected most of these conditions, so that Garrincha and the defender Orlando were able to join the team after undergoing tonsillectomies, but a few players ended up being dismissed for medical reasons.[39]

To the great good fortune of Brazil fans, the coaching staff did not strictly follow the recommendations from the psychological exams. Garrincha scored thirty-eight out of a possible 123 points on the test, marking him below average in intelligence and completely lacking in aggression. Pelé, then only seventeen, also performed poorly, leading Carvalhaes to classify him as "obviously infantile" and without "the necessary fighting spirit" and "sense of responsibility required for team spirit."[40] More veteran players, however, stepped in and argued for the inclusion of these players. Having demonstrated their skills on the field and with the backing of this core of senior team members, Garrincha and Pelé earned their spots, even after Pelé suffered a knee injury in the exhibition against Corinthians. Science did not trump talent in the build-up to the 1958 World Cup. Gosling, though, highlighted the modern work of his staff, declaring, "We will take to Sweden a team in perfect physical and mental conditions."[41]

The organization of the delegation continued on to Sweden, with CBD officials imposing a strict code of conduct. They had left out players because of suspect behavior back in Brazil and were not going to tolerate drinking, flights from the team headquarters, or other disobedience.[42] The imposing trainer Paulo Amaral, a former military man, helped keep players in line as well as in shape. Transgressions occurred, of course, but overall the climate presented a stark contrast to the turbulent and distracting 1950 camp.[43]

As the Seleção moved through the tournament, it met the goals that Havelange and Carvalho had set. Players maintained discipline from the nerve-wracking first game through a tie against England, still revered as the inventors of the sport, and on to matches against the mysterious Soviets, the gutsy Welsh, the skilled French, and the host Swedes. In the opening game, they did not panic even when their opponents dominated the ball for the first twenty minutes; their patience and self-control surprised the Austrians. The one time Nilton Santos disobeyed his coach, he produced a moment of brilliance. With Feola shouting to the defender, "Get back, Nilton, get back," Santos nevertheless glided forward, receiving a pass on the left side of goal and smoothly knocking it in with his right foot for a score.[44] Decisive plays like this, moreover, helped the team grow stronger, ultimately closing out the Cup with convincing 5–2 wins over France and host Sweden.[45] While the team was improving, two other significant shifts took place. The lineup for the first game presented a near-perfect "whitening" of the national team, an apparent reflection of the racist dossier that CBD officials had created after the 1950 and '54 defeats. All of the starters were either white or very light-skinned versions of "typical Brazilians," with "the absolutely irreplaceable *negro* Didi" the only exception to the overall rule.[46] Both Pelé and Garrincha were recovering from injuries at this point. They were soon ready, with the approval of the team doctors, but only entered the side in the match against the Soviet Union, which Brazil needed to win to guarantee its place in the knock-out round. Even then, Didi had to plead for their inclusion to Machado de Carvalho.[47] Once in the side, Garrincha and Pelé proved vital, as did the dark-skinned Afro-Brazilian Djalma Santos, who came in at right back in the final.

Didi, Garrincha, and Pelé all proved central as well to the second change, the recasting of the team as a symbol of Brazil's mulatto soccer. The tremendous infrastructure that the CBD had built to ensure victory fell largely into obscurity, as journalists, fans, and players themselves focused on the art that the Seleção had displayed on the field. Overwhelmingly, it was the *craques* who shone; indeed, the notion of the *craque* as a genius with natural gifts for producing passes and moves that lesser players could neither learn nor understand gained centrality from 1958 on, in the work not only of famous journalists and commentators but throughout the media.[48] The supposedly organic traits of the mixed-race Brazilian people, which Freyre and Mário Filho had already proposed, now seemed confirmed. The great stars of the nation were also stars of, and from, the largely Afro-Brazilian *povo*. Moreover, the victory of 1958 seemed proof that magnificent "solitary stars" could come together in a beautiful expression of the national culture and, better still, steamroll foreign adversaries.[49] As reporters noted, the Brazilians "acted in a manner that was typically their own," producing a true "show."[50] At the same time, though, what these great stars did with their skills—and their miraculously "plastic" bodies as well—became subject to new vigilance. The "maturity" and "virility" for which their coach had praised them, remained qualities they had to demonstrate in their play and in their personal lives.[51]

This mixture of adulation and vigilance marked the careers of Didi, Garrincha, and Pelé, three of the stars of 1958. The all-tournament team, selected by journalists, included all of them, plus Nilton Santos and the central defender Bellini; it was Didi (born Waldir Pereira), however, who was named the best player in the World Cup, in a decision that stirred up no controversy. As talented as the players around him were, Didi was the conductor of the team. If officials had sought a whitened team this time around, they could not leave him out, so critical were his contributions to Brazil's success—although the captaincy went to Bellini, a player of Italian descent. In 1957 it had been Didi's goal against Peru that had earned qualification to the Cup, in probably the most heralded display of a technique he invented. Known as the *folha seca* (dry leaf) because of the way it flew off his right foot only to flutter to the ground as it neared the goal line, this was his signature

FIGURE 4. Pelé, Dida, and Didi before 1958 World Cup. Coleção *Correio da Manhã*, Arquivo Nacional.

skill and one that he consistently strove to perfect. He chose to wear a special shoe on that foot, a size smaller than he normally used and one that had been broken in by a left-footed player.

It was in his reaction to another goal, Sweden's first in the 1958 World Cup final, that Didi showed a more impressive ability. Sensing that his teammates were shaken up—Zagallo later said that he had thought of the tragedy of 1950 at that moment—Didi scooped the ball out of the net, put it under his arm, and walked as slowly as he could back to the center of the field. Along the way, he calmed Zagallo, Zito, and others who seemed shaken by the unexpected score, telling them of recent games when his club had beaten Swedish sides easily. "I guarantee," one account has him saying, "these gringos can't play at all." After providing this reassurance, he then took the kick-off from Vavá and sent a beautiful, floating pass over the head of a defender and right in the path of a running Garrincha. Although Garrincha missed with his crisp shot, the moment of potential crisis had passed.[52]

This quiet leadership was part of Didi's enigmatic presence. He showed great aptitude for reading the mental state of his colleagues, gently lifting their spirits or, when this seemed impossible, planning his game strategy around them.[53] Garrincha, his teammate on the national side and at Botafogo, was one of the players who received this treatment. Didi discerned Garrincha's mood from his behavior as he dressed for a game. When the *ponta* (point, or wing forward) warmed up eagerly, Didi left him alone. When, in contrast, he put on his boots with little energy or attention, Didi knew Garrincha might be on his way to an indifferent performance and so goaded him, claiming that people had been saying that it was only after Didi arrived at the club to deliver perfect passes that Garrincha shone. Garrincha was one of the few who got away with teasing Didi, who otherwise did not tolerate much levity; he was so self-possessed that he intimidated others.[54]

On the field he evinced control of the ball and of the game as a whole. When he first came up to the first division in Rio, from his hometown of Campos, the largest city in the interior of Rio state, his cool demeanor confused coaches and diverted their attention from his masterful positioning and ball skills. He proved himself on the Seleção, however, and earned recognition as one of the country's most influential players.[55] He became part of the powerful Botafogo of the late 1950s, lining up with Nilton Santos, Garrincha, Zagallo, Quarentinha, and Paulo Valentim—so many national team members that the club became known as "Sele-fogo" (a Botafogo-Seleção). On the Seleção itself, he performed well when the side hit low points and when it conquered titles. Not only was he elected the best player at the 1958 World Cup, but he remained part of the core of Brazil's second World Cup winning side in 1962. For club and country alike he served as a classic midfield general. Indeed, one of the many epithets that journalists loved to apply to him was "Black Napoleon." Still, he commanded not by barking out orders, nor by dashing between sectors of the field. Instead, he meticulously directed his colleagues to start counter-attacks or to steer clear of trouble.[56] Another midfielder of his era, Moacir, later said that Didi played "parsimoniously." Indeed, his style contrasted sharply with that of speedier players like Moacir and Telê.[57] Didi relied on a touch that was so subtle that he did not need to play quickly. Rather, as Nelson Rodrigues wrote, he stood like a matador, holding his position before maneuvering slightly to let adversaries rush futilely by him.[58] A full-out dribble around defenders, he later said, always seemed like a last resort, something to do only when he could find no pass to "create" the play.[59]

Fans sometimes grew frustrated with his speed, thinking that he was not putting forth enough effort.[60] In response to one spectator complaining about his performance in a training session, he uttered an infamous phrase:

"Practice is practice, the game is the game" (*treino é treino, jogo é jogo*). According to Nilton Santos, Didi had simply wanted to shut up an aggressive fan, not make a statement of principles.[61] For those who doubted his commitment or who simply wanted to see their club's star in the midfield of the Seleção, however, this conjured up the image of a fundamentally lazy player, one who would not "get his shirt wet" (*suar a camisa*) for the good of the team. In truth, he often avoided overexertion in practice but demonstrated a tremendous work ethic; he exhibited great determination to perfect his passes and his free kicks, practicing them with extraordinary concentration.[62] Players who "saved" themselves during games—like the attacker Mazzola, who seemed to pull out of dangerous challenges in 1958 after he had signed a lucrative contract with Italian club AC Milan—found themselves out of the Seleção lineup.[63] Didi, by contrast, not only worked so hard that he often lost several pounds during games but also insistently challenged opponents, taking pride in the many fouls he suffered while stealing the ball.[64] His game was in fact quite rough when it had to be. In a match against Uruguay in the 1959 Sul Americano, he retaliated against his opponents' violence with flying scissor kicks. Nelson Rodrigues celebrated his tackles as a demonstration of "tremendous Brazilian fighting spirit [*garra*]."[65] His preference, though, was to play a beautiful, flowing game, running as much as he had to, but letting the ball run even more.[66]

Because of his reserved personality, Didi remained an enigma. Even on matters that changed the direction of his personal and professional life, he kept his own counsel. In 1948, just as he was moving from Campos to Rio, he married his sweetheart, Maria Eliza, nicknamed "Jóinha" (little jewel) for her beauty. By 1952, however, he began to appear in newspaper headlines because of a new romance, this time with the Bahian singer and actress Guiomar Baptista. This relationship was famously combustible—literally, according to rumors that Guiomar once tried to set Didi on fire while he slept.[67] This restrained man did not want to talk to the press about this side of his life, but he was clearly passionately in love with the very "spirited" (*geniosa*) woman who handled his business affairs.[68] He suffered so during the enforced *concentração* (closed camp) at the 1958 Cup that he staged a hunger strike just to be able to talk to Guiomar by phone. Despite the intervention of Nilton Santos, who both pleaded his case and snuck food to his room, he did not manage an exception to the rules.[69] If he remained silent on his relationship with a woman who helped him in major decisions, he was positively sanguine when it came to the troubles that marred his time at Real Madrid.

The Spanish club, like many others, coveted Didi after his display in Sweden, and in 1961 they bought his contract from Botafogo. With a roster full of stars—the Argentine-born Alfredo Di Stéfano the most galactic of all—Real saw Didi as the piece that would perfectly complete its famous attack, called the "Foreign Legion" because it contained not only Di Stéfano but the Hungarian Puskás, the Argentine Gento, and the fleet Brazilian Canário. The team demonstrated offensive firepower, with Didi emerging as a center of attention for fans when the club traveled. This caused friction, almost everyone agreed, since Di Stéfano had been boss of the team to that point. Didi found himself shut out, an exclusion possibly reinforced by racial attitudes, since he was the only black player in Real's white uniform. In any case, Didi—possibly at Guiomar's suggestion—rescinded his contract and returned to Brazil, in order, he said, to retain his position in the Seleção.[70] He certainly harbored resentment but preferred to put it to use on the field in later games against Spain.[71]

Back in Brazil, Didi continued his excellent play and was one of the leaders of the 1962 World Cup squad. The Seleção showed just a few alterations from the 1958 version; the organizing staff remained in place, and the roster included only three new players—one of whom, Amarildo, turned out to be a crucial addition, when he replaced the injured Pelé and made several game-winning plays. Didi received relatively less press than in 1958, not because of a dip in his performance but rather because others emerged as even more decisive figures. What remained, though, was the image of him as the embodiment of an Afro-Brazilianness that shone through in his marvelous passing skills and his *folha seca* free kicks. The press and fans gloried in the talent of this wonderful, cerebral midfielder. Often the praise presented a frank racial essentialism; his blackness appeared as the source of his stylish brilliance. Didi himself referred to the special qualities that Afro-Brazilians possessed, saying, for instance, that the Seleção beat the Soviet Union in 1958 because he and his teammates had quicker reflexes and a "more flexible waist" (*cintura mais flexível*)—in other words, that they had a "plasticity" that Europeans lacked.[72] Nelson Rodrigues hailed Didi's game, glorying in the way a "simple *ginga*" (swing) of his captured the essence of "eternal dance halls." More often, though, he portrayed Didi as a noble Afrodescendant leader, an "Ethiopian prince" who displayed the "racial dignity of Paul Robeson."[73] Mário Filho took a somewhat more complex racial view. Having done so much to stress the Afro-Brazilian core of the national style, Mário Filho admired Didi for having left Fluminense, where

FIGURE 5. Celebration of 1958 World Cup triumph. Coleção *Correio da Manhã*, Arquivo Nacional.

a racist club president had addressed him as *moleque* (boy). He also saw blackness in the special touch and spin Didi gave to every ball that left his foot. Because Didi's manner was so thoughtful, though, he put him in the "category of those who had stopped being black (*pretos*)." Didi went too far beyond the instinctual and became too intellectual and disciplined a player to meet Mário Filho's criteria for the ideal Brazilian—meaning Afro-Brazilian—footballer. Although less than fully "Dionysian," however, Didi received Mário Filho's support in the battle for starting places on the Seleção.[74] These mild reservations notwithstanding, Didi and his fellow World Cup winners of 1958 reinforced the impression that Brazilians played in a joyous, artistic manner that reflected the qualities of their nation's mixed-race people.

GARRINCHA TAKES FLIGHT

The champions of 1958—most of whom won the 1962 title as well—came to be seen as the truest expressions of the Brazilian style, at least until the 1970 Seleção won still more convincingly. Based on the physical "gifts" allegedly inherent to Afro-Brazilians, their *futebol* appeared to undo the "mongrel complex." That, at least, was the message that many took from their performance. Far from a weakness provoking doubts, the racial composition of the *povo* could in fact be the source of confidence. Brazil's players—and Brazilians more broadly—thus were, in a sense, not mutts who did not fit into any one racial classification, but rather a new, potent human breed that was proving itself the foundation of Brazilian progress in the world.

It was not Didi, but two other members of the 1958 Seleção who came to be the central icons of this style. In many ways, these teammates—Garrincha and Pelé—represented the pinnacle of the authentic Brazilian art of *futebol,* though their play, and their images on and off the field, also presented telling contrasts.[75] Of these two, who are often described as the greatest *craques* in Brazilian history, it is Garrincha who is perhaps the more beloved and Pelé the more idolized. Garrincha's imperfections were visible to all; his crooked legs fascinated spectators and journalists, who spoke of how he "shot straight with bent legs" and called him "the angel with bent legs."[76] News of his personal life, moreover, made him seem less like a star who had risen out of the *povo* and more like a star who remained part of the *povo*. This side of his image gave him another nickname, "the people's joy."[77] Pelé, though also from a working-class background and "marked" by Afro-Brazilian features, was almost so perfect on the field and so successful at turning sporting success into social ascension that he drew away from the *povo* and into the circles—and attitudes—of the upper classes. That said, "the inimitable *crioulo*" holds his place as the embodiment of the Brazilian style and, in the eyes of many, the best player ever.[78]

The gap between these heroes' fates was evident when the magazine *Placar* brought them together for an article in 1982. Old friends who had never lost a World Cup match while playing together, they reminisced about 1958, talked about their children (Garrincha admitted to thirteen, Pelé to three), regretted the current state of soccer, and made vague plans to meet soon.[79] By this point, though, their fortunes had taken wildly different turns. Pelé had gone on to win a third World Cup in 1970 and, after his retirement from the national team, played in the North American Soccer League (NASL), achieving fame even in a country that still regarded soccer as an odd and foreign pastime. Artist Andy Warhol, who included him as one of the subjects in his series of portraits of sports stars (fig. 6), allowed that Pelé might be an exception to his prediction that everyone would achieve fifteen minutes of fame—Pelé's status would certainly not fade.[80]

FIGURE 6. Pelé by Andy Warhol, ca. 1977. ©2013 The Andy Warhol Foundation for the Visual Arts, Inc./Artists Rights Society (ARS), New York.

Garrincha, by contrast, had slipped into near obscurity. Always a *mulher-engo* (womanizer), he left his first wife, Nair, and their kids for the singer Elza Soares in 1962. The media eagerly pounced on the *craque,* particularly when Nair's lawyer brought her to Rio to tearfully complain about the misery Garrincha's "real" family suffered back in his hometown. Elza, meanwhile, helped Garrincha take a more professional approach to his career and tried to ensure his friendly relations with Nair and his children, even as she was branded a homewrecker in the press. Despite her moral and financial support and the obvious passion the two shared, Garrincha's playing days ended sadly. Always troubled by arthrosis, he never recovered from a knee surgery he underwent in 1964.[81] He played after that, but not with the same sharpness or resilience as before. After brief appearances in the 1966 World Cup, he ended up drifting from club to club. He accompanied Elza on her tours to Europe and then back to Rio, but his lifelong alcoholism grew so severe that she ended up banning him from their home and from seeing their son after he assaulted her in a drunken fury. From that point on, his drinking intensified. Out of pity, friends found him a position teaching soccer to kids in Bangu. His final marriage, to factory worker Vanderléa de Oliveira Vieira, did not temper his vices, and he spent the remainder of his life in and out of the hospital. A poor decision led him to appear on a Carnaval float in the city of Bicas, Minas Gerais; the sight of this former idol, heavily tranquilized, wearing a Seleção jersey, and sitting next to a blond woman dressed up as the Jules Rimet trophy, saddened spectators across Brazil. Finally, at age fifty, four months after his affectionate meeting with Pelé for *Placar,* his body succumbed to alcohol-induced damage.[82]

Garrincha's death set off a flurry of claims—both on his corpse, which was buried in his hometown only after his longtime friend Nilton Santos insisted that this had been his final wish, and on his legacy.[83] In response to the poverty of Brazilian soccer at the time of his death, observers hailed him as an ultimate symbol of the true *futebol* that came from the people. Authors of "string poetry" (*literatura de cordel,* cheaply printed verse sold at markets or on the street), emphasized his humble origins, the skillful trickery of his soccer, and the way that he remained connected to the *povo.* One poet predicted that he would be universally recognized as "Saint Garrincha of Pau Grande."[84] Although this was a stretch, responses to Garrincha's death tended to skip over the deeds that had put his name in gossip columns. In this way, the plaudits by journalists, poets, and musicians revived the narrative told about Garrincha during his playing days.[85] This narrative, moreover, suggests the ways in which he was a powerful but problematic representative of the national style.

Garrincha was born Manuel Francisco dos Santos in the factory town of Pau Grande, in the interior of Rio de Janeiro. His paternal grandfather's family was Amerindian; their people, the Fulniô, were among the last forced off their own lands and into plantation labor in the northeastern state of Alagoas in the second half of the nineteenth century. His other grandparents were *cafuzos* (of mixed Amerindian and African descent), mulattoes, and *pretos.* Garrincha thus embodied the mixture of the three races that formed the legendary basis of Brazilian popular culture. Growing up in Pau Grande, a city of three thousand dominated by the textile works, he gained the nickname Mané Garrincha, after a songbird native to the area, one of the creatures that local kids hunted. Like his friends, he ran around barefoot, playing pick-up games on a bumpy field or hunting and fishing. The expectation was that they would all attend the local school, which belonged to the textile company, and proceed from there to work in the factory. Young Garrincha began this path, picking up a very basic literacy and then at age fourteen moving into the hot and loud textile mill.[86] Although he was later depicted as a peasant, Garrincha was thus a factory laborer.[87] He was not a diligent worker, though, napping in the midst of the mill's clattering machinery.[88] His soccer skills most likely saved his job, until they eventually led him out of the factory entirely. He played on the factory team, SC Pau Grande, and the bosses wanted to win.

Garrincha's genius was not obvious at first. Along with his friends Pincel and Swing, he joined in almost perpetual pick-up games, as well as turning out for the factory team. He was not the only talent in town, however; he ended up playing as a point forward because another boy beat him out for the midfield position he had occupied.[89] Garrincha, though, kept perfecting his skills. The 1962 film *Garrincha alegria do povo* (Garrincha, Joy of the People) showed him back in Pau Grande in a pick-up game, running around in just a pair of shorts, shouting to his teammates and negotiating the uneven field. As romantic as the image was, it held a great deal of truth, for he continued to go back to Pau Grande regularly until he moved in definitively with Elza.[90]

Much had changed for Garrincha by 1962. He had been recruited to play for the club Cruzeiro do Sul, in Petrópolis, and appeared for the club for two years, without quitting the Pau Grande team. Two attempts to try out for clubs in the city of Rio, first at São Cristóvão and then at Fluminense, proved futile. He never even got a look, despite the good word that an influential uncle put in for him at Fluminense. His Pau Grande team attracted attention, however, by dominating other clubs from around Rio. When Araty, a midfielder for Botafogo and at times for the Seleção, went to Garrincha's hometown with a friend, he saw the young point and recommended that his club give him a trial. As was usual, the coaching staff was less than thrilled to bring in an unknown kid, and particularly one with an obvious physical deformity; his legs bowed out strikingly to his right. The coach, Gentil Cardoso, put Garrincha up against Nilton Santos, already a star of the club and the national team. The "Encyclopedia of Football" soon saw the talent of the youngster, who kept juking by him down the sideline and reported to Cardoso, "The kid is a monster. I think it's best to sign him. Better to have him with us than against us."[91] Garrincha went right onto the team, while still traveling back and forth to Pau Grande. He needed the salary of Botafogo, but he had married Nair, who was expecting their first child. Despite the six-hour round trip commute, he managed to shine at his club, silencing early doubters who made fun of his legs—even the army had rejected him—or thought his game individualistic or unpolished.[92]

He fought his way to stardom on the Seleção as well as at Botafogo. In September 1955 he debuted for the national side in an unimpressive draw with Chile. With several other notable players at his position, his inclusion on the 1958 World Cup squad was far from certain. Julinho Botelho was good enough to have been bought by Italian club Fiorentina, and Joel was a star at Flamengo. The latter started the first two games of this Cup; Garrincha came in for the third game, against the Soviet Union, when Nilton Santos and other veterans helped convince Coach Feola to put in both Garrincha and Pelé. So dominant was Garrincha in the match that journalists labeled him the "Brazilian Sputnik."[93] The launch of the first Sputnik satellite in 1957 fueled rumors that Soviet players were "supermen trained for soccer in the laboratories of powerful Soviet technology." These modern marvels crumbled, however, before the skills of the Brazilian team reinforced by Pelé and Garrincha.[94] These two added a jolt of creativity to an already-strong squad, proving to be just the sort of "artists" that the Soviet coach Gavril Katchalin feared.[95] Garrincha remained in the side, confounding defenders who quickly saw him as one of the keys to the Brazilian offense. After a narrow win over Wales and thumping victories in the semifinal and final matches, Garrincha went back to Botafogo. There, he helped his club win the 1962 Carioca championship. He was also on the national side for that year's World Cup in Chile, where he emerged as the greatest *craque* in the tournament after Pelé was forced out with an injury. Others made telling contributions—including Amarildo, "o Possesso" (the Possessed), who stepped in for Pelé. This was, however, Garrincha's Cup, when he made his most famous plays on the biggest stage.

Throughout the peak of his playing career, he demonstrated skills that amazed observers. No one could stop him, although it is easy to see why so many thought they could; a left-footed blast in the 1962 World Cup aside, he almost inevitably went to his right before rushing goalward and launching a shot or a crossing pass. Films show how simple his moves looked but also how complicated and mesmerizing they became, repeated with subtle variations and enormous energy. Most often, in fact, he faced at least two defenders, one right on him, another a few steps back, and perhaps another forming a third line further behind. Not even Nilton Santos, reputed to be one of the best defenders in the world and Garrincha's teammate since 1953, managed to resist his feints in practice and begged not to mark him in training for the 1958 World Cup.[96]

Garrincha was most often portrayed as a simple soul with a natural genius. His hours of play and practice did not figure into descriptions of him as a player; rather, he seemed to have emerged from a rural utopia in which his skills grew unfettered. The informality of his childhood games fostered the *alegria*, the joyfulness, of the styles; for many, Garrincha maintained a naive happiness even as he became a leading figure on the Seleção. The many stories that were told about him only supported this image. On the pitch, it was said, he played out of sheer love of the game. Indeed, he did not seem to enjoy attending others' games; soccer was, he explained, something to play, not to watch. When playing, he showed little interest in tactics or the manager's advice. When coaches tried to get his attention in practices in 1958, the trainer Paulo Amaral told them not to bother; at Botafogo, he explained, they sent him off to play table tennis, since they knew he would not listen to pregame directions.[97] In fact, he appeared to operate without any planning or calculation. As Nelson Rodrigues put it, "Garrincha does not think. Everything, for him, is resolved by instinct, by the pure and irresistible jet of instinct." This was, however, an advantage, since it meant that "he always arrives first, . . . because his adversary's reasoning will never match the velocity of his instinct."[98] Indeed, one of his impulses was simply to have fun, which meant that at times he dribbled past defenders just for the joy of it. He did this in important matches, like one of the warm-up games before the 1958 Cup, in which he baffled four Italian defenders—although in this case he did end up scoring, sliding the ball between the goalkeeper's legs. It was a performance that Eduardo Galeano, echoing many earlier commentators, likened to a piece of humor by Charlie Chaplin.[99] Like Chaplin's Little Tramp, he also was credited with innocence. Others might describe what he subjected defenders to as "worse than cursing their mother," but he did not play out of malice.[100] According to Mário Filho, the journalist Sandro Moreyra tried to motivate him in a game against England by reporting to Garrincha that an adversary named Flowers had said that Garrincha was nothing. Confused, thinking that Moreyra had said "Fralda," or "diaper," and explaining that he did not like to play out of vengeance, he tried to identify "Fralda" to be able to show him how good he was. Unable to pick out Flowers/Fralda, he attempted to outplay all the opposing team, and he had a magnificent game, scoring twice to lead the Seleção to a 3–1 victory.[101] Sandro Moreyra also invented the notion that Garrincha referred to all those who tried to defend him as "João" (John), which so captured the imagination of fans that it was accepted as literal truth.[102]

If Garrincha came off as a fool in the narratives created about him, he was most often a wise fool, someone who with a bit of trickery (*malandragem*) could get the best of others without causing real hurt.[103] The nicknames he created for teammates and the teasing he dished out made everyone laugh, even the most reserved, like Didi.[104] He called Pelé "Elisa," because of Pelé's supposed resemblance to a female fan highly visible at Corinthians games. The heavy-browed goalie Castilho started as "Frankenstein" and became "Bóris," after the actor Boris Karloff. Others made fun of Garrincha as well, repeating old jokes about his physique—saying his legs were straight, but the rest of him was crooked—all of which he took in good humor.[105] Perhaps the most frequently told story about him exists in several forms; the variety reflects the enjoyment that Brazilians find in tales of his innocence. The first version I heard was this: On the way back from the 1958 World Cup, Garrincha bought a transistor radio, then a novelty in Brazil. But when a trainer playfully asked him if he understood Swedish, since all the stations the radio got were in that language, Garrincha became so disheartened that he sold the device to the trainer for less than he had paid. Other versions have him tricking someone else with the same sort of line, in other countries and in other years. His biographer Ruy Castro argues that the story refers to a joke Garrincha played on a fellow Botafogo player on a 1955 excursion. But he neither bought nor sold the radio; he was in fact taking several back for family members. He merely teasingly suggested to his companion that a radio purchased in Copenhagen would need a special valve to get reception in Portuguese.[106]

All of these narratives, in their various iterations, add up to an image of a humble man touched by genius. He played simply in order to play and in doing so showed that soccer of "pure inspiration," as poet Paulo Mendes Campos characterized Garrincha's game, could overcome not only the best efforts of opponents on the field but also the well considered tactics of European coaches.[107] For some, then, he represented the notion that the most authentic Brazilian—one drawn from the heart of the poorly educated, racially mixed majority of the population—had produced something unique and powerful in the modernizing world. Garrincha, after all, obeyed no schemes, relying on impulse and intuition. When things went his way, he showed that what seemed superfluous could be essential—in other words,

FIGURE 7. Garrincha shoots against Mexico in the 1962 World Cup. Popperfoto/Getty Images.

that the flourishes of his game were not just for show; they won games.[108] He was clearly an extreme case; not just any player could perform his moves. At the same time, though, his emergence from Pau Grande to World Cups seemed evidence that "any Brazilian player, when he untethers himself from his inhibitions," would achieve "something unique in terms of fantasy, improvisation, invention."[109] Even if club and CBD officials did not always make good use of their players, Garrincha and his colleagues comprised "the best raw material in the world."[110] They simply needed to accept themselves as they were, not try to be what they were not; as Mário Filho wrote after the 1958 World Cup, "We are Brazilians, and that is enough."[111] This recognition had given the Seleção of 1958 and 1962 what it had lacked in 1950: tranquility under pressure, and thus victory against teams from supposedly more advanced countries.[112] An English coach might look at Garrincha and judge him someone "from another world," or Russian players might consider him "something that did not exist." Brazilian fans, however, celebrated him as the real product of their nation and its *povo*.[113]

At the same time, if Garrincha served as a symbol of the potency of Brazilian tropical modernity, he was a rather unstable symbol. The problem, in the eyes especially of soccer officials, was that this "force of nature" was too unreliable to serve as a suitable basis for consistent success.[114] His innocence delighted those who saw in him a childish enjoyment of simple pleasures. This was clearest when he was on the field but also extended to his life off the pitch, where he seemed, with the glaring exception of his assault on Elza, generally free of malice.[115] Still, he hardly looked like the mature hero of a modern nation; one of his most ardent supporters, João Saldanha, thought Garrincha remained "a primitive, a bumpkin, half Indian, half savage."[116] Indeed, his image was antimodern, and thus deeply problematic for top-down modernizers who wanted to impose new tactics or technology on Brazilian players to bring them up to the level of Europeans.[117] Coaches, trainers, and *cartolas* had always been frustrated by his unwillingness to follow the most basic orders. The rapid decline of his skills after the 1962 World Cup, moreover, heightened officials' fears about relying on individual geniuses who had emerged with little or no formal training from the Pau Grandes of the country.

Some went so far as to claim that the 1966 World Cup, where the English hosts broke Brazilian hegemony, "verified the total supremacy of European soccer," though many more stressed the need for increased attention to organization on the field.[118] This meant not a mere imitation of European training, but some new system that would derive from European "advances" while making use of the Brazilian players' technical advantages.[119] For those seeking a renewal of the national style after 1966, Garrincha was either an exceptional and thus unrepeatable case or simply an example of an obsolete soccer that would no longer guarantee Brazil's lofty status in the footballing world.[120]

Neither of these negative lines of thought, however, found generalized acceptance, particularly among journalists and fans but also among coaches and officials. Many insisted that the genius of Brazilian *craques* was not an accidental occurrence but rather the natural derivative of the conditions and qualities of the Brazilian people.[121] What was needed was not a complete "renovation of values" but the discovery of new talents, since soccer "survived and lived on renovation—but principally on revelation."[122] Carlos Drummond de Andrade and others put forward candidates for the "revelations" who would take the place of Garrincha and other faded stars, the most successful of whom were the 1970 World Cup winners Gérson, Rivellino, Carlos Alberto, and Tostão.[123] João Saldanha, one of the most aggressive proponents of a playing style based on the talents of individual *craques,* approached the game as "a simple thing." Imposing too many theories would bring only "complication," not victory. The latter would come by respecting

Brazil's "magnificent production of artist-*craques*" who could more than compete with the "tanks" that European coaches were fielding.[124]

AN IDEAL INCARNATE: PELÉ, SPECTACULAR
AND RESPECTABLE

By the early 1970s this divergence of opinions transformed into a vitriolic dispute between *futebol-força* (strength soccer) and *futebol-arte* (art soccer). Garrincha would be a key reference point in those debates, but Pelé, his teammate in three World Cups and the *craque* of *craques*, played a still more influential role. So prodigious were Pelé's talents and drive to win, so great was his success at both club and national levels, so generally inoffensive was his on- and off-field behavior that he helped postpone the onset of the force versus art war. While he played, Brazil won beautifully; he was almost unassailable as a symbol of the mature tropical-modern nation. Nelson Rodrigues, cutting to the chase as was his custom, captured this sense with his assessment, "There is nothing more Brazil than Pelé."[125]

Pelé first captured world attention when he entered Brazil's match against the Soviet Union, alongside Garrincha and the midfielder Zito, in the 1958 World Cup. Zito performed well—his tireless running in the midfield showed why he was known as a *pulmão* (lung) player. Pelé and Garrincha, though, exploded with displays of amazing technical skill.[126] While the latter performed his tricks up the right wing, Pelé did a bit of everything from his position as left attacking midfielder. He scored the only goal in the next game, against Wales, before adding three in the semifinal versus France and two more against Sweden as the Seleção took its first Cup title. In the process he became the champions' leading scorer, but it was his prodigious flair that most impressed observers. His first goal, for instance, came when he received a waist-high pass from Didi, touched it lightly past the Welsh defender and tapped it in. Other goals were more pedestrian, but some stunned with their audacity. The *chapéu* (hat) move against Sweden, in which he flipped the ball over the head of his marker, twisted around the defender to meet it, and stabbed it into the net, provided one of the lasting images of the Cup. Another came shortly thereafter, when cameras caught the teenager crying happily after the Seleção's victory was complete. These tears gave him an appealing sense of vulnerability to go along with the talent and maturity that he had shown.[127]

Pelé's precocious performance startled many, including President Juscelino Kubitschek, but he had already made a name for himself in Brazil.[128] Like so many of the country's other stars, he came from the poor, brown *povo*. Born Édison Arantes do Nascimento—a name his father liked because it paid homage to inventor Thomas Edison—he preferred another spelling: Edson.[129] In any case, the pronunciation was the same, and friends called him Dico. Before achieving worldwide recognition, though, he was known as Dondinho's son.[130] His father was a professional soccer player when Pelé was born in 1940 in Três Corações, Minas Gerais. His talents never allowed him stability in his career, and the family moved to other cities in Minas before finally settling in Bauru, in the interior of São Paulo, where the club Lusitana had offered Dondinho a contract and the guarantee of a civil service job. Just as the family arrived, however, new leadership came in at the club, transforming Lusitana into the Bauru Atlético Club and reneging on the promised job for Dondinho. Still, the family opted to stay and try their luck, a risky decision because Dondinho had never fully recovered from a knee injury suffered during a brief stint at Atlético Mineiro, the only big club he ever represented. Although Dondinho's career never hit great heights, he became the star of BAC (as Bauru was known locally) and passed on his passion for, and professional approach to, soccer. Dondinho's guidance later helped distinguish Pelé's rise from that of Garrincha.

Hailed as "the bronze *craque*" in 1958, Pelé was unmistakably black and took pride in being so; he valued his color in part as a connection to his dark-skinned parents.[131] Especially as a skinny black kid, he could easily vanish into the masses that remained suspicious in the eyes of elites and officials; once, when he went out in Santos without anything to show that he was in fact part of the club, a guard barred his entry back into team headquarters. Although Bauru was a more urban environment than Pau Grande, both Pelé and Garrincha found spaces to swim, hang out with friends, and play ball. Soccer became a focus of Pelé's life just as it had for Garrincha; they both played whenever they got the chance (and made more chances by skipping school occasionally). Pelé showed his industry at age eleven, when he got together some basic tools and worked shining shoes in order to buy himself a decent ball.[132] Like Garrincha, he put together teams with friends from his neighborhood. Lacking the money to buy shoes, they played barefoot in a local tournament, impressing a local businessman who agreed to sponsor them. Now with full uniforms, including cleats, they served as the junior side of local club América. Shortly after Pelé won his first championship for this team and at the age of twelve, the club folded. This gave him the impetus to enter the junior side of BAC, where he found useful adult support.[133]

Son of a man *do ramo* (in the business), Pelé had the good fortune to come under the wing of a former Seleção player, Waldemar de Brito, then coaching BAC and serving as an inspector for the Bauru labor secretariat. Recognizing the boy's potential and his utter devotion to soccer as a profession, wanting to help his friend Dondinho, and aching to move back to the big city, Brito helped arrange for Pelé to meet the president of Santos FC. Everything was agreed on, but Pelé's mother, Dona Celeste, resisted, anxious about sending her fifteen-year old son off to live by himself in another city. Eventually, though, Pelé, Dondinho, and Brito convinced Celeste that Santos represented an irresistible opportunity for her son to pursue the career that he had chosen. In Santos, moreover, Pelé was far from alone; although he had no family nearby, he lived in the club's boardinghouse. Already raised strictly by his father to avoid smoking and drinking, this living situation allowed him to develop his game with fewer distractions than he had had back in Bauru.[134]

Though he had been a Corinthians fan, he was thrilled to join Santos. This was a major club, after all, and was coming off two straight Paulista state championships. After his first practice, the Santos staff immediately offered him a contract to join the senior team. This squad included a number of players who had appeared on the Seleção, among them the midfielder Jair Rosa Pinto, who soon served up passes that Pelé easily converted into goals; the point Pepe, who launched cannon shots with his left foot; and Zito, the side's leader and a key member of the 1958 and 1962 World Cup squads.[135] To crack into the senior team, Pelé had to win over teammates—many of whom later said that his talent had been evident from the very first—and impress coaches.[136] He suffered moments of frustration, once packing his bags and trying to leave, but managed a rapid ascent. Like other newcomers, he at first tried too many tricks, but he also demonstrated great humility and determination, along with a speed that led to the short-lived nickname "Gasolina" (gasoline).[137] He listened to those around him and then applied their lessons on the field; he also added his own moves, one of which sent starting defender Hélvio sprawling on the practice ground. Lula, coach of Santos, brought both Pelé and another newcomer, the twenty-one-year old Dorval, into the second half of an exhibition match; Dorval later formed part of the formidable core of the club in the early 1960s, but it was Pelé who caught the eye in this game, scoring four of Santos's six goals.[138]

At just sixteen years old, Pelé became a starter for Santos, remaining the central piece of a squad that built on the state titles that preceded his arrival, to add state, national, and international trophies in one of the most successful stretches that any Brazilian club has ever enjoyed. He also made himself the leading scorer in the 1957 Paulista championship and held on to that position without interruption through 1965, regaining it in 1969 and 1973. But his first explosion of promise at Santos also led to his call-up to the national team for the two-match Copa Roca in July 1957. Entering the first game as a substitute and then starting the second, he scored in both. In the latter, he formed a midfield duo with Luizinho, the Corinthians player whose spot he took on the 1958 World Cup squad. Even in the heat of this match against a bitter rival—and one that Brazil had to win to keep the trophy—the young Pelé "showed no concern . . . for the weight of the uniform." Instead, he behaved with a tranquility that made it look "like he was practicing in the Vila Belmiro (Santos's stadium)."[139]

By the start of 1958 he was disputing a place on the Seleção not only with Luizinho but also with Flamengo's Dida, an elegant player whose every goal, some said, was like a painting.[140] The latter would in fact start at the Cup until the game against the USSR. After teammates asked for Dida's replacement by Pelé, rumors spread. The less flattering hinted that the older player lacked the courage to face the Soviets; the more generous suggested he had some illness that forced him out.[141] In fact, coach Feola had hesitated to insert Pelé because of his youth and because of a minor knee injury. He might even have been cut from the squad if Dr. Gosling had not insisted on his inclusion.[142] All who saw him—Dida included—found his talent overwhelming and his maturity surprising. Nelson Rodrigues was the first to call him King (rei) in writing, after watching him score four times to lead Santos to a 5–3 win over the Rio club América. Not only skilled, Pelé was calm, even tame, Rodrigues judged, but also displayed a "virile attitude" that meant he would fear no one in Sweden.[143] This bravery led him to fight through the pains that lingered from his injury; asked when it hurt, he responded, "When I shoot." There was no question of him leaving the lineup, though, and even less of his changing his fearless style.[144]

His game was so complete that it left observers grasping for adjectives. To most, he simply represented the pinnacle of what could be achieved on the field. He was fast and strong, with the explosiveness and timing to beat others to headers. His dribbling and shot were magnificent, and he did both as comfortably with his left foot as with his right. His vision and intelligence allowed him to find open spaces for himself or to send passes precisely where teammates could best receive them. All of his skills, moreover, were magnified by his creativity and daring; he was unafraid of trying shots or moves that might not even have occurred to others. This Brazilian Edison was not, of course, the first or only inventive *craque;* Leônidas had his bicycle kick, Didi had his *folha seca*. Pelé, though, never stopped surprising other players and observers alike with his improvisations. The talented and hot-tempered Almir, who played briefly at Santos and then occasionally on the Seleção, said that he preferred playing with other stars of the day, like Coutinho or Dino Sani. Keeping up with Pelé—not just his passing but his thinking—required not only a high level of skill but also a long apprenticeship learning to anticipate his choices. Pelé, Almir said, "creates on the spot, in every game and every play he does something different, like a magician with an inexhaustible repertoire."[145] Some of his most famous moments, in fact, involved marvelous turns of skill that featured in highlight films and videos even though they did not result in goals. Two of these came in a single half in Brazil's 3–1 victory over Uruguay in the semifinals of the 1970 World Cup. When a poor goal kick by the opposing goalie landed at his feet, Pelé immediately sent a booming volley back, narrowly missing this attempt. At the very end of the match, Tostão played a through pass to Pelé; with the goalkeeper rushing out to cut the ball off, Pelé played a "dummy," letting it run past them both, before dashing around the now out of position goalie and shooting from a sharp angle. Another miss, but one of the most spectacular misses in World Cup history and, like his other try, an example of incredible decision-making speed.

Pelé did, of course, score many goals. FIFA (Fédération Internationale de Football Association) credits him with 1,281 in all, seventy-seven of which came for the Seleção. Some were mere tap-ins, others more spectacular. Playing for Santos against Fluminense in March 1961, one of his scores became the first *gol de placa* (plaque goal), after it so inspired journalist Joelmir Beting that he had a bronze plaque made and hung in Maracanã to mark what he considered a historical feat. Video of the goal does not survive, though dramatizations based on participants' testimony appear on anniversaries of the score. What we know from these memories and from contemporary accounts is that Pelé received a pass after teammate Mauro had disarmed a Fluminense player. He took the ball, turned, and "as if ignoring everything and everyone, set out [to do] the impossible," dribbling through the entire Fluminense team before firing in the goal.[146] Other players would accomplish similar scores;

José Miguel Wisnik points to Maradona's run against England in the 1990 World Cup, the Saudi player Saad Al-Owairan's against Belgium in the 1994 World Cup, Ronaldo's versus Compostela in 1996, and Lionel Messi's versus Getafe in 2007 as harkening back to the original *gol de placa*.[147] Pelé's came first, though, which not only inspired those who followed but also gave rise to a common expression: Any truly amazing achievement can be a *gol de placa*.

By the time of this score, Pelé was already widely regarded as the best player in the world. Other players received the labels of "the next Pelé" or "the white Pelé" while the original Pelé was still a teenager.[148] With fame came attention, of course, much of it in the form of the monitoring of his behavior on the field. As long as he played for the national team, he was expected to be its leader and to comport himself in a manner befitting this status. In part this meant demonstrating physical courage and determination in facing both injuries that came along with his busy schedule of games for both Santos and the Seleção, and the assaults that opposing defenders waged against him.

He had already stood up to pain in 1958, when he overcame his knee problems to shine in Brazil's first World Cup win; he would have to endure much more as his star rose. The CBD, with Havelange as president and Paulo Machado de Carvalho as vice president, tried to repeat the glory of 1958 four years later in Chile. This time, though, Pelé and Garrincha were no longer unknowns but *craques* in their peak years, on a team almost entirely made up of veterans. Indeed, this time it was the older contingent, like the thirty-three-year old Didi and the thirty-seven-year old Nilton Santos, who raised some doubts. Among the new faces was the attacker Coutinho, Pelé's teammate at Santos; their skills and familiarity with each other promised a new source of offense. They combined well until Coutinho suffered a severe knee injury in an exhibition against Wales; he remained with the team but could not regain his spot on the field.[149] Pelé, who had excelled in pre-Cup exhibitions and then at the start of the competition, soon followed him, to the horror of Brazil fans, after suffering a groin strain in the Seleção's second game of the Cup. He came back on after seven minutes on the sidelines, since the rules of the time did not allow substitutes, but he did not play again in the tournament. Garrincha stepped up to become the team's central figure, and the young and volatile Amarildo shocked everyone with his offensive dynamism.[150]

Four years later physical problems would again force Pelé out of a World Cup. He had become a target for opposing defenders early on and remained one until his retirement. Although his agility and vision allowed him to avoid many "disloyal challenges," some of the kicks and stomps hit their mark. He did not shy away from responding in kind; he gave well-timed elbows to aggressive defenders, often out of the referee's sight. Still, he could not fend off all the damaging attacks. The low point for him in this regard came in the 1966 World Cup, held in England and often described as a demonstration of the brutish force that Europeans were willing to employ against Brazilian skills. The CBD, for its part, could not mount the same sort of organization that it had put together in 1958 and 1962. Carvalho had been forced out, and with him went his detailed plans. Havelange named himself head of the delegation, and under his command, the CBD did not follow a single one of the ninety-six guidelines that Carvalho had proposed the previous year.[151] An unwieldy group of forty-five players was brought into training camp before the Cup, as coaches and other officials tried to find the right young players to blend in with the veterans. Only Pelé and the midfielder Gérson had emerged as "undisputed starters." Others seemed to have been included due to pressure from their clubs.[152] Garrincha's health problems cast doubts over his participation, in spite of promising moments, and everyone else had to fight for a place in the lineup.[153] The composition of the final squad did not convince Brazilian fans.[154] Confusion crept into the administration of the squad as well, with the CBD expressing uncertainty about its ability to meet the expenses of World Cup preparations.[155] The real dangers, though, arose once the Cup got underway. With referees letting many rough tackles go unpunished, the tournament nearly lived up to former player Vavá's wild prediction that "each game of Brazil in this Cup will be a terrible, bloody battle."[156] With goals on free kicks by Pelé and Garrincha, the Seleção beat Bulgaria in its opener, though Pelé picked up a minor injury in "a violent game."[157] Opponents simply "hunted" Pelé, as goalkeeper Gylmar later recalled, and the referees did little to stop it.[158] The brutality only increased in the next two games, both 3–1 losses, which sent Brazil home. Pelé, as ever the victim of opponents' fouls, felt so dispirited that he considered retiring from international competition.[159]

In the end, of course, he fought back, as he always did; his perseverance and courage remained in force over the course of his long career at Santos (1956–74) and through the turmoil that enveloped the Seleção before its great triumph in the 1970 World Cup. Other South American clubs had turns on the world stage, but the Santos of Pelé was one of the very few superclubs to emerge outside Europe. It thrived at all levels, from the local to the global, winning a total of ten São Paulo state championships, four Rio–São Paulo tournaments, five Brazil Cups (before the creation of the full Brazilian Championship in 1971), two Libertadores titles, and two world club championships during the Pelé era.[160] Located in the port city of the state of São Paulo, Santos FC did not have the immediate access to massive urban fan bases that clubs in the Rio and São Paulo metropolitan areas enjoyed, much less the financial infrastructure of the big European clubs. To increase revenues, club directors turned Santos into soccer's equivalent of the Harlem Globetrotters, except that Pelé and his teammates played against more consistently serious adversaries. Of course, one of the reasons for all of the tours was to keep the country's greatest star in Brazil and at Santos; this meant earning enough not only to pay Pelé himself but also to surround him with more stars. Wedging paying appearances between league and national team fixtures, the club's best played an intensely draining schedule.

Some of the club's principal members had been in place when Pelé arrived in 1956, like Pepe and Zito; still more came up through its junior ranks, like Coutinho, perhaps Pelé's best partner in attack, and Lima. The club's success helped it attract more prospects, and it developed a reputation for producing young talents. Like other clubs, it also had to play the market, bringing in and selling players. Some of these failed to pan out, but others, like defenders Mauro and Formiga and the goalkeeper Gylmar, made vital contributions. Indeed, Gylmar, who had come from Corinthians and agreed to play for only his salary (foregoing bonuses) started with Mauro and Calvet for the Santos team that unseated Real Madrid as the world's best club in the early 1960s.[161] The signing of right back Carlos Alberto Torres, who later captained the 1970 World Cup squad, gave impetus to what Pelé referred to as "a new golden period" in the second half of the 1960s, culminating in the conquest of five international trophies.[162]

Pelé, though, remained the star who amazed competitors and whose participation in exhibitions was often required for Santos to receive decent fees on their tours. By the latter part of the decade, he commanded half of the club's take for these matches.[163] Although he was earning a lot of money, he was also suffering for it, taking the field even when the medical staff had serious worries about his knees, kidneys, and ankles. The same held true on the Seleção; promoters insisted on his presence on the field before they would pay the CBD its full quota. With 1,106 appearances for Santos and 114 for the national team, he was, João Saldanha declared, "the most exploited" player in Brazilian soccer.[164]

In these same years the Seleção was being reshaped, once more around the King. Some members of the 1966 squad had matured into true *craques*, foremost among them the forwards Tostão and Jairzinho, the midfielders Gérson and Rivellino, and the Santos right back Carlos Alberto. Still, observers complained that the team lacked vibrancy.[165] At this moment João Havelange stepped in decisively, appointing new coach João Saldanha to get the Seleção back on track. This was an unlikely choice. The country was in the midst of a right-wing dictatorship, and Saldanha's links to the Communist Party were well known. Moreover, he had not coached for a decade and was one of the most caustic critics of the direction the Seleção had been taking.[166] He was, however, a respected and entertaining public figure who might restore excitement about the Seleção and dampen attacks on the CBD.[167] Nelson Rodrigues's hopeful reaction suggested Havelange had made a wise move; "For the first time," Rodrigues wrote hopefully, "the *escrete* has become a strictly technical and not political problem."[168]

Politics, however, would play a large part in bringing Saldanha down before the 1970 World Cup. From the very first announcement of his appointment, he showed why he was known as "João Sem Medo" (Fearless João). Instead of greeting his erstwhile colleagues in the press with a statement of optimism, he simply announced the twenty-two players who made up the starting and reserve lineups for his team. What he wanted, presumably, was to build a group of players confident in each other and in their place in the squad.[169] Early results were promising. Brazil sailed through World Cup qualification, winning all six games it played, scoring twenty-three goals and conceding only two.[170] The new coach lauded his players as true embodiments of the Brazilian style; not just *craques*, they were in his expression *feras* (beasts). It was through their distinctive "art and ability," he argued, and never by *futebol-força*, that the Seleção vanquished its foes in South America and would do the same in the Cup.[171] The qualifying campaign did not, however, buy him the goodwill of journalists or experienced coaches. São Paulo reporters had interpreted Saldanha's nomination as a victory for their Carioca rivals; although born in Rio Grande do Sul, Saldanha had spent most of his life in Rio. Linking his rise to Paulo Machado de Carvalho's fall, Paulistas exclaimed, "We have lost the Seleção."[172] The São Paulo–based magazine *Veja* was an influential source of criticism, labeling him stubborn and hot-headed. A long piece in February 1969 collected stories of reckless behavior in Saldanha's past as well as the poor opinions that coaches and former players expressed about his suitability to his new post.[173] Even his supporters in Rio, though, became concerned by his intensity, which veered into erratic behavior at times. Nelson Rodrigues joked that João might explode if anyone lit a match near him. Rodrigues, though, remained upbeat, arguing that Saldanha's "defects" were precisely those needed to keep Brazil from sliding back into the polite and submissive attitude that had characterized the nation in its earlier state of "underdevelopment," when Brazil was too immature to win the World Cup.[174]

As 1969 came to a close, a crisis unfolded. The tension swirling around Saldanha began to affect the team's mood. He had already publicly defied President Médici's suggestion that the attacker Dario, one of his favorites, be included in the squad; Saldanha's response was blunt: "The president selects his ministers and I select my players."[175] He soon offered a gentle qualification, saying that he was not against Dario, just "in favor of Pelé and Tostão."[176] His relationship with the press, meanwhile, approached open warfare, with each side blaming the other for "the unsustainable climate" that had been created.[177] When he cut three players for medical reasons and when Tostão, Saldanha's choice to partner Pelé in attack, had to undergo eye surgery, the group lost much of the unity the coach had fostered; individuals began to fear for their own positions on the team.[178] A stumble against Argentina in a March exhibition led to more open discord.[179] Given Pelé's centrality, it was perhaps inevitable that he would be dragged into the battles between Saldanha and his adversaries. Saldanha had in the past wildly praised Pelé as a player and denounced the burdens placed on him by Santos and the Seleção. As the besieged coach of the Seleção, however, Saldanha seemed less sympathetic to the King. He did not single him out for any negative treatment; Saldanha knew the value of Pelé. But neither did he keep Pelé out of the fray. What others took as a threat to exclude Pelé from the team was the final straw. In one of his throwaway lines, as Gérson saw it, Saldanha said that Pelé had missed a few balls during a game against Peru because of his poor eyesight. Others turned this remark into a declaration that Pelé had myopia or was in fact going blind. Saldanha's quick denials had no effect. Now it was not only his enemies in the press and in the coaching world but also the greatest player in the world who criticized him. Pelé expressed anger at the judgments attributed to Saldanha, saying that the coach knew him and his medical record—Pelé had in fact shown the beginnings of myopia as early as 1958 and had monitored the condition with leading ophthalmologists—and should have spoken directly with him if there were any fresh concerns. Moreover, the star asserted, he had recently taken the field for the Seleção with a high fever, implying that Saldanha did not value his sacrifice.[180]

In the end, though, the charge that Saldanha was not planning to keep Pelé in the Seleção proved a convenient excuse for rivals who had been scheming to force his removal.[181] After forcing Havelange to confront him directly, Saldanha departed, firing off an "Open Letter to Brazilian Soccer" to answer the charges against him and moving back into journalism.[182] His successor was Zagallo, who had coached the team in two games before Saldanha and was eager to take over on a more permanent basis. He recognized the difficulty of his circumstances. As he later recalled, replacing the leftist Saldanha and accepting Dario, General Médici's recommendation, set him up to look like a purely political appointment.[183] Seleção members later praised Zagallo for having the courage to build on much of what Saldanha had established, rather than trying to start from scratch only months before the World Cup.[184] Zagallo preferred to portray his work as a significant change, in terms of personnel and tactics, from that of his predecessor.[185] With shows of support from the CBD, which announced new medical exams to ensure the readiness of all players, he made clear that Pelé's place in the team was unassailable.[186]

Once in Mexico, the team rolled. Some members felt that they had left Brazil without their compatriots fully behind them, but their performances won everyone over.[187] Where there had been fears that the Seleção played without the velocity needed to get past European defenders, now there was praise of the artistry of the *craques*.[188] The whole team dazzled, becoming favorites of the crowds in Guadalajara, where Brazil played its first five games. Pelé was, as ever, "a spectacle apart." His daring, though by now familiar, nonetheless provided moments of surprise. In the first game, a 4–1 victory over a tough Czechoslovakia, for instance, he noticed that the opposing goalie had moved forward and, taking a pass from Tostão, tried to loop a shot in from the center circle. The shot scraped over the bar, but the attempt won applause.[189] A hard-fought win over England, the reigning champion, reassured Brazilians that their team had regained its winning spirit and could display not only technique but also cold-bloodedness.[190] Besides Pelé, fans delighted in the quick and smart passing of Tostão, the "elastic" dribbles of Rivellino, the long passes and hard shots of Gérson, the impeccable finishing of Jairzinho, as well as the hard work of Clodoaldo in midfield and the solidity of Carlos Alberto, Brito, and Piazza in defense.

Together, this Seleção captivated fans around the world. Uruguayan newspapers thanked Brazil for "saving soccer" with its exhibition of talent; observers from Europe seconded this sentiment, singling out Pelé for praise.[191]

Brazilians embraced the return of their dominance, highlighting the foundation of their footballing power in the skills peculiar to their people. "The purest soccer art," after all, came in the form of true "geniuses" like Pelé, who played with indomitable technique and joy.[192] Pelé provided a brilliant image for all of these celebrations of the tropical *brasilidade* of the 1970 Seleção and, indeed, of Brazil even at that politically tense moment. His play in this World Cup, the magazine *Placar* declared, proved once more that he was "the man who disregards all the logics of soccer, who exceeds." He also showed that he simply had a greater desire to win than anyone else.[193] This image of a Brazilian with skills beyond what anyone else could even comprehend, much less deliver, and with a pure, unshakeable drive, found general acceptance. Pelé's status as the *craque* of *craques* was beyond dispute.

What made this especially powerful in Brazil was the narrative into which observers fit the 1970 triumph. Officials and coaches would look back at the World Cup victory as the result of their careful preparation, a sense to which players like Tostão were somewhat sympathetic.[194] For most, however, the glorious campaign reflected the consolidation of a national identity based in the traits attributed to the mixed-race *povo*. Although Mário Filho did not live to witness this great victory, others portrayed it as a consummation of the processes he had described in *O negro no futebol brasileiro*. He had proclaimed the Pelé of 1962 to be "the very destiny" of the country; certainly he would have agreed with those who saw the triumphant Pelé of 1970 as the incarnation of a Brazil that was profoundly Afro-Brazilian. Nelson Rodrigues fairly shouted in his column that the "marvelously black" Pelé and his colleagues had dismantled the misguided notion that Brazilians had to play like Europeans to become protagonists on the global stage.[195]

Pelé was an especially potent symbol not only because of his unmatched prowess on the field or the sheer fact of the victories to which he had led Santos and the Seleção. Those traits made him a sports hero; his personal image, though, completed his status as an icon of Brazil's tropical modernism. His race contributed, as did his humble origins. What mattered most, though, was the sheen of respectability he maintained throughout this period. He emerged from the *povo* with attributes that middle- and upper-class Brazilians could easily embrace; as one 1965 portrait put it, he was always "the good son, the good brother, the good nephew, the pleasant companion, the loyal friend, the patient and resigned idol."[196] He held onto the lessons that his parents had given him, remained humble, dedicated to his family, his teammates, his fans, and his craft. In his autobiographies he stressed his strong devotion to his parents, depicting his efforts as founded on their support and aimed at living up to their expectations for him.[197] No one doubted that Pelé had been born with remarkable gifts—an "inexhaustible power of creation" and astounding physical abilities—but he focused hard on sharpening his skills and building a career. He was, in this regard, as much an artisan as an artist.[198]

Opportunities of all sorts rained down on this young star. When he moved out of his quarters at Vila Belmiro, he went to live with teammates at a modest local boarding house (*pensão*) owned by Dona Georgina, wife of the Santos masseur. He left only after hiring an agent, Pepe Gordo, who convinced him to find his own place and begin to take advantage of what fame had to offer. Major teams in Europe—Real Madrid and AC Milan among them—tried to buy out his contract and carry him off. In spite of the values, astronomical by the standards of the time, he remained at Santos, confirming his reputation for loyalty.[199] Staying at the club did not involve serious financial sacrifice; advertisers, film directors, and other parties saw in him the chance to make their own profits. He published his first autobiography—actually written by Benedito Ruy Barboza—in 1961 and appeared in the documentary *O Rei Pelé* the next year. Endorsement deals followed, and soon his name and image were linked to goods ranging from soccer gear to health products to televisions.[200] Not all prospects excited him, though; he refused a role in a film by prominent director Glauber Rocha. He could not, he later explained, understand how his character, a drinker and drug-user, could turn out to be the hero.[201]

While his career was taking off, he was also coming into young adulthood and experiencing romantic relationships of varying degrees of seriousness. Shortly after arriving at Santos he had met Rosemeri dos Reis Cholbi, a dark-haired white girl three years his junior. To all appearances, their dating proceeded under the watchful eyes of both Pelé's and Rosemeri's families; they were not allowed to meet alone.[202] When they finally married in 1966, it was in a small ceremony "far from the buzzing of the crowd," as the *Folha de São Paulo* put it, and certainly not the grandiose event that had been rumored. Still, the wedding was front-page news—"Pelé Marries!" was followed the next day by "Pelé and Rose in Munich." The union often appeared as an emblem of the country's supposed racial democracy.[203]

Missteps in these years did not seriously damage Pelé's public image. He had other relationships both before and after marrying Rosemeri, fathering one daughter with a domestic servant in 1964 and another with a journalist in 1968. He quickly recognized the latter, Flávia Cristina Kurtz, but refused to do the same with the former, Sandra Regina Machado, for nearly three decades, accusing her of wanting his money. (After a DNA tested confirmed his paternity in 1991, he appealed the judgment thirteen times.)[204] He suffered financial troubles, too, as his trust in Pepe Gordo turned out to be misplaced. By 1965 he had to borrow money from his club to pay off debts that bad investments had created.[205] More serious problems emerged later, but in these years, he managed to protect his image of honorability. Having put too much faith in a friend was not much of a sin, after all, and in the Brazil of the 1960s, sexual indiscretions generally did not lead to public condemnation of successful men.

In any case, he remained an icon of respectability. His fame perhaps gave him some leeway, but only because he showed himself so willing to sacrifice for his family and his country. Not only did he take care of his parents, grandmother, and brother—as well as Rosemeri and the three children she and Pelé had together—but he did what Brazil needed him to do. Most often he served the nation on the soccer field, of course, but he also fulfilled his obligatory military service with humility and obedience. The press played up the composure he showed as he carried out menial tasks, often with passersby calling to him or teasing him. The military also made use of his soccer skills in the South American Military Championship, which culminated in a violent but satisfying victory over Argentina.[206] He also avoided public political statements as the country headed into dictatorship, a stance that frustrated opponents of the regime. These critics only became angrier with him later on for his declarations that he had never faced racial discrimination and that Brazilians were not ready for democracy—or at least not ready to take voting seriously.[207] The closest he came to social or political protest in these years came when he scored his thousandth official goal in 1969. After jolting in his penalty kick, he surprised viewers with a plea: "Let's protect the children in need. . . . For the love of God, the Brazilian people can't forget their children." Hardly a controversial sentiment, his plea reminded fans that he had worked his way from poverty to success.[208]

CONCLUSIONS

Beyond the sheer joy of victory in 1970 lay the feeling that a third World Cup title marked a consolidation of modern Brazil. Not only proud Brazilians but admiring Europeans like the filmmaker and writer Pier Paolo Pasolini contrasted the joyful "poetry" of Pelé and his fellow *craques* to the unimaginative "prose" of their European rivals. Philosopher Vilém Flusser, who lived and taught in Brazil for more than thirty years after fleeing anti-Semitism in his native Prague, went so far as to say that the country's game was radically—"ontologically"—different from that of Old World styles.[209] For Brazilian commentators, the distinction between an idealized Europe and their own tropical nation had been a crucial notion since the nineteenth century. Now, though, soccer—and the magnificence of Pelé in particular—provided symbolic evidence that they had reached their own sort of mature modernity, one that might in fact be "ahead" of the modernity that Europe had achieved.[210] As poet Carlos Drummond de Andrade wrote on the eve of the final match against Italy, Pelé represented "the *povo* made athlete in the poetry / of his magical game." Far from naive about the country's problems, Andrade nevertheless experienced ecstasy at the Seleçao's triumph and felt it as a well-deserved achievement of his whole people. "To win with honor and grace / with beauty and humility / is to be mature and be worthy of life."[211]

Brazil's World Cup triumphs in 1958, 1962, and 1970 came to be remembered as inevitable achievements, rather than the struggles that they all were. Viewing the games today, though, the difficulty of the matches that led to these titles becomes apparent; even in the golden period, many of these games could easily have gone against the Seleção. The significance that the team's victories took on in Brazil, moreover, derived from the protracted and conflictive formulation of a national style and its association with a dominant sense of a national culture. The Brazilian game, based on the supposedly inherent skills and joy of the mixed-race *povo,* seemed to mark the country's emergence out of underdevelopment. That Pelé was an exceptional player, no one doubted, but observers strained to portray him as more than an "isolated fact." He seemed the latest stage of the progress of Brazil and its people, a natural successor to Friedenreich, Domingos da Guia, and Leônidas.[212]

By 1970 the buoyant optimism that had accompanied the 1958 and 1962 World Cups seemed a bit naive. The intervening years had been too tumultuous and the contemporary political and social context was far too tense, for earnest declarations that "the Brazilian could make of anything what he had of soccer."[213] If anything, this sort of phrase sounded like the propaganda in which the military regime had tried to envelope the Seleção; it contained something of the spirit of official refrains like "No one can hold this country back now" (*Ninguem mais segura este país*). Still, the undeniable achievement of the *Tricampeonato* (third championship) allowed for moments of glory and patriotism. Whether they were dark-skinned Afro-Brazilians like Pelé, mulattoes, *mestiços,* or white, the champions embodied an understanding of Brazil as essentially mixed-race. It was a multiracial Seleção—and symbolically, a multiracial nation—that conquered the world in the heroic age of *futebol.*[214]

THREE

Playing Modern

EFFICIENCY OVER ART, 1971–80

> The delirious people who yesterday hailed the players, coaches,
> and trainers of the national team had before their eyes a vision
> that went far beyond the sporting victory and its World Cup,
> which today is the Cup of Brazil. It was a vision of their force,
> their capacity, their energy formed from the energy of so many
> races. It was not ... the mere jubilation of soccer fans. It was
> support for the future of the country, the certainty that more
> difficult prizes will shine within their grasp.
>
> **JORNAL DO BRASIL, 24 JUNE 1970**

Two days after the triumph in Mexico, the national team returned home,
setting off explosions of joy. Chanting "Brazil, Brazil" and straining to catch
a glimpse of Pelé, more than 100,000 fans watched their heroes' reception in
Brasília's Plaza of the Three Powers, the hub of the federal government.
General Emílio Garrastazu Médici opened the doors of the presidential palace to the public for the first time since the military coup d'état of 1964, an
act that some journalists could only describe as a "miracle of soccer" in those
years of dictatorship.[1] A more massive celebration awaited the Seleção in Rio.
There, upward of 1.5 million people took to the streets to greet players and
coaches, turning the welcome into "the greatest carnival in history."[2]

Delirium ruled for two wild days. Without any official planning beyond
a government-granted holiday, people simply went out on foot or by car,
shouting and laughing with friends and strangers alike. The honking of car
horns joined in with the blaring music of improvised bands and the drum-
beats of parading samba schools. Events clearly went beyond the convivial at
times: forty-four people died and more than 1,800 suffered injuries in the
celebration.[3] Overall, however, ecstasy overwhelmed the city and the codes
of normal social behavior. As one observer reported, boundaries between
groups evaporated in the excitement: "This county is marvelous. ... There is

FIGURE 8. Reception for the Seleção in Brasília, 1970. Coleção *Correio da Manhã,* Arquivo Nacional.

no difference of color, there's no distinction by religion. At this moment there is no rich or poor, or black or white, or whatever you might be. You go into the bar, and there's a psychologist, who would rarely talk to you, his eyes bulging out, screaming like he's depraved and buying beers for everyone! Hugging the black guy from the pharmacy! Everybody kissing each other, all friends." The irresistible sense was, as anthropologist Arno Vogel put it: "We were Brazilians, the greatest in the world!"[4]

This transcendent feeling of national solidarity gradually faded in Rio and across the country, just as the festivities eventually wound down. Memories of the World Cup, though, colored visions of the nation in the decades that followed. Unsurprisingly, those visions were at first triumphal.[5] After the wins in 1958 and 1962 and the failure of 1966, this latest victory seemed a consecration. Brazil was now undeniably, at least to its fans, *the* country of football. The players had in fact brought a tangible symbol of this status back with them—the World Cup trophy itself, named after long-serving FIFA president Jules Rimet and set to reside permanently with the first country to win three Cups. By defeating the Italian squad in the 1970 final, Brazil also beat its rival in the race to become *tricampeões* (three-time champions). The gleaming prize that team captain Carlos Alberto held up in Mexico City's Azteca Stadium now found a home in the Rio headquarters of the CBD (Confederação Brasileira de Desportos, Brazilian Sports Confederation).

Moreover, the decisiveness of the 1970 campaign led fans to embrace the image of Brazil as the birthplace of a uniquely compelling brand of football. Indeed, for most soccer fans the 1970 team embodied stereotypes of a distinctive national style based on individual technique, startling improvisation, and a daring commitment to attacking. By completing the work of 1958 and 1962, the 1970 Seleção seemed to confirm that Brazilians would always be capable of playing like Pelé and Tostão—which in this vision meant dominating their opponents "with the purest art."[6] Romantic images of this beautiful game (*jogo bonito*) depicted Brazilians as naturally gifted with breathtaking skills and with two distinctive character traits: a naive love of the game often described simply as *alegria* (happiness), and the playful intelligence of a trickster (*malandro*).[7] With three World Cup titles to its name and the Rimet Trophy in its hands, Brazil seemed to have consolidated its place as the home of a distinct soccer that could overcome European powers and do so in a refreshingly attractive, non-European (even anti-European) way.

As this "happy moment" of national pride began to subside, however, disputes broke out over the very style that had won such widespread praise.[8] Everyone cheered for Pelé and his teammates, of course, but distinct currents of opinion emerged on how best to ensure continued success. As columnist Armando Nogueira sagely predicted two days after the 1970 World Cup, one faction came to argue that talent alone explained the country's victory, while another identified "tactical preparation" and "physical preparation" as the real reasons for Brazil's achievement.[9] The appearance of such a debate— known as the battle between *futebol-arte* (art soccer) and *futebol-força* (strength soccer)—might seem startling. The split between aficionados of art and partisans of strength, however, grew out of lines of thought that had been developing since the 1950s.

The emergence of questions about "the Brazilian style" in the early 1970s, however, also occurred in a specific historical context that turned general anxieties about the country's place among modern nations into the vitriolic art/strength arguments that broke out in the 1970s. In strictly football terms, the 1970 World Cup raised the stakes for the Seleção as it went forward; having reached the peak of world soccer, how would the country keep itself from falling?[10] Much more serious was the influence of the political climate of the era, which polarized all discussions of the nation and its culture.[11]

With the support of conservative groups at home and the United States government, senior military officers had grabbed power in the so-called Revolution of 1964 and crushed a democratic system they deemed too corrupt and weak to handle the nation's problems.[12] The advent of military rule intensified the debates over soccer, particularly because the beautiful game—the *jogo bonito*—was generally portrayed as emanating from the common folk (*povo*).

Other governments in Brazil's history had shown disdain for the populace and thought the *povo* unprepared to participate effectively in a democracy. The dictatorship (1964–85) took this distrust to new levels of brutality, though, as its leaders sought to impose their models of economic progress and social and political order from above. Building alliances with private entrepreneurs and investing heavily in massive public-sector projects like the Transamazonian Highway (begun within a month of the national team's victory in the 1970 World Cup), the regime's finance ministers pushed for, and achieved, an overall growth of the economy. Increases in the nation's economic production attained remarkably high rates—about 11 percent annually—in the period from 1969 through 1973. For the military and its sympathizers, this boom in aggregate growth outweighed the pauperization of most Brazilians. They viewed the "Brazilian Miracle" through a wide-angle lens, preferring not to focus on the impoverishment that their economic policies were bringing to the vast majority of Brazilians.[13] In fact, the government clamped down on strikes, union organizing, and other protests against the effects of the "Miracle" on the lives of the lower classes.

Within limits, the generals tolerated the formal trappings of democracy. They allowed two parties, for instance, the official one and a loyal opposition. Of course, the regime monitored the loyalty of the opposition so that no serious challenges could arise. Vigilance over the parties and over the public at large meant that the motto on the national flag, "Order and Progress," took on a sinister air. This was especially true as the dictatorship slid into increasing violence to protect its idea of order during the Médici presidency (1969–74). Having served as director of the security forces under his predecessor, Médici came out of the military's hard line, which rejected a quick return to democracy. Thus turning their backs on the stated goal of the generals who had taken power in 1964, Médici and his allies steered toward a more permanent and pervasive dictatorship.[14] Censorship of the media tightened, while tens of thousands met with exile or arrest for alleged political crimes, a term that encompassed anything the military considered potentially subversive. Torture and murder became regular features of the regime as well, with thousands ultimately subjected to physical and psychological abuse and hundreds killed at the hands of the military's agents.[15]

Even in this somber period, the military deployed propaganda agencies to win over the populace to their cause. Dictatorial though it was, the regime was not totalitarian; it worked with forces from civil society and strove to garner wide support for its plans of state-led national development. Indeed, the very term "military dictatorship" can be misleading, since it obscures the level of civilian involvement in, and tacit acceptance of, the government in the late 1960s and into the '70s.[16] A 1972 survey by the Brazilian Institute of Public Opinion and Statistics (IBOPE, Instituto Brasileiro de Opinião Pública e Estatística) suggested that regime efforts to win support had some success in the states of Rio and São Paulo, where between 81 and 84 percent of respondents registered basic approval of the Médici administration.[17] We should, of course, be skeptical of public opinion polls conducted in a time of authoritarian rule. Still, nearly thirty years later, labor activist and future national president Luiz Inácio Lula da Silva admitted that Médici most likely would have won a fair election in the early 1970s.[18]

Criticism persisted about the nature of economic growth, which increased inequality, and the expansion of government repression.[19] The Médici regime took on these reproaches directly, arguing that rapid growth was necessary first to create wealth that could be shared by all sectors.[20] At the same time, the government treated football, the national sport, as a useful tool in radio and television advertising campaigns announcing Brazil's emergence in the world. Government publicity presented the Seleção's victory as an unquestionable sign of the country's progress and unity.[21] The government pumped funds into the coffers of the national soccer confederation to support the Seleção materially while using the news media to trumpet the country's winning image.[22] Slogans like *Pra frente, Brasil* (Forward, Brazil) even seemed apt descriptions of the 1970 team's style of play. Médici was a true fan, all agreed, who "cheered just like anybody else," but he also played up this appearance to give a populist sheen to his rule.[23] He concluded his reception of the winning 1970 Seleção with an appeal to common citizens: "In this moment of victory," he declared, "I bring to the people my homage, identifying myself with the joy and emotion of all . . . to celebrate, in our incomparable Seleção, the very affirmation of the value of the Brazilian man."[24] In 1970, like governors and other politicians around the country, Médici took pains to be photographed alongside the heroes of the Seleção. He made sure to appear in civilian clothes in some of the pictures—again, to look like a regular fan. Throughout his years in power, the president enjoyed being seen sitting in the stands at Rio's Maracanã Stadium, holding a transistor radio to his ear to follow the action like an "authentic Brazilian."[25] Associating with soccer was political theater.[26]

At the same time, military leaders and the soccer establishment harbored doubts about the *futebol-arte* style that had become a trademark of Brazilian soccer.[27] The Great Brazil (*Brasil Grande*) that the military dreamed of building required planning and control in soccer as in other realms. Waiting for the next great players to emerge from the populace and take on other nations with their "natural" skills was too messy, almost too anarchic, an approach for these technocratic, profoundly antidemocratic leaders.[28] In soccer as more broadly, they insisted on "state tutelage and directed modernization."[29] This meant channeling the energies of the common people, reining in the exuberance that so many observers had praised in the 1950s and '60s. In 1975, presenting his final report as CBD president, João Havelange summed up this position in grand, paranoid, terms: "Our Dionysian football felt itself unprotected," he asserted, in the global "war against the supremacy" of Brazil.[30] To make sure the country could win this war, the *cartolas* (club and confederation directors) wanted a style based on scientific models derived from European thinking about soccer, in place of *futebol-arte.* The new approach, *futebol-força,* emphasized coordinated control of the whole field, starting with the defensive end, and downplayed individual technique. As critics were quick to note, the military wanted the national soccer team marching in lock step; they did not trust the characteristics—the creativity and *alegria* and trickery—that defined Brazilianness for most in the soccer world.

Against this backdrop the notion of *futebol-arte* took on vital, positive connotations. Because of the characterization of the 1970 squad and its style of play as coming from heart of the poor, brown-skinned majority of the population, cheering for Pelé and his teammates and for *futebol-arte* was a way of celebrating the *povo* as the real Brazil. This does not mean that fans rooted for the Seleção as a consciously antielitist or antiracist act. In fact, many of those who thought about soccer in terms of its relationship to social hierarchies had serious qualms about supporting the national team in a period of dictatorship.[31] For most supporters the Seleção was an emotional rather than political topic, separate from and above formal politics. Their fandom was, nevertheless, a usually unselfconscious identification with a romanticized common folk as distilled in the "team of the people," a label more often applied to the 1970 squad than any other in the country's history. As the poet Ferreira Gullar described enthusiasm for the national team in July 1970, "it is the *povo* hailing itself, since soccer represents nothing else but, and the stars of the Seleção are nothing less than, that: *povo*."[32] The devastating art of Pelé and his teammates thus fueled popular nationalism.

The legacy of the 1970 Cup victory, then, was not a unified collective memory, but a set of contending interpretations of the *tricampeonato* (third championship) and its legacy for Brazilian soccer.[33] These interpretations formed the schools of thought associated with *futebol-arte* and *futebol-força*. The sides differed not only on their prescriptions for restoring the sporting glory of 1958, 1962, and 1970 but also on the assessments of the capabilities of the common folk that underlay those prescriptions. If the largely Afro-Brazilian, poor, and ill-educated *povo* possessed the traits necessary to keep defeating Europeans and other South Americans—if, that is, popular "arts" were enough to win more glory for Brazil—then roll the ball out and let the new stars take over. If, in contrast, the population needed a firm hand to shape it into a force that could confirm Brazil's position as a soccer superpower in the post-Pelé era, then the authorities would intervene. This second approach—that of *futebol-força*—held the advantage of support by military and civilian elites by the early 1970s, who included soccer in what the regime called its "national policy of human resources, directed at perfecting the Brazilian in all his aspects."[34]

The art versus strength debate was thus a struggle over what modernity—embodied in the members of the modern Seleção—should look like in Brazil.[35] This protracted battle took a dramatic turn in the 1980s, when *futebol-arte* reemerged as predominant. In the 1970s, however, momentum lay with the advocates of *futebol-força*. Their vision of the modern nation disparaged traits that were conventionally deemed Afro-Brazilian and that had been identified as the basis of the national style since the 1930s. The idea of tropical or mulatto *futebol* always contained condescending and essentializing depictions of mulatto, *mestiço*, and black men, and *futebol-arte* did not break with this tradition.[36] At the very least, though, these celebrations of the Afro-Brazilian nature of the national game implied that modernization—in soccer and more generally—would have to build on the country's multiracial culture. By contrast, proponents of *futebol-força* condemned the older Afro-Brazilian style as based on a primitive individualism that could no longer ensure success in the modern era. In fact, those in charge of the Seleção in the 1970s implied that the stars and style of the past reflected a Brazilianness that had become outmoded. In short, what had been "truly Brazilian" earlier now verged on the antimodern, the backward, and the subversive. The informal cunning of stars like Garrincha would be replaced by the scientifically grounded rationality of elite experts. Looking forward from 1970, the directors of the national game acted on a deep belief that their modern Brazil needed European-style organization, based on a scientific understanding of athletes' physical capacities and of game strategies, to harness and redirect the soccer instincts arising from the people.

THE KING IS DEAD, LONG LIVE THE COACHING STAFF

The future of soccer without Pelé is the advent of a mechanistic era ... without great brilliance, without virtuosity, anything unforeseen, any madness or invention. Only the brilliance of a play carried out according to plan.

RUY CARLOS OSTERMANN

Not even the country of football easily overcomes the loss of the greatest player in the world.[37] Pelé first gave serious thought to retiring from the Seleção right after the victory in Mexico City, though his formal departure only came a year later, with appearances in exhibitions in July 1971 against Austria in São Paulo's Morumbi Stadium and Yugoslavia in Rio de Janeiro's Maracanã. Before the send-off in Rio, politicians, journalists, and common fans mounted a campaign to keep their king.[38] Despite the wide range of appeals—which continued in the thundering calls of "*Fica, fica*" (Stay, stay) from nearly 140,000 spectators in the Yugoslavia game—Pelé resolved to move on with his life. He was twenty-nine at the time of the triumph in Mexico City and knew that age and the punishment defenders had inflicted on him would diminish his physical abilities by the 1974 Cup in Germany. Playing only at the club level until finally quitting the game in 1977, Pelé could no longer anchor the Seleção.[39]

Pelé was more than a legendarily talented individual. Besides "the genius, the best player ever produced, the king, the coffee-colored *craque*," Pelé was "also the perfect player for a scheme."[40] That is, no one else could do so many things that were both remarkable as isolated feats but also crucial to the style of play that had characterized the Seleção through the 1960s. Over the course of the following two decades, many forgot this crucial aspect of Pelé's role and simply cast about for a new king to lead the country's other *craques* to international glory. None measured up, of course, but many candidates appeared. At a trivial level, it helped if a promising player's name had the right sound. The forward Reinaldo, who starred for the club Atlético Mineiro and the Seleção in the late 1970s and early '80s, seemed an obvious heir to the throne—since the first syllable of his name (*rei*) means "king" in Portuguese.[41] The gifted winger Renato Gaúcho, who emerged at the end of the 1970s and shone at several clubs (and sporadically on the Seleção in the 1980s and early '90s), shared this trait; indeed, his name could be transformed into *Rei nato*, or "natural-born king."[42] But skills that translated into wins mattered more than names or other coincidences. Thus when Zico began to lead Flamengo to victory—then as now the country's most popular club—with quick dribbles, sharp passes, and an amazing ability to bend free kicks, Maracanã echoed with choruses of "*Hei, hei, hei / Zico é nosso Rei*" (Hey, hey, hey / Zico is our king). Journalists proclaimed him the "white Pelé," but neither he nor any player since has wielded the on-field influence of the original King.[43] What Brazil and its national team needed, many observers started to believe in the 1970s, was not to replace Pelé but to figure out how to win without him.

The perceived need to change the direction of the Seleção seems surprising in retrospect. Even without Pelé, Brazil had the makings of a powerhouse. To begin with, other famously skilled and experienced stars remained from the 1970 squad. Though some—Gérson, Carlos Alberto, Rivellino—showed a certain slowing down, these "old men" had matured as leaders.[44] At the same time, stars like Clodoaldo, Paulo Cézar Lima, and Jairzinho were in their prime, and the team could also count on up-and-coming talents like Leivinha and Nelinho. Moreover, coach Mário Lobo Zagallo and his trainers were veteran hands, and the *cartolas* kept the staff largely intact. In spite of such continuities, however, advocates of *futebol-força* attacked *futebol-arte*. Rare were the voices of compromise, like that of Ivan Calvacanti Proença, the writer and folklorist who championed *futebol-arte* but hailed the idea of "*futebol-força* in the service of art," arguing that Brazil needed a "force/art communion."[45] Such pronouncements failed, however, to satisfy either side, and the direction of the Seleção became a hot issue for those who held sway in the national sports hierarchy as well as for the proverbial 90 million coaches who made up the general public.

For leaders in the military regime and other advocates of *futebol-força*, the departure of Pelé was a great opportunity. Without his vaunted magic, it was easier to justify a sweeping "remodeling" of the national style, as Zagallo put it just three days after Pelé's last game for the Seleção.[46] This reformulation was depicted at the time as the imposition of military order on the game, as cartoons from the satirical weekly *O Pasquim* suggest (see figure 9 later in this chapter). Applying lessons from U.S. and European science and from the most up-to-date European footballing strategies, the soccer hierarchy in Brazil attempted to modernize the game with the same grandiose, top-down style the dictatorship used in its "pharaonic" public works projects. Moreover, the modernity that the military targeted was clearly based on European models; the regime aimed for a progress that would make Brazil function more like the advanced nations of Europe.[47] The dictatorship was in a sense extending its overarching political initiative to the training grounds of the national team. New coaches and trainers, preferably with formal education in physical education, physiology, or related fields, would be the technocratic agents of this project, a sort of "Copernican revolution in Brazilian football."[48] Their implementation of scientific and tactical advances was highly invasive, since they sought to regulate the bodies of Brazil's soccer players and the tactical orientation of those bodies on the national team.[49] Speed, stamina, and collective schemes became fetishized as the qualities that would allow the country's players—portrayed now as too slow and too individualistic—to protect the nation's honor against the threats of physically robust and well-organized Europeans.[50] In this case, the natural resources undergoing reconstruction for the betterment of the nation were the players who almost always began their lives in the largely poor, Afro-Brazilian working classes and could now become properly modern—efficient and obedient—components of the military's Great Brazil.[51]

The first steps of this initiative came in the lead-up to the 1970 World Cup, with the methods of physical conditioning included in "Operation Mexico," the campaign that the CBD mounted to avoid a repeat of the Seleção's disastrous loss in 1966. The military had, in fact, long promoted the scientific study of physical education, setting up a Military Center for Physical Education as early as 1922.[52] Faculty and students from the Army's School of Physical Education (EsEFEx, Escola de Educação Física do Exército) formed the vanguard for the study and diffusion of physical education not only in national team sports but also in schools, factories, and community groups. Experts coming out of the military's physical education institutions played key roles in the organization of Brazilian sports, with the aim of improving the "physical aptitude" of the population to meet the needs of state-led modernization.[53] In the early 1970s, then, the regime had a range of experienced officers at their disposal. Many of these men brought their organizational know-how and scientific research to the government sports bureaucracy and specifically to the administration of the national soccer team.[54] Tellingly, they referred to team members not as players but rather as "football athletes," a terminological change that captured the orientation of the men who came to the fore in the training of the Seleção in the late 1960s and into the '70s. Referring often to empirical sciences linked to physical education, they saw Seleção members not as *craques* with skills to polish but as athletes with muscles to strengthen.[55]

João Saldanha, an iconoclast while coach of the team (1969–70) but a consistent advocate of *futebol-arte* as a journalist, later expressed appreciation for the work of the training staff of the 1970 Seleção. He singled out the introduction of altitude training as an innovation that had been helpful in preparing the team for games in Guadalajara and Mexico City. Characteristically, and quite possibly intentionally, he irritated Lamartine Pereira da Costa, the trainer whose work he most highly praised, by referring to him as "Colonel Lamartino" and by taking undue credit for Lamartine's inclusion in the coaching staff.[56] After the national soccer hierarchy removed Saldanha, the new coach, Zagallo, ceded even greater power to the technical staff in both the 1970 and 1974 World Cups. Famous as a hardworking, complementary player, Zagallo proved bureaucratically minded and compliant as a coach. He would be a good lieutenant in the rationalization of the national game.

In truth, Zagallo was one of the few members of the national team's technical staff in the 1970s without a formal military rank or advanced training in physical education. The military cast of Brazil's delegation to the 1970 World Cup was obvious. Headed by Brigadier Jerônimo Bastos, the group included also Captain Cláudio Coutinho supervising a staff with two military men, Captains Kléber Camerino and Benedito José Bonetti, and two civilians forming the physical preparation team and with Sublieutenant Raul Carlesso training the goalkeepers. One of the civilians, Admildo Chirol, said that he had supported the choice of Coutinho "because the greatest capacity in physical education [wa]s in the army."[57] Four years later, the military regime's imprint was equally strong. Zagallo returned as head coach, under the overall supervision of Admiral Heleno Nunes, who besides his military rank held the title of president of the dictatorship's official party, Arena. Nunes brought in three other military men to help oversee the Seleção. Ostensibly handling the logistics of the campaign, Nunes wielded influence on Zagallo's choice of players.[58] Meanwhile, Coutinho again headed the physical preparation department.[59] Though Zagallo remained an influential figure, he represented only the leading edge of what we can call the scientific revolution of the 1970s.

Of all these coaches and administrators, it was Coutinho who pushed the refashioning of the Seleção to its highest point when he took over as coach of the national team in 1977. Indeed, after his death in a scuba diving accident in 1981, players and journalists remembered him as a "revolutionary" because of the techniques and vocabulary he injected into Brazilian soccer.[60] Lamartine Pereira da Costa declared that Coutinho gave the impression of being "a scientist on the field."[61] His origins outside of the soccer system may have helped make him an agent of change. Like the three generals who ruled the country from 1967 to 1979, he was a *Gaúcho,* a native of the southernmost Brazilian state of Rio Grande do Sul. Unlike these commanders-in-chief, Coutinho grew up in Rio de Janeiro and showed no great interest in soccer as a child. He was athletic, an avid volleyball player and diver, but he came to soccer through his study in the burgeoning field of physical education.[62] On graduating from his military academy, he furthered his knowledge of the work of Dr. Kenneth Cooper, a physician and former U.S. Air Force colonel who popularized tests of aerobic fitness, and other foreign researchers in physiology. After completing a master's degree in physical education in France, Coutinho applied Cooper's methods to soccer players. His specific use of diagnostics like Cooper's twelve-minute run test (which measured fitness based on how far the subject could run in that time) and his general emphasis on running for his athletes ended up blurred in the public's mind. Coutinho became known as the first champion of jogging in Brazil, which was—and often still is—called "doing a Cooper."[63] Coutinho also integrated other innovations from the United States, so that Seleção players worked out on Nautilus machines shortly after their development. The Brazilian delegation arranged the installation of this high-intensity-training equipment for its headquarters in the 1974 and 1978 World Cups. Under the guidance of Coutinho and his like-minded colleagues, players ran more than they ever had while training for the Seleção and were required to build muscular strength.[64] "Doing Coopers" and other carefully monitored exercise was introduced secretly, "like contraband."[65] The focus on "working the physical" was not always welcomed by players, but persists to this day.[66]

The physical side of the renovation that Lamartine labeled "scientific" was already present in the build-up to the 1974 World Cup in Germany. Throughout his first turn as coach of the national team, Zagallo was more than happy to have his trainers pushing the players to improve their conditioning. From 1971 on, furthermore, it was clear that he intended to tweak his tactics. Executing his plans was, however, a difficult proposition. Zagallo had to deal with people's fresh memories of the 1970 side's fluid, "poetic" style—indeed, these memories were still being burnished—and with players who had become "myths" (as Zagallo himself put it) because of their performance on that team. Some of the more stubborn among them—like Rivellino and Gérson—were fixtures on the Seleção, players whose skills and fame meant that Zagallo had to include them in the team he was trying to reorganize.[67] What he wanted was to combine these willful veterans with younger talents in a more defensive scheme, one that could cope with the speed and discipline that Zagallo, like others in the national soccer hierarchy, attributed to the Europeans. Without risking a "brute change," Zagallo insisted on the collective nature of the game, with players carrying out specific tasks that their commanders—the coaches—assigned.[68] These tasks were not completely rigid; as Rivellino later recalled, Zagallo trusted that he and Gérson would know how to cover for each other when one went forward to attack.[69] At the same time, Zagallo hammered home the need for even the stars to focus on tight defense, beginning with close marking on the opponents' side of the field. As the ball moved toward the Brazilian goal, he wanted a compact defense, with everyone pitching in. Offensive moves required the kind of cooperation that Rivellino mentioned, especially on the wings. Brazilian fullbacks would no longer go bombing forward along the sidelines without teammates protecting the space they left behind. The basis of all attacks would be sharp passes, to provide "speed to exploit the few flaws of the adversary." Dribbling would most likely lead to the team getting bogged down and then losing possession. To avoid this, Zagallo's Brazil would be "running ninety minutes without . . . giving [opponents] time to catch their breath."[70]

This scheme followed the trend toward more cautious play that European teams had been developing since the 1966 World Cup in England. Coaches in Brazil had always shown an interest in tactics, generally adopting and modifying innovative schemes that arose in Europe. Up into the 1930s, the hoary pyramid still held sway in Brazil, a 1–2–3–5 system that featured the goalkeeper at the point of the pyramid, with two defenders, three midfielders, and five forwards arrayed in front of him. Like most of the rest of the footballing world, though, Brazilian coaches adopted the WM system that Herbert Chapman had developed at English club Arsenal. Introduced by Gentil Cardoso and then by European coaches who came to work in

Brazil—notably Dori Kürschner—the tactical layout found its most influential champion in Flávio Costa, coach of the Seleção in the disastrous year of 1950. Brazilian coaches did not merely ape the ideas of their European counterparts, however; the general rise of a defensive back four by the 1950s resulted from Brazilian innovations. Players did not always appreciate the 4–2–4 system that became standard in the 1950s and '60s, but this was never a rigid plan. Indeed, with input from his stars in 1970, Zagallo transformed it into a highly flexible 4–5–1, though the players' movement meant that they did not keep strictly to that shape.[71]

As early as 1971, however, Brazilian coaches and officials showed a newfound fascination with a tactical shift toward more strictly imposed specific positions and patterns. The aim was not to add offensive firepower but rather stave off opponents' scoring; in other words, the tendency was for Brazil to sink into what Eduardo Galeano called "the mediocrity of defensive soccer."[72] This was apparent in the Taça Independência (Independence Cup), which the CBD organized in 1972. Ostensibly a commemoration of Brazil's 150 years of independence, the competition was, by most accounts, somewhat hastily thrown together.[73] Former World Cup champions Germany, Italy, and England all declined invitations to take part in this "mini-Cup." Although the Seleção ended up the champion in a field of eighteen national teams plus a Selection of Africa and a Selection of CONCACAF (Confederation of North American, Central American and Caribbean Football) teams, it did so in a manner that made 1970 seem a distant past. The defense worked well, as the team played Czechoslovakia, Yugoslavia, Scotland, and Portugal— respectable powers all—without conceding a goal. The Czech coach agreed with Zagallo's assessment that including forwards in the marking scheme had made the 1972 defense better than that of the 1970 *tricampeões*.[74] Still, even with Tostão and Gérson joining fellow world champions Rivellino, Clodoaldo, and Jairzinho, the midfield and attack failed to impress, scoring only five goals in the team's three victories and one draw. As Rivellino told an interviewer before the Taça, "Everyone knows the *gringos* close ranks against us." The answer, he argued, had to come from the Brazilians' ball skills, because, "with shutting down and running, the game's better for the enemy."[75] Nevertheless, although the team had shown glimpses of the country's "beauty of unique improvisation" in a warm-up against the German club Hamburg, such moments were rare during the tournament itself.[76]

In spite of Brazil's victory, few observers liked what they had seen in the Taça Independência. Only Portugal "gave us some heat," as João Saldanha observed, holding on until Jairzinho scored in the eighty-ninth minute to give Brazil the trophy.[77] Others praised the defense but thought the Seleção slow, inhibited, or confused when the players tried to go forward with the ball; the side was not yet playing with the fluidity and organization it needed to break down vigorous European defensive game plans.[78] Like so many national teams in the years that followed, the 1972 version won but without dominating as the 1970 Seleção had done. It therefore fell subject to the damning phrase: *venceu mas não convenceu* (it won but did not convince).

Though Zagallo announced his pleasure after the Taça—shrilly suggesting that his critics were "defeatists" who should "shut their mouths"—neither he nor the soccer hierarchy found great relief in their victory.[79] It was clear that this was the last time that the Seleção would be able to use the 1970 squad as its foundation.[80] Greater evolution was needed before Brazil would be ready to mount a serious challenge in the 1974 World Cup. In fact, the changes that came about were largely unhelpful. More stars retired or fell out of favor with the coaches, from Tostão to Gérson to Clodoaldo. A nine-game tour of North Africa and Europe in June and July of 1973 failed to deliver the expected cohesiveness in the team.[81] Indeed, despite the Seleção's scientific preparation, it arrived in Germany surrounded by doubts and with remarkably low expectations, at least for a nation that had so recently claimed the Jules Rimet Cup.

The team played down to those expectations, looking anxious and disjointed throughout most of the tournament. Brazil scraped its way out of the first group stage. After uninspiring, scoreless ties against Yugoslavia and Scotland, the Seleção needed to beat Zaire 3–0. Only a goal by Valdomiro, one of the newer additions to the squad, late in the second half, completed that scoreline and took Brazil into the knockout round. Even as they managed the necessary advantage over a nation with little international tradition in soccer to that point, the Brazil team looked nervous, its players unsure how to connect with each other. The real highlight came with a 2–1 victory over bitter rival Argentina. The Brazilian midfield showed more precision and fluidity in that game than any other in the tournament—though matches against Argentina represent rare moments in which Brazilians throw their concerns for winning beautifully out the window.[82] The next game, though, pitted the Seleção against a truly innovative team, the Netherlands coached by Rinus Michels and starring Johan Cruyff. Holland's carrousel, with players switching positions in a stunning display of versatility, swept Brazil away in one of the greatest wins in Dutch football history.[83] It was also a match that nudged Brazil further along the path toward scientific modernity. The Netherlands led Brazilian officials to fear that their modernity "was not all that modern after all."[84]

After some early attempts at optimism, journalists and former players quickly pointed the finger at Zagallo for not "releasing" the players to perform the way they knew how to do.[85] Starting the Cup with two ties left some convinced that this team reflected too closely the personality of its coach. "Insecure and obedient" like Zagallo himself, the weekly magazine *Veja* judged, this team "only plays it safe, will only score goals when it is impossible to do anything else, when there is no chance to launch a sideways pass or send the ball backwards."[86] Gérson criticized the whole team and Paulo Cézar Lima in particular for not looking to go forward enough. Clodoaldo condemned the "inefficiency" and "lack of heart" he saw, especially in the midfield. Shockingly, the country of Pelé and the beautiful game had fallen into playing antisoccer—that is, trying to destroy the opponent's game with little thought of putting together effective attacks.[87] The result of this approach was dire, one journalist quipped: "Never had so many suffered so much for so few goals."[88] Though Zagallo denounced such attacks once more, he repeated the call he had issued in 1970 and again in 1971: "Brazil needs to reformulate everything."[89]

Officials—and some very anti-Zagallo commentators—agreed with this assessment. World soccer had in fact changed dramatically, with a defensive focus—condemned in Brazil as *retranca*—hegemonic. Agreeing that games were now won with harsh physicality (*no duro mesmo*), former champion Piazza aptly summarized the state of soccer in the era: "The individualism of a player is being overtaken by the spirit of the collective."[90] This described even the Dutch and their free-flowing new style. While an exception to the dominance of destructive strategies, the carrousel only functioned because of the deep commitment their players had to a cohesive team unit. Cruyff was a stellar talent, but it was the organization of the Dutch as a whole that inspired Brazilian observers. The CBD, supported by the military regime, moved to energize the shift toward greater fitness and more rational tactics. Unsurprisingly, the coaches and trainers selected by those officials embraced their orientation.[91]

The CBD did not, however, immediately turn to Cláudio Coutinho to implement their plans. Rather, they tapped a well-known club coach, Osvaldo Brandão, to take over the Seleção. Brandão's tenure represented a pause in the top-down revolution; in most ways, he seemed a step away from change. For the *cartolas* his appeal was principally his reputation as a disciplinarian.[92] He did not, by his own admission, factor players' input into his decisions. Cajoling and screaming, he tried to make himself into a leader who could unite the team.[93] Strategically, he dropped the discussion of European tactics that Zagallo's staff had tirelessly promoted. He insisted on organization and obedience, but he spent his time tinkering with the choice of players for the squad and their level of fighting spirit, not outlining new tactical paradigms. His was more the familiar style, in other words, of an old-school coach who trusted in the skills of his players. This confidence was visible in his attempt to install the first of many "magic foursomes" (*quadrados mágicos*) that the Seleção would know over the years. Brandão hoped that putting four talented and versatile players together would allow them to bring out the best in each other. His greatest contribution was the inclusion of influential new talents in the squad. Rivellino was still an important part of the midfield, but future stars like Zico, Falcão, and Roberto Dinamite made their debuts on the Seleção, and other young players like Gil and Givanildo flashed promisingly.

Brandão lasted two years at the helm. Under his guidance the national team had some impressive results, particularly in its victory over Argentina in February 1976 and its conquest of the tournament marking the U.S. Bicentennial later that year. The latter competition saw the Seleção defeat England and Italy, with all the squad's goals coming from Roberto Dinamente, Gil, and Zico. By and large, though, Brandão's schemes failed. He never managed to find consistently creative play, in spite of the skills of his magic foursome of Falcão, Zico, Rivellino, and Roberto.[94] The captain of the 1970 squad, Carlos Alberto, questioned his ability to inspire his players to move the ball quickly, while others picked away at his lineup choices.[95] When the stakes were higher, in the qualifiers for the 1978 World Cup, criticism became even sharper, and Brandão's team proved unsatisfactory in the eyes of the soccer hierarchy. The CBD seemed to believe that the country lacked individuals creative enough to pierce modern defenses without the proper organization.[96] A depressing 0–0 tie at Colombia in February 1977 was too much; the team's lack of imagination made for a very "sad Carnaval" that year.[97] Under pressure from the CBD as well as the media, Brandão abruptly resigned.

Part of the difficulty for Brandão was that the political ground of Brazilian soccer had shifted under his feet. In October 1975 the military regime reorganized the ruling structures of the soccer confederation (CBD) and its parent entity, the National Sports Council (CND, Conselho Nacional de Desportos). CBD president João Havelange had finally succeeded in his long campaign to become head of FIFA, the international soccer association, in 1974.[98] The moment seemed ripe, then, for a renewal of the scientific modernization of the national game through the reform of the sports governing system that had been in place since 1941.[99] On the surface, the formal changes in 1975 were fairly modest. The CND expanded in size, from five to eleven members. The larger council consisted, as had the older version, of presidential appointees, though the CND also included one member named by the Brazilian Olympic Committee. Moreover, the new law asserted the primacy of the national bodies (CND and CBD) over both regional soccer federations and the powerful clubs.[100] In broader terms, the expansion of the CND and its powers constituted an attempt to concentrate power over the national game in the hands of trustworthy military men, a "militarization" of Brazilian soccer.[101] In fact, the regime retained Brigadier Jerônimo Bastos as head of the CND and Admiral Heleno de Barros Nunes (who had taken office earlier in the year) as CBD president. Nunes became a dynamic and influential figure pushing for a rationalization of the national style of soccer as well as the soccer confederation.[102] Under his leadership, one of his subordinates told a reporter, the CBD would attempt not only to "create . . . a true soccer department, such as occurs in club teams," but also maintain files of "technical, medical, physical, social, professional, disciplinary, and behavioral" data about players.[103]

It was in this context that Admiral Nunes put Coutinho in charge of the Seleção. In contrast to Brandão, he possessed a slim resume as a head coach. He had, however, led the 1976 Olympic soccer team and had become the coach of Rio's "team of the masses," Flamengo, that same year. More than this experience, though, Coutinho's appointment derived from the philosophy that he had brought to bear as trainer in 1970 and 1974. Indeed, as key figures in the military and in the CBD observed, he was brought into the Seleção precisely in order to "adapt" military-sponsored "science" to *futebol*.[104] Coutinho himself declared, "Training the Seleção and commanding troops are the same thing."[105]

His style of leadership showed, however, that he believed in managing his charges "without excesses of authority," as he had put it in 1972.[106] Coutinho was certainly capable of echoing the stiff patriotism of presidential announcements during the dictatorship. On the eve of the 1978 Cup, for instance, he appeared on the popular variety show, "O Fantástico," and, dressed formally but not in military uniform, called on Brazilians to put their squabbles over lineups and other petty issues behind them. Saying that no one could doubt the sacrifice that the team had made in preparing for the competition, he appealed for national unity: "All of you and us—the CBD, players, coaching staff—want victory. The rest—differences of opinion, resentments, points of view. . . . All that rest has to be left behind." It was, he concluded, the "time for optimism, time to take the ball forward." Even in this speech, though, he characterized soccer as one of "those passions, half crazy, those manias, even the irrational ones, those delicious alienations that in truth make up the charm of life." Like this final part of his speech on "O Fantástico," his normal presentation of himself and his ideas was idiosyncratic and more charming than might be expected of a spokesman for a military dictatorship. Indeed, journalists found him intelligent and at times captivating. He was well travelled and able to answer interviewers in Spanish, French, and English, while also convincing German reporters that he understood their language though he was unable to speak it. Even his critics described him as enthusiastic and eager to discuss the game.[107]

This dynamic young coach soon took up the task of refashioning the national team. Talking frequently with team members, with an honesty that several of them later recalled fondly, he tried to "motivate the player, make him believe in the objective."[108] In addition to "working the physical," this objective meant a more complete adoption of tactics then in vogue in much of Europe. Building on the philosophical foundations of the 1974 Seleção, he envisioned a Brazilian team that would use its physical vigor to maintain a rapid pace throughout the match. Defensive coverage would again be the primary tactical focus, with even the forwards pressing opponents and trying to win the ball. As the team moved forward, players were to rely on quickly launched passes rather than creative dribbles or deceptive footwork. Following precise lines, players would run onto passes, within patterns that the coaching staff had drawn up. Even more than Zagallo, he stressed the importance of collective work. Revealing his belief that Brazil was in danger of falling fatally behind Europe, he explained, "You don't win anymore with one or two players, as you did in the past, when Pelé or Garrincha made everything easy for the rest of the team. . . . There is no more soccer of exhibition but rather the strength of an ensemble."[109]

Coutinho's greatest innovations came in the language he introduced to explain the guiding principles of his ensemble. His most famous—and later notorious—linguistic intervention was *polivalência*, or polyvalence. In practice, this just meant versatility, the ability to shift between positions to serve the overall team plan, though the uncommon word suggested an ultra-modern technical approach. He also stressed the concept of the *ponto futuro,* or future point, as central to the workings of the new Seleção. The point forward (*ponta* or *ponteiro*) position was a symbol of traditional Brazilian football, most famously occupied by Garrincha. Traditionalists called for the inclusion of true points throughout the 1970s and '80s, arguing that the team needed a player running toward the end line to send crossing passes to central attackers or dribbling his way from the side toward the goal himself. Only such a point, they held, could stretch defenses wide enough to open up attacking lanes in the middle.[110] Coutinho, however, favored the future point, which was not a player per se, but rather a location that a player would take if a teammate's pass led him deep along the wing on the opponents' side of the field. Other key principles directly incorporated English terms like "overlapping," which described the play in which a wing passed the ball ahead and then ran past his teammate to receive a return pass. Although such moves were not novelties in Brazil, as former players and other observers often noted, Coutinho's language gave a modern and rational gloss to his plans.[111]

What this meant on the field, initially, was a period of uncertainty among players, as they struggled to comprehend the neologisms of their coach. Many first responded to questions about *polivalência* and other elements of Coutinho's scheme by asking, "Poly . . . what?"[112] Forward Pepe later recounted how the coach's ideas sailed over the head of the forward Nunes. At one practice Coutinho explained what he wanted from Nunes: "Rivellino is going to retreat to the penalty box arc, right next to the zone of reason, then you immediately look for the right flank, giving preference to open spaces. Then you overtake him at speed, trying an overlapping toward the future point, and that way you receive the ball in front of the goal." Asked if he understood, Nunes replied, "I only got 'Rivellino.'"[113] When confronted individually by reporters about their coach's ideas, players predictably tried to show comprehension and diplomacy—they could hardly do otherwise and hope to remain on the team. Dirceu, who anointed himself the symbol of the team, explained to the reporters that Coutinho's principles were far from mysterious: "It's not difficult to understand the scheming of defensive pressure, not giving spaces to the enemies. Everyone has to participate equally in the game, fast and without holding the ball. Coutinho wants this and we can give it to him, easily." Like Dirceu, most broke down their coach's language into terms that any player or fan would recognize, saying that Coutinho just wanted speed, teamwork, and attention to defense.[114] As they assimilated their coach's ideas and became accustomed to his odd phrases, the players fit themselves into the ensemble as best they could.

Under its new coach the Seleção bounced back quickly from the draw with Colombia under Brandão. Playing with only ten men after Zico was red-carded, the revitalized Brazil beat Colombia just seventeen days after the tie and went on to ensure itself a place in the next World Cup by thumping Bolivia 8–0 in July.[115] As had been the case four years earlier, Brazilians in 1977 seemed desperate to reassure themselves of the Seleção's potential with a World Cup approaching, and this victory reawakened confidence. Reporters seized on the display of talents by Zico, Falcão, and Toninho Cerezo to pronounce the latest "harvest" (*safra*) of players worthy of the country's tradition of *craques*. The willingness of remarkable individuals—not just newcomers like Falcão but also veterans like Paulo Cézar Lima—to buy into Coutinho's plans also inspired confidence. They would dribble, as these two explained on separate occasions, but only when it was "indispensible" to the team's movement.[116] Even those who feared that Coutinho was too inexperienced or lacked an overall, workable scheme, could still praise the coach for having "respectable concepts," ideas that might be the basis for an eventual organization of the team.[117] Solid results against European powers encouraged many. A draw with England in Wembley Stadium provoked dismay among Europeans, who thought that Brazil had been unnecessarily violent. In Brazil, responses to the match were mixed, but nationalist voices loudly defended the team's "fighting spirit." The new Seleção was still under development, and if the players needed to scrap in order to tie with England, at least they showed the willingness to do so.[118] Other Cup victories had also come after doubts, and this commitment to the struggle could lead to further glory.[119] Some held to the belief that "the people's team is taking shape, just as in [19]70."[120]

For many observers, however, the team rarely showed anything but fight. The morning after the Seleção's qualification for the Argentina World Cup, in fact, calls for Coutinho's ouster began to appear.[121] While critics usually stopped short of that, they hounded Coutinho even before the Cup began. Journalists, fellow coaches, and ex-players all charged him with leading Brazil "down the path to the strong and ugly."[122] The England exhibition was just a particularly visible example of this. Unhappy to be criticized by Europeans for playing in ways that England, Germany, and Italy had popularized, many journalists nevertheless thought that Coutinho's plans to modernize Brazilian soccer were draining it of its most effective—and most Brazilian—aspects. Under his watch, Brazil could have no exhibition of overwhelming skill (*show de bola*), only "depersonalized" players serving as cogs in the coach's machine.[123] The defensive scheme he worked out so thoroughly was generally effective, but the team only occasionally managed to put together a fluid passing game or a dangerous attack. Even the friendly win over West Germany seemed to come in spite of Coutinho's ideas, in a five-minute span when, as one observer put it, "traditional Brazilian football was unleashed."[124] Indeed, it seemed that the team only moved the ball well when its stars resorted to the quick give-and-go passing or dribbles that they had always performed. Coutinho's principles too often shut such movement down, as they did in a loss to France in an April 1978 exhibition. After a brilliant first half with Rivellino and Zico opening up spaces in the midfield, the coach made adjustments that led to offensive "inertia" in the second half.[125] This pattern of Coutinho's clamping down on his skilled players was annoying in these preparatory matches but became fatal to Brazil during the World Cup.[126]

Coutinho's handling of his team roster added to doubts about his ability to apply his ideas.[127] If he wanted to play a hard-nosed, defensive, and European game, then why did he prefer slighter, often injured players like Zico and Reinaldo? If he favored technical skill, why then leave out Falcão and Paulo Cézar Lima? Having tried out forty-six players in game situations, he certainly had done his research; the Seleção, one editorial declared, had become Coutinho's "guinea pig."[128] Why then were there so many newcomers on his final list? It was not just the logic of Coutinho's cuts that came under attack but his honesty. He had, after all, declared that he had a team in mind, one that he himself had chosen specifically and exclusively on the basis of players' effectiveness in his scheme of play. As soon as he announced his team, however, the press assailed his choices, seeing the influence of CBD president Admiral Heleno Nunes and regional prejudices. Rumors about dissent from within the coaching staff also circulated; some officials reportedly wanted greater emphasis on individual skill.[129] Confronted with this vitriol, Coutinho rapidly released a "secondary list" of other players "who might be called at any time."[130] These debates reflected profound concerns over Coutinho's effectiveness as a coach. In spite of his confident, military bearing, he appeared out of his depth, precisely when the team was supposedly undergoing revolutionary progress.

The start of the World Cup set off furious attacks. The setting certainly did not help calm spirits. Argentina's military had set up their own dictatorship, twelve years after their Brazilian peers but with much greater violence. With the alleged aim of uprooting subversion, the Argentine military waged the Dirty War, with widespread torture and the murder of tens of thousands of their fellow citizens. Some of the games took place only hundreds of meters from torture centers, making this one of the strangest World Cups ever and certainly the grimmest.[131] Brazil, still ruled by its own *milicos* (slang for military men), never seriously considered withdrawing from "the Cup of dictatorship." Instead, it sent a Seleção designed to embody the military regime's guided modernization. For Brazil, the high point of the tournament was probably the draw between dictatorships, a scoreless tie against the host nation in the interior city of Rosario. Brazil had slipped by Austria (1–0) to progress to the second phase of the tournament after very dull ties with Sweden and Spain. The rivalry with Argentina, though, lent greater importance to the Rosario game. Even there, however, players and journalists felt that Coutinho had been too conservative and had held his team back from victory on a day they felt clearly superior to their nemesis. Brazil's participation in the Cup ended bizarrely. The Seleção managed three wins in the second phase—3–0 over Peru, 3–1 over Poland, and 2–1 over Italy—but failed to make the final when Peru collapsed, 6–0, against Argentina. Organizers had scheduled the Argentina-Peru match after Brazil's game with Poland, so that the host team knew exactly what score would send them through—and then Peru capitulated shamefully. The stench of corruption allowed Coutinho to declare his team, undefeated but out of the Cup final, the "moral champion."[132]

Brazilian observers found no solace in the injustice of its team's departure. Outrage over the Argentina-Peru result did not prevent Coutinho's emergence as the main culprit in the 1978 World Cup fiasco. The young coach was an easy target, given the extent of change he had promised and the odd, pretentious language he had used to express his ideas. His defense had worked, but his offense performed miserably, with a lower goals-per-match average than all but two other Seleções (1938 and 1974).[133] During the tournament, moreover, he made moves that contradicted the image of scientific consistency he had been cultivating.[134] Four players who had been indispensible to his scheme—Zico, Reinaldo, Rivellino, Edinho—ended up on the bench at crucial moments. He replaced two of them (Reinaldo and Edinho) at the behest of the CBD president, which suggested that he was not truly in charge of the team.[135] Mostly, he kept on talking, repeating his favorite terms almost robotically and showing the limitations of his revolutionary philosophy.

FIGURE 9. "And the Canary Seleção [Brazilian national team] takes the field . . . " José Duayer / *O Pasquim*, 7 April 1978.

After one of many delays in a press conference, his own press secretary joked, "We have to change Coutinho's batteries." The reporters took this image and ran with it, referring to the coach as "Cybernetic Couto."[136] His language itself inspired much bitter humor as well, especially his favorite term, "polyvalence." When the team looked good—as it had in some pre-Cup matches, headlines read, "Now that's what we call polyvalence."[137] When the team played poorly—as, sadly, became the general rule—reporters wrote, "Not enough polyvalence," and former players opined, "Polyvalence without goals won't do."[138] Ultimately, a consensus took hold. Coutinho's ideas had proven themselves impractical—or worse, had formed a "cage of theories" from which the real Brazilian game could not escape.[139] The coach himself came off as a false promise, citing "English theories" when he was in fact "stuck at the ABCs."[140]

According to critics, the problem was not just that he had coached poorly but that he and his backers had led the country away from the true national style. In truth, Brazil had probably achieved what it could in Argentina, given the coach and strategies that the CBD and regime had chosen.[141] The soccer hierarchy had bet on rationalization overseen by scientifically trained experts, but this, according to most observers, turned out to be merely a "farce of efficiency."[142] No one claimed that the country had another Pelé at hand, but certainly the Seleção's performance was the result of the poor application of new—many said un-Brazilian—tactics. The result of such an imposition could only be "indefinition," with players caught between the style they had learned as children and a new one that they struggled to assimilate. World Cups do not favor indefinition, of course, and the Seleção suffered, though it never lost a match in 1978.[143] In the end, it was not only the "boy coach" but also *cartolas* who came under attack. All of those in charge of the Seleção had denied what many took as a simple fact: the football that Brazil had played in the latest World Cup was far from its roots. This was of course the intention of the regime and the soccer hierarchy, which is why some observers began to call for the "rescue" of the game from the reformers.[144]

Because those in control of the Seleção stayed on, so, too, did Coutinho. Looking back from our age, when coaches come and go at a dizzying pace in Brazilian soccer, this was a remarkable nonoccurrence: surely the coach of so confused a team deserved to be fired? In fact, Coutinho only stepped down after losing another international competition, the Copa América in late 1979. To the shock of the press, Coutinho had never admitted any disappointment with the Seleção's performance in the 1978 World Cup, nor had he suffered any punishment for its failure.[145] Instead of being fired, he was eased out of the national team by means of a gentle public relations maneuver. When the CBD declared its preference for a coach who would focus exclusively on the Seleção, Coutinho gave up one of his two coaching jobs and kept the other, with his beloved Flamengo. In his 1996 memoir, Zico recalls that Coutinho became much less strident in his tactics after the 1978 World Cup, at both the national and club levels.[146] The fact that he had the opportunity to tone down his radical views, however, underscores the tremendous power that scientific coaches and trainers had gained under a military regime looking for rapid, supervised modernization, even as that modernization failed to return Brazil to the status of World Cup champion.[147]

PLAYER POWER AGAINST SCIENCE

Just months before the 1978 World Cup, art critic Jacob Klintowitz denounced the transformation that Zagallo, Coutinho, and their allies had tried to effect. For Klintowitz, the would-be reformers used a mystified Europe as their model in the transformation of Brazil. In soccer and more generally, they pushed Brazilians toward their European model of collective efficiency as a way of inculcating new patterns of behavior. They treated players and other citizens as "empty bodies" into which they would pour obedience and respect for the nation and the national team; the individual only mattered insofar as he served "reasons of state." In Klintowitz's view, then, the "scientific revolution" in soccer was nothing more than the imposition of a depersonalizing, dictatorial rule on the populace and particularly on football, a central part of Brazilian life. Language like Coutinho's was just one part of this attempt to replace existing popular culture with a new discourse that only officially recognized experts could dominate.[148]

Klintowitz's voice was not widely heard, but in its emphatic and erudite way it captured the vivid resentment that the debacles of 1974 and 1978 provoked.[149] This is not to say that *futebol-força* lacked adherents or, indeed, that it lost its battle against *futebol-arte* when Brazil returned home without a fourth World Cup trophy. Most coaches, for instance, welcomed the revolution's attention to conditioning.[150] Others held on to some of the tactical reorientation that Zagallo and Coutinho had begun, arguing that Brazil needed a greater commitment to European-style efficiency.[151] Overall, however, the poverty of offense on the Seleções of these two Cups led to calls for a return to soccer run not by technocrats but by coaches and officials who had come up through the established culture of the game in Brazil. Even more poignant were the demands for a soccer that would let players display their Brazilian skills freely, unencumbered by "artificial" schemes.[152]

Protests were not only directed at Zagallo and Coutinho. Journalists also offered more indirect criticism through reporting on the universality of Brazilians' passion for playing and watching soccer, especially a soccer of skills and art.[153] In the middle of the scientific revolution, the sports magazine *Placar* published an essay on the identification of talented kids by professional clubs. "The gringos," the editors explained, "try to reduce soccer to a mathematical formula. Here we know that talent is born."[154] This implicit identification of the scientific revolutionaries as non-Brazilian—they acted like gringos in their approach to soccer, after all—found echoes in innumerable columns, essays, and poems by a range of influential writers. In various ways, these widely read writers declared, as Ivan Cavalcanti Proença put it, "Soccer is ours. It is of our people, chosen by them."[155] Those trying to insert European methods were distorting Brazilian football, making it less Brazilian. Beyond the work of such high cultural icons, popular music and poetry reflected dismay at the direction of the Seleção. Songs celebrated artistic talents, like Jorge Ben's "Fio Maravilha," an homage to a skillful forward who helped Flamengo end a seven-year title drought. Other singers and groups like Os Novos Baianos, key figures in the consolidation of the MPB (Música Popular Brasileira, Brazilian Popular Music) genre, and Gilberto Gil captured the joy central to *futebol-arte*.[156] Pieces in *literatura de cordel* (literature on a string) took on scientific football with more gusto. One poem about the 1978 Cup, for instance, affirmed first, "Soccer is not lacking / In this noble people," before condemning Coutinho and the top-down process by which he became coach: "If the people cannot choose / The coach is just any hack."[157] As this last piece suggests, protests against the discipline of *futebol-força* easily slipped into demands for democracy. Under the military the populace certainly was not "master of itself" (*senhor de si*)—and neither was their Seleção, as another "string" poet wrote.[158]

Many players waged personal battles for autonomy against the impositions of the military-backed, scientific regime of soccer.[159] When we consider the trajectories of three stars of the 1970s—Ademir da Guia, Paulo Cézar Lima (Caju), and Reinaldo—we see examples of the forms these acts could take. Players like these did not all resist the "revolution" in explicitly political ways, but they waged persistent struggles to play and live as they thought best.

Ademir da Guia was far from a rebel. In fact, he had claim to a kind of divine lineage in his country's soccer culture. We have already met da Guia's father, Domingos da Guia, the early Afro-Brazilian star, whose brilliance helped in his country's rise to prominence in the 1930s. Against any reasonable expectation, the son achieved nearly as much fame as his father and worked tirelessly within the structures of the Brazilian game. In the process, he also inherited his father's nickname: "o Divino Mestre," the Divine Master. Born and raised in Bangu, Ademir swam and played soccer for his local club before Palmeiras, a traditional power in São Paulo football, bought his contract in 1961. His trajectory from that point forward, as he became a major star generally neglected by the national team directors, highlights the commitment by Zagallo, Coutinho, and their supporters to a particular style of play.

The Divine Master had physical attributes and technique that could have made him a centerpiece of the Seleção. His body seemed made to measure for the scientific trainers and coaches. At both club and national team levels, he impressed the technical staff with his strength and stamina. His young teammate Leivinha marveled at Da Guia's results in fitness tests in 1973, saying, "He was different from us in everything."[160] The next year, training with the Seleção, the trainer's report summed up his physical gifts: He showed "unexpected high indexes [of fitness]. He is not subject to injury. His muscles and joints have no flaws, and he shows no physical wear. He is a perfect athlete."[161] No one, moreover, doubted his skills, which were so prodigious that, according to former Santos defender Formiga, "He even entertained his opponents."[162] Entertainment was never, to be clear, his goal. Many of the people who saw him play, especially on the team he defended from 1962 to 1977, Palmeiras, referred to him as a "conductor," a player who organized his teammates and dictated the tempo of a game. As Didi had done a generation earlier, Da Guia was able to assert this degree of control in part because of what one adversary called "his elegance and intelligence on the ball." His consistency also helped; radio announcer Fiori Giglito insisted that he had seen Pelé "play badly and receive boos, but Ademir, never."[163] Like Pelé, Da Guia used his range of skills wherever they were needed on the field. One of his coaches at Palmeiras recalled, "He was one, but he seemed to be a thousand." He scored, too, even while more frequently setting up plays for others. We have only to see one of his free kicks, struck with the outside of his right foot and bending up over a defensive wall before settling into the upper right corner of the goal—to know that he possessed great touch. More remarkable, though, was his manner of taking a game over. One commentator wrote that until watching Da Guia he had not understood that a player could master not only the ball, but time.[164]

It was time, in fact, that made Da Guia seem contrary to the designs of Zagallo and Coutinho. The Divine Master had speed, as the tests of his trainers proved. During the game, however, he was the opposite of the frenetic European style so dear to the scientific revolutionaries. More than any other player in the 1970s, he displayed the cadence of the traditional Brazilian game. Watching a video of him, you have to force yourself to notice how much ground he covers; he is not being outrun. But he stands out, like a calm center in the middle of a frenzied game. One of Brazil's foremost poets of the era, João Cabral de Melo Neto, was moved to write of Da Guia's pace, "Ademir imposes with his game / the rhythm (and the weight) of lead, / of the slug, of slow motion, / of a man caught in a nightmare." In that rhythm, though, he tied up "the most restless adversary."[165] This ability to control the game won him plaudits at the 1974 Ramón de Carranza Trophy in Spain. Leading his Palmeiras to victory in a tournament that also featured Santos with Pelé and Barcelona with Dutch legend Johan Cruyff, Da Guia was named the best player of the competition by the Spanish press.[166]

Da Guia's mastery was in the end too different from the efficiency that Zagallo and his allies sought. With their emphasis on delimited roles for players within a set plan, they were not interested in a player who could manage the game like an orchestra conductor. Moreover, in spite of his ability to move the game along, he seemed an icon of the slowness that they wanted to eradicate from the national style. They wanted displays of scientific modernity, not artistic "recitals."[167] As a result, one of the outstanding talents of the era played only sixty minutes for his country in a World Cup. That opportunity came only in the third-place match against Poland in 1974, a game that few people in Brazil cared about. Even then, he was replaced fifteen minutes into the second half. As a final insult, Zagallo lied to reporters about his reasons for the substitution, alleging that Da Guia had asked to come off because of fatigue.[168]

Da Guia did not question Zagallo's move publicly. It just was not in his nature to do so, as he often explained. No rebel, the Divine Master simply played as he knew how, representing on the field an alternative to the style of soccer that became hegemonic on the Seleção during the '70s. He did not take up any cause except victory for team, but he symbolized a more organic-seeming Brazilian efficiency. This meant that international fame eluded him, but he remains a beloved member of the *futebol* pantheon. By contrast, Paulo Cézar Lima and Reinaldo gained meaningful space on the Seleção in spite of being openly political. Certainly they were, like Da Guia, *craques*. But Paulo Cézar and Reinaldo consciously took on the conservative forces that dominated soccer and politics during the dictatorship. Ultimately, their transgressive behavior—real and rumored—caused problems for them, but both found their way onto the national team because coaches believed they could fit these two forwards into a modern style of play based on rationally devised collective schemes.

Paulo Cézar Lima (later called Caju) grew up in one of the slums, or *favelas,* that poor and industrious residents of Rio had been building on the steep hillsides of the city's rugged geography since the nineteenth century. Because the *favela* where he was born, Cocheira, ran down into the middle-class neighborhood of Botafogo, he ended up playing with kids of other classes and races. He wrote of his early pick-up games on the street, "I was the poor one, but the poor one who played the best and the one everybody asked for." Despite the poverty and the racial discrimination that he faced early on—doormen forced him to use service entrances when visiting middle-class acquaintances—he lived out a nearly impossible dream through soccer. From playing on the street, he managed a tryout with Flamengo's indoor soccer team and won a spot on the team. There he performed well enough to be called "Pelezinho" (little Pelé) for a while. He also made friendships that carried him far away from the favela. His friend Fréderico happened to be the only child of a former player who had become a trainer for the club Botafogo. After Fred invited him to celebrate Christmas and the New Year at his house, Paulo Cézar became a fixture there. When Fred's father, Marinho Rodrigues de Oliveira, became trainer of the Honduran national team, he invited Paulo Cézar to go live with them in Tegucigalpa. Paulo Cézar followed his adoptive "second family" to Honduras and then to Colombia when Marinho got a new job there. In Colombia as in Honduras, soccer officials invited him to seek naturalization so he could play on their national teams. Marinho wouldn't hear of such a thing and kept both Fred and Paulo Cézar with him. When Marinho moved to Peru to train its national team, however, Paulo Cézar returned to Brazil. Marinho arranged a tryout for him at Botafogo, where he not only won a spot but soon became a starter on a team filled with famous veterans.[169]

Paulo Cézar played for Botafogo from 1966 through 1972, his longest tour of duty at any club. In all, he played for six clubs in Brazil—with two spells each at Botafogo and Gremio—plus Olympique de Marseille in France and the California Surf in the United States. He also played on the Seleção in both the 1970 and 1974 World Cups, though not, to his great disappointment, in 1978. At every club he impressed with his quickness and skills as a left-sided forward before almost always leaving acrimoniously. Flamengo fans remember him as an obvious *craque,* with one asserting that "even the sound of the ball, when he passed it, was different."[170] It is hard to judge how much of his itinerancy was due to a difficult personality and how much arose from his refusal to bend to the powerful club directors who treated even stars poorly. His first departure, from Botafogo in 1972, seems to have been an example of the latter. The team president had promised Marinho that he would pay Paulo Cézar $100,000 when he joined the senior professionals. After playing on that squad on tour to Chile, Peru, Colombia, and Mexico, however, Paulo Cézar returned to find the president claiming to have made a partial payment earlier, and the young star went home with less than half the money he was due.[171] Bad-faith management of this sort was typical of the era, as journalists and former players attested.[172] At other clubs, though, Paulo Cézar was the source of conflict. As he later wrote, he placed tremendous importance on having a "marvelous ambience" wherever he played. When he judged the climate less than marvelous, he made a "bohemian" departure—just taking off.[173] Before leaving, he showed up late for team

FIGURE 10. Paulo Cézar Caju outside the Flamengo training ground, 1972.
Agência O Globo.

buses after spending too long at the beach, passed nights in dance clubs, and
faked injuries to avoid playing. He has characterized himself as "very combative" and prone to outbursts that were not in his professional interest.[174]
Late in his career he began to have problems with cocaine and alcohol, which
affected his health and play.[175] While training with Gremio for the 1983
Intercontinental Club Championship—a tournament that pitted the
European and South American club champions against each other—he
seemed so apathetic that Renato Gaúcho, famous for his own late-night
exploits, confronted him. Frustrated by Paulo Cézar's lazy practice the day

before the final, Renato yelled, "If you don't run tomorrow, I'll punch you right in the face five minutes into the game and then kill you in the dressing room."[176] Whatever the balance of causes, Paulo Cézar seemed to live in an "interminable personality crisis."[177]

Paulo Cézar was far from the only problem player in these years. What stands out about him, however, is the range of his transgressions. He entered, first of all, into public political debates. Most famously, he wrote a column for the satirical magazine *O Pasquim* in the late '70s. Under the pseudonym "Nariz de Ferro" (Iron Nose), he took on the repression of the military dictatorship directly. Elsewhere, though, his politics took less conventional, though equally provocative, forms. As we have already seen, he challenged the norms of behavior for soccer players by refusing to be just another obedient body. Caju's early run-in with the director of Botafogo taught him, he later said, not to trust club officials, and he showed little of the subservience that *cartolas* expected of players. His behavior fell short of systematic rebellion; by treating his contracts with the same cynicism that club directors exhibited, however, he tried to win greater autonomy for himself.[178] He loved soccer but fought against those he felt were exploiting him.[179]

Paulo Cézar's defiant nature was irksome to almost everyone but also inspired other players. Dionísio, labeled the "Black Wonder" (Maravilha Negra) when he played at the club Atlético Mineiro, admired Paulo Cézar because "he takes responsibility for all his actions."[180] Indeed, this declaration by the Black Wonder points to a key feature of Caju's politics: he assumed a provocative public image as a self-assured Afro-Brazilian man. His self-presentation was key; he put so much care and money into cultivating his style that some journalists denounced him as a spoiled child, a dandy, or a diva.[181] He spent extravagantly on fashion and ate at Maxim's in Paris— hardly sins, as João Saldanha wrote in his defense, and behavior that would not have attracted notice if done by a white player. Paulo Cézar, however, stood out like "a black cat on a field of snow."[182] Fully aware of this fact, he made his appearance into an assertion of his pride in his race and his accomplishments. Though others sported Afros in the early 1970s, for instance, he may have been the first player to wear self-consciously "Black Power" hair. He certainly set himself apart when he dyed his Afro the color of cashew, thereby also earning the nickname "Caju" (cashew).[183] His bold fashion statements, from his wildly patterned suits to patchwork bell-bottom jeans, aviator sunglasses to platform shoes, showed that he was not afraid of attention. He had mixed with the jet set while playing in Europe and favored the latest styles imported from France—never those made in Brazil, his friends swore.[184] When he posed for magazine photographers in those clothes—or just leaning shirtless against his imported sports car—he may have been flaunting the privileges he had won, but he was also making a political statement: he was a proud, strong, black man who had made it out of the *favela*.

Nothing about Caju's public image could have pleased officials of the regime, who saw their revolution as a struggle to cleanse the nation morally as well as politically. By 1975 it seemed clear that powerful figures in the CBD—and, it was rumored, in the military itself—were trying to veto him from the national team. In that year Admiral Heleno Nunes, CBD president, explained that the country needed "a Seleção of men, of players with defined personality, with character."[185] Paulo Cézar certainly did not possess the sort of personality that the admiral had in mind. Still, in spite of his politics, Paulo Cézar was able to play significant minutes in two World Cups, unlike the stoic Ademir da Guia. Indeed, Paulo Cézar's time on the Seleção indicates that reformist coaches, from Zagallo to Coutinho, thought his considerable talents useful to their projects. On club sides and even on the national team, he occasionally recalled the brilliant playfulness of Garrincha. On one memorable occasion in the 1971 Rio state championship, for instance, he received the ball in front of the goal and with two defenders behind him, performed a series of *embaixadas*—bouncing the ball up repeatedly on one foot, as any player might do for fun—before turning quickly to shoot. His opponents from Botafogo were furious, and even the directors of his own team, Fluminense, thought that he had gone too far and "disrespected" the game.[186] When he was focused, however, Paulo Cézar was a dangerous, quick presence on the left side of the attack, a good scorer but better still at finding ways to send crossing passes in to center forwards. On the Seleção he also proved a very cooperative, complementary player. Perhaps surprisingly, given his hardheadedness, he willingly changed positions to work with Rivellino in 1972 and to open up a space for Edu on the 1974 squad.[187] This attitude, together with skills that allowed for real versatility, made him an attractive option for Zagallo in the 1970 and 1974 Cups and for Coutinho up to the very final roster cut in 1978. In his heart of hearts, he remained a *futebol-arte* stylist, affirming that "soccer, without *alegria*, without freedom, does not exist" and remaining supremely confident in his technical qualities.[188] Coutinho did not seem to mind his off-field preferences or his love of a more technical soccer; indeed, shortly after taking over the Seleção, Coutinho declared that Paulo Cézar would have great freedom on the left flank.[189]

Ultimately, though, Coutinho kept this provocative player off the squad and even off his "second list" of potential substitutes. It may be that this was an act of an obedient junior officer following orders from Admiral Heleno Nunes. It may also be that, as the World Cup drew nearer, Coutinho's anxieties led him to opt for a more defensive player to shore up his tactical scheme.[190]

The example of Reinaldo, another rebellious *craque,* suggests that Coutinho most likely did not cut Paulo Cézar in 1978 because of his own political intolerance. Reinaldo was a favorite of Coutinho's, part of his "base squad" in spite of the forward's history of questionable fitness and his bold statements against dictatorship and racism in Brazil.[191] The sixth of eight children of working-class parents in a small town in the interior of the state of Minas Gerais, Reinaldo followed an older brother into soccer. Their father, a railroad worker, encouraged his children's education but also helped his sons pursue football. The family often spent time with relatives in Rio, where Reinaldo saw his brother play on Botafogo's junior team. His own career began back in Minas, however, where he became one of the greatest stars in the history of Atlético Mineiro. Reinaldo remained at Atlético from 1971 until the tail end of his professional life, when he had brief and unhappy stays at Palmeiras and other clubs in Brazil, Sweden, and Denmark before retiring in 1987.[192]

His talent and his unfortunate tendency to injury were both obvious early on. At his tryout for Atlético, when he was only fourteen, he won over the team's trainers, including future Seleção coach Telê Santana, with his technique. Playing brilliantly in his first phase on the senior squad, the "baby *craque*" became a fan favorite from 1973 to 1976. Although renowned for his humility, he later spoke proudly of his skills. "My style then," he told a biographer, "was extremely technical, versatile, short and quick dribbles." João Saldanha marveled at his ability to maneuver in tight spaces; for Reinaldo, the columnist wrote approvingly, a patch of grass the size of "a handkerchief was like a huge ranch."[193] His amazing ability to find holes in opposing defenses often led to scores; he led the national league with twenty-eight goals in 1977, a record that lasted twenty years.[194] His attacking work cost him dearly, however, as angry rivals took out their frustrations on his legs. By 1975, still just eighteen, he was already suffering the knee problems that would make the next decade a cycle of injury, surgery, and recuperation. Unfortunately, he was ill served by team doctors, who submitted him to radiation therapy early on and by 1976 decided to remove cartilage from both of his knees in order to prevent later injuries. This operation only increased the wear on these joints; the radiation apparently did nothing in spite of the exposure to carcinogens it involved.[195] When his health allowed, Reinaldo shone as one of the best players in Brazil. So undeniable was his talent, in fact, that even fans in Rio and São Paulo, whose strong regionalism often manifested itself in a profound hatred of players from outside their cities, ended up supporting him. More astonishing still was the praise he received from the officials overseeing the remodeling of the national team. Admiral Heleno Nunes, for instance, proclaimed Reinaldo "the best forward in Brazil and one of the best in the world" on the eve of the 1978 World Cup.[196]

What makes the admiral's approval remarkable was Reinaldo's public political persona. As a young player, he later admitted, he did not have that much to say about politics. He elaborated firm positions, however, and he acted on them even in the face of possible repression. In 1978 he became the first athlete to speak out openly against the military regime in an interview in *Movimento,* a magazine run by the revolutionary movement MR-8.[197] He demanded a return to full democracy, since "the people have the right to vote and to select their government." Linking soccer and national politics, he declared, "intelligent players distress carnivals, just as an enlightened people distresses government authorities."[198] In a period when the emergence of new labor organizing and other opposition had the military feeling vulnerable, Reinaldo's words drew great attention. When the Seleção made a ceremonial visit to the presidential palace before leaving for the Cup in Argentina, President General Ernesto Geisel greeted Reinaldo gruffly. "So this is the boy," he said to the Minister of Education and Culture, before advising Reinaldo, "Soccer players should stick to playing soccer and not involve themselves in politics."[199] The president did not, however, shake the player's resolve; if anything, Reinaldo moved toward greater radicalism afterward. Reinaldo commemorated his goal in the 1978 World Cup with a Black Power salute, as he had been doing for some months on smaller stages. A conscious adaptation of the actions of U.S. runners Tommie Smith and John Carlos in the 1968 Summer Olympics, Reinaldo's gesture was, he later asserted, not just for Black Power but "for socialism, revolutionary."[200] Whether primarily antiracist or anticapitalist or both, his raised right fist was a daring symbol in that "Cup of Dictatorship," as well as a sign of a life in politics. After his decline as a player—a period in which he, like Caju, abused cocaine and alcohol—he entered formal leftist politics, eventually being elected to the Minas state assembly on the Workers' Party (PT, Partido dos Trabalhadores) ticket, after the end of the dictatorship. In 1978, with that activism still in the future, some observers thought Reinaldo "the only player with a political vision" on Coutinho's Seleção.[201]

In spite of Reinaldo's politics, Coutinho treated him as "indispensable" to the Seleção he took over in 1977.[202] Coutinho believed that the attacking combination of Reinaldo and Zico would provide the agility that the team needed in front of goal.[203] Reinaldo, for his part, eagerly supported Coutinho's plans. He admired Coutinho for being "committed to the future," and so friendly and thoughtful that he led Reinaldo to reject "that impression that people gave when they talked about military guys on the Seleção."[204] The two men spoke only about soccer and Reinaldo's duties on the team. With great determination and none of the selfishness that might be expected of a league-leading scorer, he followed Coutinho's orders, tracking back on defense as the coach wanted. Coutinho went to great lengths to ensure that Reinaldo would be able to fill his role on the national team at the World Cup in Argentina. Coutinho and his staff paid special attention to Reinaldo's attempts to strengthen the muscles around his ever-troublesome knees.[205] Ultimately, Reinaldo did not deliver the firepower that Coutinho had hoped for, and Admiral Heleno listed him as one of the three players to be replaced in the lineup after the team's dispiriting first two games.[206] With the team falling into disarray, Coutinho agreed to bench this forward he had championed.

The Copernican revolution in Brazilian soccer, then, contained spaces for certain great talents. The deciding question was how well a player would fit into the schemes that Zagallo, Coutinho, and their allies tried to impose. Ademir da Guia, the Divine Master, may have been one of the best players of his era, but his skills on the ball, extraordinary athleticism, and calm professionalism were not enough to win over the proponents of *futebol-força*. He was too old-fashioned and perhaps too dominant a figure on the pitch to become a cog in the scientific machine. Paulo Cézar Caju, though not as transcendent a talent as Da Guia, played with skill and filled a role in the reorganized national team. His pugnacity and his ostentatious presentation of himself as an Afro-Brazilian man, independent and proud, may have kept him off the 1978 Seleção, but only after he had been a part of the prior two World Cup squads. Reinaldo, finally, was a great attacker who played with art but also actively tried to mold his game to fit the plans of a coach he admired—and admired precisely because of the coach's dedication to a particular modernization. Reinaldo's commitment to the reorientation of the country's football even outweighed his other revolutionary stances, in particular his denunciations of two entrenched features of Brazilian society in the late 1970s, dictatorship and racial inequality.

CONCLUSION

The attempts to force the game toward a particular modernization from above, which reached their peak under Coutinho, failed to restore the optimism that Brazil's triumphs in 1958, 1962, and 1970 had inspired. After the 1978 World Cup the national team was in disarray, "shattered."[207] The eventual removal of Coutinho from the Seleção raised hopes that a new approach would more effectively draw on the skills that had made Brazilian players famous. By about 1980, more fans, coaches, and even CBD and government officials were willing to put their faith in the "something more" often attributed to Brazilian players.[208] For much of the 1980s the Seleção rediscovered the glories of the skills long defined as Afro-Brazilian, embracing the *futebol-arte* style based on the exhibition of Brazilian talent. Because those glories did not include victory in the World Cup, however, *futebol-força* made an unfortunate comeback at the end of the decade. Cláudio Coutinho and his collaborators had not killed off *futebol-arte,* but neither had their failures eliminated the allure of a top-down, scientific modernization of the national game.

FOUR

Risky Beauty

ART AND THE OPENING OF BRAZIL IN THE 1980S

Discipline was made for little toy soldiers and not for men. And
soccer must be passionate, because it is played by human beings.

NELSON RODRIGUES

From 1978 through 1990, Brazil managed to lose five World Cups in a period
when only four World Cup tournaments were held. This remarkable feat
came about because thieves managed to make off with the Jules Rimet
Trophy in 1983. The Seleção of 1970 had brought the prize home as an ostensibly permanent symbol of its footballing excellence. However, officials of the
Brazilian Soccer Confederation (CBD, Confederação Brasileira de Futebol)
had mysteriously chosen to display the original and guard a copy in a safe, so
it was the actual trophy that disappeared in the theft. The consensus theory
was that this symbol of the soccer glory was melted down as so much gold.[1]
This incident outraged and embarrassed Brazilians. The "string" poet
Franklin Maxado Nordestino went so far as to label Brazil the "ex-country of
football" in the wake of the crime.[2] In the face of persistent political turmoil,
economic uncertainty, and social inequality, many had clung to the saying
"only soccer works in Brazil"; by highlighting the ineptitude of soccer's governing body, the robbery deprived them of this not particularly optimistic
belief. "Not even soccer works in Brazil," might have been the new slogan.

Even more demeaning, though, were defeats on the field, especially in the
1978 and 1990 World Cups, when the Seleção displayed "a sad and repressed
futebol."[3] Those two performances sit like grim bookends on either side of the
turbulent decade of the 1980s. The 1978 and 1990 national teams were shaped
by a dour scientism that embraced two ideals: to apply the expertise of physi-
ologists and other scientifically trained professionals to the transformation
of players into more efficient athletes, and to adopt the most up-to-
date European tactics. For members of this school of thought, known as

futebol-força (strength soccer), the objectivity of science was beyond question. Guided by this powerful model, those in charge of the Brazilian game had pressed for a controlled, top-down modernization of soccer before 1978.[4] At the end of the next decade Sebastião Lazaroni brought lofty credentials to bear in his own attempt to impose science on the Seleção. He had earned a doctorate in physical education with a dissertation that focused on the *líbero,* a free-roaming defender then very much in vogue in European football, particularly in Italy and Germany.[5] Like his predecessor Cláudio Coutinho, Lazaroni sought to rein in the skills, the *arte,* that had captivated fans of the Seleção during the golden age of Brazilian football.

In the early 1980s, however, art allowed the national game to regain much of the luster that had faded since Brazil's resounding victory in Mexico City in 1970. Once again, Brazil could claim to be "the country of football with samba in its veins."[6] This revitalization was not principally manifest in international triumphs by the Seleção, which lost even when it played well in the 1982 and 1986 World Cups. Glories came at the club level, however, beginning with Flamengo's defeat of traditional English power Liverpool in the world club championship in 1981 and continuing on to Gremio's repetition of that accomplishment against Hamburg two years later. More important than these titles were the philosophical and stylistic changes that characterized *futebol* for much of the 1980s. First evident at Flamengo in Rio and Corinthians in São Paulo, the reformulation of Brazilian soccer took its most famous form on the national teams that Telê Santana conducted in 1982 and 1986. As Paulo Roberto Falcão, one of the stars of the Seleção in these years, later put it, Telê "rescued art, beauty, and talent."[7] Brazilian soccer thus enjoyed a brilliant revival of *futebol-arte* (art soccer), before the shift back to *futebol-força* under Lazaroni at the end of the decade.

Art was exactly what made Telê's national team inspire enthusiasm at home and abroad. Not all of scientific soccer fell by the wayside; almost everyone agreed that soccer had to be different now, with conditioning and speed accepted as indispensable features of the era. The consensus was that "in modern soccer, ability by itself isn't worth much."[8] After all, as Paulo Cézar Caju said, "Even Germans use ability."[9] Still, most observers agreed that the inherent skills of Brazilian players remained unsurpassed—and that it was only logical to recognize these skills as the foundation of the national style. The widely shared hope was, as the midfielder Zenon confidently predicted in 1979, that Brazilians were emerging from "the psychosis of *futebol-força*," a style that was "appropriate to Europeans and didn't work [for

Brazil]." Once again, "talent spoke loudest," and training and tactics would support, rather than supplant, the passion and artistic gifts that issued from the heart of the *povo*.[10]

The grace, ingenuity, and overall quality of Telê's *craques* revived belief in a style of soccer that was uniquely Brazilian and efficient in its own fashion. The 1982 Seleção in particular promised to recover the country's glorious footballing tradition. Indeed, before the Seleção lost to Italy in the "Tragedy of Sarriá"—as the 3–2 defeat on 5 July 1982 came to be known in Brazil—it fueled comparisons to Brazil's previous World Cup winners. Even after that defeat, many critics considered that squad one of the strongest teams—along with Hungary in the mid-1950s and the Netherlands in the 1970s—not to have taken home the trophy.[11] The feeling that Brazilian soccer had returned to its roots, however, focused on the style that the Seleção displayed. This position found its way into the CBF's annual report in 1981, which hailed Brazil's "reencounter with its vocation," which it called "creative, free, happy" soccer.[12] More flamboyantly, it appeared in the presentation by the samba school Beija Flor, which in spring 1986 paraded to the theme "The World Is a Ball" (*O mundo é uma bola*)—with the requisite, gaudy celebration of a samba-fueled soccer. "The art is to play ball," the school's theme urged, "go to the Cup and make Carnaval."[13] Political cartoonist Agner put the 1982 team's stylistic orientation in provocative focus when he contrasted two of the country's most visible leaders. Agner drew then-president General João Baptista de Oliveira Figueiredo pronouncing into one microphone, "We remain faithful to the ideals of 64," while Telê declares into another, "I remain faithful to the ideals of 58, 62, and 70." Agner's playful barb here suggests the common feeling that in the realm of soccer—and perhaps more generally—the country had outgrown the military's initiatives of the 1970s.[14] This liberation of the game from heavy-handed and artificial schemes accompanied a loosening of the military regime's grip on politics and society. *Abertura*—opening—was the order of the day in soccer and more generally.

In all realms *abertura* proceeded in fits and starts. The two generals who followed Médici promised to lead the country to democracy, but many in the government felt the country still needed military guidance to achieve "order and progress," the dual goals emblazoned on the national flag. Some military men, in fact, resisted the political opening with acts of terror against civilians. This violence, coupled with a weakening economy, ultimately turned much of society against the regime. The dynamic labor movement that had emerged in the late 1970s was joined by church, student, and indigenous groups in pressing for a return to democracy in the early 1980s. When this change came in 1985, it followed a wave of demonstrations, the most spectacular of which brought millions to the streets of big cities to demand direct elections. Still, the postdictatorship New Republic had no clear agenda other than to be democratic. The economy went into an inflationary spiral that draconian stabilization plans failed to halt, while both street crime and political corruption reached unfortunate new heights. The Constitution of 1988 outlined a modern, democratic Brazil, but in practice its provisions remained largely aspirational; the country found itself mired in crisis.

The victory of art in the national sport was also unsatisfying. The reemergence of *futebol-arte* in the 1980s seemed at first glance like a rediscovery of the lost ideals of the 1958 to 1970 period. In practice, however, it reflected the complex relationship between soccer on one hand and politics and society on the other during the years of *abertura*. Overall, *futebol-arte* seemed to embody freedom in an era when freedom was very much the focus of public attention. In practice the national sport provided a means for critiquing authoritarianism, most often as a symbol of the empowerment of players and, by extension, of citizens. In this regard, soccer gave people a space and language—both of them ostensibly apolitical—for discussions of power relations in the country. For some, soccer was inextricably implicated in authoritarian structures. Others held out hope for the "emancipatory dimensions" of the game, in which the humblest could become heroic figures and common fans had a freedom of expression unavailable to them in the formal political world. For those who believed in soccer's democratic capacity, the style of play evident at Flamengo and Corinthians and then on the Seleção under Telê was evidence that governments had never managed to turn the sport into a mere "opiate of the masses," though they had certainly tried.[15]

More visibly than before, soccer became a direct—not merely symbolic—part of national political processes. Most figures from the world of *futebol,* from players to coaches to fans, stuck to passive roles or avoided public political stances in the waning years of dictatorship.[16] Many at least tacitly supported the military. Pelé's assertions that the Brazilian people were unprepared for democracy are perhaps the most notorious examples of this tendency, though Gérson was also known for his reactionary politics.[17] *Cartolas* (club and confederation directors), meanwhile, often formed tight links to the regime. At the same time, some players, commentators, and administrators entered directly into the political fray of the *abertura*. Many of these worked with the opposition media, the newly formed Workers' Party

(Partido dos Trabalhadores, PT), or the campaign for direct elections.[18] Sócrates, who starred for Corinthians and captained the 1982 Seleção, represented the extreme here. As an organizer and leader of movements to democratize both the Corinthians clubhouse and the overall political system, he stood out as "a sincere representative of liberty, a Brazilian who inaugurated critique and self-critique on the field and in politics."[19]

Whether in the explicit forms that Sócrates embodied or in more diffuse and symbolic ways, the resurgence of *futebol-arte* in the early 1980s became part of a project to push Brazil toward a more politically and socially democratic modernity. Often romantic—Telê was hailed as a kind of "Don Quixote of *futebol-arte*"—this initiative was largely reactive, in that it came about in response to the projects that the military had pursued in soccer and other realms. Indeed, in its "content"—the stylistic elements it promoted—it was conservative, embracing old notions of Brazil's tropical cultural makeup. What was new was the use of traditional conceptions of *futebol-arte* in the context of efforts to remake the nation after almost two decades of dictatorship. Ultimately, of course, the prodemocracy movement failed to deliver full citizenship, just as *futebol-arte* failed to restore Brazilian hegemony in world soccer.[20] Nevertheless, *abertura* set the stage for more substantive democratization and a more pragmatic soccer style—and another World Cup victory—in the 1990s.

A LITTLE ROOSTER AND A PHILOSOPHER LEAD THE "POPULAR" CHARGE

During the uneven progress of *abertura,* two clubs and two stars presented visions of a revived tropical nation. Of the two teams, Flamengo and its great *craque* Zico, the "Little Rooster of Quintino" (after the Rio neighborhood, Quintino Bocaiuva, where he grew up), followed a more conventional path toward success. With a group that had emerged largely from the club's youth system, this most popular of Rio's big clubs built steadily toward victories at the state, national, and international levels, practicing a modified version of *futebol-arte.*[21] Meanwhile, the largest club in Brazil's largest city, Corinthians of São Paulo, launched a more expansive project to unite success on the playing field with a revamping of its administrative structures. Dubbed "Corinthian Democracy" by Washington Olivetto (who later claimed that he had not invented the term but merely "perceived" it), an advertising executive and supporter of the movement, this initiative created beautiful soccer and a model of direct democracy with Sócrates as the face of both art and democracy.[22] Together, then, these clubs exhibited the key elements of the emerging soccer ethos of the day: success and art, tied in various ways to calls for active citizenship.

The differences between the clubs' positions in *abertura* soccer became apparent when they met in Rio's Maracanã Stadium on 17 April 1983. Flamengo won 5–1, thanks in large part to Zico's "exhibition of touches, dribbles, goals."[23] What stuck out about the encounter, though, were the attitudes of the players on the opposing sides. The game was Flamengo's first under coach Carlos Alberto Torres, who had captained the 1970 national team. Speaking modestly, Carlos Alberto said that Flamengo's win came not because of anything he had done and that the score reflected a great deal of luck. His players gave journalists a different version of events. For them, Carlos Alberto had brought a renewed sense of freedom both on and off the field.[24] The club's veteran goalkeeper, Raúl, explained, "He came to a tense team. He remembers that we're all adults, that each one can resolve his own problems, and that the group is what matters."[25]

Flamengo's directors must have felt euphoria, though with an admixture of relief, after the game. Their team had built steadily from about 1972, accumulating trophies at the state level in Rio that year as well as 1978, 1979, and 1981, in addition to winning the Brazilian Championship in 1980, the tenth year of that competition. They followed up this national title with a continental one in the Copa Libertadores of 1981 before capping off their run with victory over the European club champion in the December 1981 Intercontinental Cup in Tokyo. The team carried on with two more national titles in 1982 and 1983, an accomplishment that marked Flamengo's displacement of Internacional of Porto Alegre (which had won the Brazilian league in 1975, 1976, and 1979, the last of these the only undefeated campaign in league history) as the dominant club side in the country.[26] Still, Flamengo was unable to reconquer the Libertadores, and some feared a slippage, particularly since Zico was among those *craques* being targeted by European teams.[27] Indeed, club president Dunshee de Abranches enlisted government help to arrange a deal in which Coca Cola and other firms would ensure extra wages to keep the *craque* at Flamengo.[28] Still, the expectation of Zico's departure remained, and journalists speculated about candidates to succeed the "King of Maracanã."[29] The demolition of Corinthians, then, suggested that Flamengo's cycle of success, begun in the early 1970s, was not yet over.

This success brought more than just trophies to the club; it consolidated Flamengo's status as the most popular and, at least in the eyes of its supporters, the most Brazilian side in the country. Assertions of the equation of Flamengo with Brazil—phrased succinctly in 1981 by string poet Raimundo Santa Helena, "To be FLAMENGO is to be BRAZIL"—showed Carioca chauvinism, to be sure.[30] Beyond that, though, the identifications of Rio and Brazil that appeared in mainstream culture portrayed Rio as the heart of "tropical" Brazil.[31] Fans of other clubs contested the exaltation of Flamengo. To take but one example, the columnist Luis Fernando Verissimo, a supporter of Internacional in his home state of Rio Grande do Sul, jested that Zico's talents were really only suited to his home city. "Zico is an abstract entity created by the collective unconscious of Maracanã," he had one of his characters declare; on the national team, "if [an English defender] gets close to him, Zico falls down."[32] Paulistas aimed less good-natured criticism at Zico, as indeed they tended to do with most stars from Rio teams.[33]

In truth, though, not even regionalist opposition kept the 1980s from becoming known as "the Zico era" and Zico from being called "the most brilliant player to emerge in the country" in the two decades after 1970.[34] More to the point here, he led his club in the period of its greatest national and international triumphs and forged "a marriage of great love" with the "nation" of Flamengo supporters.[35] The squad was full of artful players, but "on a team of monsters, [Zico] was THE monster."[36]

It was not only the skills that Zico displayed but also his lifelong emotional connection to the club that gave a special savor to Flamengo's prominence. The youngest of five children, Arthur Antunes Coimbra gained the nickname Zico when the affectionate diminutive his family used for him, Arthurzinho, blurred into Arthurzico. Like his siblings, he was virtually born into Flamengo. His father, known as Seu Antunes (Mister Antunes), was a fanatic supporter of the club, proudly holding membership number 737, and taking Zico and his other sons with him to cheer for the team in person. The earliest game Zico remembers was the final of the Rio–São Paulo tournament of 1961, in which Dida scored in Flamengo's 2–0 defeat of Corinthians. For the eight-year-old Zico, the image of his hero's goal stuck in his memory.[37] Despite his father's enthusiasm for the club, though, he insisted that his sons pursue their studies and not try to build careers in soccer. The boys' grandparents—three of them from Portugal, with one grandmother from an Italian family—had established a certain respectability in their working-class neighborhood. As Zico wrote in an autobiography, "Soccer players at that

FIGURE 11. Zico at Flamengo, 1978. Luiz Pinto/Agência O Globo.

time [the 1950s] had a reputation as ... bohemians ... bums."[38] The boys played whenever they were not in school, Zico recalls, forming their own team, Juventude (Youth), that "demolished" other neighborhood teams. The talents of the brothers won out over their father's preferences, and four of them went on to play professionally. Zico accompanied his older brother Edu to practices at the club América, where the coach tried to bring the skinny, twelve-year-old Zico into the team. Everything was set for Zico to join Edu at América, but the radio sportscaster Celso Garcia, who had seen Zico score nine goals in an indoor soccer game, convinced him to try out at Flamengo.

After presenting himself at the club's headquarters in the Gávea neighborhood, Zico scored twice. His efforts earned him an immediate invitation to join Flamengo's academy (*escolinha*), so that at age fourteen he had entered "the club of his heart."[39]

The arrival of Zico coincided with a changed orientation of the club. Like Rio's other big clubs, Flamengo had relied heavily on stars bought from other teams in the 1960s. From approximately 1972 on, coaches elevated more players from the junior categories. This policy never enjoyed unanimous acceptance among either fans or club officials, but several of the stars of the 1970s and early '80s came up from within the club together. The midfielder-turned-left defender Júnior, for instance, was brought in about the same time as Zico; others, like the midfielder Andrade, goalie Cantarelli, defenders Rondinelli and Leandro, the forward Tita, and the left forward Júlio César (whose twists and turns down the side of the field led fans to nickname him "Uri Geller," after the spoon-bending magician then gaining fame), joined the senior squad by the end of the 1970s.[40] There were remnants of the old guard, like Paraguayan defender Reyes, purchased from Atlético of Madrid, as well as other stars who had been brought in. Most of the famous hires stayed only briefly, as was the case with Paulo Cézar Caju, the forward Dario (Dadá Maravilha), or defender Carlos Alberto Torres. Others, like goalie Raúl Plassmann, center forward Cláudio Adão, and midfielder Paulo César Carpegiani (who coached the team from 1981 to 1983 after retiring as a player), stayed on to become fixtures in the national and international championship teams of 1978 to 1983.

It was this team that signaled Brazil's resurgence in world football. Radio announcer José Carlos Araújo later recalled watching Flamengo in the early 1980s with "the feeling that I was cheering for the national team, that this was Brazil there winning a world title." Similarly, journalist Roberto Assaf asserts that the club's victory over Liverpool in 1981, "was important for Flamengo, it was important for Brazil soccer itself. It was as if we were saying, 'Our *futebol* is still alive, we could still be world champions.'"[41] More than just the fact of the win, it was Flamengo's style that harkened back to the great national teams of the past; this was a team that opened up opposing defenses with beautiful passes and exquisite dribbles. Carpegiani's move from player to coach established a period of stability in which the club strengthened its playing identity. Forceful personalities like Raúl, Cláudio Adão, and Júnior helped the group maintain its focus, shining especially in tough matches. Perhaps the greatest challenges were away games in the Copa

Libertadores; Brazilian teams had rarely done well when faced with hostile crowds and unsympathetic referees in other South American countries. As Flamengo forward Lico later explained, the Libertadores loomed like a test of Brazilian masculinity: "I say that you have to prepare yourself like a man for the Libertadores if you want to win. They think that if they squeeze, many Brazilian players will go limp [*dão uma afrouxada*]."[42] Flamengo's 1981 victory made it only the third Brazilian club to win the competition; after Pelé's Santos managed a double (1962–63), thirteen years passed before Cruzeiro became the second champion from Brazil.

The Libertadores trophy came to Rio at last partly because Flamengo showed they were "real men," as Júnior later put it.[43] Most notorious was the team's response to the repeated "disloyalty" that players of Cobreloa, Flamengo's Chilean opponent, displayed in the three matches that made up the 1981 final. After Flamengo won the first game in Maracanã, the teams moved to Santiago for the second leg. There, Cobreloa players committed numerous violent fouls, most of which the referee opted not to call. Intimidated, Flamengo played poorly and lost for the first time in that year's tournament. In the last game, however, the *Rubro-Negro* (Red-and-Black) went ahead 3–0 in the neutral setting of Montevideo's Centenario Stadium. Without hope of overtaking the Brazilian side, Cobreloa defender Mario Soto landed a punch right in Tita's face, directly in front of the Flamengo bench. Carpegiani had had enough. He sent in the substitute Anselmo, telling him he did not even need to warm up, since he would not be in the game for long. Anselmo, who remembered that the coach told him simply "Go smash the guy," did as ordered, marching over and striking Soto. The red card that Anselmo received provoked a melee in which Soto and his teammate Jiménez were also sent off. Although Anselmo's expulsion meant that he missed the rest of that match as well as the Intercontinental Cup, he was hailed as a hero by his colleagues and Flamengo fans more generally; Carpegiani insisted that Anselmo be part of the delegation to Tokyo.[44]

Such brutality—understood as justifiable defense by Flamenguistas—was, however, atypical of the team.[45] Generally, they stuck to their art and rejected the *anti-futebol* of the Montevideo final, becoming a kind of Brazilian version of the flowing and versatile Netherlands of the mid-1970s.[46] Their style proved devastating even against Liverpool's renowned pass-and-move scheme. Carpegiani boldly played all four of his *fantasistas*—Zico, Lico, Adílio, and Tita—and the team helped revive the belief that the "fluency and poise in possession" could lead Brazilian soccer back to international glory.[47]

Once more, as João Saldanha wrote the day after Flamengo's victory in Tokyo, Brazilians showed that they could make "the ball obey."[48]

At the Flamengo-Corinthians match in Rio in 1983, a similar playing philosophy but quite a different climate prevailed in the visitors' locker room. Corinthians had not been known for its beautiful style, but the Timão ("Great Team," a nickname of Corinthians) of the early '80s played *futebol-arte*. The talk at the São Paulo club was also of freedom, but Corinthians players and officials were pressing a much more difficult and explicitly political project. They were attempting to create a living democracy in the midst of a dictatorial regime and, perhaps just as vexing, in the world of club football.

Throughout the history of professional soccer in Brazil, *futebol* clubs had been about as democratic as the country as a whole. That is to say, both clubs and country held periodic elections that promised more popular involvement than they delivered. This pattern was particularly striking at Corinthians, the team of the masses in São Paulo and, before the advent of Corinthian Democracy in 1981, a glaring example of boss rule. The democratic experiment (1981–85) was, in fact, an aberration in the history of a club presided over by three imperious figures from the mid-1940s to the early 1980s: Alfredo Ignácio Trindade, Wadih Helu, and Vicente Matheus. The last of these, widely known to be "attracted by the pleasure of command," held on until the man he had set up to be his puppet turned on him and cleared the way for the start of the democratic revolution.[49]

While Flamengo symbolized the triumphant return of a fluid, tropical style of play with a relaxed administrative climate, Corinthians challenged authoritarian structures of power in the club and, metaphorically, in the country as a whole. Corinthians won trophies in these years but never came close to Flamengo's record of victories. Although the Timão had made it to the Brazilian league finals in 1976—the year thousands of its fans staged the "Corinthian invasion" of Rio by taking over that city's streets before a semi-final victory over Fluminense—that second-place finish was the best Corinthians would manage until its first national championship in 1990.[50] The Corinthian Democracy team rose only as high as fourth in 1982 and 1984. At the state level, though, Corinthians won the Paulista championship in 1977 for the first time in twenty-three years and then repeated the feat in 1979, before conquering back-to-back state titles (1982–83).[51] The difference between the trophies of the late '70s and those of the early '80s derived from the manner in which they were won. Under Corinthian Democracy—and with skilled players like Sócrates, Wladimir, Zenon, and Casagrande—the team played a more "beautiful" brand of soccer than had been typical of Corinthians in the past. The club's mass of fans had been more obviously focused on results and hard work than was true at other clubs, but the heyday of Corinthian Democracy presented them with a team that played artistically, as if "to music."[52] From 1981 to 1985, the team asserted the "ludic, joyous, and pleasurable" possibilities of soccer, as Sócrates put it, and celebrated their goals so emphatically that they thrilled supporters of the Timão, even those politically aligned with the dictatorship.[53]

The overtly political nature of Corinthian Democracy always made it a tenuous experiment. It grew out of the cracks of an old system of paternalism, at a time when the club presidency fell into the hands of an official open to the idea of refashioning its structure. For two decades, Wadih Helu and Vicente Matheus had vied for control, beginning with Helu's betrayal of Matheus. While serving as Matheus's vice president, Helu put together a coalition capable of beating his patron in the 1961 club elections. Helu's backroom dealings paid off, and he grabbed and then held on to power for ten years, until Matheus forged his own bloc and drove his former second-in-command from office.[54] Back at the helm, Matheus strove to make the club revolve around himself, using his own money to fund the purchase of players and declaring, "For directing Corinthians, I'm the one. If they don't let me, no one else will do."[55] His centralizing personality persisted even when he was forced to stand aside in the elections of 1981.[56] Regulations prohibited him from running for the presidency again, and this time he was told by a club lawyer that he would have to abide by them. His response was to put Waldemar Pires, who had served as his vice president since 1977, up for the office; Matheus would run for the vice presidency. His aim here was obvious: to bar Helu's faction from returning to power while positioning himself as an *éminence grise*.[57]

For many Corinthianos, Matheus was a "folkloric" figure, someone who cheated but did not steal and who was always ready to fight for the club.[58] Eventually, however, his maneuvering drove away allies, most importantly the new club president. In late 1981 Pires turned against his longtime patron and decided to take back the power that Matheus had been exercising informally. To calm fans' doubts about "who was president in fact and who was president in name only," as he put it, Pires chose a new director of football from outside Matheus's circle of influence.[59] Adilson Monteiro Alves was the son of a longstanding member of the club hierarchy but also, at thirty-five years old, young to assume such a post. More strikingly, as Sócrates put it, Adilson "didn't know a damned thing about soccer."[60] The new director of football admitted as much, saying that he "had never entered the dressing room," much less had any role in sporting decisions.[61] What Adilson had to offer was a willingness to listen to players and an ability to form friendships with individuals from different groups at the club. Committed to dialogue, he turned his introduction to the team and coaches into a six-hour-long discussion.[62]

Open-ended debates about matters large and small were at the heart of the Corinthian Democracy movement, then, from its very start. With Adilson and sympathetic administrators in place, a core of politicized players set about trying to regularize processes of debate and voting on virtually all issues affecting the club, from the selection of coaches and new players to the division of game bonuses among starters, reserves, and others. The president, Pires, functioned as a shield, behind which democratic structures proceeded to replace old paternalistic and authoritarian ones. With Pires's protection, explained Sérgio Scarpelli, director of finances, "our aim was to decentralize."[63] Wladimir, a left defender who had risen through the junior ranks to the first team at Corinthians by 1973, summed up the essence of the initiative as "the participation of all at almost every level of decision making for the group."[64] Described by later commentators as "a utopian socialist cell" or as "merely an attempt by players to return to what they had been before the dictatorship," the movement was in fact a radical experiment in direct democracy and a repudiation of the infantilization of players by *cartolas* like Matheus.[65]

This democracy depended on the willingness of the group to conduct honest, often lengthy discussions. Adilson and the leaders among the players benefited from the arrival of a coach who favored dialogue on his team. Mário Travaglini joined Corinthians near the end of the club's disastrous 1981 season, having coached Portuguesa de Desportos the previous year. Upon his appointment at Portuguesa, he had declared, "I have never taken the so-called 'hard line,' and I like to discuss with players the best strategy to adopt."[66] He brought this disposition to Corinthians, where he was welcomed eagerly by Wladimir and other influential players.[67] Other members of the technical staff embraced the new spirit at the club. Hélio Maffia, a trainer (*preparador físico*), described his experience in glowing terms. Unlike his colleagues who had gained so much power over the course of the 1970s, this conditioning coach (and professor of physical education) remembered his time in Corinthian Democracy as his "best moments in soccer." During those years, Maffia recalled, "I learned to hear what was being said. Everyone spoke and everyone listened." This openness was not only a good in itself, he explained, but it allowed him to "demand more of the athletes, since I knew the return would be guaranteed."[68] Players supported this perception, attesting that having to explain—and at times defend—themselves before teammates made them feel more invested in taking care of themselves and in maintaining their focus on team needs.[69] In other words, the process of consensus building led to firm decisions for the group to obey.

Obedience was not, however, easy to come by. The initiative being attempted was unprecedented, and, even if it "moved in parallel" with the political *abertura* underway in the country as a whole, it was an assertion of democracy in the midst of dictatorship.[70] Some players rejected the project out of hand or openly called for the return of Matheus. Others were more interested in individual than collective goals. As Corinthian Democracy began, the group held a series of closed-door meetings, from which came the decision to sell off players who either opposed the new regime of "self-rule" (*autogestão*) or were deemed, in Wladimir's phrase, "extremely individualistic."[71] Many of those who remained or arrived later took relatively passive roles in meetings among players and administrators.[72] Some of these, like the defender Mauro or the midfielder Biro-Biro, looked back favorably on the democratic project. Mauro told an interviewer, "Things have improved a lot. . . . Players feel more gratified." Biro-Biro, whose determined style on the field made him a favorite of the working-class followers, offered a grudging acceptance, declaring, "I don't understand much about politics, I don't want to. But it's freedom for everyone to speak, discuss, etc. Everyone, not just some."[73] Here we can detect a hint of the resentment that would become a threat to the existence of Corinthian Democracy; some players felt that a few men—Adilson, Sócrates, Wladimir, Casagrande—held the real power in the club, comprising a farcical "democracy of four."[74]

These four were the face of Corinthian Democracy, appearing frequently in the press and in public forums. Of all these figures, though, Sócrates stood out as the preeminent leader of the movement and of the team. Born in Belém, Pará, the state capital near the mouth of the Amazon, he bore a grand, portentous-sounding name: Sócrates Brasileiro Sampaio de Souza Vieira de Oliveira. Early on, his success in the intellectual world seemed more assured than any sporting career. He started elementary school at five, only to have to repeat that year when his family moved to Ribeirão Preto, a city in the interior of São Paulo. After finishing up at the Marist school in Ribeirão, he went on to graduate in medicine in 1977—hence, one of his nicknames, "Doutor" (Doctor). As he explained, he joined the ranks of the club Botafogo de Ribeirão Preto casually: "I played in the junior level, all my friends from school went; I ended up staying."[75] Even then, though, he felt torn between his passions for medicine and soccer. When he came back from vacation in 1973, he was set to start his residency and hoped to become an orthopedist. The starter in his position at Botafogo broke his collarbone, however, and Sócrates made the momentous decision to pursue *futebol* seriously.[76] By 1977 he helped Botafogo win the first round of the state championship, a huge achievement for a team from the interior. The following year, spirited off by Vicente Matheus before his rivals at São Paulo FC could reach Sócrates, the Doctor joined Corinthians.[77]

At Corinthians he stood out not only because of his name and medical degree, but also because of his obvious talents and unusual physique. Rail-thin and six foot three, *Magrão* (skinny, another nickname) he was and would remain throughout his career. He also played with an almost impossibly erect posture that former *craque* Zizinho once jokingly said made him look like Frankenstein.[78] At first, by his own admission, he was virtually an "antiathlete." That is, he lacked the strength and conditioning of the professionals he found himself taking on. His technical creativity saved him. "I used whatever I could just to give a touch—butt, knee, elbow, . . . heel"—anything to keep the ball moving sharply up the field.[79] His skills with the heeled back-pass later led Pelé to pronounce famously, "Sócrates plays better backward than others do forward." He worked to refine his skills. He never, though, allowed himself to be turned into one of the finely tuned athletes that the scientific revolutionaries of the 1970s had sought.[80]

More than perhaps any of his colleagues—with the possible exception of the free-spirited Casagrande—Sócrates asserted his right to control what he or others did with his body. He smoked and drank, though he knew these were unhealthy choices for a footballer. Appearing on a popular TV show in the last months of his life, he admitted with disarming directness that he was an alcoholic. Drinking had been, he told another interviewer, "a companion with whom to live through part of the madness of this society."[81] During his career, however, he talked about alcohol and smoking in political terms, equating them with freedom of thought. "They don't want me to drink, smoke, or think?" he said. "Well, I drink, I smoke, and I think."[82] Physical autonomy was, after all, one of the central causes that he championed. For a while he dared to challenge the pass system (*lei do passe*) by which clubs held the rights to players and according to which players could only move if another club "bought" them.[83] One of the most egregious infringements on player freedom, the pass system nevertheless occupied Sócrates only briefly.[84] Instead, Sócrates turned his attention to the abolition of the *concentração,* the closed training camp that Brazilian teams imposed on players even before home matches, calling it "out of date" and saying, "Now, each one knows what is best for himself."[85] Indeed, locking the players up as though in a prison was, he argued, counterproductive, since "when the team is *concentrado,* the players want freedom and know they will have it only after the game." Rather than focusing their minds on the game, it fostered thoughts of escaping to have a drink or look for sex.[86] Not all of his teammates united with him in abandoning the *concentração;* he joked that ending this practice would leave comrade Wladimir's wife "desperate, telling him, 'Go back to the *concentração.*'" More seriously, though, he recognized that staying with teammates at the club, under the supervision of trainers, was an ingrained habit among many players, however repressive he found it.[87]

His opposition to the *concentração* paled before his profound commitment to democracy. With Adilson and Wladimir, he believed that "the power of soccer is in its group of athletes" and that soccer players should be able to exercise the full rights of citizenship. In many instances, this meant that he would be outvoted; in the case of the *concentração,* for example, the group ultimately decided to eliminate it for married players but not for single men, "because players, coaches, and officials decided together that this was best."[88] Above all, though, what mattered was openness: "Everyone is consulted, we lay out the problems and later there is a vote. This is how we began to work with our directors, and there was really an *abertura* even in the coaching staff. There [you see] the results of a victory of democracy."[89]

Collective decision making, he believed, was needed for people to gain "consciousness," knowledge of the structures of power that shaped their lives. Although he knew that a broader education would be necessary to spread democratic education throughout society, he claimed, "we can also transform society through soccer." This was very much how he approached Corinthian Democracy: as a means of fomenting democratic processes in a specific but not isolated context. Given the low indexes of literacy and especially of political knowledge in Brazil, soccer could serve a tutelary function.[90] After all, "the discourse of soccer, the language of soccer, is something that reaches all of society." Talking about the logistics of running the club, he later claimed, left them "discussing the country through *futebol.*"[91]

FIGURE 12. Sócrates wearing "Corinthian Democracy" on his jersey, 1983. Jorge Araújo/Folhapress.

In fact, Sócrates and others from the club were, indeed, discussing the country's political situation in much more overt ways. One way they used to transmit their messages was the uniforms that the players wore during games. In the early 1980s teams met great resistance to the use of any advertising on their uniforms; a 1977 survey found almost 70 percent of fans opposed to publicity on team jerseys.[92] Only in the wake of Flamengo's world club triumph did the national sports bureaucracy approve the club's contract with Toyota for this purpose, first in games outside the country and later in Brazil.[93] Under Adilson, Corinthians followed suit.[94] Given the group's political leanings, however, Corinthians uniforms would not just carry sponsors' names but political messages on their backs. As the elections of late 1982 approached, the club's players wore slogans "Vote on the 15th," urging people to participate in elections, and "Corinthian Democracy" itself. In response, the government quickly banned the use of political propaganda on uniforms, and soon Corinthians players appeared with the logos of cleaning products or car parts companies.

This incident failed to diminish the group's "democratic daring."[95] Indeed, several players tried both to deepen and widen their project. Internally, Wladimir and Zé Maria ran for the club's council of directors in March 1983. With Sócrates and Casagrande as energetic campaign workers, Zé Maria won his election and thus assumed a lofty position in the traditional hierarchy.[96] After Travaglini resigned later that year, the players held a closed meeting and voted to make Zé Maria, by then retired as a player, the new coach. For journalist Marco Antônio Rodrigues, it was in this moment that "Corinthian Democracy reach[ed] its apex: players attain power. A rare moment in Brazilian soccer: the players had the right to choose their new coach; they had in their hands all the power to decide the command of the team."[97] Several players also contributed to efforts to organize unions of professional players across the country. Emerging in Rio, São Paulo, and other major cities in 1976 and 1977, this syndicalism attracted star players from a range of clubs and with a range of political views. All, however, took as their overarching aim what Sócrates summarized as gaining "for the laborers of soccer, who are we players, participation in the running of their work."[98] As Zico declared in accordance with this Corinthian ideal, "In Brazil, soccer players don't have the right to behave like normal citizens," and only by collective action could they claim that right.[99]

This interest in organizing on behalf of democratic rights led figures from Corinthians to align themselves with opposition groups in the years of *abertura*. Coach Mário Travaglini, as well as the players Wladimir, Vagner, Casagrande, Sócrates, and Zé Maria supported various antimilitary political parties.[100] Beyond formal politics, though, these players held meetings with the Metalworkers' Union in São Paulo, one of the dynamic forces in the burgeoning trade union movement and in the creation of the Workers' Party. The metalworkers put together a meeting called "Soccer in Debate!" at which Sócrates and Wladimir faced tough questions about their political positions. Ultimately, though, factory laborers and footballers left impressed with their shared commitment. As Lula said while transitioning from president of the Metalworkers Union to gubernatorial candidate in São Paulo, "Corinthians is proving to the whole Brazilian people and principally to the critics of 'Corinthian Democracy' that it is possible to have the rights of assembly, liberty, and autonomy."[101] Two years after sitting down with the metalworkers, Sócrates, Casagrande, Wladimir, and other players from the team took to the streets as part of the massive campaign for direct national elections, the "Diretas Já!" (Direct Elections Now) movement that drew millions to marches in São Paulo and many more cities across the country. At a climactic rally in São Paulo on 16 April 1984, the players took their turns addressing the massive crowds—estimates were as high as two million people—who cheered them wildly. Sócrates, who like Zico had been sought after by several

Italian teams, declared, "If the National Congress does not approve the direct elections amendment, I will leave the country." If the measure passed, though, he would stay on to help build democracy.[102] The failure of "Diretas Já!" was a staggering setback for Sócrates, as for so many of his compatriots. As the Doctor later explained, he felt "extremely frustrated," since it had seemed "the moment for the country to take flight" toward real democracy.[103] Instead, he fulfilled his pledge and left to play for the club Fiorentina, spending two rather unhappy years there among players he found to be "excellent professionals, but [whose] game lacks joy."[104]

Sócrates' move to Italy removed the principal leader of the democratic experiment and thus represented a tremendous challenge for those who stayed at the club. Before it even gained the name Corinthian Democracy, the movement had always suffered pressures. Press coverage was often ferocious, though the democratic ideal enjoyed support in the newspaper *Folha de São Paulo* and especially in the magazine *Placar,* where editor Juca Kfouri worked to protect Corinthian Democracy.[105] Most of the media condemned it as a "misgovernment" or just a "mess." Journalists who were used to the heavy hand of traditional *cartolas*—and who had developed sources of information (and perhaps favors) in the old system—resented the control that Adilson and the players maintained over the flow of information about the team.[106] These critics pounced eagerly on any evidence of dissent or improprieties in the team.[107] When Casagrande was arrested for cocaine possession in December 1982, or when Casagrande and Sócrates were found drinking beer on the training table in February 1983, much of the press pointed to the incidents as proof of indiscipline. Neither the explanations that Casagrande and Sócrates offered—Casão (as he was called) said the cocaine had been planted on him by the police and Sócrates said that as an adult he could drink beer when he wanted to—nor the public support by celebrities could dissuade the media from presenting the club's situation as verging on anarchy.[108]

The club's performance on the field was another target for critics. Team leaders tried to separate their sporting and democratic aspirations, as when they displayed a banner that read "Win or lose, but always with democracy" before a match against São Paulo. At other times, though, team members argued that democracy would improve their quality of play. Freedom brought with it responsibility, Adilson said, and meant the team's stars had to answer for bad games.[109] Moreover, club players were aware that "the survival of the project depend[ed] fundamentally on results on the field."[110] When the team did poorly, opponents blamed Corinthian Democracy and its flattened power structure. After the defeat to Flamengo, for instance, a reporter opined, "Under Matheus, heads would roll."[111] Clearly, Sócrates later noted, "without beautiful soccer, good results, and titles," this experiment in democracy would be crushed by the "retrograde" culture of soccer.[112]

Elements of that culture had not, after all, melted away. In and around the club headquarters, furthermore, old threats persisted. Pires had tried to integrate elements of both factions of the old regime, supporters of Helu as well as of Matheus.[113] Matheus, who had once declared, "Corinthians needs me more than I need it," could not, however, be easily pacified. He schemed against Pires and Adilson before finally, in July 1982, launching an attempted coup d'état against their administration. Only with the assistance of an injunction issued by a civil judge did Pires manage to fend off Matheus's assault.[114]

The range of opposition lent Corinthian Democracy a certain fragility, in spite of the vociferous commitment of its leaders to their "revolutionary project."[115] In order to complete the dismantling of old power structures, new administrative processes had to be established quickly. Here the decentralized and direct democracy was both blessing and curse. On the one hand, it gave supporters the sense that they could contribute to the project. On the other, the very novelty and openness of the project left it vulnerable to factionalism.

Tensions in the locker room had occasionally appeared but came to a head with the arrival of goalkeeper Emerson Leão. An experienced goalie who had started for the Seleção at two World Cups and won numerous state and national titles, Leão found himself unwanted at the start of 1983.[116] In the belief that "every great team starts with a great goalkeeper," Adilson moved to purchase Leão's rights from Gremio of Porto Alegre.[117] As he later admitted, Leão was known to be a difficult character, "*um sujeito chato*" (an annoying guy); Adilson nevertheless proceeded, hoping that "what mattered were the ninety minutes on the field and there, yes, he was great."[118] Adilson's eagerness led him, however, to circumvent the normal decision-making processes. He did not raise the question of Leão in a full meeting, but instead sought the advice only of those players—five or six—who had played with the goalie.[119] Reactions to this maneuver were immediate and heated. Teammates spoke up in support of goalie Solito, who had been state champion on the team the previous year. Graver still was the discontent with the antidemocratic process by which Leão had been brought to the club. Wladimir, who had talked over the matter with Adilson, agreed that he "should have consulted the whole group." Those who had not been heard were understandably upset.[120]

Disappointment with Adilson's betrayal of the democratic ideal was compounded by disgust at Leão's behavior. Looking back, some players argued that Leão made important contributions. Juninho thought he actually helped keep discussions open, "because [Leão] thought differently than most participants." Zenon, by contrast, focused on Leão's excellence on the pitch; even if "his arrival really agitated [matters], ... he was always a great professional and was essential to ... the results that sustained Corinthian Democracy."[121] Wladimir politely recalled Leão as having "a very controversial personality, very singular," but admitted that the goalie caused a "setback" for the movement.[122] The leaders of Corinthian Democracy tried to win Leão over, having him share a room with the politically reliable Solito.[123] Despite these attempts Leão never joined in what he called "the beautiful experiment"; in fact, he succeeded in creating "two [factions]: one of Leão and the other of Sócrates." This was a fight that Leão could not win. Sócrates was too important to the team, in both footballing and political ways, and so the new goalkeeper found himself sold off to Palmeiras.[124] His final verdict on his year at the Timão: "Corinthian Democracy never existed."[125]

The inclusion of a player capable of such an assertion serves as a final reminder of the difficulty of what was being attempted at Corinthians from 1981 to 1985. It was tempting to skirt direct democracy in the interest of assembling the most talented *futebol* team possible. In 1983, for instance, Adilson said the club had been "able to overcome deficiencies with unity and spirit, as well as some brilliant individual performances." With the addition of a few great talents, he believed, "Corinthians will form a good team."[126] In his efforts to build a champion, Adilson was not as democratic as he had promised to be. At the same time, though, he was neither as authoritarian as Matheus nor as entrepreneurial as other *cartolas*. Across the city, officials of São Paulo FC were trying to transform their club into a *futebol-empresa* (soccer corporation). They wanted a more professional and efficient business enterprise.[127] Adilson, by contrast, declared early on that "a club is not a capitalist enterprise and thus its end is not to make a profit."[128] If he faltered in his handling of Leão, he did not in the end repudiate the central goal that he and his colleagues shared: the consolidation of direct democracy.

They hewed to their cause as long as they could. Slowly, though, the core of the movement gave way, as Casagrande departed for São Paulo FC and other players were sold off elsewhere in 1984 and 1985. Combined with the team's waning success on the field, this dissipation of the democratic leadership gave hope to the old *cartolas* and even convinced Pires to shift toward a more traditional mode of administration.[129] The club brought in a new coach, Jorge Vieira, who considered Corinthian Democracy "true anarchy."[130] Despite public manifestations of support, the democratic experiment fell apart, and its slate of candidates met defeat in the 1985 club elections. The old guard, still with ties to right-wing political parties, had to leave club headquarters through the back door to avoid the protests of angry fans. They returned through the front door, however, and set out to undo what Corinthian Democracy had done.[131]

To this day Corinthian Democracy remains "a chapter apart."[132] At the time, players from other clubs took note of what was happening at Corinthians, and some tried to bring at least a semblance of this democracy to their own teams. Members of Fluminense and Internacional initiated dialogues with club officials about lineups and tactics.[133] The experiment that Sócrates, Wladimir, Adilson, and their colleagues had embarked upon did not, however, have lasting impact on club hierarchies.[134] Still, the project served as a beacon in the context of the first half of the 1980s, highlighting soccer's links with politics more explicitly than at any other point in the country's history and inverting the "Brazilian practice of regulated citizenship, highly exclusionary and controlled from above," if only briefly.[135] The ultimate failure of Corinthian Democracy as the seed of a new participatory politics in soccer does not take away from its role as a symbol of democracy in the waning years of military rule.[136]

ROMANCE AND THE "LACK OF MALICE": THE 1982 SELEÇÃO

Flamengo and Corinthians were (and remain) clubs of the masses, with powerful collective identities. Even so, the Seleção is the national team, with an association with Brazil and Brazilianness that supersedes, without eliminating, club loyalties. Thus some fans may wear the red and black of Flamengo or the black and white of Corinthians to a Seleção match, but they are there to cheer on the national team, and they are small islands in a sea of yellow. The opening of soccer styles and administration occurring at the club level was remarkable, but developments in the Seleção took *abertura* soccer to a larger symbolic stage. Changes at the national level in fact were almost as startling as the advent of Corinthian Democracy. The military government and its allies in the national soccer bureaucracy, after all, had included the Seleção in their efforts at top-down modernization. When the orientation of the national team shifted from the scientific revolution of the 1970s to the return of *futebol-arte* in the early '80s, it was thus a dramatic transformation that promised a move away from dictatorship.

It would be hard to portray the rise of *futebol-arte* on the Seleção as democratic in a strict sense. The shift in the stylistic orientation of the national team certainly did not bubble up from the players or the population at large. In the wake of the defeats between 1971 and 1978, the government decided to reorganize the country's sporting bureaucracy. The National Sports Council (CND, Conselho Nacional de Desportos) stayed in place as the oversight body for all sports, but *futebol* received its own entity, the Brazilian Soccer Confederation (CBF, Confederação Brasileira de Futebol).[137] This new football bureau was headed by Giulite Coutinho, who gave a civilian face to the bureaucracy but did not shake up the paternalistic structures of administration.[138] At the same time, it was this CBF chief who chose Telê Santana, the coach who led the Seleção to embrace a fluid, technically rich game at the 1982 World Cup.[139] As glorious as Telê's team would be, though, his transformation of the Seleção was a more strictly symbolic part of *abertura* than Corinthian Democracy.

Like Mário Zagallo, Telê had played as an inside forward, a point who cut in to help pressure opponents as a first line of defense. Telê never reached the national team, however, remaining a very good club player, despite a strikingly thin frame (he was five foot six and 125 pounds in his early days at Fluminense) that led fans to call him "Fiapo," or "Piece of Thread."[140] The differences between the men appeared when Telê got his chance to remake the national team and opted for greater offense and not the defensive blockade that Zagallo had tried to mount in 1974.[141] Indeed, the hope that Telê brought to supporters of the Seleção was that Brazil would play the beautiful game once more.

In early 1980, when Telê took over the national team, Brazil was in desperate need of an injection of optimism. Not only had the Seleção failed to win, or even play cohesively, while following the scientific doctrines during the 1978 World Cup, the team finished a poor third at the 1979 Copa América. By February 1980, Telê had become the consensus candidate to assume leadership of the Seleção.[142] After he became coach, results generally redeemed this support. When the Seleção suffered defeat to the USSR, some were ready to sound alarms; after all, the location (Maracanã) and score line (1–2) were the same as the 1950 Maracanazo—and the game took place just one day short of the thirtieth anniversary of that event.[143] Other than this unpleasant reminder of the fragility of national success, 1980 was a good year overall, with solid victories over Chile and Uruguay at home and two wins over Paraguay, the second a 6–0 massacre in Goiânia.[144] By May 1981, *Veja* heralded "the ascension of the Brazilian team," declaring that it was "also the ascension of coach Telê Santana."[145]

More than Telê's early record, though, it was his philosophical orientation that excited many observers. By contrast to Cláudio Coutinho, he did not promise a reformulation of the national game, nor did he speak in neologisms or present foreign schemes as the best way forward. Coutinho talked of polyvalence; Telê, of versatility.[146] In the 1970s the coaching staff treated Europe like the source of modern ideas; by the early 1980s, under Telê, Europeans were colleagues with whom useful "interchanges" could be arranged.[147] The foundation of the team should build on the skills and spirit that defined the nation: Telê wanted "a *craque* who is also a warrior."[148] On that basis, Telê sought to create a Brazilian squad that would face Argentina and Germany and other powers "without fear."[149] This belief—like the tactical scheme he would implement—was based, he said, primarily on a recognition of the "good individual value" of his players. "Technically," he told one interviewer, "we are among the best in the world, if we are not the best."

He did not, however, simply turn the team over to his stars.[150] Rather, he pushed to impose a faith in "working as a group," something he said Brazilian players took time to accept. Indeed, he praised Europeans for their greater collective orientation, declaring, "If Brazilian players had the tactical discipline of the Europeans, perhaps we would reach perfection in soccer."[151] His aim was not to turn Brazilians into Germans, though, but to find a Brazilian scheme that would give his *craques* space "to develop individual maneuvers" while not just "letting [the opponent] play."[152] This fluid conglomeration of outlandishly talented individuals represented a break from the controlled modernization of the 1970s and moved toward a tropicalized "high modernism."[153]

Both his upbeat attitude and his tactical ideals, he explained, had been shaped by conversations with the team: "I spoke a lot with the players. I opened things up and everyone wanted to know what I think, what I want, what my philosophy and my intentions are. Beyond that, I trust in the work that we are doing."[154] Sócrates later characterized Telê as the "most democratic" coach he had known, precisely because of this openness to discussion.[155] The new coach did not, however, transform the administration of the Seleção into a national-level version of Corinthian Democracy. He had a well-earned reputation for hard-headedness and showed himself particularly stubborn when it came to his choice of players and key strategic options. Before taking over the Seleção, for instance, he declared, "I can't prevent a director from choosing the team. But, if he does it, I leave. I don't accept suggestions; if they have to cut off my head, let it be because of my own mistakes."[156] In sum, the coach who oversaw the rebeautification of the Seleção's game listened to his players but also imposed his strict control over the members of the team.[157]

Often his inflexibility protected his players from officials or the press. In a famous episode from his time coaching at Fluminense, he threatened to walk out when the *cartolas* decided that players could no longer use the front, "social" entrance to the club. When one official tried to assure Telê that this was not aimed at him, only the players, the coach announced that he would quit immediately unless the rule was changed. The rule stood, and so Telê left in protest, making sure to go out a back door.[158] He also assumed responsibility for discussing disciplinary matters directly with players, never leaving this task to club officials.[159] At the same time, the heavy demands he made of his players led to disputes over matters of discipline. He was sympathetic to their concerns and had spoken out against the *concentração* as an unnecessary and patronizing institution in the 1970s. At the 1982 Cup, he let some players leave the team compound, to the surprise of observers.[160] He insisted, however, that players respect their teammates and the rules that he set, rules that he considered essential to the success of the group. Both open-minded and hardheaded, Telê found his time on the Seleção marked by conflict.

The nature of the battles that flared up between Telê and certain players reveals much about this icon of *futebol-arte*. His dispute with the forward Serginho Chulapa, for instance, highlights his rejection of violence on the soccer field. More a rugged finisher than a clever, darting attacker, Serginho was one of the most effective scorers in the late 1970s and early 1980s. He possessed, however, a notoriously short temper, a side of his personality that he said reflected the abuse that he had suffered as a child. It also guided him on the streets of Casa Verde, the São Paulo neighborhood in which he grew up and where he was "leader of his gang" and given to "many fights."[161] Although he believed that soccer "saved" him from a life of crime, Serginho committed more than his share of assaults on the pitch.[162] One incident in particular led to his banishment from the Seleção for much of 1981. In the league final that year, Serginho's São Paulo faced Gremio, whose goalkeeper was Leão—the same who opposed Corinthian Democracy from within the club. At the time Serginho had problems with hemorrhoids and had taken to using women's sanitary pads to help contain the bleeding. For Leão, this was too easy an opportunity to provoke Serginho, and he shouted, "What's wrong, blackie (*negão*)? You menstruating?" and called the forward a "little woman." Serginho struck out, kicking the abrasive goalie in the face. This "aggression against a professional colleague," as Telê described the act, was more than the coach could bear.[163] Telê was certainly not alone in his concerns about the perceived rise in aggressive fouls, both in Brazil and internationally. Whereas others spoke out about it, with some even proposing rule changes to rid soccer of a plague they saw as destroying the beauty of the game, Telê acted on his belief by cutting Serginho.[164]

Telê's arguments with three very skilled players—the point Renato Gaúcho, the fullback Leandro, and the forward Reinaldo—show also that he set the terms for his team's *futebol-arte*. Renato emerged by the early 1980s as a tremendous right forward who at times drew comparisons to Garrincha.[165] Although he grew up a supporter of the Porto Alegre team Internacional, he ended up becoming an icon of their great rival, Gremio. His work on the wing was a key factor in Gremio's capturing second place in the Brazilian championship of 1982 and winning the Copa Libertadores and the Intercontinental Club title the following year. He rejected the common image of him as irresponsible, saying, for instance, "I'm young, they say I'm a *moleque* (urchin), but ask Telê if I don't do everything that the coaching staff asks."[166] Renato's exuberant style off the field, though, ultimately caused problems with Telê. A late night of drinking with friends and teammates in February 1986 almost led to his removal from the Seleção. Only the intervention of the right back Leandro bought Renato a second chance. He failed to heed Telê's stern warning, though, that if either Leandro or Renato showed further indiscipline, they would be cut, "with no going back."[167] Renato found himself off the final roster for the 1986 World Cup after breaking curfew again. Leandro responded with a dramatic act of solidarity and refused to travel with the team.[168] With its coach enforcing his code rigidly, the Seleção would have to make do without two great talents on the right side of its lineup.

This blow-up served as a reminder that Telê demanded total command over his squad. This meant that he could choose his tactical scheme and his players. Famously, he adamantly refused to lay out his team—in 1982 as in

1986—with fixed point forwards. The television comedian and talkshow host Jô Soares used "Put in a point, Telê!" (*Bota ponta, Telê!*) as the punch line to years of jokes, and others made the same request in serious as well as comic ways.[169] The *ponta* was, after all, a symbol of the old and "true" Brazilian style, so the criticism leveled at Telê's lack of point forwards by the great *ponta* Garrincha could have been damning. The coach, though, stuck to his plan, trying to come up with a scheme that would allow his players to play Brazilian in a manner that fit their specific talents. He exhibited confidence in their skills and in their ability to adjust to changing game conditions. To enjoy this trust on the field, however, they had to work very hard to earn his trust off the field. When he judged that a player had fallen short—like Renato—Telê simply replaced him.[170]

His exclusion of Reinaldo in 1982, though, was troubling in what it revealed about the convictions of the coach in these years of *abertura*. One of the great forwards of the era, Reinaldo promised to be one of the principal weapons of the Seleção in the World Cup. Moreover, Telê knew him well, having promoted the forward to the professional team at Atlético Mineiro in 1973.[171] After working to ensure the forward's fitness, though, Telê left him off the squad.[172] Reinaldo's precarious health might have explained his omission in earlier Seleção matches, but this time the reason was his off-field behavior. Telê had declared that he wanted not only players with good technique and a strong tactical sense, but also "correct behavior in the *concentração* and in relationships."[173] In the coach's evaluation, Reinaldo had become too invested in politics. As he declared in a November 1981 interview, "The only thing Reinaldo knows how to do is play soccer. But people have put it in his head that he's an intellectual. . . . So Reinaldo, instead of training and undergoing physical therapy, goes to Brasília to give lectures, is being interviewed all the time."[174] Perhaps just as damning in the coach's view, Reinaldo did not hide his friendships with the openly gay radio personality Tuti Maravilha; Telê criticized Reinaldo for having a "faggot friend."[175] Reinaldo, for his part, saw nothing wrong with his political activities or his friendships; neither impinged on his "professional performance," he noted.[176] For Telê, however, they were at odds with his idea of proper discipline, which demonstrates that this champion of *abertura* soccer was not only uninterested in party politics—as he admitted—but also fundamentally conservative, perhaps reactionary, in his cultural politics.[177]

If the national team coach did not embrace the social and political movements of the early 1980s, he nevertheless presented an energetic assertion of a tropical-modern Brazil. The context of dictatorship had turned an embrace of the old visions of race and *futebol* into a progressive stance. Telê certainly wanted to protect and encourage what he thought of as essential "Brazilian talent" and use it to impel the Seleção to international glories. To accomplish this, as Falcão phrased it in his bland praise of the coach, Telê brought together "a qualified group" and gave them a "suitable formation."[178] To others in the country and elsewhere, the change in the Seleção under Telê was glorious; German coach Jupp Derwall, after confronting Telê's *craques* in 1981, told the press, "We lost to a team with a brilliant game and intense movement." Brazilians, too, were eager to believe that the Seleção had rediscovered, as Gérson put it, "the true essence of Brazilian soccer."[179]

Most commentators agreed that the difference between Brazil and all other teams but Argentina came down to sheer talent; the Brazilians had many more *craques* than the Europeans.[180] The most obvious strengths lay in the fullbacks—Júnior on the left and Leandro (and later Edevaldo) on the right—but especially in the midfield, which was the heart of the team.[181] Indeed, the team "had too many players" in the latter sector.[182] To begin with, alongside Sócrates was Zico, then rivaling Maradona as the greatest star in the world.[183] Beyond these two icons, the team had Falcao, who had gone on to earn the nickname "King of Rome" for his play at AS Roma, as well as Toninho Cerezo, a sharp and versatile player with tremendous stamina. The generation had other star midfielders as well, so many that Telê struggled to discover the best combination of *craques* for the middle of the pitch. Paulo Isidoro and Batista ended up mostly as substitutes but also started occasionally and made important contributions in big tournaments.[184]

This group excited national passions from the Mundialito of January 1981 onward.[185] The fluidity of the team as a whole and the fighting spirit of players like Isidoro and Batista led observers to speak about "Brazilian artists" and "magicians."[186] Criticism flared up when the Seleção slipped up in exhibitions or even in scrimmages, but overall a cautious euphoria began to take hold.[187] Victories in a three-game tour of Europe, particularly a 3–1 defeat of France, led many to hail the "impeccable soccer" that the team displayed, "like in the old days."[188] With some urging caution, the general sense was that the squad had "reaffirmed Europe's respect for Brazil."[189] As the squad hit its stride, in fact, the comparisons to the champions of 1958 and 1970 become commonplace.[190]

Thus Brazil was anointed favorite before the 1982 Cup, a status that its last exhibition, a 7–0 massacre of the Republic of Ireland, confirmed.[191] The opening game against the Soviet Union, a come-from-behind victory, sparked some anxieties. Two more victories in the group stage, over Scotland and New Zealand, left Telê demanding that the squad "justify its favoritism on the pitch."[192] Still, optimism only grew more exuberant as the Cup progressed.[193] As the string poet Alvarus Moreno wrote, "The Brazilian fan / . . . / prepared a Carnaval / for the day of victory."[194] Journalists from Brazil and other countries dubbed the Seleção "the greatest" team in the Cup and a *"time de cinema"* (team worthy of the movies).[195] Spirits soared even higher with a convincing 3–1 victory over Argentina, Brazil's greatest rival, in the first game of the knockout phase.[196] With Falcão and others blending hard tackling into their passing game, Brazilians judged that their team had subjected the defending champions in a "last tango to a samba rhythm."[197]

The Seleção was the darling of much of the world press, as well as fans from other countries, many of whom picked up on tropical images of the country. On game day in Barcelona, "everyone was wearing the yellow jersey of Brazil. . . . There were even *blocos,* small samba schools."[198] Brazilian papers at home delighted in relaying the praise that their colleagues elsewhere heaped on the Seleção, much of which focused on the *arte* of Telê's squad. After the narrow win over the USSR, for instance, one Madrid paper to concluded that "in the end samba was imposed."[199] For Brazilians as well as others, the decisive traits of this Seleção was its joyful application of specifically Brazilian skills.[200] They did not carve up their opponents surgically, but overwhelmed them with their clever, unpredictable passes and runs and inimitable touches and dribbles, their "refined and mischievous game."[201]

Having dispatched Argentina in a satisfying fashion, Brazil now needed only a tie against Italy to advance. Telê, however, sent his team out to win. The euphoria surrounding the Seleção made this seem a reasonable choice; the general attitude was that "Brazil can only lose to itself."[202] What followed, though, was a tragedy that eliminated the widely loved Seleção from the Cup. Before the match and in most recollections to this day, Brazil versus Italy was a classic confrontation between *arte* and *força*.[203] The flow of the game did not bear out this simplification; Italy was a team with talented players who sought out goals and did not fall back into a defensive shield. Led by Paolo Rossi, recently returned from a two-year ban for his involvement in a match-fixing scandal, Italy came into the game an underdog.[204] Seleção members found, to their surprise, that their adversary went on the offensive.[205] Italy scored first when Rossi headed home a cross by Cabrini in the fifth minute. Almost as shocking as the timing of the goal was the slow build-up by the Italians that preceded it; this was not the game the Seleção had anticipated. Sócrates brought his team back with a slashing shot from a nearly impossible angle on the right of goal. When Cerezo played a lazy lateral pass on his own side, Rossi intercepted it and with a long right-footed drive put Italy in the lead again. Brazilian spirits revived when Falcão maneuvered outside the Italian area and nailed a precise, left-footed shot into the opposite top corner of the goal. The Seleção was safe again; a tie would still see it through to the semifinals. To the dismay of Brazil and fans of its team around the world, though, Rossi marked his third goal in the 75th minute, redirecting a shot by Tardelli. Brazil's desperate individual responses led to one clear chance, a sharp header by Oscar near the end of the game. Italian goalkeeper Dino Zoff saved it, however, holding the ball in front of his body to make it clear to everyone that it had not crossed the goal line.[206]

Reactions in Brazil resembled those in 1950; once again, "a dream of Brazilian *futebol* ended."[207] Optimism exploded, sending shards of blame everywhere; rarely did anyone make the obvious argument that Italy deserved to win because it had played better.[208] Nationalist egotism portrayed the loss as an unanticipated disaster that must have derived from Brazilian mistakes or overconfidence.[209] Those who followed this line of thinking often focused on Cerezo's misplaced pass, which set up Rossi's beautiful second goal, while still others more broadly judged that Brazil had simply not "found its samba rhythm, its total football" against a disciplined opponent.[210] Few questioned the talent of the Seleção, glorying even in defeat at the manner in which Brazil had "enchanted the world with the beauty and joy of a magical soccer of subtle touches, rich in plasticity and creative imagination."[211]

Nonetheless, it was the coaching philosophy behind this soccer that became the main target of criticism.[212] The most frequent complaint was that Telê had too boldly or naively pursued a dynamic, attacking football. He had not injected the "cunning" needed to win, going for a beautiful victory instead of the simple tie that would have allowed a team of great talents to bring home a fourth World Cup trophy.[213] In these arguments, the conflict over *futebol-arte* and *futebol-força* came to a boil once again. Various voices urged Brazil not to be "goody-goody," but rather to "play ugly," since "beauty alone is not enough, we need to defend."[214] Against these declarations appeared others calling for a smarter form of *futebol-arte*. João Saldanha, for instance, wrote disingenuously, "the Cup was not difficult to win" if only the coach had made the proper use of the handful of great players at his disposal and the technical staff had prepared the whole team well enough.[215] Other observers from Brazil and beyond simply applauded Telê and his team for courageously pursuing an ideal of beauty. They had lost, of course, but they had done so "on their feet," not giving way to their brutal or cynical enemies but defending the *jogo bonito*.[216] Poet and columnist Carlos Drummond de Andrade produced the most lyrical paean to the 1982 team's efforts: "If the Seleção went to Spain, land of mythical castles, only to grab the cup and bring it back in a suitcase, as exclusive and inalienable property of Brazil, what merit would there be in that? In truth, we went out of hunger for the uncertain, the difficult, the fantastic, and the risky and not to collect a stolen object."[217] Given the emotional and symbolic investment in the national team's success, this rejection of a venal pragmatism did not satisfy many fans. A good number agreed with Milton Cruz's later assessment: "For me, a good Seleção is one that wins."[218] Brazil wanted to be champions again, after all; the question was still how to do so in a way that was both effective and somehow authentically Brazilian.

This question lingered after the end of the 1982 Cup, even as the country turned its attention more directly to the strains of the late *abertura*. Telê departed, as he had planned to do, to coach the club Al Ahli in Saudi Arabia, helping to institute "Arab soccer" as an El Dorado for Brazilian coaches and players, a place where they would find the riches that service in the domestic league did not provide.[219] Before leaving, though, he made very clear his sadness over the loss to Italy but also his convictions regarding the essence of the country's soccer. Accepting the errors that he and his players had made in Sarriá, he swore, "If I had it all to do again, I would repeat the same methods. . . . I defend *futebol-arte* with intransigence."[220]

DROPPING OFF: THE 1986 AND 1990 WORLD CUPS

Telê's removal of himself from the national scene facilitated the calming of debates over the Seleção's performance against Italy. With this symbol of *futebol-arte* generally out of the public eye, the national game moved on, though without any clear, new direction. The CBF remained in the hands of Giulite Coutinho, who turned first to Carlos Alberto Parreira, one of the products of the military-sponsored scientific modernization of the 1970s, to take over the Seleção. Parreira's teams did not perform poorly, losing only two of the fourteen games under his guidance. Fully half of those matches were ties, however, leading the press to nickname Parreira "King of the Draw."[221]

The team drifted along under two other coaches until the eve of the qualifying matches for the next World Cup, when Giulite, with broad, but not unanimous, public support, called Telê back.[222] The project that the coach adopted in the run-up to the 1986 World Cup was much the same as the one he had used in 1982. The focus was again on making the best use of the skills of the Brazilian *craque;* as he told a reporter, "This Cup will be decided more by technique, by *arte,* by ability than exactly by physical condition."[223] This was more than a tactical assertion, however; he was intent on using most of the key players from the 1982 squad and felt the need to justify this reliance on veterans. Indeed, the core of the Seleção consisted of four *craques* from the last campaign: Sócrates, Zico, Falcão, and Júnior. Sócrates in particular went out of his way to try to work new talents like midfielder Josimar and defender Júlio César into the squad, but observers worried that the Seleção depended too heavily on aging players who would have to play at altitude in Mexico.[224] Watching these players he knew so well, Telê nevertheless convinced himself that the old guard retained the vitality to help him realize his dream: "I am on the Seleção once more to be world champion; and I want my team playing beautifully and scoring many goals."[225]

With Telê back in command, the Seleção hit lofty heights in 1985 and then in the 1986 Cup. Qualification came with such ease that Telê declared, "We have the best team in the world."[226] Indeed, the early stages of the tournament gave a measure of hope to Brazilian fans.[227] Sócrates, Falcão, and Zico demonstrated great imagination, if not the physical vitality of 1982. Telê, meanwhile, evinced growing confidence in some of his younger charges, with Josimar emerging as a new star and displacing Falcão for much of the competition.[228] As long as the veterans continued to show their genius at times while also paying more attention to their defensive responsibilities, the team might still establish its "collective art."[229] The efforts of young and old members of the Seleção could not, ultimately, overcome France, a national team that Brazilian journalists had often approvingly characterized as the "Brazilians of Europe."[230] With a powerhouse midfield led by Michel Platini and Luis Fernandez, France matched Brazil in the first half. In the second, though, the Seleção began to fall apart, losing at last on penalty kicks and sealing the fate of a "generation without glory."[231]

Unlike the experience of 1982, Brazil's loss in 1986 appeared disheartening but fair. Telê's team had completed "an excellent campaign" but simply came up short; the veterans had done their best while their "cycle" met its inevitable end.[232] More significantly, Brazilian journalists and officials seemed to feel once more that "South American soccer was backward in relation to Europe."[233] This was the position that had led to the attempted scientific revolution of the 1970s under the generals. At the close of the 1980s, it fueled another rationalist adventure, with a reprise of *futebol-força,* this time under Sebastião Lazaroni.

Lazaroni's hiring showed the same sort of top-down decision-making and faith in technocratic solutions that had flourished in the 1970s. Lazaroni's appointment in January 1989 was part of the program that Ricardo Teixeira, the son-in-law of former CBD and then FIFA president João Havelange, had begun to implement even before his formal election as the new head of the CBF.[234] The new coach reentered the national scene after coaching Al Ahli in Saudi Arabia, Telê Santana's former club, and was plunged into a political morass. Surveys suggested a huge amount of support remained for Telê, while only 3 percent of those polled named Lazaroni as their choice to head the national team.[235]

Lazaroni did what he could to soothe the situation, declaring his respect both for Telê and the others who had followed him.[236] Once in place as the sole head coach, moreover, he pledged to build on the foundation that his predecessors had lain, by combining Brazilian skill with European tactical cohesion.[237] In practice, however, the change that Lazaroni represented quickly became obvious. In terms of management style, Lazaroni played into the paternalistic politics of the CBF. Even before he coached his first Seleção game, he had been part of an outrageous CBF maneuver, by which Eurico Miranda had named fully thirty-nine players to the team. Eurico's motivation in creating this "false Seleção," the press charged, was to drive up the transfer prices of the athletes he had indicated; he was a *cartola* himself and apparently eager to help out his fellow *cartolas.*[238] In the midst of such machinations, Lazaroni behaved like a good "little lamb."[239]

But it was in strictly footballing terms that the distance between Lazaroni and Telê was most apparent. Despite his occasional arguments that he was an offense-minded coach—even an advocate of *futebol-arte*—he set up a system that valued the construction of a solid defensive wall above all else. To accomplish this, he moved to a 3–5–2 system, adopting tactics then prevalent in Italy, Germany, and Argentina. The back three defenders included a free-roaming *líbero,* who could come forward if the play was far up the field but generally stayed in the back, shoring up any defensive gaps he might see. The presence of a defensive midfielder just ahead of the back three further bolstered the Seleção's protection of its own goal, so that the system was effectively a 5–3–2 that "shut down spaces on defense and facilitated the capture of the ball in the midfield, but has a hard time occupying positions on the attack, leaving its two forwards in an unequal battle against three or four defenders."[240] The strikers were often left far away from the rest of the team and expected to pounce on any balls that might be sent up to them in a counterattack. When they missed chances, Lazaroni criticized them for it in the press. As a result, his relationship with several of the promising young forwards of the new generation—especially Romário and Bebeto— was strained.[241]

Compared to Telê, he was unconcerned with working on quick movement or with fostering versatility among his players; he wanted his team to line up just as he planned—and he often stressed the importance of planning.[242] He rejected Dutch "total football" as too focused on offense. Instead, he demanded "total participation" on defense. In this little bit of linguistic pickiness he recalled his predecessor Cláudio Coutinho, and, indeed, as with Coutinho, the press soon poked fun at Lazaroni's language, dubbing it "Lazaronês."[243]

Whatever label we place on Lazaroni's soccer, it produced decidedly mixed results before the 1990 World Cup. After a tedious display in his first game inspired home fans to boo, he managed to guide the Seleção to its first Copa América triumph in forty years. This "resurrection" of Brazil prevented Lazaroni's replacement by Falcão and, more significantly, ensured the continuation of the "Lazaroni Plan," as the magazine *Istoé* termed his scheme, through the 1990 World Cup.[244]

Brazil's participation at this competition is widely remembered as one of the more shameful performances in the history of the Seleção. The squad contained talented players, some of whom would be key parts of the World Cup–winning Seleção of 1994. Lazaroni, like Cláudio Coutinho in 1978, failed to convince Brazilian observers of the worth of the reforms he was applying and then failed to deliver victory. Somewhat unfairly, the defensive midfielder Dunga became the icon of Lazaroni's scheme. Dunga's sins were nothing more than carrying out the duties the coach assigned to him while explaining—more directly than the coach ever did—the need for a move away from "spectacle-soccer." As the midfielder stepped up in public and as his coach heaped generous praise on his grasp of the tactics of the modern game, 1990 became known as the "Dunga era," which served from that on as a mark of contrast to the preceding "Zico era."[245] The Seleção's ultimate elimination from the Cup came, sadly enough, on the occasion of its best performance in the tournament. Against its greatest rival, Argentina, the team succumbed to a brilliant pass by Maradona, who had been effectively marked up to that point, to his teammate Claudio Caniggia.[246]

This was a bitter loss, but it provoked nothing like the disappointment of 1982 or the general resignation of 1986. In fact, the end came as a "defeat foreseen," although this did not stem the flow of condemnations of Lazaroni and Dunga.[247] Their idea of modern soccer, critics charged, had produced a Brazil with "very little Brazilian" in it.[248] It was particularly galling that an Argentine, Maradona, had shown the value of *arte*.[249] Like Coutinho's ideas in 1978, Lazaroni's *futebol-força* plan seemed to work only in isolation from the vagaries of a real game.[250] In 1990, the "science of football boots" gave the world a Brazil playing timid soccer, a display far worse than the ambitious failures of the Telê years.[251] To the shame and anger of Brazilians, it also shut off the possibility of Brazilian *craques* leading the Seleção to victory; it was, in the end, a soccer philosophy of disdain for the inherent popular talents— the *arte*—of the Brazilian nation.[252]

CONCLUSION: FROM ANTICLIMAX TO ANTIFOOTBALL

If the 1982 Seleção had captured some of the guarded optimism of the *abertura* period, the World Cup teams of 1986 and 1990 reflected the age of the New Republic. A time of uncertainty and anxiety, when the definitions of citizenship and democracy were up in the air, this was also a period of dramatic, top-down, and unrealistic attempts to right the ship of the nation.[253] In sporting realms, the greatest legacy of these efforts lay not in any intentional accomplishment but rather in a coincidental achievement; the faded beauty of the aging 1986 Seleção and the sudden turn to Lazaroni's scientism in 1990 helped exhaust the debates between *futebol-arte* and *futebol-força*. Art seemed to grind down by the end of Telê's tenure; under Lazaroni's leadership, force came back with a new version of scientific soccer. This time, though, *futebol-força* returned as a farce. The art versus force conflict never died out completely, but by the start of the 1990s, the acrimony that characterized the 1970s and early 1980s now seemed an artifact of the dictatorship.

FIVE

The Business of Winning

BRAND BRAZIL AND THE NEW GLOBALISM, 1990–2010

There are 160 million Brazilians, and one more, Nike, cheering for a five-star Brazil. Today and forever.

NIKE AD, 1998

In early 2006 Nike launched a worldwide marketing campaign that urged viewers, "*Joga bonito*" (Play beautiful). A massive collaborative effort by Nike and Google, *Joga bonito* included not only fast-paced TV commercials hosted by former France and Manchester United great Eric Cantona but also a social networking site that was complex by the standards of the time. Although much of the visual content featured famous players from other countries—France's Thierry Henry, England's Wayne Rooney, Portugal's Cristiano Ronaldo, and Sweden's Zlatan Ibrahimovic—the star of the campaign was Brazil, most often embodied in the dribbling, trick-performing Ronaldinho Gaúcho. One of the central ads, titled "Joy," features images of Ronaldinho playing *futsal* (a form of indoor soccer) as a kid in Porto Alegre and then again when he was at the height of his footballing powers and the two-time World Player of the Year.

The Brazilianness on display in the campaign is an updated version of the tropical modern identity constructed in the golden era of the Seleção. Another commercial, "Teamwork," makes this clear as it follows Seleção members from the team bus into the dressing room as they prepare, presumably for a World Cup match, and casually put their *arte* on view. Ronaldinho and the other team members at the heart of the commercials—Ronaldo, Roberto Carlos, Robinho, Adriano—are all Afro-Brazilians; white players appear as if by accident in fleeting shots. The emphasis is on playfulness and setting up teammates, with a childish delight, to improvise further maneuvers and keep the play going. They trap and pass the ball in fanciful ways, like angelic *malandros,* tricking locker room attendants and a referee, but gently and without malice. Meanwhile, a version of the 1960s international hit "Mas que nada," reimagined by Brazilian performer Sérgio Mendes and by hip hop artist will.i.am of the Black Eyed Peas, provides an energetic and recognizably Brazilian rhythm for the crisp visual editing. Even the elements of the campaign that did not make use of Seleção players or musical references to Brazil, rely on the myth of the country as the home of the beautiful game. The campaign, though aimed at a global audience and with Cantona speaking English, culminates in the invocation, in Portuguese, "Joga bonito."[1]

Brazil had not, however, been heeding this command consistently since the mid-1980s. Individual *craques* continued to produce moments of magic that sent observers into rapture. Brazil's defeat of England in the 2002 World Cup featured a glorious free kick by Ronaldinho that confounded goalkeeper David Seaman and inspired columnist Armando Nogueira to proclaim, "Brazilian soccer comes down to this: pure electricity. Just like a verse that comes from a divine breath, the dribble, the curved or backheeled pass are inventions that reason does not know."[2] Brazilian teams also compiled a record to make any other country envious. The Seleção made it to the finals of three consecutive World Cups (1994, 1998, 2002), winning two of those matches, while club sides São Paulo (1992, 1993, 2005), Corinthians (2000), and Internacional (2006) added world club championship titles to those conquered in previous decades by Santos, Flamengo, and Gremio. Still, the arrival of more trophies could not dispel the sense of rupture between what Brazilian soccer was and what it had been.

The dynamics of globalism in the 1990s and early 2000s caused Brazilians to worry that what set their soccer apart might be swept away in the waves of commercialization that characterized these years.[3] Their national style and its allegedly inherent traits seemed more disconnected than ever from the lives of real Brazilians and even from the soccer that the country's clubs and national side exhibited; "brand Brazil" had been born.[4] Anyone with sufficient means could make their virtual Ronaldinho Gaúcho pull off incredible feats in a video game.[5] At the same time, players flooded out of Brazil to leagues great and small, leaving fans at home to wonder how to cheer for these migrants, or whether to do so at all, when they took the field for the national team.[6] Could Brazilians who spent most of their lives abroad even retain their *brasilidade,* or would the skills that made them so marketable be lost in a world that was at the same time homogenizing and fracturing?[7]

Brazilians were not, of course, the only ones grappling with the effects of the new globalism that has flourished since the last decades of the twentieth century. The expansion of markets, facilitated by the pro–free trade ideology loosely termed "neoliberalism" and by rapid developments in communication technologies, set off dire warnings about globalization's threats to national and local identities.[8] In fact, Brazilian governments began to embrace neoliberalism only in the early 1990s under President Fernando Collor, who argued that removing tariff barriers and privatizing state enterprises would sweep away "the discredited and abrogated forms of protectionism, paternalism, and populism that burden our society."[9] It was with the economic and political stabilization achieved under one former leftist, Fernando Henrique Cardoso, and continued under the first "worker-president," Luís Inácio Lula da Silva, that neoliberalism truly took hold. Lula in particular tried to blend meaningful social programs with business-friendly policies, but his Workers' Party administration accepted the supremacy of the market.[10] Even with neoliberalism triumphant, however, traditional notions of racial, regional, and national identities showed signs of revitalization, with new media often useful tools in their strengthening.[11] Lumped together as "glocalization," these reactions against the universalizing thrust of the changing economy appeared in soccer as in other cultural, social, and political realms.[12]

The advent of the new globalism posed new challenges to understandings of *futebol* and what it represents. To some, the symbols of tropicalized Brazil, "Carnaval-*mulata*-samba-soccer," were "losing little by little the appeal that they had possessed" by the 1990s.[13] Other sports like Formula 1 racing, tennis, and volleyball certainly gained media attention as well as fan support, particularly when Brazilian individuals or teams excelled in them.[14] In this crowded sporting culture, though, soccer remains the national sport, and the *jogo bonito* survives as the dominant stylistic ideal, as depictions in films, glossy books, and museum exhibitions suggest.

Discussions of *futebol* in the postdictatorship and neoliberal era have often revolved around two matters: producing a style of play that combines a recognizably Brazilian flair with international competitiveness and bringing business logic to the organization of the national game. These facets of globalizing *futebol* shaped the careers of four of the many "R's" prominent in recent decades: the *craques* Romário, Ronaldo, and Ronaldinho Gaúcho, and the *cartola* (club or, in this case, confederation director) of *cartolas,* Ricardo Teixeira. All of these figures lived at the interface between the domestic game and processes of globalization.

The early 1990s were difficult times for the Seleção. Former star Paulo Roberto Falcão succeeded Lazaroni as coach, promising renewal based on the revelation of new *craques*. Memories of his own exploits at Internacional of Porto Alegre and AS Roma and on the Seleções of 1982 and 1986 suggested Falcão would steer the national team toward success based on *arte*. His tenure was, however, brief and uninspiring. After scraping into the knockout round of the 1991 Copa América, Brazil managed a second-place finish. The team lacked a coherent style, though, and Falcão's faith in its members was not widely shared. Very quickly the CBF brought in an old hand, Carlos Alberto Parreira, to take over the Seleção, with an even older hand, Mário Zagallo, as his technical advisor. Together, the two of them set about implementing what others in Brazil disparaged as "soccer of results" (*futebol de resultados*) and what they considered the ideal way to win in the 1990s.[15]

The problem, though, was that positive results remained hard to come by in this period. The qualifiers for the 1994 World Cup went down to the final game, with Brazil needing to beat Uruguay in Maracanã, the very stadium and the very opponent that had produced defeat in the 1950 World Cup. Adding to the tension around the team was the situation of Romário de Souza Faria, the gifted striker who had been kept off the team since December 1992, when he objected to being a reserve in an exhibition match.[16] Parreira had started the Cup elimination process poorly, and the Baixinho (Shorty), as Romário was affectionately known, became the symbol of missing vitality. With Brazil's status as the only country to have qualified for every World Cup on the line, Parreira and Zagallo relented, calling the prodigal attacker back to the Seleção. Although Zagallo justified the forward's exile as a useful lesson, Romário was hailed as a returning hero of "true Brazilian *futebol*."[17] His confidence shone through in the decisive match, with Romário scoring both goals in a 2–0 victory. The second score was especially thrilling. Running on to a through ball, Romário touched the ball to his right, out of reach of the Uruguayan goalie, and then ran around to slice it home. Not only beautiful, this goal recalled Pelé's famous dummy in 1970 (when he let the ball run past him and the opposing goalkeeper, before catching up to it and launching a shot), though Romário pointed out a key difference: "Pelé didn't score, but I did."[18] The triumph brought temporary relief to Brazilian fans, who anointed this forward the "savior of the fatherland."[19]

In an era of "results soccer" Romário's skills and savvy served as proof that Brazil was still Brazil, that the DNA of the beautiful game survived. At the same time, both his on- and off-field behavior recalled the stereotypes of tropical *brasilidade* developed in the mid-twentieth century. He rose from the poor suburbs of Rio to play at big clubs in Rio and Europe. From Jacarezinho, where he was born in 1966, his family moved to the neighborhood Vila da Penha when he was just three years old. His footballing career began on the local youth team that his father, Edevair, put together with a friend to keep their kids occupied.[20] Dubbed Estrelinha da Vila da Penha—because Edevair considered all kids to be "little stars" (*estrelinhas*)—the team was where Romário first showed his hunger for the ball and for scoring.[21] After being turned away as too skinny at Vasco da Gama, Romário passed in a tryout at the smaller club Olaria in 1979. Soon, though, his reputation attracted the attention of scouts from Vasco, and he transferred there in 1980, climbing to the professional ranks five years later. In his first season on the full team he was the second-leading scorer in the Brazilian championship, taking over first place the following year while playing alongside club icon Roberto Dinamite.

By 1988 he became a *Selecionável*, a player worthy of a spot on the national side. In the Seoul Olympics that year Brazil failed once more in its quest for a gold medal in soccer, but the team contributed key players for later World Cup squads.[22] The main attackers went straight to the Seleção, first under Carlos Alberto Silva and then Lazaroni. Both coaches seemed to appreciate the ways in which Bebeto and Romário complemented each other. Bebeto covered a lot of ground with long, smart runs, while Romário focused intensely on picking his spots to "kill" the game with a quick shot or pass.[23] By early 1990, however, Lazaroni had decided to bet on a completely different attacking pair, Careca and Muller. Romário had recovered from an ankle injury, but both he and Bebeto played sparingly in 1990.[24]

By that time, Romário was part of the wave of Brazilian players moving to Europe in search of high salaries. First at PSV Eindhoven and then at Barcelona, the Baixinho kept up his scoring ways. PSV paid US$5 million for his transfer—and sent head coach Guus Hiddink to Brazil to expedite the transaction. In his three years at the Dutch club, Romário made good on that fee, the highest to that point for any Brazilian, by tallying 174 goals and leading PSV to three straight national league championships. His disenchantment with life in Eindhoven, together with his prodigious goal record, led to a move to Barcelona in 1993. Playing now with Hristo Stoichkov and other strong-willed stars, Romário showed himself to be, in the words of his coach and Dutch legend Johan Cruyff, "a genius in the box."[25] Still, despite his protestations to the contrary, he was deeply unhappy living in Europe.[26] Recognizing the opportunity to bring the country's biggest star back, Flamengo entered into months of complicated negotiations. Finally, with Romário's encouragement and financial backing from Brazilian companies, the Rio club assembled an offer that Barcelona accepted, and the *craque* returned home in early 1995.[27]

Romário and many of those around him said he had never really left. In 1995 he proclaimed, "Nothing compares to Brazil and to Rio de Janeiro. The people are happy, the weather is delicious, the beach, friends."[28] When he was not in Rio, Romário tried to recreate it in Europe with his friends from home and a few teammates, mostly other Latin Americans or the occasional Italian.[29] While still in Barcelona, he searched for beaches where he could hang out with friends as he loved to do in Rio; despite a few promising locations, nothing ended up satisfying this desire.[30] What set him apart from the hundreds of other Brazilian players plying their trade around the world was that he had the means to maintain a close connection to home. As he declared while at PSV, "I work in Holland, I live in Rio."[31] In his time in Eindhoven and Barcelona, he not only flew back to Rio often—more often and for longer periods than club officials wanted—but also paid for friends and relatives to come stay with him. He was one of the first "air-shuttle *craques*," players who spent as much time as they could in Brazil while under contract to clubs in Europe.[32]

It was not only officials at PSV and Barcelona who found Romário a frustrating figure. He was certainly a player of exceptional gifts, one of the greatest Brazilian players since Pelé in almost every observer's estimation. Tostão offered this evaluation in 2007: "Since Pelé is a separate case, Romário deserves to go down in history as the greatest scorer of all time—or the greatest Brazilian scorer. Aside from Pelé, he is the forward who most enchanted me." Others stressed that he was much more than just a goal poacher. His 1994 Seleção teammate Branco countered those who claimed that "the ball finds" Romário by saying, "No way, he finds the ball in the exact right place."[33] He remained a fantastic scorer at the end of his career, leading the Brazilian league in goals at the age of thirty-nine. At the same time, he generally avoided work that might have improved his overall game. He owned up to his dislike of running or practicing in general. While at PSV he told a Dutch journalist, "The day of a game for the Europa Cup, they order me to wake up at 9:00 to come here and run for six minutes. What is that? It doesn't help anything."[34] Looking back in 2004, he noted casually, "I was never an athlete."[35] Those who managed or played with him agree that he always missed as much training as he could, relying on the explosive speed and sense of positioning that he had picked up as a kid.[36] These abilities served him well; as José Miguel Wisnik writes, he "always demonstrated boredom with discipline, but passion for efficiency."[37]

Efficiency had very much been the watchword of scientifically minded trainers and coaches since the 1970s. Parreira had been one of the scientific revolutionaries, and as Seleção coach promoted rationalization in the national game. Parreira declared his love of "the true Brazilian style" but thought it best not to get caught up in "dreaming about a soccer that hasn't existed for a long time." Brazil had to embrace advanced techniques of physical conditioning, psychological preparation, and tactics.[38] These innovations, he argued, helped his team play an updated version of "the purest Brazilian soccer." Pointing to his 1994 squad, he explained, "There is nothing more Brazilian than this Seleção with a line of four defenders, marking by zone, going forward through touch passing and not booming the ball down the field ... Whoever compares Brazil to Germany either hasn't seen Brazil or [hasn't] seen Germany, or doesn't understand soccer, or isn't being fair."[39] His plain language contrasted with the odd jargon Coutinho and Lazaroni had adopted, making Parreira seem a reasonable reformer instead of a revolutionary.

Parreira's results-oriented ideal was to position well-conditioned players to defend aggressively all over the field. In other words, despite his outline of the abstract Brazilianness of his team, the 1994 Seleção focused on shutting down opponents.[40] This was in effect the "Dunga era" brought to a successful conclusion. When Brazil received the trophy, it was in fact Dunga who first held it above his head, as team captain. For those who watched his Seleção struggle through the qualifiers and then win the Cup only on penalty kicks in the final, the "Dunga-ness" of the Parreira years went beyond the defensive midfielder's leadership role. After all, playing next to Dunga was Mauro Silva, another tough tackler. Farther up the midfield, Parreira insisted on the ball-hawking Zinho and, for a while at least, the more stylish Raí, younger brother of Sócrates, as the main attempt to solve "the crisis of creativity" in the midfield.[41] When Raí failed to provide the playmaking that Parreira had hoped, he gave way to Mazinho, a more solid if less electric option.[42] In front of the tightly packed defense and midfield, Parreira pragmatically deployed

Bebeto and Romário. This decision put the lie to Parreira's declaration that "goals are just a detail" (*gol é apenas detalhe*), a phrase that subjected him to showers of derision. Withstanding charges that he was "un-Brazilian," Parreira saw Bebeto and especially Romário finish off counterattacks with incisive final touches.[43]

Parreira remained vigilant over Romário, assigning the straight-laced Dunga as his roommate and minder.[44] To the surprise of many, Dunga and Romário got along well both on the field and off, and the Baixinho—at least outwardly—accepted his coach's dictum that "in no circumstance can individual interests overwhelm those of the group."[45] Indeed, Romário minded his behavior during the competition, keeping what Parreira deemed his "strong personality" under wraps, or at least out of the public eye. He did make little "escapes" from the team compound with friends from home; as one of them explained, "Being closed up in the *concentração* . . . was not to his liking."[46] Still, Romário held ranks in a Brazilian team marching steadily, if not brilliantly, through the tournament.

The Seleção's campaign ultimately resulted in the Tetra (fourth championship) but did so in a way that did not fully satisfy fans. As Ruy Carlos Ostermann noted wryly, in 1990 Germany had "invented a manner of winning the World Cup without having to play soccer, which would be imitated rigorously and decisively by Parreira/Zagallo in '94."[47] As they celebrated their team's victories, Brazilian fans harbored misgivings about the Seleção's style. In a tournament that supposedly reversed the trend toward antisoccer, Brazil won by allowing the fewest goals and stealing the most balls from adversaries.[48] Parreira kept his team on the defensive, counting on providential moments of offensive brilliance to create wins. In the quarterfinal, fullback Branco came up with one such instant, when his free kick rocketed the Seleção past a Dutch team that had come back from a two-goal deficit. As miraculous as that shot seemed, Romário supplied even more "magic" with his goals, "decisive at the right time, most guaranteeing victories."[49] In two games against Sweden, for example, he pierced a solid defense with darting attacks that ensured a draw in the group stage and delivered victory in a semifinal match. Such moments were hailed as evidence that the old Brazilian style survived in Romário. He did not win the Cup by himself, as some analysts claimed and as he at times implied; he did not even produce the only crucial goals. His role was, however, much grander; he was seen, at the time and in later accounts, as an injection of the true nature of the Brazilian *povo* in an otherwise rather bland and formulaic team.[50]

However much Romário played the "good boy" during the tournament, he continued to perform the role of "*malandro* of Vila da Penha."[51] Indeed, his behavior often illustrated the liminality of the stereotype of the Carioca rogue. He showed, for instance, a deep commitment to adventures with friends, dribbling around the rules officials tried to set for him, letting himself be filmed handling and discussing handguns on the beach.[52] Although not known to drink or smoke, he indulged in other pleasures, going out to clubs and bars, always looking for women.[53] He was very much a *mulherengo* (womanizer), he freely admitted, and cheerily supported a sexual double standard for men and women.[54] Moreover, although he did not use drugs, he admitted to having friends involved in drug trafficking and saying that they were part of the *povo* and thus, presumably, just like anyone else.[55] He also showed an adolescent sense of humor that led him to put up crude caricatures of Zagallo and Zico in the bathroom of his nightclub (fittingly called Café do Gol), a temper that led him to fight publicly with teammates during games and more formidable enemies like a *torcida organizada* (organized fan group) when he was playing for Vasco in 2002, and an active acceptance of the paternalistic and corrupt ways of old *cartolas*.[56]

These misdeeds, however, did not hurt his image. If anything, in fact, his roguish behavior made him appear more down-to-earth. Carlos Heitor Cony dubbed him "the synthesis" of the country's soccer since 1970: "Brazilian football—in its best moments—is exactly that which Romário does: pisses on hotel windows, prays in the chapel of São Conrado. But on the pitch, he embodies all the demons of our soul—and wins."[57] Romário echoed this sense, declaring, "I am difficult because I am authentic."[58] When he played well, his indiscretions made him more lovable to those who saw in him someone who had fought his way from the streets to global fame without forgetting his origins. The press adhered to this image of Romário as part of the *povo*, emphasizing his generosity to family and friends, to whom he gave jobs, trips, and expensive gifts; his devotion to his old neighborhood, where he had a social services institute created (the Instituto Romário de Souza Faria); and his open love for simple pleasures like the beach and pursuing women. When he suffered because of his fame, enduring muggings, car thefts, and the kidnapping of his father just months after the 1994 World Cup, his display of both sentiment and bravery made him seem both vulnerable and admirable.

After the safe return of his father, Romário declared, "Romário isn't going to change at all," and he kept his word.[59] His celebrity attracted hangers-on, and his wealth allowed him to indulge his taste for expensive cars. He did not, however, disappear into the global media but stayed just where he wanted to be, playing in Rio.[60] He extended his career as long as he could and always remained a highly visible presence in *futevôlei* games. At the same time, he was honest and outspoken, traits that were attractive precisely because they felt so un-Brazilian. That is, Romário said what he felt, acknowledging his high opinion of himself, in a society where such frankness was frowned upon.[61] This did not always mean outrageous boasting; after the World Cup qualifiers, for instance, he told the press, "I am a guy like many others around here, trying my luck in soccer. It's just that I play better than them."[62] At other times, he punctuated his bravado with tearful sentiment, as when he declared himself moved at having seen "the people smile" because of the Cup that he had delivered.[63] He was also capable of using the World Cup title to claim a higher place for himself in soccer history than former greats who "understood everything about the game" but had not made Brazil champion, as he had done.[64]

His exploits made him a folk icon, besieged by advertisers and celebrated in "string" poetry and popular music.[65] The affection directed at Romário recalled that of an earlier "King of Rio," Zico, though the two were very different. Zico was a model of hard work, with a personal life that was startlingly free of scandal. His commitment to the game led him into politics. In the early 1980s he worked in the movement to unionize players. A decade later, he became National Secretary of Sports and proposed a sweeping reform of soccer administration.[66] At the close of his brief venture into politics, he turned to coaching, establishing a youth academy in Rio while managing the national sides of Japan and Iran. Romário never considered coaching, but he, too, entered politics when he finally called an end to his playing career. As a congressman for the Brazilian Socialist Party (PSB, Partido Socialista Brasileiro), he has emerged as a combative protector of the rights of the common fan. The transformation was unlikely; after all, he had not only reveled in his *malandro* image, but also rapped about it with fellow attacker Edmundo in the 1995 "Rap dos Bad Boys" (Bad Boys Rap). In spite of his sharp suits and stylish glasses, though, the new Romário remained provocative, merely transferring his rebellion to more acceptable political spaces.

Romário, like Zico before him, marked an era in Brazilian soccer history but enjoyed a preglobalized celebrity. Zico is perhaps more warmly remembered in Brazil and elsewhere, though Romário also features on many lists of all-time stars in spite of his often truculent behavior. Both were protagonists at major clubs and on the Seleção and both seemed to embody the *jogo bonito*. In the end, though, their career peaks came too early—and Romário stuck too close to his Carioca roots—for them to become global brands.

RONALDO NAZÁRIO, PHENOMENON OF GLOBALISM

Brazil itself had long been a sort of brand, a reference point for advocates of creative soccer. In the second half of the 1990s, though, the star forward Ronaldo—who became Ronaldinho to distinguish him from the defender Ronaldão at the 1994 World Cup and then reverted back to Ronaldo when he started to play in Spain two years later—took the stage as a world celebrity of a new sort. As quick and skillful as Zico or Romário, he played with a power that neither of them could match. Moreover, the timing and manner in which he became famous meant that he became a more profoundly globalized icon than either of these other *craques*. Known as "o Fenômeno" (the Phenomenon) for his brilliant runs around and past defenders, he was also a phenomenon of marketing.[67]

No one could claim that Ronaldo was the greatest celebrity in Brazilian soccer. Pelé's position in that regard remains unassailable. When Ronaldo returned from Europe in 2008, however, he was not only a wealthy celebrity but also a walking brand. His yearly earnings had reached US$32 million, US$23 million of which came from endorsements. He had served as the centerpiece of Nike's initial efforts to dominate the global soccer market as it had done with running and basketball in the United States. He had his own marketing and investment firm, Grupo R9, to watch over his many business ventures. It was this team of advisors who sought to create an image that transcended the sports world. In part this entailed using his stardom for charitable causes, which he began in earnest after the 1998 World Cup. In 1999 he made a very public visit to Kosovo, where he met with victims of warfare in the region and donated tens of thousands of dollars for the construction of a school.[68] The following year the United Nations named him a Goodwill Ambassador, a position that he used to promote various social initiatives. While pursuing these causes, he and Grupo R9 cared for his marketing power. Because of his personality, his good works, and the worldwide popularity of soccer, his principal agent asserted in a 2007 interview, Ronaldo enjoyed a lucrative position "on a global scale ... independent of religion, culture, race, ethnicity, social class, or sex."[69] This degree of fame left him isolated, and this young man who once described himself using the language of computing—"I programmed myself to be the best in the world"—sought anonymous connections on the internet. He played games but also entered chat rooms to strike up conversations; he particularly enjoyed breaking online conventions by using his own name, knowing that no one would believe it was really him.[70] From a beginning that recalls the origins of earlier stars, Ronaldo had created a career that put him at the center of profound transformations of soccer from an international sport into a globalized and intensely commodified entertainment industry.[71]

Three factors—in addition to the considerable coincidence of timing—allowed Ronaldo to achieve this status, and all three were in evidence by the time he was seventeen. First, he was, and remains, a highly likable character radiating an *alegria* that was always appealing and became "product-friendly" when he established himself as a star.[72] Second, with the initial guidance of two ex-bankers and former Seleção forward Jairzinho, he carved out an innovative path toward fame and wealth in the sporting world. Finally, he was a sensation on the pitch, scoring goals and winning major titles for all but one of the seven professional clubs he represented, in addition to helping Brazil to victory in two of three consecutive World Cup finals and earning FIFA's World Player of the Year prize in 1996, 1997, and 2002.

It is vital to recall these sporting glories today, when the name Ronaldo has come to refer most often to the Portuguese star Cristiano Ronaldo and when Brazil's Ronaldo Luís Nazário de Lima has taken up a very public, but at times awkward, life off the field of play. Ronaldo retired from the game in 2009, tearfully declaring, "I lost to my own body." He had long suffered from hypothyroidism, which made him prone to weight gain, but had avoided taking the normal medication for the condition so that he would not break any antidoping regulations.[73] By that time, though, he had become a figure of fun, the punch line of many fat jokes in Brazil; the *fenômeno* had become the *fofômeno*—the phenomenon of pudginess.[74] He took on the issue of his weight not only with his explanation of his retirement but also by subjecting himself to the potential humiliations of reality TV documenting his attempts to lose weight. Not just a marketing ploy, he explained, his appearance on "Medida Certa" (The Right Size) would help him get fit for a charity exhibition, the Match Against Poverty, played in December 2012 between the Friends of Ronaldo and the Friends of Zidane.[75]

The older images of Ronaldo linger on, however, in highlight clips and video games, as well as in fans' memories, of perhaps the most brilliant player since Pelé and Maradona. Born in the Rio neighborhood Bento Ribeiro—home also to actress and TV star Xuxa and Formula One great Ayrton Senna—Ronaldo quickly became as well-known for timidity as for his skills in pickup games (*peladas*).[76] Unable to sit still for long, much less to keep up with his schoolwork, this quiet, buck-toothed kid shed his awkwardness in tough *peladas* with older boys. His exploits in neighborhood games led to an invitation to play *futsal* for the Valqueire Tênis Clube, in the next *bairro* (neighborhood) over. Despite its elegant name, this was a modest starting place, but Ronaldo made the best of it. Since all other positions were taken when he arrived, he first played in goal. As the season proceeded disastrously, the coach turned his goalie into a forward and was rewarded for this act of desperation: Ronaldo scored four of his team's five goals in a win over the league leaders. More to the point, he caught the eye of the scout Fernando Gordo, who convinced Ronaldo's mother to allow her son to move to a more prominent *futsal* club, Social Ramos. There the prodigy continued to pour in goals—166 in his first season. Still lacking in confidence off the pitch and with little social life, he dreamed of playing for Flamengo, the club of his idol Zico. Not yet thirteen years old, Ronaldo summoned up the courage to show up at Flamengo for an open tryout. Although he did this without telling anyone who might have put in a good word on his behalf, Ronaldo passed the first cut. He would not even make it to the next phase, however; since his parents had separated, money was tighter than ever at home, and he could not afford the bus fare back to Flamengo's headquarters the next day.[77]

Within a few months, though, he found a place on a proper, albeit much smaller, soccer club, São Cristóvão. As he had done in previous debuts, Ronaldo scored in his first game for the team. His talents won admirers, among them the 1970 Seleção star Jairzinho, who became the team's coach. Although his place as the "discoverer" of Ronaldo is disputed, Jairzinho proved vital not only for recognizing potential in the fifteen-year-old, but also for putting Ronaldo in touch with the majority shareholder of the multi-pronged business venture that bore Jairzinho's nickname, Furacão Emprendimentos (Hurricane Investments).[78] A fervent fan of Jairzinho and his old club, Botafogo, Reinaldo Pitta was a former bank manager and businessman who in turn enlisted another former banker, Alexandre Martins. Together, Pitta and Martins steered Ronaldo outside the normal channels by which the "passes" of promising players were bought by bigger clubs. These bankers-turned-agents proposed instead that Ronaldo sell them his pass for US$7500 and sign a ten-year contract with them. They would be responsible for promoting his career and negotiating with clubs and sponsors, receiving in return 10 percent of all deals he would sign during that time. Once again, Ronaldo's mother resisted at first, though his father saw merit in the arrangement and thought Pitta and Martins of good character. Eventually both parents agreed to allow their son to enter into this contract and thus start his professional career in a novel way, as part of an enterprise that brought Ronaldo's transfer and image rights together and largely kept control out of the hands of *cartolas*.[79]

Since Ronaldo had to play for clubs, the freedom he and his agents enjoyed was of course limited. It was, however, greater than what most budding stars had. Moreover, the agreement survived because all parties to it—Ronaldo, Pitta, and Martins—performed their duties vigorously. On the pitch Ronaldo proceeded as he always had, with skill and cool determination. After a tip by Jairzinho, scouts for the national under-seventeen team watched him score some of his forty-four goals for São Cristóvão, and he found himself part of the junior Seleção competing in the South American championship. Prolific as ever, he emerged as the tournament's top scorer, leaving Pitta and Martins to calculate which first division club would provide the best next step for their partner. Interest abounded, but neither the powerhouse of the era—São Paulo under coach Telê Santana—nor Ronaldo's childhood preference—Flamengo—signed him. Rather, Cruzeiro, one of the big two clubs in Minas Gerais, paid about US$20,000 for 55 percent of his playing rights, a deal that decreased the club's risk but also left a significant portion of Ronaldo's pass in his group's hands. After further service on the under-seventeen national squad and a brief trial on Cruzeiro's junior team, he joined the full professional side of a major club at age sixteen.

The velocity of Ronaldo's ascent concerned some of those around him. His coach at Cruzeiro, former Seleção manager Carlos Alberto Silva, took care so that his forward would not lose his bearings. Silva complained to the press that he needed a more experienced attacker, so that Ronaldo would not take his place on the team for granted. Once he recognized that Ronaldo's head would not be turned by favorable press or his access to the trappings of middle-class life—a new car, videogames and other toys, braces put on his teeth by renowned orthodontist Dr. Eustáquio Araújo (who also happened to be a Cruzeiro fan and coach of the national *futsal* team)—Silva began to label Ronaldo the club's great revelation. His scoring continued to the point that the sports press began to take notice; he appeared in a preview of the 1994 Brazilian championship (the Brasileirão) as "the *matador* Ronaldo, who at seventeen was one of the sensations of the last Brasileirão."[80]

Despite such notices, he was a virtual unknown to many Brazilians. His inclusion in the 1994 World Cup squad thus elicited general surprise.[81] His tender age inspired a few hopeful comparisons to Pelé, who had first played in a World Cup while also only seventeen. Unlike Pelé, however, Ronaldo did not take the field for the Seleção in 1994. FIFA president João Havelange, Brazilian president Itamar Franco, and some journalists posited that he might be a useful addition to the team, but he played poorly in practice. More to the point, his coach had already opted to rely on Romário and Bebeto.[82] Ronaldo was part of the Cup-winning squad, in any case, and experts predicted that he would form part of the attacking duo that would lead Brazil in France four years later.[83] In spite of support from presidents and pundits and his first appearances in TV ads, he remained a non-entity as the Seleção worked its way to victory.[84]

He won his laurels soon enough in Europe. His first move took him to Romário's former club in the Netherlands, PSV. The older forward showed no real faith in Ronaldo on the Seleção but gave him sound advice in this regard. Other European clubs offered more, but the young star went to the Dutch powerhouse, which paid Cruzeiro an extra US$1 million after he was called up to the Seleção.[85] Still following the path that Romário had blazed, he scored prodigiously for PSV before moving to Barcelona. From that point on, though, his direction diverged from Romário's. Ronaldo stayed in Europe, playing for both sides of great rivalries in Spain (Barcelona–Real Madrid) and Italy (Inter–AC Milan). More significantly, he worked with his marketing team to groom his image in a way that never seemed to interest Romário.

It was in these years that Ronaldo experienced the two great high points but also the nadir of his playing career: his rise to global stardom by 1996, his return at the 2002 World Cup, and, between these two, his mysterious breakdown in the final game of the 1998 World Cup. The first peak came in the single season he spent at Barcelona (1996–97). He had transferred to the Catalan club despite great initial success at PSV, where he scored in his first game—as had become his pattern—and gone on to break Romário's single-season goal record. He had some trouble settling into Eindhoven life, unable to learn Dutch and having to listen to quarrels between his working-class mother and his upper-class girlfriend, both of whom had moved with him

FIGURE 13. Ronaldo in action for FC Barcelona, April 1997. Shaun Botterill/
Getty Images.

from Brazil. His discontent deepened in the wake of his first knee injury.
After undergoing surgery to clean up the cartilage in the joint, he wanted to
be back in the starting side soon. His coach, however, resisted. When
Ronaldo began to voice his frustrations, declaring that he would play for
Barcelona "even for free," the move became inevitable.[86] By the time he met
up with his teammates at the 1996 Summer Olympics in Atlanta, PSV had
sold him to Barcelona.[87] There, he exploded on the field, leaving observers
grasping for praise worthy of what they were witnessing.[88]

Video clips of Ronaldo's achievements at Barcelona are, thanks to the
internet, endlessly available. Perhaps the most stunning of them, which

occurred in a rather modest game, would have been lost in a previous age, like so many feats of earlier *craques*. During a match on 12 October 1996 between Barcelona and Compostela, a relatively young club then eighteen places behind league-leading Barça, Ronaldo displayed the combination of skills that characterized his game. Taking a pass just to the left of the midfield circle, he set off on a weaving run through the opposition. Increasingly desperate Compostela players attempted to tackle him, kicking at the ball and at Ronaldo, some pulling on his jersey. With close control of the ball and abrupt changes of direction, rhythm, and pace, Ronaldo weaved and powered his way some fifty yards, finally shooting crisply past the diving goalkeeper. His display of touch, cutting ability, force, and explosive drive toward the goal were amazing to those who saw the game and continue to be so to those viewing highlight clips. His combination of astounding propulsion and the tricks of the great dribblers—showing the ball to defenders only to fool them with a subtle feint or an unexpected combination of taps and spins—made him a perfect image of *arte* married to *força*.[89] Biographers have added up the statistics of this particular demonstration of his talents: "fourteen seconds with the ball at his feet, sixteen touches on the ball, five adversaries dribbled past, thirty-four steps, forty-six meters covered with the ball."[90] Brazilian weekly *Veja* patriotically exclaimed, "Since the time of Garrincha and Pelé, nothing like this had been seen."[91]

If he did not repeat his performance from that victory against Compostela, he filled the 1996–97 season with dazzling achievements. His thirty-four goals made him the top scorer in the First Division; he added thirteen more goals in other competitions to help Barcelona collect trophies for the Copa del Rey and the European Cup Winners' Cup. He finished the year with a second straight FIFA World Player of the Year award and was generally held to be the greatest player in the game. As he turned twenty-one commentators were likening him to an "extraterrestrial," while his teammate Pizzi explained, "I play football; Ronaldo plays something different altogether," and his coach, the experienced Bobby Robson, unabashedly declared that his forward was in fact "the new Pelé."[92]

Unlike Pelé, Ronaldo would never stay long at a single club. Ronaldo sought a transfer away from Barcelona in 1997 just as he had pressed for a transfer to the Catalan club the previous year. He had become the center of attention at Barça, with some fans worrying about a growing "Ronaldo dependency." He nevertheless felt underappreciated by Barça officials, who were slow to sign him to an improved contract and believed a hefty buyout clause would keep him at the club. The price stipulated in this clause—US$32 million—did not deter Internazionale of Milan, which swooped in for the striker. The move was a sensational publicity gain for Inter. Ronaldo continued to play at a high level at his new club, although defenders showed the physical intensity for which Italy's Serie A was known. As he explained shortly after arriving in Italy, "They start by surrounding you, then they grab hold and, if they can, they smash you. Always in every game there are at least three players keeping an eye on me. Since I'm fast, I sometimes manage to escape. But most of the time one of them ends up with the ball."[93] Once accustomed to the style of the league, he began to find the net, ending up with twenty-five goals in thirty-two games in Serie A and nine more in fifteen matches in other competitions. It was in this first year at Inter that journalists dubbed him "the Phenomenon" (Il Fenomeno). Despite this glorious moniker, his goals, and the Uefa Cup trophy he helped win for Inter, Ronaldo's career descended from the first of his playing peaks.

Coming into 1998, both Ronaldo and the Seleção appeared ready to build on past successes. The World Cup in France held great promise for Ronaldo in particular.[94] With the 1994 World Cup, two World Player of the Year trophies, and club titles at both PSV and Barcelona on his resume, Ronaldo had a strong claim on a place among the greatest stars in history. In spite of some tenderness in his knee, the Cup promised to be "Ronaldo's time." Brazil, meanwhile, had held the top spot in FIFA's ranking of national sides since its win in the 1994 World Cup. Ronaldo, moreover, was just one of a strong generational "harvest" of talent. Players who had been key parts of the 1994 squad remained.[95] To this pool had been added players who, like Ronaldo, had fulfilled secondary roles in 1994, such as the midfielder Leonardo, and emergent talents like Edmundo, fullbacks Cafu and Roberto Carlos, the flashy winger Denílson, and Barcelona's latest Brazilian star, Rivaldo. Coach Mário Zagallo, quirky and abrasive, had won World Cups as a player, manager, and technical advisor. He eagerly explained that luck was on his side once more.[96] Just before the last match in 1998, he declared, "No one will take the Penta [fifth World Cup title] away from us."[97]

As one of the favorites, Brazil was expected to move through the Cup with relative ease. Instead, the Seleção struggled to make it out of the group stage, losing its last match to Norway. Confident as ever, Zagallo characterized the result as a "defeat on the road to the Penta."[98] Few observers shared his faith, especially when it came to light that Ronaldo had been experiencing knee pains since an exhibition match just eleven days before Brazil's first game in the World Cup.[99] The team's most convincing performance came in a 4–1 win over Chile, a team that had managed just three ties in the group phase but which counted on two talented strikers in Marcelo Salas and Iván Zamorano. Two of Brazil's four goals came from Ronaldo, just as he had predicted to his coach before the game. Afterward, Zagallo asked incredulously, "So, it's just ask, and you do it?" Playfully, Ronaldo said yes, adding, "So always ask."[100] He scored just once more in the Cup, as the Seleção won two tough matches against the skilled squads of Denmark and the Netherlands. After the latter victory on penalties, only host France blocked Brazil's conquest of a fifth World Cup.

For the French team, the drama of the championship game came with an easy 3–0 victory and the celebrations that poured out into the streets afterward. Their coach had correctly noted the Brazilian defense's inability to handle high balls into the box; two of the French goals came on headers by Zinedine Zidane.[101] Brazil supporters, however, fell into confusion. Some sought consolation in their status as the only four-time Cup champions. The 1994 conquest of the Tetra, these fans felt, had cemented the country's place as the team of the twentieth century.[102] Furthermore, if they lost, at least it was to a worthy opponent, one with an elegant style and a racial and ethnic diversity that made them seem almost Brazilian.[103]

The loss of the Penta had, however, major repercussions, which eventually extended to an unprecedented investigation into the workings of *futebol*. What set this off was not the loss to France itself, but the circumstances surrounding it and especially Ronaldo's participation in the match. No Cup had seemed so easy for Brazil to win, some ventured; it was only a "work of destiny" that kept the trophy from staying in Brazilian hands. As TV commentator Luciano do Valle put it during the final, Ronaldo and the rest of the Seleção were "unrecognizable" in their lack of creativity and determination.[104] The precise causes of this poor performance remained very much in doubt.

The first hint of something unusual came when Zagallo handed his roster card to match officials. Instead of Ronaldo, the document listed Edmundo as Bebeto's partner in attack. The replacement of this document with a new one that restored Ronaldo's name in its customary spot only increased the confusion.[105] Slowly, the outline of a story emerged: Ronaldo had been ill the night before the game, which explained why he seemed "a mere shadow of the *craque* who usually decides games with blasting shots."[106] What exactly happened was unclear, despite efforts by journalists, physicians, and politicians to uncover the story. It certainly did not help that Ronaldo was at first unconscious and then groggy while others tended to him. As Dunga told an interviewer a year later, "Not even [Ronaldo] himself knows" what happened to him.[107]

The timeline of events that fits most of the testimony—and versions varied—begins in the hotel room shared by Ronaldo and left back Roberto Carlos. It was a few minutes after 2:00 in the afternoon, rest time for players on the day of the Cup final. Roberto Carlos noticed that Ronaldo was making strange faces and told him to "knock it off," before realizing that this was more than his roommate's normal playfulness. Suddenly worried, he ran into the hallway in search of help. There he yelled to Edmundo, "Call Dr. Lídio [Toledo, team physician], Ronaldo's sick!" Edmundo took off in search of the doctor, screaming, "Ronaldo's dying" as he went. The "convulsion," as it came to be known, lasted only about two minutes. In that short time, other players, panicked by Edmundo, crowded around Ronaldo, with César Sampaio forcing Ronaldo's mouth open and holding his tongue to make sure his airway was not blocked.

Dr. Lídio arrived within three or four minutes of Roberto Carlos's initial shouts, joining the players and the antiterrorism guards who had all squeezed into the room. Trained as an orthopedist, Dr. Lídio had the team's clinical physician, Joaquim da Mata, summoned. Together, they decided to let the player remain in his bed instead of rushing him to a hospital; this contradicted the advice that Dr. Lídio received from a neurologist friend he called in Rio. Toledo and Mata also chose not to inform Zagallo about the crisis, even after Zico heard about matters and asked if they had told the coach. Sometime about an hour after the onset of the incident, Zico encountered Ronaldo outside the room; the forward, unaware of what had happened to him, remarked, "I don't know what's going on with me. My body's all hard, I feel dizzy. I woke up and felt like I'd taken a beating." His teammates had agreed not to tell him about the convulsion. The meal passed in silence, no one able to eat. Dr. Joaquim and the scout Gilmar Rinaldi decided to take Ronaldo out for some light exercise, with midfielder Leonardo along to observe. The other players took heart when Ronaldo remembered that he had promised to help Gilmar with his computer, but their worries returned at hearing him declare that he was too tired to do so and went to take another nap. By this time Dr. Lídio finally talked to Zagallo, telling him simply that Ronaldo was out of the final. The coach, furious at not having been alerted earlier, held a scheduled team meeting anyway, trying to find inspiration in stories of previous Seleção triumphs that had followed last-minute injuries.

In spite of Zagallo's efforts, players continued to worry about Ronaldo, fearing even that he was dying.

Dismayed and distracted, the rest of the team went to the stadium around 6:00 P.M., while Ronaldo was at last taken for a detailed exam at the Lilas Clinic. There, however, a CAT scan and other tests revealed nothing, and Ronaldo began to argue that he should be allowed to play. Shortly after 8:00 P.M. the forward entered the dressing room, smiling and working on Zagallo to insert him in the lineup. "I'm fine," he declared. "Don't keep me out of it." Reassured by Dr. Lídio that the hospital tests showed no problems, Zagallo gave in to his star's wishes. After all, he felt he had no choice: "The best player in the world asks to play, the doctors approve, what am I going to do?" Ronaldo took the field that evening as if nothing had happened.[108]

Something had, of course, occurred, and it affected Ronaldo and the entire Seleção, although French goalkeeper Fabien Barthez thought they "didn't look different, just a little tired."[109] In Brazil, however, theories of all sorts popped up, ranging from the plausible but unproven to the outlandish. Two of the country's leading magazines, *Veja* and *Placar,* mounted comprehensive investigations into Ronaldo's convulsions. The general-interest weekly *Veja* found that Ronaldo had succumbed to an excess of stress. After explaining the normality and utility of some degree of stress in daily life, the magazine's reporters argued that he had fallen "victim to a nervous crisis" that left him in the tragic situation of "feeling his body crumble just when control over it was most necessary."[110] A year later, *Placar* argued strongly that the convulsion had in fact been a grand mal (or tonic-clonic) seizure. However, *Placar* presented stress as just one of five possible factors that brought about the seizure and focused instead on the misdiagnosis and inappropriate treatment that Ronaldo had received from the Seleção medical team.[111] Whether they claimed that he had been overwhelmed by the responsibilities placed on him or overtaken by a seizure, both investigations posited a very human weakness in a player who had to that point seemed almost superhuman.[112]

Neither medical explanations nor the humanization of the superstar, however, calmed the waters. Ronaldo emerged from the France debacle not only as a *craque* with common frailties but also as the pawn of powerful forces. Indeed, the conspiracy theory with the greatest staying power revolved around financial and political influence. Many came to believe that Nike, sponsor of the Seleção since 1994, or CBF President Ricardo Teixeira, acting at the behest of Nike, had insisted that Ronaldo play, whatever his physical condition. Teixeira was apparently present in the dressing room before the match, but Zagallo, loyal to his superior, eagerly asserted his sole responsibility for the inclusion of Ronaldo in the starting lineup. "I decided and that's it," he claimed, asserting that the choice had been his duty as coach and as a man. His macho gesture—as Zagallo described it himself—did not deflect attention from the possible role of Nike and its alleged lapdogs in the CBF.[113] In fact, before Ronaldo had the chance to redeem himself at the next World Cup, speculation about Nike's control over the Seleção would, in combination with more concrete scandals, turn the player's convulsion into a catalytic moment for Brazilian soccer.

While this crisis was brewing, Ronaldo returned to the playing field. All too soon, however, further problems put his career in jeopardy. The pain that had flared up in his knees during the World Cup in France came at end of the season with Inter and in the midst of preparations with the Seleção. Just as the 1998–99 Serie A calendar was kicking off back in Italy, Ronaldo suffered a crunching hit directly on his knee by an AC Milan defender. The incident sharpened both Ronaldo's pain and anxiety. As he had done in 1996, Ronaldo consulted with Nilton Petrone, known as Filé, an enigmatic physical therapist who had come to Ronaldo's attention through another sage recommendation by Romário. Filé combined the mainstream training he had received with acupuncture and other elements of "Eastern medicine" that he had taught himself. Often at odds with the official physicians and trainers of the national team—most notably the long-serving Dr. Lídio, who had little time for Filé's opinions—the therapist enjoyed Ronaldo's confidence. Examining Ronaldo's knees in 1998, the therapist found the same problems he had diagnosed two years earlier: the development of the player's thigh muscles was so exaggerated that it produced instability in his joints. His knees were structurally sound, Filé pronounced. Rather, the force of the muscles around the knee—a force that Ronaldo's dedicated training while at Barcelona had aggravated—exposed the components of his knees, especially the tendons, to dangerously imbalanced stresses.[114]

Under pressure from Inter's coaching staff as well as fans, the attacker tried to play through his discomfort, at one point feigning a minor ankle problem in order to distract from his ongoing knee issues. After Inter lost in the Champion's League second round, the club hired a new coach, Marcelo Lippi, and contracted the Italian forward Cristian Vieri for a massive fee that was US$20 million more than the team had paid for Ronaldo. When Ronaldo failed to race back to Inter after playing for Brazil in the 1999 Copa

América, Lippi benched him. With Vieri in good form, the coach did not want to rely on the Phenomenon. Finally back on the field, Ronaldo scored goals but also earned his first red card in Italy. In the midst of this difficult stretch came a horrific moment: after converting a penalty against Lecce, Ronaldo stepped in a hole on the pitch. That trivial incident brought a halt to his efforts to become the world's best player once more; the damage to his knee was so severe that he had to undergo another operation. Lippi told reporters that Ronaldo would not be missed.[115]

The coach of the Seleção, Wanderley Luxemburgo, was of a different view. He saw Ronaldo as vital to Brazil's qualification for the 2002 World Cup. When assembling the team for a game against Ecuador, he left a spot open for the attacker. Before Ronaldo could play for his country, however, he had to prove himself for his club. In the midst of his marriage in Rio and his wife Milene's pregnancy, the Phenomenon had worked conscientiously in his physical therapy, so much so that Milene joked that she was living with a "cyborg." His efforts would not, however, pay off. In his first game back on Inter's side, just six days after the birth of his son Ronald (named not for his father but for Ronald McDonald, logo of the fast-food chain Ronaldo and Milene loved), his knee gave way as it never had before. Entering as a second-half substitute, he survived one hard tackle and made a handful of touches on the ball before trying one of his familiar moves. This time, though, he crumpled to the ground as his right patellar tendon tore apart. Graver than his previous injuries, this one required another surgery and a longer and more intense period of recuperation.[116]

Before Ronaldo's second knee operation, conducted in Paris in late 1998, he had expressed relief that his "year of suffering" was coming to an end.[117] This latest surgery deepened his pain. Although he remained optimistic in public, much of the press evinced concern about his future. Tostão, who had retired early because of recurring eye injuries and had become a physician, urged him to be realistic in his expectations. As other journalists concurred, Ronaldo would probably never regain the strength and the confidence that had characterized his playing style.[118] Certainly, his physical troubles confirmed Ronaldo's own declaration: "I am not a robot," he reminded fans.[119] Along with a new wave of sympathy for the hero, Ronaldo's injuries provoked dismay among supporters of the Seleção, who bemoaned the disappearance of a "Ro-Ro" attacking duo made up of Ronaldo and Romário. Fans, coaches, and fellow players held on to hopes that Ronaldo would recover in time for the 2002 World Cup.[120]

The national team was, however, in such a woeful state in 2000 and 2001 that Brazil's presence at the Cup was in doubt. In 2000 the country once again fell short in its quest to win Olympic gold in men's soccer. The loss was particularly dispiriting this time round, since it came at the hands of a Cameroonian side that finished the game with only nine men on the field. Moreover, the coach, Luxemburgo, had resisted Romário's ardent pleas to play on the team. As the full Seleção turned to World Cup qualifiers, further nerve-racking results followed, with defeats to Ecuador, Uruguay, Bolivia, and Argentina coming in 2001 alone. Luxemburgo gave way to Emerson Leão and then to Luiz Felipe Scolari, with the latter voicing his fears that Brazil's unmatched record of participation in every World Cup was in imminent danger.[121]

Felipão (Big Phil), as Scolari was known, called up Ronaldo even when he was still injured, as a way of making clear that the "Scolari family" on the Seleção included Ronaldo. Felipão needed the firepower that the two-time World Player of the Year could provide; this need approached desperation with the exclusion of Romário. The star of the 1994 Seleção had, in his coach's eyes, proved himself unreliable and deceitful. Scolari had made Romário captain of the team in his first match as Seleção coach. After a loss to Uruguay in that game, Romário begged out of the Copa América, which started in Colombia just eleven days later, alleging that he needed an eye operation. Instead, Romário went on vacation in the Caribbean. Felipão was not moved by Romário's public apologies. Exercising his right to choose the members of the Seleção family, he left Romário out and banked on Ronaldo's recovery.[122]

Brazil managed to battle its way into the 2002 World Cup, though as in 1993, only by winning its very last qualifier.[123] Almost three years since his last appearance on the Seleção, Ronaldo started slowly on the field as he continued his intense conditioning off the pitch, putting in three sessions of therapy per day as the Cup approached.[124] The forward did not score for the team until its last warm-up match, a 4–0 win over Malaysia that failed to convince the Brazilian press in spite of the score line.[125] Until Ronaldo began to prove himself in Cup matches, much of the media resisted pinning the nation's hopes on him.[126]

Despite their initial skepticism about Ronaldo's health, journalists generally still hailed him as a true *craque,* one of the few players on the 2002 team who displayed "true Brazilian soccer" and thus did not "deserve to be condemned for the era in which they lived."[127] Over the course of the tournament, Ronaldo suffered through spells in which he showed the effects of his injuries. In key moments, however, he flashed skills that recalled his phenomenal past, ultimately making himself the Cup's leading scorer with eight goals in seven games.[128] Most impressively, though, Ronaldo roared in the final, tapping in a rebound and later thumping home a ball that Rivaldo let slide by with a brilliant dummy move. German goalkeeper Oliver Kahn had seemed an impregnable force, but Ronaldo and Brazil made him look ordinary.[129]

Despite these and his other goals, the Phenomenon did not display the same dynamism that had awed opponents and fans in 1996 and 1997. Still strong, he finished with authority but no longer made fantastic runs like the one against Compostela six years earlier.[130] Nevertheless, his dedication to physical therapy allowed him to become the main offensive threat on the first five-time-champion national team in the world. At the club level as well, his image regained its sheen, and he found himself transferred from Inter to Real Madrid.[131] As happened later when he moved to AC Milan, this transaction landed Ronaldo on a team filled with other global stars (Zinedine Zidane, Figo, Raúl, and Brazilian fullback Roberto Carlos in Madrid; Paolo Maldini, Andrea Pirlo, and the up-and-coming Brazilian attacking midfielder Kaká in Milan).[132] FIFA recognized his achievements in 2002 by awarding him his third World Player of the Year prize. This title, like the World Cup championship, represented "the victory not only of the *craque* but also of the man."[133]

The shining highlights of 2002 gave way, unfortunately, to a bumpy slide for Ronaldo. Despite his frail knees, he remained a cornerstone of planning for the 2006 World Cup. Once again in charge of the team, Carlos Alberto Parreira envisioned a "magic quartet" of Ronaldo, Ronaldinho Gaúcho, Kaká, and the powerful attacker Adriano. The formation, however, failed to deliver.[134] After a few impressive wins, Parreira's Seleção played a rather tepid Cup, falling to France in a 1–0 quarterfinal. Perhaps the most notable achievement was the mark that Ronaldo set with a goal against Ghana, which made him the top scorer in World Cup history. The team, by contrast, left the impression that it had not taken the competition seriously enough and had thus stumbled to a "fiasco."[135]

In the same period, Ronaldo strove in vain to carve out a dominant spot for himself at Real Madrid and then AC Milan. Worse, injuries hobbled him again, and his age and (as he later characterized it) hypothyroidism hampered his recovery. He put on weight, which only subjected his often-damaged knees to greater risk when he did play. No longer wanted at Milan, he opted to join the ranks of stars returning to Brazil. There, *cartolas* drooled over the commercial prospects that his image promised for any club. In these waning days of his playing career, he retained enough marketing power to negotiate a novel deal with Corinthians. Grupo R9 ensured that Ronaldo would receive a large portion of new sponsorship revenue the club received after his arrival. In part the arrangement treated him like any potential advertising space; greater visibility commanded higher fees. Thus it cost much more to place a logo on the team's jersey than on other parts of the uniform. Ronaldo's share of the revenues also varied, from 30 percent of the price of an ad on a sleeve to 80 percent of the prices for logos placed on uniform shorts and socks. At the same time, the forward was the impetus for the club's opening dozens of Corinthians stores at which these advertising-laden products were sold.[136]

By this point Ronaldo was a new sort of star who stayed out of politics but focused on marketing ventures. Along the way, he made missteps, from his very public breakups with several blonde girlfriends (two of whom later posed in Brazilian *Playboy* as the "Ronaldinhas") and divorce from Milene to media storms that arose over his patronage of a Brazilian prostitute in Italy in 1999 and of three transvestite prostitutes in Rio in 2008. Although the last of these incidents led *Veja* to compare Ronaldo unfavorably to Kaká, with his middle-class manners and evangelical Protestant beliefs, the Phenomenon never became a villain. His geniality allowed him to preserve the impression that he was "a good boy," and he and Grupo R9 made sure to capitalize on this image.[137]

RICARDO TEIXEIRA: ARTICULATING A BRAZILIAN GLOBALISM

After his retirement Ronaldo became involved with preparations for the 2014 World Cup, supplying a friendly face for the increasingly expensive and contested efforts to mount a sporting mega-event. Often the former *craque*'s activities included appearances with Ricardo Teixeira, the boss of bosses in Brazilian soccer for twenty-three years, from his contested election as president of the CBF in 1989 until his forced resignation in March 2012. As Teixeira's formal role—if not his informal influence—waned, he named Ronaldo to the Local Organizing Committee for the 2014 World Cup.[138]

Ronaldo's connection to the former CBF president was not surprising. After all, the forward took part in four of the six World Cups during Teixeira's tenure at the CBF. His moments of bad publicity never troubled the national team—one reason, perhaps, that Teixeira confided to Ronaldo as the latter prepared for his final appearance on the full Brazil side, a June 2011 friendly against Romania, "You were the best Seleção player since I've been running the CBF."[139] Moreover, the *craque* was a focal point of the increasingly commercialized *futebol* that emerged by the 1990s, and Teixeira strove to make the best of the opportunities that the new game presented. At the same time, however, the Ronaldo-Teixeira relationship highlights not only the explosion of the global game but also the perpetuation of old politics in Brazilian soccer. Marketing, media, and investment ventures coexisted with "the exchange of favors between friends and relatives and . . . the law of the most clever," as Tostão described the bases of "the Brazilian model" of power relations in soccer and other realms.[140] In other words, Teixeira sat atop a mixed model of development in *futebol,* in which global market forces rubbed against the rule of a national elite.[141]

Teixeira's career as a *cartola* began with his marriage to Lúcia Havelange, daughter of the longtime CBD/CBF and FIFA president. This family connection helped him in his bureaucratic rise. Although Ricardo and Lúcia separated in 1998, João Havelange always lent his support to Teixeira, in part to maintain relations with his grandchildren (who, contrary to custom, bore the last name of their maternal grandfather and not their father). This backing started when Teixeira was working in finance and continued as he moved into soccer governance.[142] Havelange ushered Teixeira into the upper circles of the CBF and into the Executive Committee of FIFA. The father-in-law bristled, however, at Teixeira's dream to take over as president of FIFA after 2006, insisting on the reelection of Sepp Blatter, but he helped to make the younger man's career.[143]

When he first came to power in the CBF, Teixeira declared that the president of the confederation had to be, above all, a competent administrator. Few would have disagreed with this point. After all, crusading journalists had been denouncing soccer officials in Brazil as the "disorganizers" of the game since the 1940s.[144] Not even the coming of the dictatorship in 1964 curbed the corruption of the system. In fact, the military regime expanded the Brasileirão, as the first truly national competition was known, to win over potential opponents and to reward allies. As the saying went, "Where ARENA [the military's political party] does badly, one more team in the National championship; where it does well, one more also."[145] By the late 1970s, this policy resulted in a ludicrously bloated competition, with massive and miniscule clubs thrown together in a ninety-four-team tournament.

In the first years after the return to civilian rule, the administration of the national game fell into even greater disarray. The CBF found itself nearly bankrupt and riven by internal strife, as the Rio and São Paulo soccer federations struggled to share power. So dire were the CBF's finances, in fact, that its president declared in July 1987 that it would be unable to organize the Brazilian championship that year. Within days the largest clubs founded the "Club of 13." This entity proved a combative advocate for its members' interests; their prevailing concern was establishing greater autonomy in relation to the CBF. This latter body soon stepped back in to the fight, asserting that the Brasileirão would proceed but only under CBF regulation. The struggles that followed saw two clubs, Flamengo and Sport Club Recife, claiming the national title, a conflict that has never been fully resolved.[146]

With this history of incompetence behind and with new commercial opportunities ahead, the time was ripe for the sort of effective administration that Teixeira promised. It soon became evident, however, that he would focus his energy and acumen on the dark arts he once described as "articulation."[147] What he meant by this discreet term was the sometimes subtle, sometimes vicious politicking of an old-style boss. His tactical repertoire was vast but familiar: weaving coalitions, peddling influence, distributing patronage, manipulating elections, intimidating opponents. Most of his actions, as one would suspect, took place out of public view. At times, however, some came to light and revealed the double game he played, as he tried to fend off threats to his power while reaping profits from the changing global business climate. One of his overwhelming aims was to increase the autonomy of the CBF in relation to both the Club of 13 and the federal government. His campaign against the Club of 13 began with a gesture of cooptation. Stepping in to public view as CBF president even before his formal election, he named Eurico Miranda, then vice president of the club Vasco da Gama and a founding member of the Club of 13, as the confederation's new Director of Soccer.[148] At the same time, he used patronage to shore up his support among regional federations. Most impressively, he distracted press attention away from these maneuvers by announcing a new coach, Sebastião Lazaroni, for the Seleção and promising to reveal the roster of players who would soon take on Chile and Venezuela in World Cup qualifying matches.[149] All in all, he made a spectacular debut in CBF politics.

He built on this early success by cultivating key allies. Through loans and direct payments—from his own as well as CBF coffers—he supported political campaigns.[150] Favors also flowed from his headquarters, with the CBF flying his friends to Seleção matches or hosting them at a restaurant he owned in Rio. Through such gestures he cultivated a group of allies in Congress known as the "soccer faction." At the same time he nurtured his ties to federation bosses, since they held the power to reelect him. To placate these regional leaders, he sent them money ("aid to affiliated federations") and organized the Copa do Brasil (Brazil Cup), a knock-out tournament involving teams from all state federations.[151] While introducing a major new competition to the country, he defended state tournaments, thus compounding the scheduling burden on clubs and players.[152]

At times the machinations of Teixeira's CBF exposed the national game to ridicule. Perhaps the most infamous incident came after the conquest of the 1994 World Cup. Having finally achieved the Tetracampeonato, the Seleção faced charges of corruption or, at the very least, unseemly opportunism, on its return to Brazil. The delegation included not only players, coaches, and training staff, but CBF officials and thirty-seven invited guests—"cousins, secretaries, neighbors." Together, the members of this party brought back more than seventeen tons of baggage. Scandal arose not from the size of the load, which required twenty men and two hours of work to be moved off the plane, but from the delegation's refusal to pay customs duties on this muamba (contraband). Teixeira brazenly insisted that, as national heroes, the group should not be subject to normal regulations. The director of the customs service tried to hold up the baggage until the proper fees were paid—a stance that a majority of Brazilians supported—but Teixeira ultimately won out. The conquerors and their hangers-on thus cheated the government out of some US$1 million in revenue.[153] Teixeira correctly calculated his ability to leverage World Cup triumph against federal law.

It was also on the back of the 1994 Cup that Teixeira formed one of the relationships that symbolized the new era of Brazilian soccer. Two years after Brazil's fourth championship, Nike, already the sponsor of Ronaldo, proposed to join Coca-Cola in backing the entire national team. Eager for the profits and global projection that this association offered, Teixeira agreed to the deal, with the marketing firm Traffic Assessoria e Comunicação serving as intermediary. Teixeira signed the contract secretly—refusing to divulge where the pact had been finalized—so that its provisions and even its value only emerged years later.[154] Essentially, for about US$160 million, the CBF guaranteed that the Seleção would wear Nike gear, appear in Nike advertising, and take part in fifty exhibition matches over the following decade. Nike committed US$150 million in "sports marketing," as well as a further

US$1 million to provide transportation for CBF delegations anywhere in the world and US$10 million to buy out Umbro, which had been the official supplier of sporting material to the CBF. The Seleção, with at least eight top players, had to meet opponents chosen by Nike at sites chosen by Nike on the "Nike World Tour." When Teixeira later negotiated a smaller quota of games, he also agreed to a US$14 million reduction in payments from Nike. Finally, the contract provided for a possible extension, for an additional four years and US$43 million, to which both parties agreed.[155]

For Teixeira, the Nike contract represented not only a financial windfall but also one of the signs that he had righted the CBF's ship. Partnerships with major multinational and national corporations over the course of Teixeira's presidency resulted in a tremendous influx of revenue, perhaps quadrupling the CBF's intake by 2000.[156] After Brazil won in 2002 and the CBF began a more concerted pursuit of World Cup hosting rights, the support of these companies increased. When FIFA granted the 2014 World Cup to Brazil, Teixeira positively glowed, declaring that it was his "point of pride" that "the biggest companies in the world—the biggest meat company, the biggest insurance company, the biggest brewery, the biggest bank in Brazil, the biggest news publishing company, everyone, sank millions into a dirty thief, this crook here."[157]

Because they involved the national confederation, the CBF's endorsement deals attracted great media attention. The 1990s began, however, a period of heavy, direct investment by large corporations at the club level as well. Companies had long sought to benefit from ties to popular clubs and had been advertising on team jerseys since the early 1980s. Now, however, corporations like Parmalat, Coca-Cola, and General Motors; investment and marketing firms like ISL, Traffic, and HMTF (Hicks, Muse, Tate & Furst); and banks like Banco Excel-Econômico, Bank of America, NationsBank, and Opportunity positioned themselves as major powers at many clubs around the country. Indeed, some of them dug in at multiple clubs; not only Palmeiras, for instance, but also the moderately sized Juventude of Caxias, Rio Grande do Sul, and the smaller Etti of Jundiaí, São Paulo, all became Parmalat teams.[158] The Swiss-based marketing firm ISL, with strong ties to the CBF and FIFA, came to back two major clubs, Corinthians in São Paulo and Cruzeiro in Belo Horizonte.

Throughout the 1990s, both clubs and companies experimented with forms of investment. Many agreements went far beyond advertising to include ownership and/or direct control over core portions of club activity.

The traditional Bahia became the first limited liability corporation in Brazilian soccer, when the bank Opportunity established a majority stake in November 1997. Larger and presumably more lucrative clubs like Vasco da Gama followed the pattern, with most of the shares in Vasco bought up by NationsBank in March 1998. More intriguingly, corporations took over marketing at clubs, as ISL did at Flamengo, and even directed football operations, as Opportunity did at Bahia and HMTF did at Corinthians.[159]

The opening of opportunities provoked mixed reactions in the Brazilian press and also among *cartolas* and their partners in the investment community. An injection of market logic had, in fact, been hailed by some observers as a necessary remedy for the inefficiencies and corruption that permeated soccer in the country.[160] *Futebol-empresa* (enterprise soccer), as this goal was commonly known, promised to create efficient enterprises out of informal societies directed by volunteers who lacked professional training in sports administration and marketing but who had a firm commitment to the politics of patronage.[161] As neoliberalism gained momentum in Brazil (and throughout much of the world) in the late 1980s, the allure of *futebol-empresa* only grew stronger in Brazil. By turning clubs into companies able to compete in the globalizing economy, so this vision had it, the model would wrench the "backward" and "decadent" administration of *futebol* into a market-based modernity. This belief required an idealization of business practices as purely rational and separate from clientelism. Nevertheless, by the 1980s and '90s, the professionalization of administration became the aim and means of modernization.[162]

The precise degree of control that HMTF, ISL, and the other agents of this professionalization had over daily footballing decisions in the peak years of direct investment was never clear, but it concerned many observers. Occasional allegations of corporate officials' interference in footballing matters—such as the contracting of players—sparked protest in the press.[163] A nationalist critique took shape: the takeover of clubs by multinational corporations stoked fears that foreign companies would gain control of resources that were vital to Brazil's well-being. Selling clubs, in combination with the export of players to foreign leagues, appeared as a sort of "liquidation" of the Brazilian game.[164] Moreover, clubs became dependent on the companies that provided them with abundant funding; if investors pulled out, the clubs would face financial crises. This risk became reality when a post–Parmalat Palmeiras dropped to the second division of the Brasileirão in 2002, and a post–MSI Corinthians followed it down in 2007.[165]

Cartolas recoiled from any talk of government oversight of the globalizing game. When two major reform projects emerged in the 1990s, the CBF and its congressional allies attacked ferociously. The first of these proposals came from Zico during his time as Secretary of Sports. The final version of this reform, the Lei Zico of 1993, showed the influence of the "soccer faction." The law merely allowed clubs to become limited-liability corporations, rather than requiring such a change. Moreover, the law did not eliminate the pass system but called for a study of the "values, criteria, and conditions" necessary for the gradual extinction of the pass system.[166] Four years later another former *craque,* Pelé, put forward a more invasive project for change. Teixeira and his allies again called together their forces to fight the latest reform project. This time, however, his opposition proved incapable of eviscerating the proposal.[167] Clubs were now compelled to become business enterprises, and professional soccer players were no longer subject to the pass system.[168] After the 1998 passage of the Lei Pelé, the *cartolas* launched a campaign of passive resistance, concocting amendments to the law and, most consistently, going about their business as if the provisions of the law simply did not exist. That is, they continued to buy and sell players, effectively asserting rights that federal law now denied them.[169]

The grinding battle over the interpretation of the reform showed the *cartolas'* desire to have globalization two ways. They wanted the growth that the *futebol-empresa* ideal promised, but they also wanted to maintain the clientelism that had brought them to power. In sum, they strove to work out a sort of crony capitalism that selectively adapted elements of neoliberalism. By the 2000–01 season, however, this system lost its appeal for many corporate partners, who began to withdraw.[170] The fear seems to have been that doing business with *cartolas* was too risky. In David Goldblatt's sharp assessment, "foreign capital was effortlessly outmaneuvered by their Brazilian counterparts who really did take the money and run."[171]

In spite of the concerted efforts of both investors and *cartolas,* the dark side of the new *futebol* became apparent by 2000. Reports of improprieties in soccer had appeared in the press throughout the previous decade. Episodes of match fixing by the head of the CBF commission of referees and evidence of tax evasion by individual players, clubs, and the CBF president tarnished the image of the beautiful game.[172] In the years when hundreds of millions of dollars flowed into *futebol,* both clubs and the CBF slipped deeply into debt.[173] It was, however, the specter of Nike's control over the national team—with rumors about the company's role in the choice to play Ronaldo in the World Cup loss of 1998 still reverberating—that inspired full-blown congressional inquiries (CPIs, Commissions of Parliamentary Inquiry) in both the Chamber of Deputies and the Senate.[174]

In one sense, the CPIs did little more than supply detailed confirmation of what most suspected about soccer in Brazil. They did not result in the conviction or immediate resignation of top officials. The publication of evidence about the criminal activities of leading figures, however, had a broader political impact; it represented a step toward transparency.[175] Both houses of Congress forced *cartolas,* players, coaches, team doctors, agents, marketing executives, auditors, and others to testify on the inner workings of *futebol.* Aside from comic moments here and there—the most famous coming when a congressman asked Ronaldo who had been in charge of guarding Zidane in the 1998 World Cup final—the CPIs proceeded with rigor and seriousness, refusing to take at face value any easy or vague explanations of irregularities.[176]

The probes paid off with evidence of profound corruption in the CBF and specifically in the dealings of its president, who treated the entity as his personal fiefdom. The "lack of democracy and transparency" at the CBF came out clearly in testimony about the contract with Nike. Teixeira acted as the sole and ultimate authority in decisions touching on all sectors of CBF operations. Testimony about the Nike contract revealed, for instance, that he had appeared alone, without other CBF officials or even a lawyer, to finalize negotiations.[177] One of the most surprising details that emerged was the central role of the marketing firm Traffic in the contract. Teixeira had not previously made public details of his relations with Traffic and its president, José Hawilla. Both CPIs expressed dismay at the degree of control over the national sport that the contract ceded to corporations.[178] Neither commission determined that Nike had been directly responsible for the disastrous defeat to France in 1998; both, however, suggested that the corporation had gained undue influence over the Seleção in general, a fact that may have increased pressures on Ronaldo and thus affected his health and performance.

The Nike contract served as an entry point into wider practices. The CPIs identified a number of suspicious—and some clearly illegal—actions taken under Teixeira's direction. According to the confederation's own regulations, as established in a 1994 assembly and not subsequently revised, the CBF remained legally a nonprofit organization. As such, it was not allowed to pay salaries to its officials. Not only did CBF officials receive regular salaries, however, they also took home bonuses.[179] Beyond the illegal remuneration of its officials, Teixeira's CBF also engaged in dubious financial maneuvers.

Between 1995 and 2001, for instance, the CBF purchased gold in the international market. Although Teixeira later assured the Chamber CPI that these transactions had proceeded at rates and in the manner set by law, he did not explain why the CBF had carried out these "foreign transfers" or identify the recipients of the money they involved.[180] The CBF also took out a series of high-interest loans from the New York–based Delta Bank and paid them back on a schedule that was more beneficial to Delta than to the CBF. Teixeira insisted that the terms of the loans were within the normal range for the time; the CPIs concluded that they were "disadvantageous," verging on the "extortionate."[181]

The uncertain nature of many of Teixeira's personal business ventures concerned congressional investigators, of course, but it was his administration of the CBF that piqued the greatest worries.[182] A series of unexplained transactions hinted at a generalized lack of financial oversight within the organization itself. The Senate CPI found that, contrary to the CBF's own statutes, Teixeira governed without a budget. Teixeira asserted that he had contracted a well-known firm to conduct an independent audit, a claim that the firm denied.[183] What this meant is that in the period from 1994 to 2001, when CBF revenues expanded tremendously, its directors set no budgets and kept no records—none that they were willing to produce, in any case. How, then, this influx of money coincided with mounting debts at the CBF, could only be a matter of speculation.

These revelations all pointed to a reckless lack of rational administration, in the best of cases, in Teixeira's CBF. More damning possibilities included not only money laundering and tax evasion but also illicit gain. Senator Álvaro Dias concluded that the supreme body of soccer organization in Brazil was nothing more than "a den of crime, revealing disorganization, anarchy, incompetence, and dishonesty."[184] Since the CPIs were not prosecutorial bodies, they pursued the facts but could only recommend actions. Among their proposals was a call for Teixeira's resignation, along with the adoption of a series of legislative reforms aimed at preventing the mismanagement that he had perpetrated.[185]

Teixeira did not resign, however, until early 2012, and business went on without much visible change.[186] The Nike contract emerged "unharmed," and Teixeira signed other major sponsorship deals. The largest of these, with the brewing giant AmBev, included payments of some US$8 million to intermediaries who were friends of Teixeira's.[187] The supreme *cartola* survived even when charges of his participation, with Havelange, in more massive fraud and money laundering schemes appeared in connection to the marketing firm ISL. The bankruptcy of ISL in 2001 attracted the interest of Swiss regulators as well as European journalists; although the case remains unresolved, allegations persist that Teixeira and Havelange received between US$12 million and US$60 million in illicit deals with the company, which in 1996 had purchased television rights for the 2002 and 2006 World Cups.[188] Still, Teixeira held on as pressures mounted—capped off with a "mega Twitter" campaign at the start of 2012—before finally resigning as CBF president. He remained on the CBF payroll even then as a consultant. With José Maria Marin, a survivor from the days of military rule, taking over as president, few expected significant changes, although they hailed the end of Teixeira's direct control.[189]

Teixeira retained his grip on the national game in part because of his extraordinary "articulation" of political and business alliances. He also benefited from the distraction that Brazil's victory in the 2002 World Cup and its selection as host of the 2014 World Cup provided. Coming as they did in the wake of the CPIs' reports, these triumphs effectively bestowed on Teixeira the traditional Brazilian description of an acceptably corrupt leader: "He steals but he delivers" (*rouba mas faz*).[190] More broadly, he helped set the parameters of Brazilian soccer's globalization. Market logic became an overweening ideological force by the 1990s and shaped the drawing of new rules for the sport's administration in the country. At the same time, however, leaders like Teixeira ensured that day-to-day practices would not reflect neoliberal visions. Rather, the modernization of the game through the market coexisted with the clientelism that had always characterized *futebol* politics in Brazil. This modernization merely increased the stakes in political and business contests played in familiar patterns.[191]

RONALDINHO GAÚCHO: "LOOK WHAT HE'S DONE!"

During the boom years of investment under Teixeira's CBF (1997–2001), another "R" burst on the scene as the latest potential savior of the national game. When Ronaldo's injuries and Romário's personality threatened to deny the presence of two creative forces on the Seleção, Ronaldo de Assis Moreira revived hopes that traditional *alegria* could prosper in the globalized game. He represented in this regard the best hope to hold off the waning not only of Brazil's dominance but also its influence on worldwide soccer style; he combatted, unconsciously, "the decline of the dribbler."[192] At the same time, Ronaldinho Gaúcho, as he became known to distinguish him from Ronaldo, lived out many of the reforms that first Zico and then Pelé had pushed. His move to Europe in 2001 challenged the *cartolas'* grip on the flow of talent and wealth.

Ronaldinho's background echoed that of many *craques* who had preceded him, though his professional trajectory made him the most globalized Brazilian star yet. He was born into poverty but also into *futebol,* growing up in working-class suburbs of Porto Alegre as the youngest child in a family of Gremio fanatics. With his parents both laboring hard at various jobs, Ronaldinho was raised in an extended family. His grandmother and sister were among those who delighted in putting him in Gremio uniforms and encouraging him to kick a ball. It was in family spaces, in and around the tin-roofed houses in which they lived, that Ronaldinho began to play.[193]

Although he has retained close ties to his family, it was his older brother Roberto, known professionally as Assis, who came to serve as a "second father" following their dad's death in early 1989.[194] Nine years older than his brother, Assis was by that time constructing his own successful playing career. After earning a spot at Gremio, he rose up through the club's ranks to the full professional side, eventually playing for other big clubs in Brazil (Fluminense, Vasco, and Corinthians) as well as teams of moderate size in Portugal, Switzerland, Mexico, Japan, and France. Technically gifted, he was also known to be somewhat of a difficult personality. He turned his hard-headedness to the care of his younger brother, becoming not only his champion but his agent as well.[195]

Ronaldinho was the great hope of the family, as Assis realized.[196] Like Ronaldo and others before him, he made his first mark indoors, playing *futsal.* In Ronaldinho's case, a visual record of his prodigious skills became familiar to much of the world, via the Nike commercial "Joy," which formed part of the Joga Bonito campaign. The ad cuts between scenes of Ronaldinho playing *futsal* at ages ten and twenty-six, showing not only that his talent was evident early on but also that he maintained his playfulness into adulthood; indeed, the commercial ends with the message, "Never grow up, my friends." The young Ronaldinho showed early versions of many of the moves that he later used on the Seleção and at Gremio, PSG, Barcelona, AC Milan, and other clubs. Nike's packaging of these images, moreover, hints at the public persona that Ronaldinho created, with the help of his brother and other advisors. Talent, inspired always with an *alegria* reminiscent of Garrincha, and innocence—these traits would feature prominently in his play on the

FIGURE 14. Ronaldinho Gaúcho during a training session at the 2005 Confederations Cup. Ivo Gonzalez/Agência O Globo.

pitch but also in the marketing of "R10," an appellation that graced his own model of Nike shoes and positioned him as the next Ronaldo.

Like Ronaldo Nazário, Ronaldinho Gaúcho rose to fame in sudden fashion. His career at Gremio made him much more familiar to Brazilian fans than his predecessor. With two dribbles still remembered in Porto Alegre since they came against World Cup champion Dunga, who had returned to captain Internacional, Gremio's great rival—he helped his club win a state championship in 1999, two years after playing a key role on Brazil's world champion under-seventeen squad. The true announcement of his arrival, however, came in an easy win by the full Seleção over Venezuela in the Copa

América. He scored only one of his team's seven goals that day, but he did it with a spectacular heel-flick of the ball over a defender followed by a sharp shot past the goalie. Rebroadcast repeatedly on TV highlight shows, the move fanned hopes that Ronaldinho would be able to team up with Ronaldo and perhaps Romário as well.

This trio never formed a united attack for the Seleção, but Ronaldinho Gaúcho was cast as a central part of other magic offensive formations. When Felipão led the Seleção into the 2002 World Cup, he included the young attacking midfielder from Porto Alegre as a "third 'R,'" alongside Ronaldo and Rivaldo. Once again, Ronaldinho produced moments that seemed to mark him as a carrier of *jogo bonito* genes.[197] Two of these came in a quarter-final against England, one of Brazil's strongest matches in the competition and one that saw the Seleção win despite Ronaldinho's expulsion just fourteen minutes into the second half. With Brazil a goal down, Ronaldinho made an elastic dribble past left back Ashley Cole and set up Rivaldo to score. Just four minutes after the break, Ronaldinho stepped up to take a long free kick from the right of the England goal. He sent a floating ball up over the experienced keeper David Seaman, dropping it in so unexpectedly that many thought he had meant the ball to be a cross rather than a shot. He asserted, however, that the ball had done precisely what he intended, and it was hailed as a revival of Didi's *folha seca* technique.[198]

Although he missed the semifinal because of a red card and played somewhat anonymously in the final, Ronaldinho emerged from the 2002 World Cup as a new star in world soccer. He returned to France, where his club, PSG, had narrowly missed out on qualifying for the Champions League. PSG coach Luis Fernandez later said that his star played without the same focus or motivation after Brazil's World Cup triumph.[199] Although he did not deliver the on-field rewards that PSG officials had dreamed of, his performance in the 2002–03 season made him a target to follow in the footsteps of Romário, Ronaldo, and Rivaldo at Barcelona.[200] The Catalan club beat out both Real Madrid and Manchester United, purchasing his contract for US$30 million, with an annual salary of US$4 million.[201] Like his predecessors, Ronaldinho shone at Barça. With four fellow Brazilians—Edmilson, Belletti, Sylvinho, and Deco—he led the club up the league table to second in 2004 and then in the following season helped Barcelona conquer the Spanish League for the first time since 1999. The year 2006 saw Ronaldinho's Barça claim a second straight title as winner of not only La Liga but also of the Champions League.

Barcelona proved to be the high point of Ronaldinho's club career and the basis of his global fame. It was there that he applied the "technical maturity" that the England match had forced on him.[202] This is not to say that he reined in his exuberant style. Indeed, as Felipão observed, he continued to improve his technique as well as his conditioning.[203] So brilliant was he, in fact, that he twice earned FIFA's Player of the Year award, in 2005 and 2006. From this point onward, however, his play declined at all levels. In 2006 the World Cup loomed invitingly, and Brazilians pointed to Ronaldinho as a principal reason for their team's position as favorites.[204] Rather than the team's main attraction, however, he became its greatest disappointment.[205] Carlos Alberto Parreira, coaching the national team again, sent in various "magic quartets," but none worked very well. Of the players enlisted in these schemes, it was Ronaldinho whose failure to meet expectations was most egregious, since at age twenty-six he was in his footballing prime.[206] Rather than an innovative force scoring and setting up teammates, he turned out to be "just a midfielder" who did not make things happen by himself or in combination with teammates.[207] Setting a record for the fewest goals scored by anyone wearing the number 10 jersey for Brazil in a World Cup—the number worn by Pelé and Zico and other greats—he won the vote for "the worst of the Seleção."[208]

The fault that many observers pointed to at the World Cup, apathy, seemed also to creep into Ronaldinho's play for his club. An injury cut at his contributions at Barcelona in 2007, and soon his departure seemed a certainty. Barcelona officials and fans had hailed Ronaldinho as soon as he signed with the club. His dedication to nightlife in the Catalan city, however, led journalists to allege that he was losing his focus on the field. Like Romário and Ronaldo, he apparently avoided drug and alcohol problems, but he found himself caught out partying during the nights—and sometimes even the mornings—before matches.[209] Because this development coincided with the emergence of a generation of promising players from the club's famous youth academy, Barça leadership decided to sell him. Turning down a bid from Manchester City, he went instead to AC Milan. His short spell at Milan saw him reduced to a substitute in most games. His subsequent and still shorter time at Flamengo restored him to star status but also bolstered his image as a gifted *fantasista* who loved music and nightlife too much for the good of his game. Whatever the reasons, he became "just a good player" after Barcelona, though he commanded the wages and sponsorship deals of a superstar.[210]

At his best, however, Ronaldinho represented, in José Miguel Wisnik's wonderful description, an "anthology" of the most notables skills of great Brazilian *craques:* "the elastic dribble of Rivellino, the *chapéu* of Pelé, the free kicks of Zico, the 'shell' pass of Ademir da Guia, the cut-back finish of Romário, the back heel of Sócrates, the *folha seca* of Didi, the stepover of Denílson and generation 2000."[211] As this last reference suggests, Ronaldinho had contemporaries who dazzled spectators with flashy moves, with the left-footed attacker Denílson and the versatile Robinho among the most notable. Like Ronaldinho, Denílson and Robinho reminded commentators of past greats and, in particular, greats who had exhibited invention and foresight on the field.

Denílson, who appeared on the scene a few years before Ronaldinho, inspired comparisons to Garrincha. Like this former *craque,* Denílson was a master of the dribble, a "mystic with his feet on the ground."[212] Certainly, the early stages of his career led many to see him as another great talent who could join with Romário and Ronaldo to lead the Seleção to new glories. Only seventeen when he broke into the first team at São Paulo in 1994, he impressed with speed and skill. His club performances led to his inclusion on the Seleção. Flashing great potential on the national side, Denílson became the most expensive player in history to that point when Spanish club Real Betis purchased his contract for US$30 million in 1997.[213] His star on the rise, he became a regular inclusion on the Seleção, with a place on the 1998 and 2002 World Cup squads. In both of those international tournaments and at Betis, however, he struggled to become a player that coaches could build a team around.[214] He functioned best as a substitute, entering games when tired defenders were unable to shut down Denílson's feints. Fresh-legged and sharp-witted opponents, however, merely watched his step-overs and waited for him to push the ball, usually to his left, before intervening. In the judgment of Tostão, his "monstrous ability" never elevated him to the status of a true *craque.*[215]

Robinho, by contrast, turned himself into more of a well-rounded player, quieting those who worried that he might be merely "the new Denílson."[216] Unlike his predecessor, he bore a special mark; Robinho grew up as the brightest star in a group known as the *meninos da Vila* (kids from the Vila, referring to the club's home stadium, the Vila Belmiro) at Santos, Pelé's old club. Moreover, Pelé had observed Robinho training with fellow *meninos* like Diego, Renato, and Elano in a practice and pulled him aside, expressing his hope that he would follow in the King's footsteps. As soon as he made it to the first team, Robinho began to deliver on his promise, helping the club to the 2002 Brasileirão title, the first since 1968; they won a second in 2004. As it turned out, this meteoric rise was only the start of a new period of talent production at Santos; Robinho and his cohort would soon be followed by that of Neymar and Ganso.

By that time, however, Robinho had made his way to big clubs in Europe, by way of some extravagant transfers. He moved to Real Madrid in July 2005, impelled not only by the lure of wealth and visibility but also of safety. His mother, Marina da Silva Souza, had been kidnapped and held for thirty days in late 2004, until Robinho, with the help of agent Juan Figer, paid a ransom of some 500 million Brazilian reáis (approximately US$185,000).[217] This combination of push and pull factors led him to pressure Santos for a transfer to Real.[218] There, he impressed initially by calling for the ball, striving to lead a team of galactic stars, including Zinedine Zidane, Real icon Raúl, David Beckham, and four fellow Brazilians: Ronaldo, attacker Júlio Baptista, left back Roberto Carlos, and, briefly, coach Wanderley Luxemburgo.[219] Nowhere, however, did Robinho manage to claim a permanent starting position, despite his displays of "diabolic" skills. At Madrid, Manchester City, and AC Milan, as well as on the Seleção under Carlos Alberto Parreira in 2006, he was a frequent part of the first eleven, but faded to the reserves from time to time.[220] Many critics called for him to start at the 2006 World Cup, citing the "lightness" and "agility" he brought to the offense, but he could not push his competition out.[221] Perhaps he earned greatest recognition on the Seleção after Dunga took over as coach in 2006. Symbol of "results soccer," Dunga came to treat Robinho as a reliable veteran who could add touches of flash without disrupting "the collective."[222]

Robinho, however, did not gain his fame as a role player, though he has demonstrated dedication to team goals throughout his career. Rather, it is his *ginga*—his swing—and his ball tricks that are the basis of his celebrity. Unlike Ronaldinho, he has not filled out physically but looks very much like the slight kid from his first stint at Santos. More than Denílson or anyone else, Robinho comes close to matching Ronaldinho in playful juggling. He has featured in many of the same ads as Ronaldinho, including one 2006 spot that Eric Cantona introduces by asking simply, "Three Brazilians and a ball; what else do you need?" With Roberto Carlos as the third and least inventive, Robinho and Ronaldinho keep the ball up, catch it behind their heads and trap it behind their knees; together, the teammates perform an ideal of Brazilian skill in its joyful magnificence.

The trajectory of these great dribblers—Denílson, Robinho, and Ronaldinho—descended eventually to a realm of unfulfilled hopes. All three have had their time as the "next *craque*," though perhaps only Ronaldinho has lived up to such predictions. Even he, however, failed to become the basis of a successful Seleção; after serving as a useful, promising part of the 2002 champions and one of the symbols of overconfidence and lack of application in the 2006 World Cup fiasco, he did not even make the 2010 squad.[223] In 2010 Dunga resisted pressures from the media and allegedly from CBF officials to reinstate Ronaldinho. Instead, he called on Robinho and Kaká, the latter having become the most recent Brazilian to be named World Player of the Year (2008) and then to star at AC Milan.[224] In his exile Ronaldinho worked hard to win back a spot on the national team, particularly after leaving Flamengo and trying to shake off his reputation for on-field lethargy and off-field partying at the club Atlético Mineiro. Indeed, he won election to the "Best Eleven" of the Brasileirão at Flamengo in the 2010–11 season and again at Atlético in later seasons.[225]

Generally, though, he became more a static picture of genius than a fluid attacking threat. With his mobility declining, he has relied on superb footwork to hold off the defenders descending on him. His subtle touches can lead to sharp passes to teammates, but increasingly also to loss of possession. Fans savor his footwork in such open play but also grow frustrated at the way the game sometimes stops at Ronaldinho instead of speeding up through him. His free kicks are the one area in which he has remained capable of consistent brilliance. Overall, however, he—like Denílson before and Robinho still—has become reduced to his technique. As considerable as the components of his game are, they too often lack what Brazilians refer to as "objectivity"—in other words, they seem an enjoyable, if aimless, bit of entertainment. Ronaldinho, *craque* though he was, has become more the magician of Nike commercials and avatar in video games, than dominant force on the pitch. As Tostão has argued, however, fans would do well to appreciate his magnificent peak than to worry about his "brusque fall"; the real "mystery," and one worth pondering, is how anyone could show the football he did in the 2004–05 season.[226]

Far more complicated and less savory was the business of soccer in which Ronaldinho and other players of his generation have been immersed. Ronaldinho was a trailblazer in the reformulation of the Brazilian market in soccer talent, helping to ease the movement of players from (and later back to) the country. Although he grew up in a Gremio family and played devotedly at the club for fourteen years, he was ready to move to Europe before he turned twenty-one. With Assis, who had personal experience of several European leagues, Ronaldinho calculated that France might be a good entry point for a long and lucrative career abroad. Against the wishes of Gremio's *cartolas,* the brothers negotiated a "precontract" with PSG, to go into effect at the end of Ronaldinho's existing contract with Gremio, on 15 February 2001 and signed in semisecrecy (the news leaked out in France) in December 2000.[227] Two days after the expiration of Ronaldinho's formal link to Gremio, PSG announced their agreement with the *"petit* Ronaldo."[228] No longer bound to his childhood club, Ronaldinho intended to take up a position with a new employer, just as an employee in another profession might do. The difficulty for all parties, however, lay in the uncertainty of the moment at which he tried to act on this desire. The Lei Pelé had been approved by this time, but its abolition of the pass system was not to go into effect until 26 March 2001. For months Gremio fought to hold onto its star. After initial victories that promised to keep Ronaldinho from leaving, however, came a series of defeats in Brazilian labor tribunals and then at FIFA.[229] Finally, by the start of August, with the player having already moved to Paris, an agreement emerged. Gremio lost its "revelation" but at least received some financial indemnification—nothing like the US$38 million the Porto Alegre club had sought, but more than the nominal penalty that FIFA had contemplated imposing. In the end, PSG paid less than US$10 million in a deal that Gremio condemned as an act of "piracy."[230]

With the protections of the pass system removed, it is no surprise that Brazilian clubs worried about footballing privateers. The migration of players in search of wages began before the professionalization of soccer in Brazil and carried on afterward.[231] Fans, journalists, and *cartolas* showed a rare degree of consensus on the potential harm that emigration of stars could do to both club and national sides. Many blamed the drain of talent for declining attendance in the 1980s and '90s; particularly in times of economic crisis, it did not make much sense to pay to see teams that consisted, in a sense, of reserves and young promises. Meanwhile, the stars' unfamiliarity with each other also seemed a huge obstacle to the formation of a cohesive Seleçao.[232] In the end, though, most beloved *craques* left to seek their fortunes outside Brazil, so that by the 1990s the country became the major exporter of footballers in the world. In 2011, some 1,061 players carrying Brazilian passports (many with additional passports, often from Italy, which opened up spots for them at teams in the European Union) participated in 108 leagues—a figure that omits those who have become naturalized citizens in Portugal, Croatia, the Netherlands, Germany, Japan, and other countries.[233]

If Ronaldinho was merely following a well-established pattern in this way, he was also bringing some of a Europe's "Bosman revolution" to Brazil. Twenty-one years before Ronaldinho arrived in Paris, a Belgian player named Jean Marc Bosman had sued for the right to sign for the second-division French club US Dunkerque-Littoral after his contract with Belgian side RFC Liège expired. After protracted legal battles, he won his case in 1995, in a decision that promised a free labor market for soccer players across Europe. Although this freedom could not shed all restrictions, it affected working conditions in the richest leagues in the world. The original provisions of the Lei Pelé envisioned a similar transformation in Brazil, although *cartolas* limited this change.[234] In the end, though, the precedent that Ronaldinho's case set—relatively small compensation for the loss of a highly valuable player— forced clubs to employ one resource they had in abundance: creativity.[235]

The approaches that clubs adopted varied of necessity; in the globalizing labor market, they faced not only increased player power but also other wealthy and innovative forces in the shape of agents and other intermediaries. "Superagents" had already been at work, arranging transfers behind the scenes, assembling coalitions of individual and corporate investors to buy contracts—or some percentage of their total value—and shifting players between clubs. Much of this, as the CPI in the Senate found in 2001, took place outside the bounds of any nation's laws. In the seven years that the CPI examined, some 2,061 Brazilian footballers left to play in other countries. Many of them took indirect routes with the help of agents like the Uruguayan Juan Figer. Figer admitted before CPI members that he moved players out of Brazil to Europe via his home country. Registering them temporarily at Uruguayan clubs that existed only on paper, he argued, was a normal business practice.[236]

Indeed, as the new century progressed, related schemes spread, with not only Figer but other cosmopolitan figures like the Portuguese Jorge Mendes, the Israeli Pini Zahavi, the Argentine Gustavo Arribas, and the Iranian-born and London-based Kia Joorabchian ushering players to and from Brazil. The complexity of their arrangements, which involve webs of agents and at times the use of banks in fiscal paradises like Gibraltar and the British Virgin Islands, means that it is difficult to ascertain who even holds the rights to a player's contract, much less how much revenue these rights produce for the parties in any transfer.[237] Club officials, then, have had to find ways of working with agents and investors who might be multinational and transnational, individual and corporate.

Diplomacy has become key as *cartolas* cultivate lines of contacts within Brazil and beyond, relying on agents and "money men" who know the seams of financial and sporting legislation in the country and around the world. At times clubs have used these connections to their benefit, bringing in players who would otherwise have been too expensive. Because intermediaries can at times put up obstacles to club transactions, though, they are also targets of distrust. Koorabchian placed two Argentines, Javier Mascherano and Carlos Tévez, at Corinthians in 2005; the move helped the club win the Brasileirão that year as Tévez was named the best player in Brazil. Nevertheless, the club's fortunes faltered in 2006, ending in an exit from the Libertadores. More seriously, both Joorabchian and the firm he represented in Brazil, MSI, came under legal scrutiny, with Kia being accused of money laundering and racketeering. The tumult shattered the bloc of *cartolas* in power at the club; ultimately, the superagent plucked his players out and sent them to English club West Ham United. There, as in São Paulo, club officials could do little more than resent the control that go-betweens have attained in globalized soccer.[238]

Creativity has also meant procreation, as new clubs have appeared with the primary—and at times exclusive—goal of gathering players, showcasing their talents, and selling them in other countries. Some of these are initiatives of big clubs, participating in the lower levels of state championships. These B teams have the dual tasks of preparing young players for the principal squad and putting them "in the shop window" (*na vitrine*)—on view for scouts of European clubs.[239] These projects have parallels in European leagues, but they also reflect the strategies that agents and marketers already had in place in Brazil. These intermediaries have turned themselves into principals by inventing stand-alone clubs, teams that lack ties to established clubs. One of the best known of these is RS Futebol Clube, established in 2001 not far from Ronaldinho's hometown. Owned by marketing company Talento S/A, RS FC trains players between five and fifteen at its Carpegiani Soccer Academy and those over fifteen and headed toward professional contracts at its Athlete Training Center. The club has its own colors—yellow, green, and red—and a foundation story based on Paulo César Carpegiani. Highly credentialed as a player and coach, Carpegiani accepted the invitation of an entrepreneur who was looking to set up this new entity in order "to spread soccer and discover new talents," making use of Rio Grande do Sul's reputation for "seriousness, work, and competence." What is so different about RS FC and other such clubs mounted recently with the help of marketing firms like Traffic, is that their focus is clearly not on competing in CBF-regulated tournaments. Instead, they send players into official games, but only as part of a broader plan of producing salable goods, in the shape of young players who ply their trade almost entirely out of the sight of Brazilian fans.[240] All such initiatives represent the efforts of entrepreneurs to give unprecedented form to the ideal of the *futebol-empresa*. The new globalism of the game in the 1990s onward has thus reached deep into Brazilian soccer, not only injecting the logic of the market into familiar structures but weaving new webs of commerce.

CONCLUSION

Those trying to place Ronaldinho in the history of *futebol* might see his career as a final dissection of Brazilianness into distinct, idealized technical abilities; not the complicated and at times error-filled performance of real players or teams, but a set of extractable and imitable skills.[241] The prevalence of these traits in pop culture highlights the ever more pervasive marketing of stereotypes of the "true Brazil game," of course, but at the same time suggests the paradox of early twenty-first century *futebol,* as signaled by Luis Fernando Verissimo: "To be played correctly it needs to inhibit the individuality of the player and sacrifice his personal brilliance for the sake of solid organization. But defenses have become so organized that they can only be defeated by individual initiative—that is, by that which is forbidden."[242]

Since the early 1990s coaches of the Seleção have tried to resolve this dilemma by embracing tightly controlled styles of play that appear more and more detached from Brazil's own mid-century tropical modernism. Along with fans, though, they have always hoped that some Ronaldinho or Robinho would emerge at a key moment and cut through the enemy with an "anti-modern" dribble.[243] Ultimately, though, an emphasis on organization, the collective, and tactical sophistication—all terms linked to an idealized Europe in different periods over the last century—have coexisted, conflictively, with celebrations of the tropical, childlike joy, and artful in *futebol;* the tension between these constructs is what has long given Brazilian modernity its defining and discomfiting energy.

Changing political-economic conditions in Brazil and around the world in the 1980s and thereafter gave players, club and confederation officials, agents, and other actors reason to value certain qualities that had become commodities. Players able to exhibit the Brazilian qualities that could fetch good prices had every incentive to emphasize these skills and attitudes. For fans of Brazil, the problem became even more serious than Verissimo's paradox; they had to worry that their idols, their clubs, and their country might sell their soul while marketing their swing.

———————

Mega-Brazil

In Rio, Sports Mean the Future.

In June 2013, hundreds of thousands of Brazilians transformed the Confederations Cup into grand theater. Normally low on sporting drama, the tournament has served as a chance for national coaches to fine-tune their teams and for FIFA (Fédération Internationale de Football Association) and local organizers to work out logistical kinks a year before the start of the World Cup. In the 2013 version, however, the participating teams brought an uncharacteristic level of quality and passion to most games. The final, in which Brazil swept aside Spain, the 2010 World Cup champions, was precisely the matchup and display of quality soccer that promoters had dreamed of. In the end, Brazil dominated Spain, a country that had displaced the Seleção as standard bearers of the beautiful game, taking its fourth Confederations Cup title with a 3–0 score line. If it did not mark a sea change in global soccer, the result at least raised the possibility of Brazil's return to the status of protagonist in world competitions.[1] It was off the field, however, that the greatest shocks came. Rather than a simple logistical warm-up for FIFA and local organizers, the 2013 Confederations Cup emerged as the occasion for protests in hundreds of cities and towns across Brazil. Far from a unified movement, this conglomeration of "mini-protests" presented challenges not to soccer or the World Cup per se, but rather to the lack of representation of the Brazilian public in government decisions, including those about the management of the national game.[2] In the process, the Confederations Cup (Copa das Confederações) became the Demonstrations Cup (Copa das Manifestações) and set off questions about the form that modernity had taken in Brazil, as well as about the practices of FIFA in running the world's most popular sport.

The protests began innocuously. Before the opening of the Confederations Cup itself, small crowds gathered in major cities to denounce hikes in bus fares.[3] Police repression of demonstrators quickly provided a further cause for public complaints. By the time the tournament was under way, massive groups were taking to the streets against a vast array of abuses. Dismissed initially as vandalism by political figures in São Paulo and Rio, the demonstrations witnessed a surprisingly low degree of violence by those taking part in the marches.[4] Nevertheless, the protests included daring moves, like the attempted invasion of state government palaces in São Paulo and Rio and of the national Congress in Brasília. Indeed, the dynamism and sheer size of the countrywide upsurge took everyone by surprise.[5] More Brazilians participated in these demonstrations in 2013 than at any time since the prodemocracy movement in the early 1980s and the protests against the corrupt presidency of Fernando Collor in 1992.[6] The 2013 actions addressed a much wider range of issues than these public campaigns, but in a broad sense the three moments of contestation shared an overarching concern. In 2013 Brazilians were once more demanding a deepening of democracy, with transparency in their government's dealings and real attention to the needs of common citizens.

The setting of the Confederations Cup provided part of the novelty of 2013. The international soccer tournament not only drew a global audience but also presented a focus for Brazilians' criticisms of the direction their country had taken. Corruption and mismanagement in the preparations for the 2014 World Cup had always been expected by observers in Brazil and elsewhere.[7] Coming at a time of mounting frustrations over the cost of living as well as the misdeeds of the political and business elites, however, the Confederations Cup—as part of the World Cup process—acted as a catalyst for denunciations of a wide range of abuses. Individual politicians came under fire, most visibly with the booing of President Dilma Rousseff at the first match of the competition, but protestors condemned government misrule more generally, the brutality of police forces (especially the military police), and the extraordinary powers granted to FIFA in return for the right to hold the World Cup in Brazil. These were only a few of the concerns expressed; indeed, as some signs declared grandly but vaguely, the protesters hoped to accomplish nothing less than "changing Brazil."[8] The general desire, as expressed on social media and in demonstrations, was to get people to "come to the streets" and force politicians to react positively to citizens' needs.[9]

FIGURE 15. Protester holding a sign that reads "I will give up the Cup! I want money for health and education!!!" Rio de Janeiro, 16 June 2013. TASSO MARCELO/AFP/Getty Images.

MEGA-EVENTS IN BRAZIL

This sort of public expression was notably absent in 2007, when FIFA announced that the 2014 World Cup (and thus also the 2013 Confederations Cup) would take place in Brazil. The news brought forth an uncomplicated outpouring of national pride, though the success of the country's bid was far from a surprise. As early as 2003 FIFA had made clear its intention to grant the event to a South American nation, and behind-the-scenes negotiations during the selection process had left Brazil the sole candidate by the time of the final vote on 30 October 2007. Exuberant patriotism, nevertheless, accompanied the news, with then President Lula pledging pointedly that the Brazil World Cup would be one that "no Argentine could find fault with."[10] Just two years later, the country managed a precious double when the International Olympic Committee chose Rio over Madrid, Tokyo, and Chicago as the site of the 2016 Summer Olympics. This time Lula went even farther in his comments, proclaiming that the "victory," coming after more than a decade of campaigning, signaled that Brazil was becoming a "first-class" nation.[11]

The country was not new to staging international events. In soccer alone, Brazilians could boast of having hosted the Copa América in 1989 and its predecessor, the Campeonato Sul Americano, three times, beginning with the 1919 championship that helped to establish the symbolic relationship between the sport and the nation. When the country hosted the 1950 World Cup, this link came back to haunt Brazilian fans, of course, after the Seleção met unexpected defeat. More recently, the 2007 Pan American Games in Rio served as evidence that the Brazilian Olympic Committee (COB, Comitê Olímpico Brasileiro) marshaled in its bid for the 2016 Olympics. The country had also been home to major nonsporting events, including two United Nations conferences on development and the environment (Eco-92 in 1992 and Rio+20 in 2012) and five iterations of the World Social Forum.

None of these, however, approached the World Cup and Olympics in sheer magnitude or complexity. Both are true mega events training the gaze of global audiences on host countries. In this regard, they also serve as marketing opportunities. Private and public sectors alike seek to portray the most positive possible image of their nation to the world, while tucking anything potentially negative out of sight. Such promotional efforts benefit from an association with the universalist ideals that the International Olympic Committee (IOC) and, to a lesser extent, FIFA have promoted.[12] These international governing bodies cast sports as a means of fostering physical and moral health among individuals and peace between countries. Adept local agents tap into these notions, which are, after all, such abstractly optimistic ideals that they typically do not spark public criticism. At the same time, both the World Cup and the Olympics are predicated on nationalism, serving as a stage for competition between athletes representing specific countries. Even in the age of new globalism, when soccer and other sports show signs of "denationalization" because of the flow of players, coaches, ideas, and capital around the world, these mega-events remain at the same time nominally transnational and effectively *inter*-national.[13]

Like previous host countries, Brazil treated national and international goals as complementary. It tacitly accepted the overarching aims of FIFA and the IOC, framing its bids and subsequent publicity in terms that support the stated purposes of these entities. Controversially, Brazilian politicians also made significant legal and logistical concessions to these international entities, as part of the price for receiving the Cup and the Olympics. Nationalist discourses, though, dominated plans for both events. One strain focused on the purported benefits the competitions would bring, in what former Minister of Sports Orlando Silva called a "shock of development," and in a shift in attitudes toward Brazil that would foster longer-term gains in tourism and other business sectors.[14] The other major logic was the one reflected in Lula's initial reactions to the good news he received in 2007 and 2009. Government and business leaders used the mega-events as evidence that Brazil has achieved a version of modernity recognized by the global community.[15] In this telling, the country of the future, despite undeniable social and political problems, was at long last reaching its potential. The two lines of argument present a basic contradiction: were the events the means or the acknowledgment of Brazilian development? Marketers left this question open, but the unspoken assertion was that the World Cup and the Olympics would not only affirm but also consolidate the achievement of modernity.

The juggling of aims has been common to all hosts, and the effort to display the host country's emergence as a major world force has been particularly evident in the mega-events held in other nations in the BRICS (Brazil, Russia, India, China, South Africa) group.[16] These are all countries that have aspired to make the jump from rising power to superpower—or, in the case of Russia, to regain the latter status—while managing the internal social and political stresses that have accompanied their growth. The specificity of the Brazilian case comes out, however, when placed against the history of *futebol* and the pursuit of tropical modernity. In one sense, obtaining the rights to two mega-events represented the culmination of an effort dating back at least to the formation of the first Seleção in 1914—namely, to demonstrate through sports that Brazil has become *gente grande* (big people, or grown-ups).[17] The campaigns to stage the World Cup and Olympics show, however, that the divisions that have marked the formation of the national game, even its golden period of incredible international triumphs, persist. The protests that began in June 2013 are in this regard only the most visible evidence that Brazilian modernity remains both a conflictive process and an elusive goal.[18]

SOCCER AND THE BRAZIL WORLD CUP

The confirmation of Brazil as host of the 2014 World Cup provided cause for patriotic celebration, certainly, but also a welcome distraction for those following the Seleção closely. Officials had long lobbed for the rights to the 2014

Cup, asserting that "the best soccer in the world must also be the greatest," and that this latter distinction could come only by organizing the tournament for the first time since 1950.[19] The Seleção's performance in 2006 brought the question of Brazil's on-field supremacy into doubt, but the prospect of 2014 meant that Brazilians could at least temporarily forget the failure of the heavily favored 2006 team, along with charges that its stars had simply not shown the dedication, the "love of the uniform," that fans had expected of them. Indeed, as soon as FIFA president Sepp Blatter held up the card with Brazil's name on it, the 2014 Cup became the focus of Brazilian hopes. The 2014 tournament, in this way, preempted that of 2010.[20]

It often seemed that fans and commentators had relatively low expectations for the 2010 World Cup. To be sure, like those before it, this competition catalyzed nationalist feelings more intensely than any national holiday, as Édison Gastaldo noted.[21] Still, the squad coached by Dunga did not inspire the deep affection that the 2006 team had enjoyed before the Cup. Dunga's Seleção achieved a solid winning record, qualifying more easily than the champions of 1994 and 2002 had done, and only went out in a tough game against the Netherlands, a traditional power in the sport. Never, though, did Dunga convince observers that his tightly regulated, counterattacking Seleção was authentically Brazilian. Had he brought home the trophy, he might have been forgiven his pragmatism, as had occurred with Carlos Alberto Parreira and Luiz Felipe Scolari. Defeat, though, transformed the criticisms he had suffered into a sweeping sense that he had rejected the beautiful game. The strongest evidence presented in support of this was his refusal to include promising young talents, particularly Neymar and Paulo Henrique Ganso, and former World Player of the Year Ronaldinho Gaúcho in the side.[22]

When Mano Menezes replaced Dunga shortly after the close of the World Cup in South Africa, then, he faced rekindled hopes and reinvigorated expectations.[23] With the World Cup coming home, it was crucial that Brazil assemble a squad that could reconquer the title.[24] Ideally, Mano would do this in the manner he had promised, constructing a Seleção that would live up to the country's reputation for skillful soccer. For a brief time, he seemed able to oversee the renovation that this would require. With former stars like Ronaldinho and Kaká in apparent decline, Mano turned to Neymar, Ganso, the midfielder Oscar, and other youngsters. The potential they flashed encouraged critics, even when they lost an exhibition match to Argentina. Mano was unable, however, to maintain that early momentum. Injuries hampered the progress of forward Alexandre Pato and reduced Ganso to a "virtual" *craque*.[25]

Neymar and Oscar continued to impress, but their youth and the lack of reliable veterans around them meant that they simply could not deliver every game. By the time the Olympic team lost in the gold-medal match to a well-organized Mexican side, it was clear that Mano was losing the support of the public and CBF (Brazilian Soccer Confederation) officials.[26]

Contemplating Mano's departure from the Seleção, some observers allowed themselves to wonder how Brazil could follow the path of FC Barcelona and the Spanish national team, the new standard-bearers of technical soccer.[27] A few went so far as to imagine what Barça coach Pep Guardiola might do with the Seleção, particularly after he reportedly expressed his willingness to take the Brazil job if it were offered to him.[28] New CBF president José Maria Marin, who had stepped in after Ricardo Teixeira's resignation, showed no sympathy for these fantasies. An old right-wing political hand—he had served in Congress for the military's party during the dictatorship—Marin rejected the idea of a foreign coach and instead brought back Luiz Felipe Scolari to head the national team, in the hope that he might replicate his success of 2001 and 2002.[29]

The good will that Felipão had earned in his first turn at the helm of the Seleção protected him, for a while, from critics. When it became clear that he could not quickly reverse the downward course the team had fallen into under Mano's command, however, doubts emerged. Former World Cup winners expressed worries that Felipão's Seleção was "unstylish" or simply not good enough to beat any but the weakest opponents. Jairzinho and Ronaldo separately asserted that the country's soccer had hit its lowest point ever.[30] Experienced stars had faded, while new revelations seemed unprepared to lead the team to victory. The highly visible and abundantly talented Neymar, in particular, came under intense scrutiny. Scouted by major European clubs since the age of thirteen and hailed as "the next King" at the age of eighteen, he had become a symbol of the authentic national style, as Romário had been in 1994. With neither the team nor its most popular star showing signs of improvement, some commentators began to condemn Neymar before he even had the chance to "save the fatherland" with his skillful play. In response to this perceived injustice, editors of the magazine *Placar* put an image of a crucified Neymar on the cover of their October 2012 issue.[31]

The Seleção's triumph in the 2013 Confederations Cup restored hope to many Brazil fans. Neymar shone brightly, demonstrating his commitment to working his individual skills into Scolari's organization of the squad. His efforts were crucial to the development of a consistent, collective scheme for the first time since 2010. As Tostão noted after Brazil's victory over Italy, Scolari's team had given "its first show of maturity." The win over Spain inspired spectators to shout, "The champion is back," while leading a sanguine Carlos Alberto Parreira to remark, "We may not be the best in the world, but we are capable of taking the Cup."[32]

MEGA-*BRASILIDADE* AND DEMOCRACY

The rebirth of admiration for Scolari's Seleção, however, gives a somewhat misleading impression of the importance of actual soccer in these years. Athletic performance and results matter during and after competitions, but the buildup to a World Cup or Olympics focuses public attention on the logistics of preparation.[33] These include technical questions about projects to build stadiums, improve transportation, and accommodate visitors. They also touch on profound questions about the methods of decision-making and the terms of national representation. Debates about these matters began from the launch of efforts to acquire hosting rights and grew more heated as organizers' plans for the two mega-events came into public view. The complicated deals between private firms, international organizations, and all levels of government proceeded with very little transparency. In twenty-first-century Brazil, this could only lead to contestations of various sorts. As the World Cup drew closer, communities affected by construction projects began to lodge protests against measures that organizers considered essential to the success of the Cup and the Olympics. Activists and intellectuals added their support for these protestors and offered critiques of the predictions of economic gains that would accrue to the country. Thus, in spite of the best efforts of FIFA, the IOC, and Brazilian officials, what emerged was a political debate so vibrant that it led FIFA secretary general Jérôme Valcke to note, in an undiplomatic moment, "sometimes less democracy is better for organizing a World Cup."[34]

Democracy, however, was a well-established feature of Brazilian modernity by the early twenty-first century. The election of Lula in 2002 and his successor Dilma in 2010 brought to power a party that had advocated government transparency and direct participation and had delivered them to an impressive degree, at least at the municipal level. The ascension of the Workers' Party (PT) thus encouraged many Brazilians to hope for a more active kind of citizenship than they had enjoyed under previous administrations. While expanding social programs that effectively redistributed income downward, though, the PT also engaged in energetically business-friendly practices. As the country moved toward the World Cup and Olympics, this balance seemed to shift away from the social-democratic and toward a heavily top-down management of more clearly neoliberal initiatives. In short, the government entered into deals with national and multinational firms to carry out massive physical reforms, taking on increasing portions of the ever-rising expenses of these projects and giving in to pressures to enact legislation that gave FIFA and the IOC wide powers in host cities, and doing all this without any specific public mandate or clear financial reckoning.[35]

There was no shortage of work to be done. In spite of the country's rich soccer culture and overcrowded calendar of matches, not a single stadium in Brazil met FIFA standards for a World Cup in 2007.[36] All twelve of the cities chosen to host games, moreover, needed improvements to their transportation and tourism infrastructures, as well as renovations of practice facilities for the participating teams. Organizers multiplied the difficulties they faced by opting to spread the event out across so much of the national territory, even to areas where large stadiums were almost certain to become underused white elephants after 2014. With spectators and teams having to travel not only to Brazil but also to fly extensively within the country, the stress on airports emerged early on as a potential weak point. Security, finally, was a necessary and thorny problem, as hooliganism and terrorism joined the more familiar reality of everyday crime in Brazil on the list of threats.[37]

To many common citizens, the methods that government officials and event organizers adopted to address these monumental tasks quickly came to seem an assault on their democratic rights. Romário, the former player turned congressman, became a leading critic of the CBF, FIFA, and government. His assertion that this would be "a Cup in Brazil but not for Brazilians" struck a chord with much of the public.[38] Although his initial point of reference had been high ticket prices that would keep regular Brazilian fans from attending matches, he and other observers and activists developed this complaint into a broad argument that the World Cup was not being set up to benefit—or even include—local people.[39]

Indeed, acting on behalf of its partners at FIFA and in the private business sector, the government enacted measures that seemed aimed at clearing out real Brazilian citizens to open space for glittering monuments to an idealized Brazilian modernity. Organizers of the 2007 Pan American Games had been relatively moderate in their approach to the occupation of urban spaces. Police had made incursions into *favelas* and killed suspected drug traffickers, but generally both government agencies and the organizing committee had tried to keep unpleasant realities of city life literally out of sight. They had, in fact, constructed walls to block poor neighborhoods from the view of spectators watching matches and races.[40] The mega-events of 2014 and 2016, by contrast, occasioned more extreme and invasive measures.[41] Particularly galling was the policy of *remoções,* the forced evacuations of communities or the demolition of schools and other public buildings, all to clear the way for new arenas and the parking, shopping, and public spaces around them. Scholars like Raquel Rolnik, urbanist and United Nations Special Rapporteur on Adequate Housing, attested that these moves contradicted Brazilian law. The *remoções,* they charged, proceeded without the reasonable alternative shelter or compensation that the 2001 Statute of the Cities (Estatuto das Cidades) demanded.[42] Community activists, meanwhile, tried to map out the tens of thousands of homes threatened by *remoções* from Porto Alegre in the far south to Natal and Fortaleza in the northeast and Manaus in the Amazon.[43] Like many of the initiatives foreseen in the plans for the Cup and the Olympics, these moves put particularly vulnerable parts of the populace at risk.

As the spiritual heart of *futebol,* Maracanã Stadium in Rio emerged as a center of struggles over the orientation of Cup preparations. The project of building a new Maracanã held tremendous symbolic power, especially since the original stadium had been hailed as a modern marvel in 1950 and remained the principal physical legacy of that year's World Cup.[44] Organizers clearly intended to awe the world again in 2014 and were willing to bull through any obstacles to achieve that effect. In this part of Rio's North Zone, it was not only the homes of poor residents that seemed impediments to progress. Training facilities used by some of the country's top swimmers and track-and-field athletes and a public school also faced destruction. The school caught public attention both because it was a relative success story in Rio's chronically underfunded educational system and because of its name. The plan to demolish the Escola Municipal Arthur Friedenreich suggested the 2014 World Cup officials' lack of respect not only for area residents, but also, symbolically, for the memory of the first great soccer star in the country.[45]

In the end, politicians demurred on the issue of the Friedenreich school and the track-and-field facility, promising to replace the first and renovate the second, instead of eliminating them. The announcement of these changes did not, however, reassure neighborhood residents and activists. Rather than political victories, these decisions could turn out to be nothing but empty rhetorical gestures by imperious authorities. Indeed, preparations for the mega-events of 2014 and 2016 witnessed an increasing concentration of power in the hands not only of high-ranking politicians and business elites in Brazil but also of FIFA and the IOC. Together, these elements of the much-vaunted public-private alliance imposed policies from above, in the name of marketing the country as an efficient and modern nation.[46] In practice, this tendency meant that the costs of construction projects shifted largely from private to public accounts. This flew in the face of earlier government assertions that the financing of stadiums, in particular, would be left entirely to private firms. Between 2007 and 2013, though, costs of preparations for the mega-event soared, and the federal development bank had to pick up much of the tab; private companies proved unwilling to risk their own money.[47] At the same time, the state conceded key power to nongovernmental interests. In spite of a series of protests and legal challenges, Maracanã was privatized, initially becoming the property of the very firm that had been contracted to study the economic viability of the stadium project.[48]

FIFA, meanwhile, extracted its own substantial concessions from the Brazilian government. Brazil would have to build stadiums to standards set by the international sporting body, while also exempting FIFA's activities in the country from all taxes. More galling still to Brazilian nationalists were the "zones of exclusion," in which FIFA gained virtual sovereignty over commercial and other activities within two kilometers of World Cup stadiums. Thus, while Brazil was spending billions of dollars to put on a soccer show, it was also giving up significant control over that show. It is no wonder, in these circumstances, that citizens began to demand "FIFA standard" public education and health services and to ask, "Whose World Cup?"[49]

TROPICÁLIA FOR SALE

The top-down nature of policy making has also brought about changes in the image of tropical modernity. The tropical has been reduced, overwhelmingly, to abstract and decorative features, rather than essential and defining traits of the nation and its historical evolution. References to older conceptions of a mixed-race civilization have appeared in publicity materials, but only fleetingly and as part of a broader notion of diversity within the nation. Brazil still has a culture influenced by Afro-Brazilian and Amerindian peoples, as signaled by official displays at the Casa Brasil (Brazil House) that the CBF set up in Johannesburg during the 2010 World Cup and the performance of samba in the closing ceremony of the 2012 London Olympics.[50] These depictions of Brazil as multicultural imply unity, but not one based in racial mixture. The *brasilidade* marketed in both the World Cup and Olympic initiatives is no longer essentially mulatto or *mestiço* culture but plural and more vaguely integrated, as though the nation no longer needed a singular, racialized identity to unite its many parts. As Lula wrote in the official World Cup bid, the new Brazil is a "nation marked by the tolerance of races, of beliefs, a nation marked by peaceful coexistence and by diversity in all fields."[51]

This conception represents a step away from the notion of a fundamentally mixed-race nation and toward a recognition of the multiple racial and ethnic identities that have become meaningful parts of public political discourse in Brazil. At the same time, however, it lumps all of these identities together as "diversity," not dwelling on any of them but moving the viewer or consumer quickly on to images of Brazil as a dynamic and mature nation. To connect the old tropical Brazil to the Brazil capable of staging mega-events, organizers have relied on the term "passion." Passion has been featured in the Olympic bid, which was titled "Live Your Passion," and has subsequently showed up in the promotion of the World Cup as well.[52] Falling close to stereotypes of Brazilians as driven by their emotions, passion gestures to Brazil's financial might but also the energy and warmth of its people. Official representations tend to focus on the willingness of public and private sectors to promote business ventures that will be lucrative but also environmentally responsible. The rich culture of the *povo*, understood for so long as the source of the tropical essence of Brazil, has taken a backseat to images of Brazil's natural beauty—its palm-lined beaches and verdant rain forests—in portrayals of the country's tropicality. These references presumably seem safe, in the sense that they are unlikely to call up images of poverty or crime (so common in news about Brazil since the late 1980s), while providing a distinctive, Brazilian imagining of the World Cup and Olympics. Organizers might prefer to keep the Brazilian common people out of sight—and certainly out of decision-making processes—but they need to craft a Brazil that will function as an effective brand.[53]

The official projects for these two mega-events suggest just how much has changed since Brazil hosted the 1950 World Cup. Brazilians put national pride on the line in the 1950 competition, as the reaction to the Maracanazo makes clear, but the demands for infrastructural improvements were modest.[54] At that time, World Cups were international events; since then, though, they have grown into globalized mega-events that mobilize political and financial capital on a scale that would have been unimaginable in the

FIGURE 16. Protester kicking a tear gas canister, Rio de Janeiro, 16 June 2013. Alexandro Auler/
LatinContent/Getty Images.

mid-twentieth century. These mega-events remain opportunities for countries to promote themselves, although once again the marketing potential has
expanded enormously. Perhaps the most striking shift in the Brazilian case
involves the national image that organizers have embraced. In the Brazil of
1950 an explicitly racialized collective identity, based on claims of a national
culture linked directly to the mixed-race populace, had gained traction. As
the country prepares to host the 2014 World Cup and the 2016 Olympics, this
tropical-modern ideal looks quite different; the cleaning-up of Brazil's image
for global consumption has washed away much of what had represented the
tropical in earlier periods. The Brazil that mega-event planners have formulated veers away from the *povo,* treating it more as a source of potential con-
sumers, in a best-case scenario, or as a threat to measures ensuring progress,
in more pessimistic reckonings, than as the foundation of authentic national
identity.

This mega-Brazil represents an assertion of the country's economic and
political triumphs on the world stage. It remains to be seen, however, if it will
serve as the basis for a new dominant sense of *brasilidade,* particularly after
the end of the World Cup and the Olympics. Indeed, in light of the demonstrations that began before the 2013 Confederations Cup and continued on

after it, with the sporadic but at times brutal acts of violence that accompanied them, the legacy of these mega-events is anything but certain.[55]

Soccer's central place in Brazilian culture, by contrast, endures. Despite occasional charges that the game itself had been irredeemably tainted by the profiteering of Brazilian politicians and national and international sports institutions, support for *futebol* and for the national team retained its force during and after the 2013 protests. Declarations that the unrest was "not about soccer" or "not against the Seleção" came to be nearly as common as messages that Brazilians had not taken to the streets over bus fares alone. Indeed, one of the most moving features of the Confederations Cup was the singing of the national anthem, particularly the choruses that rang out after the musical accompaniment had stopped.

As patriotic displays and the success of the national team stoked emotions inside the "FIFA standard" stadiums, protestors and bystanders found themselves the targets of tear gas and rubber bullets from police shock troops in the streets outside. Soccer did not cause the recent conflicts that tore through the country, just as it did not cause any of the other social and political conflicts that have marked Brazilian history since the sport first appeared in cities in the late nineteenth century. Once more, though, soccer provided a space and an opportunity for debates over the nature of Brazil's modernization. The relationship between soccer and nation persists and with it the complex, overlapping discussions of power relations in the country of football.

NOTES

INTRODUCTION

Epigraph: Jorge Vasconcellos, org., *Recados da bola: Depoimentos de doze mestres do futebol brasileiro* (São Paulo: Cosac Naify, 2010), 230.

1. "Por futebol vistoso, Mano quer Brasil protagonista," 8 Aug. 2010, accessed 10 Aug. 2010, www.gazetaesportiva.net/nota/2010/08/02/647750.html.

2. Marco Antônio Janeiro Calmulur and Antonio Jorge Gonçalves Soares, *A memória da Copa de 70: Esquecimentos e lembranças do futebol na construção da Identidade nacional* (Campinas: Autores Associados, 2009), x, 1–3.

3. Simoni Lahud Guedes, "O 'povo brasileiro' no campo de futebol," *A Margem* 1, no. 3 (1993): 5.

4. Simoni Lahud Guedes, "O Brasil nas Copas do Mundo: Tempo 'suspenso' e história," *Aquinate* 3 (2006): 163–72, and *O Brasil no campo de futebol: Estudos antropológicos sobre os significados do futebol brasileiro* (Niterói: EDUFF, 1998), chap. 2; José Miguel Wisnik, *Veneno remédio: O futebol e o Brasil* (São Paulo: Companhia das Letras, 2008), 19–28; Hans Ulrich Gumbrecht, *In Praise of Athletic Beauty* (Cambridge: Harvard University Press, 2006), 68; Arno Vogel, "O momento feliz: Reflexões sobre o futebol e o ethos nacional," in *Universo do futebol: Esporte e sociedade brasileira,* Roberto DaMatta et al. (Rio de Janeiro: Pinakotheke, 1982), 75–115; cf. Michael Oriard, *Reading Football: How the Popular Press Created an American Spectacle* (Chapel Hill: University of North Carolina Press, 1993), 1–25.

5. Roberto DaMatta, "Antropologia do óbvio: Notas em torno do significado social do futebol brasileiro," *Revista USP: Dossiê Futebol* 22 (1994): 10–17; Hilário Franco Júnior, *A dança dos deuses: Futebol, sociedade, cultura* (São Paulo: Companhia das Letras, 2007), 11.

6. Guedes, "O 'povo brasileiro.'" Compare with Roger Magazine, "'You Can Buy a Player's Legs, but Not His Heart': A Critique of Clientelism and Modernity among Soccer Fans in Mexico City," *Journal of Latin American Anthropology* 9, no. 1 (2004): 8–33; Laurent Dubois, *Soccer Empire: The World Cup and the Future of France* (Berkeley: University of California Press, 2010), 21–22 and passim; Grant Farred, *Long Distance Love: A Passion for Football* (Philadelphia: Temple University Press, 2008); C.L.R. James, *Beyond a Boundary* (Durham: Duke University Press, 1993).

7. On urban violence in these years see *Cidade de Deus* (City of God), dir. Fernando Meirelles (2002); Anthony W. Pereira, "Public Security, Private Interests, and Police Reform in Brazil," in *Democratic Brazil Revisited,* ed. Peter R. Kingstone and Timothy J. Power (Pittsburgh: University of Pittsburgh Press, 2008), 185–208; Teresa P. R. Caldeira, *City of Walls: Crime, Segregation, and Citizenship in São Paulo* (Berkeley: University of California Press, 2000). See also Roberto DaMatta's analysis of the negative connotations of the word *cidadão* (citizen), "'Do You Know Who You're Talking To?' The Distinction Between Individual and Person in Brazil," in *Carnivals, Rogues, and Heroes: An Interpretation of the Brazilian Dilemma,* trans. John Drury (Notre Dame: University of Notre Dame Press, 1991), 137–97.

8. This continues in scholarship as well; see Wisnik, *Veneno,* 421.

9. Kim B. Butler, *Freedoms Given, Freedoms Won: Afro-Brazilians in Post-Abolition São Paulo and Salvador* (New Brunswick: Rutgers University Press, 1998); Flávio Gomes and Petrônio Domingues, eds., *Experiências da emancipação: Biografias, instituições e movimentos sociais no pós-abolição (1890–1980)* (São Paulo: Selo Negro, 2011); Maria Arminda do Nascimento Arruda, "Dilemas do Brasil modern: A questão racial na obra de Florestan Fernandes," *Raça, ciência e sociedade,* org. Marcos Chor Maio and Ricardo Ventura Santos (Rio de Janeiro: FIOCRUZ / CCBB, 1996), 195–217.

10. Carlos Halsenbalg and Nelson do Valle Silva, "Notes on Racial and Political Inequality in Brazil," in *Racial Politics in Contemporary Brazil,* ed. Michael Hanchard (Durham: Duke University Press, 1999), 154–78; Edward E. Telles, *Race in Another America: The Significance of Skin Color in Brazil* (Princeton: Princeton University Press, 2006). Useful broad treatments of race and nationality in Brazil include Emília Viotti da Costa, *The Brazilian Empire: Myths and Histories,* 2nd ed. (Durham: Duke University Press, 1988); Thomas E. Skidmore, *Black into White: Race and Nationality in Brazilian Thought* (New York: Oxford University Press, 1974), and "Racial Ideas and Social Policy in Brazil, 1870–1940," in *The Idea of Race in Latin America, 1870–1940,* ed. Richard Graham (Austin: University of Texas Press, 1990), 7–36; Micol Seigel, *Uneven Encounters: Making Race and Nation in Brazil and the United States* (Durham: Duke University Press, 2009).

11. David Goldblatt, *The Ball is Round: A Global History of Soccer* (New York: Riverhead Books, 2008), chap. 5.

12. Roberto Ventura, *Estilo tropical: História cultural e polêmicas literárias no Brasil* (São Paulo: Companhia das Letras, 1991); Lúcia Lippi Oliveira, *A questão nacional na Primeira República* (São Paulo: Brasiliense, 1990).

13. Frederick Cooper, *Colonialism in Question: Theory, Knowledge, History* (Berkeley: University of California Press, 2005), chap. 5; Monica Pimenta Velloso, *História e modernismo* (Belo Horizonte: Autêntica Editora, 2010), 11; Octávio Ianni, *A idéia do Brasil moderno* (São Paulo: Brasiliense, 2004), 120–21, 150.

14. Ventura, *Estilo,* 36–41; Florencia Garramuño, *Primitive Modernities: Tango, Samba, and Nation,* trans. Anna Kazumi Stahl (Stanford: Stanford University Press, 2011), 40–41.

15. Garramuño, *Primitive Modernities,* 74–75.

16. The quotation, attributed to José Lins do Rego, appears in Jair de Souza, Lucia Rito, and Sérgio Sá Leitão, *Futebol-arte: A cultura e o jeito brasileiro de jogar* (São Paulo: Empresa das Artes, 1998), 230–31.

17. Roberto DaMatta, *O que faz o brasil, Brasil?* (Rio de Janeiro: Rocco, 1999), and "Esporte na sociedade: Um ensaio sobre o futebol brasileiro," in *Universo do futebol,* DaMatta et al. (Rio de Janeiro: Pinakotheke, 1982), 19–41.

18. Freyre, *Interpretação do Brasil: Aspectos da formação social brasileira como processo de amalgamento de raças e culturas,* trans. Olívio Montenegro and org. Omar Ribeiro Thomaz (São Paulo: Companhia das Letras, 2001), 183.

19. Guedes, "O 'povo brasileiro' no campo de futebol"; Ronaldo Helal, "Mitos e verdades do futebol (que nos ajudam a entender quem somos)," *Insight Inteligência* 52 (2011): 70–71; José Sergio Leite Lopes, "'The People's Joy' Vanishes: Considerations on the Death of a Soccer Player," special issue, *Journal of Latin American Anthropology* 4, no. 2 and 5, no. 1 (2000): 78–105.

20. Waldenir Caldas, "O futebol no país do futebol," *Lua nova* 3, no. 10 (1986): 24; Antonio Jorge Soares and Hugo Rodolfo Lovisolo, "A construção histórica do estilo nacional," *Revista Brasileira de Ciências do Esporte* 25, no. 1 (2003): 129–43; DaMatta, "Esporte na sociedade"; Wisnik, *Veneno,* 221–32.

21. Michael George Hanchard, *Orpheus and Power: The Movimento Negro of Rio de Janeiro and São Paulo, Brazil, 1945–1988* (Princeton: Princeton University Press, 1994), esp. chap. 3.

22. Antonio Risério, *A utopia brasileira e os movimentos negros* (São Paulo: Editora 34, 2007), 309.

23. Olívia Maria Gomes da Cunha, "Black Movements and the 'Politics of Identity' in Brazil," in *Cultures of Politics, Politics of Cultures: Re-Visioning Latin American Social Movements,* ed. Sonia E. Alvarez, Evelina Dagnino, and Arturo Escobar (Boulder: Westview, 1998), 220–51; Michael Hanchard, "Black Cinderella? Race and the Public Sphere in Brazil," in *Racial Politics in Contemporary Brazil,* ed. Michael Hanchard (Durham: Duke University Press, 1999), 59–81; Peter Fry, "O que a Cuidicila Negra tem a dizer sobre a 'política racial' no Brasil," *Revista USP* 28 (1995): 122–35; and on parallel processes in popular music, Bryan McCann, *The Throes of Democracy: Brazil Since 1989* (Halifax: Fernwood Publishing; London: Zed Books, 2008), chap. 4; Idelber Avelar, "Mangue Beat Music and the Coding of Citizenship in Sound," in *Brazilian Popular Music and Citizenship,* ed. Avelar and Christopher Dunn (Durham: Duke University Press, 2011), 313–29.

24. Ronaldo Helal and Antonio Jorge Soares, "O declínio da pátria de chuteiras: Futebol e identidade nacional na Copa do Mundo de 2002," *Anais XII COMPÓS—Associação dos Programas de Pós-Graduação em Comunicação Social* (Recife: UFPE, 2003): 401–12; Tiago Lisboa Bartholo, Antonio Jorge Gonçalves Soares, Marco Antonio Santoro Salvador, Felipe Di Blasi, "A patria de chuteiras está desaparecendo?" *Revista Brasileira de Ciências do Esporte* 32, no. 1 (2010): 9–23; Fernando Cardoso, "Quem torce para o Brasil?" 12 Oct. 2011, accessed 14 Oct. 2011, www.goal.com/br/news/619/especiais/2011/10/12/2708285 /quem-torce-para-o-brasil.

25. Roberto DaMatta, *A bola corre mais que os homens: Duas Copas, treze crônicas e três ensaios sobre futebol* (Rio de Janeiro: Rocco, 2006), 164–65.

26. On the contextual workings of race, see Livio Sansone, *Race Without Ethnicity: Constructing Race in Brazil* (New York: Palgrave Macmillan, 2003). On the integrative workings of *futebol,* see esp. Janet Lever, *Soccer Madness: Brazil's Passion for the World's Most Popular Sport* (Prospect Heights, IL: Waveland Press, 1995).

27. Marcel Diego Tonini, "Negros no futebol brasileiro: Olhares e experiências de dois treinadores," *Oralidades: Revista de História Oral* 7 (2010): 125–46; Bruno Otávio de Lacerda Abrahão and Antonio Jorge Soares, "O que o brasileiro não esquece nem a tiro é o chamado frango de Barbosa: Questões sobre o racismo no futebol brasileiro," *Movimento* 15, no. 2 (2009): 28.

28. Cf. Wisnik, *Veneno,* esp. 420–29.

CHAPTER 1

Epigraph: Milton Pedrosa, *Gol de letra* (Rio de Janeiro: Gol, n.d.), 117–19.

1. "150 mil pessoas cantaram," *O Globo,* 14 Jul. 1950; Ademir Menezes in Jorge Vasconcellos, org., *Recados da bola: Depoimentos de doze mestres do futebol brasileiro* (São Paulo: Cosac Naify, 2010), 102; Leonardo Turchi Pacheco, "Memórias da tragédia: Masculinidade e envelhecimento na Copa do Mundo de 1950," *Revista Brasileira de Ciências do Esporte* 32, no. 1 (2010): 30.

2. Fábio Franzini, "Da expectativa fremente à decepção amarga: O Brasil e a Copa do Mundo de 1950," *Revista de História* 163 (2010): 264.

3. "Morreu de emoção," *O Globo,* 17 Jul. 1950.

4. Paulo Perdigão, *Anatomia de uma derrota* (Porto Alegre: L&PM, 1986), 168.

5. "Pelé: 'Eu, tricampeão,'" *Placar,* 20 Aug. 1971, 14; Edson Arantes do Nascimento, with Orlando Duarte and Alex Bellos, *Pelé: The Autobiography* (London: Simon & Schuster, 2006), 46–48; *Pelé eterno,* dir. Anibal Massaini Neto (Brazil, 2004).

6. Perdigão, *Anatomia,* 37; Cláudio Vieira, *Maracanã: Templo dos deuses brasileiros* (Rio de Janeiro: Construtora Varca Scatena, 2000), 172.

7. "Atuando com grande entusiasmo e espírito de luta, a representação uruguaia venceu o IV Campeonato Mundial de Futebol," *O Estado de São Paulo,* 18 Jul. 1950; Vieira, *Maracanã,* 172.

8. *O Estado de São Paulo,* 18 Jul. 1950, in Perdigão, *Anatomia,* 172.

9. Geneton Moraes Neto, *Dossiê 50: Os onze jogadores revelam os segredos da maior tragédia do futebol brasileiro* (Rio de Janeiro: Objetiva, 2000), 91; Roberto Muylaert, *Barbosa: Um gol faz cinqüenta anos* (São Paulo: RMC Comunicação, 2000); Bruno Otávio de Lacerda Abrahão and Antonio Jorge Soares, "O que o brasileiro não esquece nem a tiro é o chamado frango de Barbosa: Questões sobre o racismo no futebol brasileiro," *Movimento* 15, no. 2 (2009): 13–31; Jô Soares, "1950 era assim: Olé, olé, olé e gol," in *A copa que ninguém viu e a que não queremos lembrar,* ed. Armando Nogueira, Jô Soares, and Roberto Muylaert (São Paulo: Companhia das Letras, 1994), 68; *Djalma Santos (depoimento, 2011)* (Rio de Janeiro: CPDOC, 2011), 16.

10. Perdigão, *Anatomia,* 61; Barbosa, Jair Rosa Pinto, Zizinho, and Ademir Menezes in Vasconcellos, *Recados da bola,* 52–102.

11. *Anuário Esportivo Brasileiro* (1950), 94–95, quoted in Arno Vogel, "O momento feliz, reflexões sobre o futebol e o ethos nacional," in Roberto DaMatta et al., *Universo do futebol: Esporte e sociedade brasileira* (Rio de Janeiro: Edições Pinakotheke, 1982), 95.

12. Freyre, "Foot-ball mulato," *Diario de Pernambuco,* 17 Jun. 1938; José Sergio Leite Lopes, "Class, Ethnicity, and Color in the Making of Brazilian Football," *Daedalus* 129, no. 2 (2000): 239–70.

13. Araken Patusca, with Marinho U. de Macedo, *Os reis do futebol* (São Paulo: n.p., 1945), 73; Tomás Mazzoni, *História do futebol no Brasil (1894–1950)* (São Paulo: Edições Leia, 1950), 181.

14. Albert Laurence, "'Les Brasiliens, rois du football' para os franceses desde a visita do 'Paulistano', em 1925," *Última Hora,* 23 Oct. 1963.

15. "O C.A. Paulistano passou hontem pelo nosso porto e os uruguaios também," *O Imparcial,* 12 Feb. 1925; "Uma entrevista de Friedenreich," *O Imparcial,* 4 Mar. 1925.

16. Patusca, *Os reis,* 113–62; Waldenyr Caldas, *O pontapé inicial: Memória do futebol brasileiro* (São Paulo: IBRASA, 1990), 162.

17. Abrão Aspis, *Futebol brasileiro: Do início amador à paixão nacional* (Porto Alegre: Evangraf, 2006), 77.

18. Patusca, *Os reis,* 92–93; "Brasil 7-França 2," *O Imparcial,* 16–17 Mar. 1925; Tony Mason, *Passion of the People? Football in South America* (London: Verso, 1995), 32–33.

19. Aidan Hamilton, *An Entirely Different Game: The British Influence on Brazilian Football* (Edinburgh: Mainstream, 1998), 19–34; José Moraes dos Santos Neto, *Visão do jogo: Primórdios do futebol no Brasil* (São Paulo: Cosac & Naify, 2002), 27–29.

20. Hamilton, *An Entirely Different Game,* 67–78; David Goldblatt, *The Ball is Round: A Global History of Soccer* (New York: Riverhead Books, 2008), 48–49.

21. Mazzoni, *História,* 26.

22. Mazzoni, *História,* 17; Santos Neto, *Visão do jogo,* 33–36; Aspis, *Futebol brasileiro,* 35–36; Claudio Nogueira, *Futebol Brasil memória: De Oscar Cox a Leônidas da Silva (1897–1937)* (Rio de Janeiro: Editora Senac Rio, 2006), 39.

23. Richard Graham, *Britain and the Onset of Modernization in Brazil, 1850–1914* (Cambridge: Cambridge University Press, 1972), 122.

24. Traces of these elitist values remain in the form of the Charles Miller Trophy, which the national soccer confederation awards annually to the player who best exemplifies good sportsmanship—an honor that recalls the toast that Cox made after the first matches between São Paulo and Rio clubs in 1901, when he hailed Miller as "the best all-round sportsman" of the competition. Hamilton, *An Entirely Different Game,* 44.

25. Aspis, *Futebol brasileiro,* 38.

26. Mazzoni, *História,* 21–24.

27. Rosane Feijão, *Moda e modernidade na belle époque carioca* (São Paulo: Estação das Letras e Cores, 2011); Jeffrey Needell, *A Tropical Belle Époque: Elite Culture and Society in Turn-of-the-Century Rio de Janeiro* (Cambridge: Cambridge University Press, 1987).

28. Mario [Rodrigues] Filho, *O negro no futebol brasileiro,* 4th ed. (Rio de Janeiro: Mauad, 2003), 34.

29. Leonardo Affonso de Miranda Pereira, *Footballmania: Uma história social do futebol no Rio de Janeiro, 1902–1938* (Rio de Janeiro: Nova Fronteira, 2000), 33.

30. Rinaldo Cesar Nascimento Leite, Coriolano P. da Rocha Junior, and Henrique Sena dos Santos, "Esporte, cidade e modernidade: Salvador," in *Os sports e as cidades brasileiras: Transição dos séculos XIX e XX,* org. Victor Andrade de Melo (Rio de Janeiro: Apicuri, 2010), 227.

31. Fábio Franzini, "A futura paixão nacional: Chega o futebol," in *História do esporte no Brasil: Do Império aos dias atuais,* org. Mary Del Priore and Victor Andrade de Melo (São Paulo: Editora UNESP, 2009), 113.

32. Gilmar Mascarenhas de Jesús, "Fútbol y modernidad en Brasil: La geografía histórica de una novedad," *Lecturas: Educación Física y Deporte* 3, no. 10 (May 1998), accessed 1 Apr. 2012, www.efdeportes.com/efd10/geoc.htm; Thacia Ramos Varnier et al, "A emergência dos clubes esportivos em Vitória," *Esporte e Sociedade* 7, no. 20 (Sep. 2012): 101; Raphael Rajão Ribeiro, "Em busca de um campo: O futebol belo-horizontino e a transformação dos espaços na cidade (1904–1921)," in *Campo e cidade na modernidade brasileira: Literatura, vilas operárias, cultura alimentar, futebol, correpondência privada e cultura visual,* org. Maria Eliza Linhares Borges (Belo Horizonte: Argumentum, 2008), 97–125; Mazzoni, *História,* 36.

33. Aspis, *Futebol brasileiro,* 53–54; Nogueira, *Futebol Brasil memória,* 37–38; Arlei Sander Damo, *Futebol e identidade social: Uma leitura antropológica das rivalidades entre torcedores e clubes* (Porto Alegre: Editora da Universidade / UFRGS, 2002), 39–40; Silvana Vilodre Goellner and Janice Zarpelon Mazzo, "Esporte, cidade e modernidade: Porto

Alegre," in *Os sports e as cidades brasileiras: Transição dos séculos XIX e XX,* org. Victor Andrade de Melo (Rio de Janeiro, Apicuri, 2010), 189. On similar events that year in Campinas, see Mazzoni, *História,* 25.

34. Ricardo de Figueiredo Lucena, *O esporte na cidade: Aspectos do esforço civilizador brasileiro* (Campinas: Autores Associados, 2001), 109.

35. Lucena, *O esporte,* 91.

36. On cycling, Goellner and Mazzo, "Esporte, cidade e modernidade: Porto Alegre," 181–83; Victor Andrade de Melo, "Das touradas às corridas de cavalo e regatas: Primeiro momentos da configuração do campo esportivo no Brasil," in *História do esporte: Do Império aos dias atuais,* org. Mary Del Priore and Victor Andrade de Melo (São Paulo: Editora UNESP, 2009), 77–82; on automobiles, Joel Wolfe, *Autos and Progress: The Brazilian Search for Modernity* (New York: Oxford University Press, 2010).

37. Melo, *Cidade sportiva,* 78.

38. [Rodrigues] Filho, *O negro,* 48; João do Rio in Victor Andrade de Melo, "Sportsmen: Os primeiros momentos da configuração de um público esportivo no Brasil," in *A torcida brasileira,* org. Bernardo Borges Buarque de Hollanda et al. (Rio de Janeiro: 7letras, 2012), 38.

39. "Sports," *Jornal do Brasil,* 16 Sep. 1911; Ricardo Pinto dos Santos, "Uma breve história social do esporte no Rio de Janeiro," in *Memória social dos esportes: Futebol e política: A construção de uma identidade nacional,* org. Francisco Carlos Teixeira Da Silva and Ricardo Pinto dos Santos (Rio de Janeiro: Mauad Editora / FAPERJ, 2006), 34.

40. Mazzoni, *História,* 25.

41. Roberto Porto, *Botafogo: 101 anos de histórias, mitos e superstições* (Rio de Janeiro: Revan, 2005), 29.

42. [Rodrigues] Filho, *O negro,* 49–50.

43. *Estatutos da Liga Metropolitana de Sports Athleticos* (Rio de Janeiro: Typ. Leuzinger, 1907), 13.

44. Lima Barreto, "Sobre football," *Bras Cubas,* 15 Aug. 1918.

45. [Rodrigues] Filho, *O negro,* 34.

46. Ibid., 36.

47. Pereira, *Footballmania,* 40–41; Goldblatt, *The Ball,* 131–32; Henrique Sena dos Santos, "Notas sobre a popularização do futebol em Salvador, 1901–1912," *Esporte e Sociedade* 5, no. 6 (2010/2011): 3–4.

48. Gregg P. Bocketti, "Italian Immigrants, Brazilian Football, and the Dilemma of National Identity," *Journal of Latin American Studies* 40 (2008): 275–302; José Renato de Campos Araújo, *Imigração e futebol: O caso Palestra Itália* (São Paulo: Editora Sumaré / FAPESP, 2000); Rodrigo Caldeira Bagni Moura, "O futebol em Belo Horizonte na décadas de 1920 e 1930: As partidas e diversões, os sururus e outras tramas," *Recorde: Revista de História do Esporte* 4, no. 1 (2011): esp. 22.

49. José Sérgio Leite Lopes, "Class, etnicidade e cor na formação do futebol brasileiro," in *Culturas de classe: Identidade e diversidade na formação do operariado,* org. Claudio H. M. Batalha, Fernando Teixeira da Silva, and Alexandre Fortes (Campinas: Editora da Unicamp, 2004), 133.

50. Plínio Labriola Negreiros, "A cidade excludente e o clube do povo," *Revista de História* 163 (2010): 213; João Paulo França Streapco, "'Cego é aquele que só vê a bola': O futebol em São Paulo e a formação das principais equipes paulistanas: S.C. Corinthians Paulista, S.E. Palmeiras e São Paulo F.C. (1894–1942)" (Master's thesis, Universidade de São Paulo, 2010), 37–40.

51. *Diário de Notícias,* 11 Jun. 1906 and *Gazeta do Povo,* 11 Jun. 1906, quoted in Sena dos Santos, "Notas," 14–15; Joel Rufino dos Santos, *História política do futebol brasileiro* (São Paulo: Brasiliense, 1981), 25–26; and Pereira, *Footballmania,* 135–36. On capoeira see Matthias Röhrig Assunção, *Capoeira: The History of an Afro-Brazilian Martial Art* (London: Routledge, 2005).

52. Negreiros, "A cidade," 211.

53. *Diário de Notícias* (Salvador), 7 Nov. 1906, in Leite, Rocha Junior, and Santos, "Esporte, cidade e modernidade: Salvador," 234; Negreiros, "A cidade," 212; Santos, "Notas," 14, 16. On the "ideology of vagrancy," see Lúcio Kowarick, *Trabalho e vadiagem: A origem do trabalho livre no Brasil* (São Paulo: Brasiliense, 1987).

54. Santos Neto, *Visão do jogo,* 53.

55. Uassyr de Siqueira, "Clubes recreativos: organização para o lazer," in *Trabalhadores na cidade: Cotidiano e cultura no Rio de Janeiro e em São Paulo, séculos XIX e XX,* org. Elciene Azevedo et al. (Campinas: Editora da Unicamp 2009), 300–301; cf. Pereira, *Footballmania,* 256–58.

56. Fatima Martin Rodrigues Ferreira, "Futebol de fábrica em São Paulo" (Master's thesis, Universidade de São Paulo 1992), 42–46.

57. [Rodrigues] Filho, *O negro,* 37.

58. Marcos Guterman, *O futebol explica o Brasil: Uma história da maior expressão popular do país* (São Paulo: Contexto, 2009), 46.

59. Renan Almeida Barjud, "Raça em jogo: O negro no futebol campineiro no início do século XX" (Undergraduate thesis, Universidade Estadual de Campinas, 2008), 37; Pereira, *Footballmania,* 272.

60. Mazzoni, *História,* 90; Negreiros, "A cidade," 214–21.

61. Gilmar Mascarenhas de Jesús, "O futebol da *Canela Preta:* O negro e a modernidade em Porto Alegre," *Anos 90* 11 (1999): 149–50.

62. Streapco, "'Cego,'" 169–70.

63. Kim D. Butler, *Freedoms Given, Freedoms Won: Afro-Brazilians in Post-Abolition São Paulo and Salvador* (New Brunswick: Rutgers University Press, 1998), 221.

64. Barjud, "Raça," 39 and 39n96; Bruno Otávio de Lacerda Abrahão and Antonio Jorge Gonçalves Soares, "A imprensa negra e o futebol em São Paulo no início do século XX," *Revista Brasileira de Educação Física e Esporte* 26, no. 1 (2012): 68.

65. Abrahão and Soares, "A imprensa negra," 68–69; Barjud, "Raça," 39–40.

66. [Rodrigues] Filho, *O negro,* 32.

67. Adriana Oliveira de Freitas, "Abalou Bangu! A Fábrica Bangu e a república nascente (1889–1914)" (Master's thesis, Universidade Federal do Espírito Santo, 2005).

68. [Rodrigues] Filho, *O negro,* 32. Carregal was not the first Afro-Brazilian to play at a big football club; Ponte Preta AA had several mulatto and *preto* players in 1900. Santos Neto, *Visão do jogo,* 70.

69. Lopes, "Classe," 132; [Rodrigues] Filho, *O negro,* 90–99.

70. "Gazeta dos sports," *Gazeta de Notícias,* 10 May 1907; Pereira, *Footballmania,* 66–67.

71. "Gazeta dos sports," *Gazeta de Notícias,* 26 June 1907; Santos, "Uma breve história," 41–42.

72. Pereira, *Footballmania,* 66–67.

73. Alexandre da Costa, *O tigre do futebol: Uma viagem nos tempos de Arthur Friedenreich* (São Paulo: DBA Editora, 1999), 13.

74. "As commemorações jubilares de Friedenreich," *Folha da Noite,* 4 Jul. 1934.

75. Decio de Almeida Prado, "Recordações de Leônidas (da Silva)" (1961), in *Seres, coisas, lugares: Do teatro ao futebol* (São Paulo: Companhia das Letras, 1997), 189–90.

76. Costa, *O tigre,* 18–19.

77. Newton César de Oliveira Santos, *Brasil X Argentina: Histórias do maior clássico do futebol mundial (1908–2008)* (São Paulo: Editora Scortecci, 2009), 61.

78. "Os 'cracks' da 'Copa Roca' de 1914," *A Gazeta Esportiva,* 8 Dec. 1945; "A carreira gloriosa do mais perfeito e famoso futebolista brasileiro de todos os tempos," in Thomaz Mazzoni, *Almanaque esportivo: 1939* (São Paulo: n.p., [1939]), 9.

79. "Salve Brazileiros!" *Vida Sportiva,* 31 May 1919.

80. "Recorder é viver . . . ," in Mazzoni, *Almanaque,* 83–91; Mazzoni, *História,* 41; Roberto Sander, *Sul-Americano de 1919: Quando o Brasil descobriu o futebol* (Rio de Janeiro: Maquinária, 2009), 25–27; Alexandre de Costa, "O primeiro rei do futebol," *Revista de História,* 2 Dec. 2011.

81. "As nossas victorias," *Vida Sportiva,* 7 Jun. 1919.

82. Santos, *Brasil X Argentina,* 81.

83. Fábio Franzini, *Corações na ponta da chuteira: Capítulos iniciais do futebol brasileiro (1919–1938)* (Rio de Janeiro: DP & A Editora, 2003), 41–42; Sander, *Sul-Americano,* 25–27; Costa, "O primeiro rei"; Mazzoni, *Almanaque,* 7, 9; Mazzoni, *História,* 41.

84. [Rodrigues] Filho, *O negro,* 60; J. Victtor, *A discussão do Pó-de-Arroz com o Urubu* (Rio de Janeiro: Academia Brasileira de Literatura de Cordel, n.d.).

85. Arthur Friedenreich papers, Rio de Janeiro. My special thanks to Cesar Oliveira for allowing me access to this collection.

86. [Rodrigues] Filho, *O negro,* 61.

87. [Rodrigues] Filho, *O negro,* 60–61; Anatol Rosenfeld, *Negro, macumba e futebol* (São Paulo: Editora Perspectiva, 2000), 98

88. Rosenfeld, *Negro,* 98–99; [Rodrigues] Filho, *O negro,* 112.

89. "Café com leite," *O Imparcial,* 10 Jan. 1920.

90. "Futebol," *O Imparcial,* 7 Feb. 1919; Costa, *O tigre,* 28.

91. Caldas, *O pontapé,* 43; Costa, *O tigre,* 25.

92. Sander, *Sul-Americano,* 72.

93. Leonardo Affonso de Miranda Pereira, "Pelos campos da nação: Um *goal-keeper* nos primeiro anos do futebol brasileiro," *Estudos Históricos* 19 (1997): 23–40; Silva, *Futebol Brasil memória,* 123.

94. Cited in Pereira, "Pelos campos," 28.

95. [Rodrigues] Filho, *O negro,* 74–75.

96. "O amor entrou em campo," *Correio da Manhã,* 13 Apr. 1970.

97. Compare Pereira, "Pelos campos," 36.

98. Pereira, "Pelos campos," 32–33; "O amor entrou em campo," *Correio da Manhã,* 13 Apr. 1970.

99. Fernando Azevedo in Carlos Guilherme Mota, *Ideologia da cultura brasileira (1933–1974)* (São Paulo: Editora Ática, 1985), 78.

100. Maurício da Silva Drumond Costa, *Nações em jogo: Esporte e propaganda política em Vargas e Perón* (Rio de Janeiro: Apicuri, 2008). The appropriation of samba remained a struggle for the state; Bryan McCann, *Hello, Hello Brazil: Popular Music in the Making of Modern Brazil* (Durham: Duke University Press, 2004), chap. 2; Daryle Williams, *Culture Wars in Brazil: The First Vargas Regime, 1930–1945* (Durham: Duke University Press, 2001), 84–87; Hermano Vianna, *The Mystery of Samba: Popular Music and National Identity in Brazil* (Durham: Duke University Press, 1999), esp. 41–42.

101. Gregg P. Bocketti, "Brazil in International Football, 1900–1925," in *Negotiating Identities in Modern Latin America,* ed. Hendrik Kraay (Calgary: University of Calgary Press, 2004), 79; Pereira, *Footballmania,* 139.

102. Santos Neto, *Visão do jogo,* 94; Ivan Soter, *Enciclopédia da Seleção: As Seleções Brasileiras de Futebol, 1914–2002* (Rio de Janeiro: Folha Seca, 2002), 25–26.

103. "Foot-ball," *O Imparcial,* 11 Jul. 1914; Pereira, *Footballmania,* 140–41.

104. "Pall-Mall Rio: foot-ball," *O Paiz,* 4 Sep. 1916, quoted in Pereira, *Footballmania,* 147.

105. Peixoto, "A educação nacional," in *Poeira de estrada: Ensaios de crítica e de história,* 2nd ed. (Rio de Janeiro: Francisco Alves, 1921), 285–88; Leonardo Affonso de Miranda Pereira, "O jogo dos sentidos: Os literatos e a popularização do futebol no Rio de Janeiro," in *A história contada: capítulos de história social da literatura no Brasil,* org. Sidney Chalhoub and Leonardo Affonso de M. Pereira (Rio de Janeiro: Nova Fronteira, 1998), 203.

106. Pereira, "O jogo dos sentidos," 210–13.

107. Netto, "Innovação brasileira," *Sports* 1, no. 1 (Nov. 1919); "Campeonato Sul-Americano—ligeiras considerações," *O Estado de São Paulo,* 30 May 1919; Franzini, "As raízes," 6.

108. "O Campeonato Sul-Americano de 1919 termina com o magnifico triumpho dos brasileiros," *Correio da Manhã,* 30 May 1919.

109. João Manuel Casquinha Malaia Santos, "'Diplomacia do pé': O Brasil e as competições esportivas sul-americanas de 1919 e 1922," *Tempo e Argumento* 3, no. 2 (Jul. / Dec. 2011): 60–61; Diego Santos Vieira de Jesus and Valéria Lima Guimarães, "Muito além da festa: O VI sul-americano e as relações internacionais no centenário da independência do Brasil," in *1922: Celebrações esportivas do centenário,* org. João Manuel C. Malaia Santos and Victor Andrade de Melo (Rio de Janeiro: 7letras / FAPERJ, 2012), 53–54.

110. Denaldo Alchorne de Souza, *O Brasil entra em campo! Construções e reconstruções da identidade nacional (1930–1947)* (São Paulo: Annablume, 2008), 33; Ricardo Pinto dos Santos, "Comemorando o Brasil: Que Brasil?" in Santos and Melo, *1922,* 176; "Os esportes no Centenário—Porque o Brasil tem feito má figura no Campeonato—Friedenreich diz duras verdades," *Diário de Notícias* (Salvador), 28 Sep. 1922; *Careta* (Rio de Janeiro), 7 Oct. 1922, 42.

111. Gilberto Agostino, "Nós e *Ellos, Nosotros y Eles*: Brasil X Argentina: Os inimigos fraternos," in *Memória social,* org. Silva and Santos, 64; and on preparations for the royal visit, see Sueann Caulfield, *In Defense of Honor: Sexual Morality, Modernity, and Nation in Early Twentieth-Century Brazil* (Durham: Duke University Press, 2000), 48–78.

112. Santos, *Brasil X Argentina,* 86–93.

113. "O Seleccionado Brasileiro—Os elementos de côr como indesejaveis!" *O Estado de São Paulo,* 18 Sep. 1921.

114. "Para o campeonato sul-americano," *Correio da Manhã,* 17 Sep. 1921; "O sul americano: Negros e mulatos," *O Paiz,* 27 Jul. 1921; Santos, *Brasil X Argentina,* 96; Pereira, *Footballmania,* 174–79.

115. Santos, *Brasil X Argentina,* 97; Pereira, *Footballmania,* 177–78.

116. Costa, *O tigre,* 67.

117. Paulistas referred to the CBD, headquartered in Rio, as an unloving "stepmother" (*madrasta*). Boris Fausto, *O crime no restaurante chinês: Carnaval, futebol e justiça na Sao Paulo dos anos 30* (São Paulo: Companhia das Letras, 2009), 152.

118. Mazzoni, *História,* 221–23; Caldas, *O pontapé,* 198–200.

119. Mazzoni, *História,* 247–49; Soter, *Enciclopédia,* 52–53.

120. "Rescaldo da Copa foi desastrosa," *Última Hora,* 7 Apr. 1964.

121. João Lyra Filho, *Cachimbo, pijama e chinelos: Memórias* (São Paulo: Editora Edaglit, 1963), 263–64.

122. Franco Júnior, *Dança,* 80; Lamartine Pereira da Costa and Plinio Labriola, "Bodies from Brazil: Fascist Aesthetics in a South American Setting," *International Journal of the History of Sport* 16, no. 4 (1999): 167.

123. Decreto 23.532, 19 Oct. 1933, *Coleção das Leis da República dos Estados Unidos do Brasil,* 1933, vol. 4 (Rio de Janeiro: Imprensa Nacional, 1934).

124. Pereira, *Footballmania,* 335.

125. Fábio Franzini, "As raízes do país do futebol: Estudo sobre a relação entre o futebol e a nacionalidade brasileira (1919–1950)" (Master's thesis, Universidade de São Paulo, 2000), 44.

126. Costa, *Nações em jogo,* 58–59; Souza, *O Brasil entra,* 48–49.

127. *Jornal dos Sports,* 8 May 1934.

128. "Pode-se ir a Paris por 500 réis," *A Gazeta,* 6 Apr. 1938; Souza, *O Brasil entra,* 62–63; Franzini, *Corações,* 70–71.

129. Decreto-lei 3.199, 14 Apr. 1941, *Diário Oficial da União,* 17 Apr. 1941.

130. Souza, *O Brasil entra,* 85.

131. "Alberto Byington Júnior fala sobre a transmissão do campeonato Mundial de Futebol," *A Gazeta,* 4 Jun. 1938.

132. "Os brasileiros precisam vencer a superstição das estreias," *Jornal dos Sports,* 4 Jun. 1938.

133. "O jogo Brasil-Polônia e a confraternização das colônias," *A Gazeta,* 8 Jun. 1938.

134. "Estrangeiros, mas brasileiros," *A Gazeta,* 7 Jun. 1938.

135. "O jogo Brasil-Polônia e a confraternização das colônias," *A Gazeta,* 8 Jun. 1938; and compare "Tudo contra o Brasil," *Jornal dos Sports,* 10 Jun. 1938.

136. "A palavra de entusiasmo do Ministro da Educação," *Correio da Manhã,* 15 Jun. 1938; Plínio José de Labriola Campos Negreiros, "A nação entra em campo: O futebol nos anos 30 e 40" (PhD diss., Pontifícia Universidade Católica-São Paulo, 1998), 277–81.

137. Velloso, "Os intelectuais e a política cultural do Estado Novo," in *O Brasil republicano,* vol 2, *O tempo do nacional-estatismo: Do início da década de 1930 ao apogeu do Estado Novo,* org. Jorge Ferreira and Lucilia de Almeida Neves Delgado, 5th ed. (Rio de Janeiro: Civilização Brasileira, 2012), 172.

138. "O treino de hontem em Caxambu," *A Gazeta—Edição Esportiva,* 4 Apr. 1938, in Franzini, "As raízes," 47. Not all members of the 1938 Seleção shared a sense of patriotic uplift; Luizinho and Leônidas da Silva in Franzini, "As raízes," 49.

139. *Jornal dos Sports,* 8 Mar. 1938, quoted in Machado, "Bola na rede," 24.

140. "A comissão explica porque escalou certos elementos," *O Globo,* 24 Jun. 1931; Leonardo Affonso de Miranda Pereira, "Domingos do Brasil: Futebol, raça e nacionalidade na trajetória de um herói do Estado Novo," *Locus: Revista de História* 13, no. 2 (2007): 194–95; Thomaz Soares da Silva (Zizinho), *Verdades e mentiras no futebol* (Niterói: Imprensa Oficial, 2001), 27.

141. Aidan Hamilton, *Domingos da Guia: O Divino Mestre* (Rio de Janeiro: Gryphus, 2005), 73.

142. [Rodrigues] Filho, *O sapo de Arubinha: Os anos de sonho do futebol brasileiro* (São Paulo: Companhia das Letras, 1994), 16–17; José Miguel Wisnik, *Veneno remédio: O futebol e o Brasil* (São Paulo: Companhia das Letras, 2008), 199.

143. Zizinho quoted in Kleber Mazziero de Souza, *Divino: A vida e a arte de Ademir da Guia* (Rio de Janeiro: Gryphus, 2001), 39; Hamilton, *Domingos,* 73, 104.

144. Mário [Rodrigues] Filho, "Aquele 'dribbling' de Domingos," *O Globo,* 8 Sep. 1931; Hamilton, *Domingos,* 74–75.

145. Hamilton, *Domingos,* 30–32.

146. Hamilton, *Domingos,* 24, 35–37; *O Imparcial,* 12 Aug. 1928; Domingos da Guia, Depoimentos para a posteridade, MIS-RJ, 1967.

147. Souza, *Divino,* 17.

148. Pereira, "Domingos," 198–99; Domingos da Guia, Depoimentos.

149. Pereira, "Domingos," 200; Hamilton, *Domingos,* 87.

150. Domingos da Guia, Depoimentos; Pereira, "Domingos," 202–3.

151. Domingos da Guia, Depoimentos.

152. Pereira, *Footballmania,* 324.

153. "Não tenham ilusões: Cada jogador é um monstro," *Última Hora,* 3 Jun. 1957; Hamilton, *Domingos,* 174–77.

154. Quoted in Hamilton, *Domingos,* 190.

155. "Jogadores, pretos e sem cartaz, sao perseguidos pelo juiz Mário Viana," *Última Hora,* 10 Jun. 1957; "Kruschner foi o 'coveiro' de Fausto," *Última Hora,* 6 Jun. 1957; "Porque Flavio barrou Leônidas em 48," *Última Hora,* 22 Jun. 1957; "O cavalário de Gentil é a pele escura," *Última Hora,* 8 Jun. 1957.

156. "Passe: Mercado de escravos," *Última Hora,* 14 Jun. 1957.

157. "Concentracao. Prisao sem grades," *Última Hora,* 17 Jun. 1957.

158. "Tudo que possuo, devo ao futebol," *Última Hora,* 15 Mar. 1952; Pereira, "Domingos," 213.

159. Cesar C. Gordon Jr., "História social dos negros no futebol brasileiro: Primeiro tempo: 'Essa maravilhosa obra de arte fruto da mistura,'" *Pesquisa de Campo* 2 (1996): 89.

160. "Garotos-propaganda," *Folha de São Paulo,* 14 Dec. 2000.

161. Domingos da Guia, 1998, quoted in Pereira, "Domingos," 210–11.

162. On the myth of Leônidas, see Souza, *O Brasil entra,* 117–70.

163. "Leônidas conta a sua vida nas canchas de foot ball," *O Globo,* 17 Sep. 1931; Pereira, *Footballmania,* 312–13.

164. "Memórias de Leônidas: Da bola de meia aos primeiros 5 mil réis," *Última Hora,* 25 Mar. 1964.

165. Ribeiro, *Diamante,* 24.

166. "Eu não irei para o América," *O Globo,* 17 Oct. 1931.

167. [Rodrigues] Filho, *O negro,* 188–90; Robert Levine, "Sport and Society: The Case of Brazilian *Futebol,*" *Luso-Brazilian Review* 17, no. 2 (1980): 238.

168. Ribeiro, *Diamante,* 36–47.

169. "Tempos de Leônidas," in Orlando Duarte and Mário Vilela, *São Paulo FC: O supercampeão* (São Paulo: Editora Companhia Nacional, 2011), 77–110.

170. [Rodrigues] Filho, *Copa Rio Branco de 1932* (Rio de Janeiro: Irmãos Pongetti, 1943), 138; Ribeiro, *Diamante,* 71.

171. "O 'Diamante Negro,'" *A Batalha,* 4 May 1932; Ribeiro, *Diamante,* 39.

172. *A Gazeta,* 23 Mar. 1938, quoted in Felipe Morelli Machado, "Bola na rede e povo nas ruas! Estado Novo, Imprensa esportiva e torcedores na Copa do Mundo de 1938: O futebol construindo a 'nação,'" *Recorde: Revista de História do Esporte* 4, no. 1 (2011): 26.

173. "Zarzur, Leônidas, Luna e outros multados pela Censura," *A Batalha,* 1 Sep. 1932.

174. Roberto Sander, *Anos 40: Viagem à década sem Copa* (Rio de Janeiro: Bom Texto, 2004), 64–67.

175. Ribeiro, *Diamante,* 170–89.

176. See esp. Prado, "Recordações."

177. "Malabarista e artilheiro prodigioso," in Mazzoni, *Almanaque,* 34–37.

178. Wisnik, *Veneno,* 183.

179. Jeffrey Needell, "Identity, Race, Gender, and Modernity in the Origins of Gilberto Freyre's *Oeuvre,*" *American Historical Review* 100, no. 1 (1995): 51–77.

180. Júlio Barata noted that "Dr. Gilberto Freyre has already taken advantage of the triumph over the Czechs to prove that the African element is an excellent reinforcement for our race"; "O meu palpite," *A Batalha,* 16 Jun. 1938.

181. "Foot-ball mulato," *Diario de Pernambuco,* 17 Jun. 1938.

182. See also "Prefácio à 1a. edição," [Rodrigues] Filho, *O Negro,* 24–26; "A propósito de futebol brasileiro," *O Cruzeiro,* 18 Jun. 1955; "Ainda a propósito de futebol brasileiro," *O Cruzeiro,* 25 Jun. 1955; "Futebol desbrasileirado?" *Diário de Pernambuco,* 30 Jun. 1974; *Novo mundo nos trópicos,* 2nd ed. (Rio de Janeiro: Topbooks, 2000 [orig. English ed. 1945; orig. Portuguese ed. 1963]).

183. His grand narrative of Brazilian history appears in *Casa-grande e senzala,* 2nd ed. (Rio de Janeiro: Schmidt, 1936 [1933]); and *Sobrados e mucambos: Decadência do patriacalismo rural e desenvolvimento do urbano,* 3rd ed., 2 vols. (Rio de Janeiro: José Olympio, 1968 [1936]).

184. *Novo Mundo,* 143.

185. Roberto Ventura, *Estilo tropical: História cultural e polêmicas literárias no Brasil, 1870–1914* (São Paulo: Companhia das Letras, 1991), 66–68; Thomas E. Skidmore, *Black Into White: Race and Nationality in Brazilian Thought* (Durham: Duke University Press, 1993), esp. 184–92; Tiago Maranhão, "Apollonians and Dionysians: The Role of Football in Gilberto Freyre's Vision of Brazilian People," *Soccer & Society* 8, no. 4 (2007): 513. On uses of "scientific" racial theories from the North Atlantic, see Lilia Moritz Schwarcz, *O espetáculo das raças: Cientistas, instituições e questão racial no Brasil, 1870–1930* (São Paulo: Companhia das Letras, 1993); Nancy Leys Stepan, *"The Hour of Eugenics": Race, Gender, and Nation in Latin America* (Ithaca: Cornell University Press, 1991).

186. "O treino dos scratchs, hontem no stadium do Fluminense," *A Batalha,* 11 Jul. 1931; Silva, *Mil e uma noites,* 148–49.

187. Freyre, "Prefácio," 25.

188. Freyre, "Ainda"; and on his later focus on Garrincha see Jorge Ventura de Morais and José Luiz Ratton Júnior, "Gilberto Freyre e o futebol: entre processos sociais gerais e biografias individuais," *Revista de Ciências Sociais* 42, no. 1 (2011): 102.

189. Vianna, *The Mystery,* 1–9.

190. [Rodrigues] Filho, *Copa do Rio Branco,* 32, 7.

191. Fatima Martin Rodrigues Ferreira Antunes, *"Com brasileiro, não há quem possa!": Futebol e identidade nacional em José Lins do Rego, Mário Filho e Nelson Rodrigues* (São Paulo: Editora UNESP, 2004), 52.

192. *Jornal dos Sports,* 16 May 1949, in Antunes, *"Com brasileiro,"* 65.

193. Ruy Castro, *O anjo pornográfico: A vida de Nelson Rodrigues* (São Paulo: Companhia das Letras, 1992), 154.

194. Gordon Jr., "História social," 71.

195. Castro, *O anjo,* 132–33.

196. He added two chapters, "The Confirmation of the Black" and "The Time of the Black," to the second edition, published in 1964.

197. Souza, *O Brasil entra,* 171–94.

198. [Rodrigues] Filho, *O negro,* 215–18; Souza, *O Brasil entra,* 171–94; Gordon Jr., "História social"; Lopes, "Class"; Silva, *Mil e uma noites;* Maranhão, "Apollonians"; Roberto DaMatta, "Esporte na sociedade: Um ensaio sobre o futebol brasileiro," in DaMatta et al., *Universo do futebol,* 19–42.

199. Nicolau Sevcenko, "A capital irradiante: Técnica, ritmos e ritos no Rio," in *História da vida privada no Brasil*, vol. 3, *República: Da Belle Époque à era do radio*, org. Sevcenko (São Paulo: Companhia das Letras, 1998), 581.

200. Paulina L. Alberto, *Terms of Inclusion: Black Intellectuals in Twentieth-Century Brazil* (Chapel Hill: University of North Carolina Press, 2011), 110.

201. Vianna, *The Mystery of Samba*, esp. 41–42; Jorge Caldeira, *A construção do samba* (São Paulo: Mameluco, 2007), esp. 94–105; McCann, *Hello, Hello Brazil*, esp. 52.

202. There was a notable Carioca orientation in soccer, as there was in samba and Carnaval; Arlei Sander Damo, "Ah! Eu Sou Gaúcho: O nacional e o regional no futebol brasileiro," *Estudos Históricos* 23 (1999): 87 117; Alberto, *Terms of Inclusion*, 109, 111.

203. Tiago Fernandes Maranhão and Jorge Knijnik, "*Futebol mulato:* Racial constructs in Brazilian football," *Cosmopolitan Civil Societies Journal*, 3, no. 2 (2011): esp. 66; cf. Needell, "Identity, Race."

204. Pereira, *Footballmania*, 340.

205. Antonio Risério, *A utopia brasileira e os movimentos negros* (São Paulo: Editora 34, 2007), esp. 299–323.

206. Luiz Henrique de Toledo, "Didi: A trajetória da folha-seca no futebol de marca brasileira," in *Memória afro-brasileira*, vol. 2, *Artes do corpo*, org. Vagner Gonçalves da Silva (São Paulo: Selo Negro Edições, 2004), 86–87; Rosenfeld, *Negro*, 87; Pereira, *Footballmania*, 319–21.

207. "A tragédia do futebol brasileiro: A seleção de todos os tempos," *Última Hora*, 1 Jul. 1957; compare Gordon Jr., "História social," 81–83.

208. Maranhão and Knijnik, "*Futebol mulato*," esp. 63.

209. Robin E. Sheriff, *Dreaming Equality: Color, Race, and Racism in Urban Brazil* (New Brunswick: Rutgers University Press, 2001), esp. 4–11.

210. Cf. Pereira, "Pelos campos," 36.

CHAPTER 2

Epigraph: Mário [Rodrigues] Filho, *Copa do Mundo, 62* (Rio de Janeiro: Edições O Cruzeiro, 1962), 335–36.

1. *1958: O ano em que o mundo descobriu o Brasil*, dir. José Carlos Asbeg (Brazil, 2008).

2. Hornby, *Fever Pitch* (New York: Riverhead Books, 1998), 38. Armando Nogueira described the 1970 team as "the ideal of soccer" at the time; *Bola na rede*, 2nd ed. (Rio de Janeiro: J. Olympio, 1974), 162.

3. Marcos Chor Maio, "A questão racial no pensamento de Guerreiro Ramos," in *Raça, ciência e sociedade*, org. Marcos Chor Maio and Ricardo Ventura Santos (Rio de Janeiro: FIOCRUZ / CCBB, 1996), 179–93.

4. Roberto DaMatta, *Carnavais, malandros e heróis: Para uma sociologia do dilema brasileiro* (Rio de Janeiro: Zahar Editores, 1983). On areas of "softer" and "harder" discrimination, see Livio Sansone, *Blackness Without Ethnicity: Constructing Race in Brazil* (New York: Palgrave Macmillan, 2003).

5. "A Seleção de todos os tempos," *Última Hora*, 1 Jul. 1957.

6. Roberto Sander, *Anos 40: Viagem à década sem Copa* (Rio de Janeiro: Bom Texto, 2004).

7. On the 1950 defeat and national honor, see Arno Vogel, "O momento feliz, reflexões sobre o futebol e o ethos nacional," in Roberto DaMatta et al., *Universo do futebol: Esporte e*

sociedade brasileira (Rio de Janeiro: Edições Pinakotheke, 1982), 108; on disbelief, see "Permanece a onda de descrença em torno da representação do Brasil," *Folha da Noite,* 14 Apr. 1953; "O que falta não é sistema de jogo, é jogo mesmo," *Folha da Noite,* 21 Sep. 1954.

8. "O quadrúpede de 28 patas" and "Complexo de vira-latas" in Nelson Rodrigues, *À sombra das chuteiras imortais: Crônicas de futebol* (São Paulo: Companhia das Letras, 1995), 50–52.

9. Nelson Rodrigues, "O triunfo do homem," in *À sombra,* 58–59; Sander, *Anos 40,* 5; Armando Nogueira, *O homem e a bola* (Rio de Janeiro: Globo, 1988), 39.

10. Charles A. Perrone and Christopher Dunn, "'Chiclete com Banana': Internationalization in Brazilian Popular Music," in *Brazilian Popular Music and Globalization,* ed. Perrone and Dunn (New York: Routledge, 2001), 16–18; Ruy Castro, *Bossa Nova: The Story of the Brazilian Music That Seduced the World,* trans. Lysa Salsbury (Chicago: A Capella, 2000); Robert Stam, *Tropical Multiculturalism: A Comparative History of Race in Brazilian Cinema and Culture* (Durham: Duke University Press, 1997), 166–79, 213–31.

11. James Holston, *The Modernist City: An Anthropological Critique of Brasília* (Chicago: University of Chicago Press, 1989); Guilherme Wisnik, "Doomed to Modernity," in *Brazil's Modern Architecture,* ed. Elisabetta Andreoli and Adrian Forty (London: Phaidon, 2004), 22–55.

12. Thomas E. Skidmore, *The Politics of Military Rule in Brazil, 1964–1985* (New York: Oxford University Press, 1988), chap. 1; Joel W. Wolfe, *Working Women, Working Men: São Paulo and the Rise of Brazil's Industrial Working Class, 1900–1955* (Durham: Duke University Press, 1993), chap. 6; Murilo Leal, *A reinvenção da classe trabalhadora (1953–1964)* (Campinas: Editora da UNICAMP, 2011), chap. 6.

13. Jorge Ferreira, "O governo Goulart e o golpe civil-militar de 1964," in *O Brasil republicano,* vol 3., *O tempo da experiência democrática: Da democratização de 1945 ao golpe civil-militar de 1964,* org. Jorge Ferreira and Lucilia de Almeida Neves Delgado, 4th ed. (Rio de Janeiro: Civilização Brasileira, 2011), 343–404; Shawn C. Smallman, *Fear and Memory in the Brazilian Army and Society, 1889–1954* (Chapel Hill: University of North Carolina Press, 2002), chap. 8.

14. Miguel Archanjo Freitas Júnior, "Razão e paixão no futebol: Tentativas de implementação de um projeto modernizador," in *Futebol e globalização,* org. Luiz Ribeiro (Jundiaí, SP: Editora Fontoura, 2007), 213–33, and "No meio do caminho: Tensões presentes nas representações sobre o futebol e o ideal da modernidade brasileira na década de 1950" (PhD diss., Universidade Federal do Paraná, 2009).

15. On the spread of radio and TV audiences, see Esther Hamburger, "Diluindo fronteiras: A televisão e as novelas no cotidiano," in *História da vida privada no Brasil,* vol. 4, *Contrastes da intimidade contemporânea,* org. Lilia Moritz Schwarcz (São Paulo: Companhia das Letras, 1998), 448–49.

16. Nelson Rodrigues, *A pátria em chuteiras: Novas crônicas de futebol* (São Paulo: Companhia das Letras, 1994).

17. Mário [Rodrigues] Filho, "O que nos falta," *Jornal dos Sports,* 5 Jul. 1957.

18. "Barbosa: 'Em cinqüenta os desmandos vieram de cima,'" *Última Hora,* 14 Jan. 1958.

19. Rafael Casé, *O artilheiro que não sorriu: Quarentinha, o maior goleador da história do Botafogo* (Rio de Janeiro: R. Casé, 2008), 47–48.

20. Eduardo Valls, *1956: Uma epopéia gaúcha no México* (Porto Alegre: WS Editor, 2005); Ivan Soter, *Enciclopédia da Seleção: As Seleções Brasileiras de Futebol* (Rio de Janeiro: Folha Seca, 2002), 106, 117–19, 131, 136.

21. Tom Cardoso and Roberto Rockmann, *O marechal da vitória: Uma história de rádio, TV e futebol* (São Paulo: A Girafa, 2005), 139; Freitas Júnior, "Razão," 214–15.

22. Ernesto Rodrigues, *Jogo duro: A história de João Havelange* (Rio de Janeiro: Record, 2007), 60–61.

23. Cardoso and Rockmann, *O marechal,* 147–49.

24. Ernesto Rodrigues, *Jogo duro,* 62; Cid Pinheiro Cabral and Ruy Carlos Ostermann, *O admirável futebol brasileiro: A história da evolução e das grandes passagens do futebol brasileiro* (Porto Alegre: Edição de Gaúcha, s.d.), 67–68; "Plano inovador leva o Brasil ao topo," *Folha de São Paulo,* 4 May 2008; Hilário Franco Júnior, *A dança dos deuses: Futebol, sociedade, cultura* (São Paulo: Companhia das Letras, 2007), 133.

25. Ernesto Rodrigues, *Jogo duro,* 62.

26. "Dominados os campeões do mundo," *Folha da Noite,* 17 Apr. 1952; "Campeonato Pan-Americano de Foot-ball—o Brasil vence, brilhantemente, os campeões do mundo por 4 × 2," *Última Hora,* 17 Apr. 1952; "Mantida a hegemonia—derrotados outra vez os campeões do mundo," *Folha da Noite,* 16 Mar. 1954.

27. João Lyra Filho, *Taça do Mundo, 1954* (Rio de Janeiro: Irmãos Pongetti, 1954), 52–53.

28. Nelson Rodrigues, "Freud no futebol," *Manchete Esportiva,* 7 Apr. 1956, 10; Freitas Júnior, "Razão," 216.

29. Roberto Porto, *Didi: Treino é treino, jogo é jogo* (Rio de Janeiro: Relume Dumará, 2001), 43–44; Nilton Santos, *Minha bola, minha vida* (Rio de Janeiro: Gryphus, 2000), 74; "Relatório: Realismo ou preconceito?" *O Globo,* 18 May 2008; Marcos Guterman, *O futebol explica o Brasil: Uma história da maior expressão popular do país* (São Paulo: Contexto, 2009), 125.

30. "Joao Havelange na porta do 'inferno': 'Sou a favor de Solich mas não contra os outros'" and Nelson Rodrigues, "A ideia fixa de 1950," *Última Hora,* 23 Jan. 1958; "O ponto de vista do supervisor Paulo Machado de Carvalho: 'Apoio Flávio Costa porque a experiência tem valor inestimável num "mundial,"'" *Última Hora,* 24 Jan. 1958; "O 'scratch' já tem treinador: Feola, mas agora está faltando um assessor," *Última Hora,* 11 Feb. 1958; "A C.B.D. ontem hoje e amanhã," *Manchete Esportiva,* 25 Jan. 1958, 37–42; cf. "De caráter pessoal a carta do presidente," *Correio da Manhã,* 8 Apr. 1958; "Provocou uma reunião secreta e pede resposta ao presidente," *Última Hora,* 8 Apr. 1958.

31. *Dino Sani (depoimento, 2011)* (Rio de Janeiro: CPDOC / FGV, 2011).

32. "Encontro com JK para decisão sôbre a verba do Copa do Mundo," *Última Hora,* 17 Mar. 1958; "Segunda feira, no Palácio Rio Negro, audiência com o Presidente J.K.," *Última Hora,* 29 Mar. 1958; Freitas Júnior, "Razão," 217–18. Havelange and Carvalho contributed their own money when Italian clubs delayed their payments; Guterman, *O futebol,* 124; Cardoso and Rockmann, *O marechal,* 165–66.

33. "Dr. Hilton Gosling: 'Levaremos para a Suécia um selecionado em perfeita condição física e psicológica,'" *Última Hora,* 22 Apr. 1958; Freitas Júnior, "No meio," 125–26.

34. Geraldo Romualdo Silva, "Roteiro do médico para o scratch não morrer de saudade," *Jornal dos Sports,* 14 Aug. 1957.

35. Guterman, *O futebol,* 122; Ruy Castro, *Estrela solitária: Um brasileira chamado Garrincha* (São Paulo: Companhia das Letras, 1995), 135.

36. Nascimento, *Pelé,* 82–83; José Macia (Pepe), *Bombas de alegria: Meio século de histórias do Canhão da Vila,* 2nd ed. (Santos: Realejo Edições, 2009), 33.

37. "Começarão os exames dos jogadores brasileiros," *Última Hora,* 5 Apr. 1958; "Apenas Jadir e Atlair não foram aprovados nos exames," *Última Hora,* 8 Apr. 1958.

38. Castro, *Estrela,* 132; and cf. Guterman, *O futebol,* 122. Estimates of the number of extractions range from thirty-two to more than 400.

39. "Garrincha e Orlando viajam para Araxá," *Última Hora*, 22 Apr. 1958; Castro, *Estrela*, 136–37; "Apenas Jadir e Atlair não foram aprovados nos exames," *Última Hora*, 8 Apr. 1958.

40. Castro, *Estrela*, 136–37; Santos, *Minha bola*, 76–78; Almir Albuquerque (o Pernambuquinho), *Eu e o futebol* (São Paulo: Editora Abril, 1973), 55.

41. "Dr. Hilton Gosling: 'Levaremos para a Suécia um selecionado em perfeita condição física e psicológica,'" *Última Hora*, 22 Apr. 1958; "Hilton Gosling em Florença: 'Estado físico invejável dos atletas brasileiros,'" *Última Hora*, 28 May 1958.

42. *Dino Sani, (depoimento 2011);* Sandro Moreyra, *Histórias de Sandro Moreyra* (Rio de Janeiro: Ed. JB, 1985), 100–101; Renato Pompeu, *Canhoteiro: O homem que driblou a glória* (Rio de Janeiro: Relume Dumará / Ediouro, 2003).

43. Zizinho, Depoimentos para a posteridade, Museu da Imagem e do Som, Rio de Janeiro, 1985; *Dino Sani, (depoimento 2011)*.

44. Santos, *Minha bola*, 75; *1958: O ano*.

45. Helmut Senekowicz, in *1958: O ano*.

46. Porto, *Didi*, 44; Toledo, "Didi," 107.

47. Didi and Carvalho in *1958: O ano*.

48. *Garrincha, alegria do povo*, dir. Joaquim Pedro de Andrade (Brazil, 1962).

49. Nelson Rodrigues, "Originalidade gaga," in *A pátria*, 131–32; compare Nelson Rodrigues, "O brasileiro é o melhor," *Última Hora*, 16 Jun. 1958; Armando Nogueira, *A ginga e o jogo: Todas as emoções das melhores crônicas de Armando Nogueira* (Rio de Janeiro: Objetiva, 2003), 191; João Saldanha, *O trauma da bola: A Copa de 82 por João Saldanha* (São Paulo: Cosac & Naify, 2002), 40.

50. "Garrincha, o indomável; Didi, arquiteto da grande vitoria," *Última Hora*, 16 Jun. 1958.

51. "Mocidade e confiança, forças do 'scratch' que levamos à Suécia," *Correio da Manhã*, 20 May 1958.

52. Didi in Jorge Vasconcellos, org., *Recados da bola: Depoimentos de doze mestres do futebol brasileiro* (São Paulo: Cosac Naify, 2010), 184; Porto, *Didi*, 94; cf. Castro, *Estrela*, 176; Vieira, *Maracanã*, 75; Zagallo, Zito, Didi in *1958: O ano*.

53. Didi in Vasconcellos, *Recados*, 178.

54. Castro, *Estrela*, 107.

55. "Campeonato Pan-Americano de Foot-ball—o Brasil vence, brilhantemente, os campeões do mundo por 4 × 2," *Última Hora*, 17 Apr. 1952; Ribeiro, *Didi*, 38–39; Soter, *Enciclopédia*, 89–90.

56. For instance, "Itália queria que Didi fôsse 'oriundo,'" *Manchete Esportiva*, 21 Jun. 1958, 12.

57. Moacir in *1958: O ano*; Mário [Rodrigues] Filho, "O ideal de 16 de julho," in *O sapo de Arubinha: Os anos de sonho do futebol brasileiro* (São Paulo: Companhia das Letras, 1994), 202–5.

58. Nelson Rodrigues, "Meu personagem da semana," *Manchete Esportiva*, 4 Apr. 1959, 8.

59. Didi in Vasconcellos, *Recados*, 178.

60. Nelson Rodrigues, "Meu personagem da semana," *Manchete Esportiva*, 12 Jul. 1958, 8.

61. Porto, *Didi*, 77.

62. [Rodrigues] Filho, "O ideal de 16 de julho," 203; Castro, *Estrela*, 102.

63. Cabral and Ostermann, *O admirável*, 70; Santos, *Minha bola*, 75–76

64. Quoted in Casé, *O artilheiro,* 109.

65. Nelson Rodrigues, "Meu personagem da semana," *Manchete Esportiva,* 4 Apr. 1959, 8; the cover of this issue had a picture of one of Didi's wild tackles. See also Albuquerque, *Eu e o futebol,* 58; Porto, *Didi,* 107–9.

66. Nelson Rodrigues, "Meu personagem da semana," *Manchete Esportiva,* 4 Apr. 1959, 8; Didi quoted in Toledo, "Didi," 95.

67. Ribeiro, *Didi,* 30–31, 34–35, 44–45; "Até uma passagem a Paris destinada a Guiomar," *Gazeta de Noticias,* 23 Feb. 1956; "Os três mistérios da seleção brasileira," *Última Hora,* 5 Apr. 1958.

68. Castro, *Estrela,* 100; Toledo, "Didi," 92; Nelson Rodrigues, "Meu personagem da semana: Didi e Guiomar," in *O berro impresso das manchetes* (Rio de Janeiro: Agir, 2007), 369–70.

69. Porto, *Didi,* 89–90.

70. Toledo, "Didi," 110; Ribeiro, *Didi,* chap. 7; Porto, *Didi,* 115–17; Didi in Vasconcellos, *Recados,* 178–79.

71. Djalma Santos in Vasconcellos, *Recados,* 118; [Rodrigues] Filho, *Copa do Mundo, 62,* 144–47.

72. Didi in Vasconcellos, *Recados,* 182.

73. Nelson Rodrigues, "Meu personagem da semana," *Manchete Esportiva,* 4 Apr. 1959, 8; Nelson Rodrigues, "A mãe dos pernas-de-pau," "Garrincha, passarinho apedrejado," "O escrete de loucos" in *A pátria,* 58–59, 77, 81; Nelson Rodrigues, "Brasil X Áustria" and "Meu personagem da semana: Didi" in *O berro,* 72, 261–62.

74. Mário [Rodrigues] Filho, *O negro no futebol brasileiro,* 4th ed. (Rio de Janeiro: Mauad, 2003), 321; Mário [Rodrigues] Filho, *Viagem em torno de Pelé* (Rio de Janeiro: Editora do Autor, 1963), 163. Mário was among those who felt that Didi needed to run more during games; see "Didi dos nossos sonhos" in *O sapo,* 226–29. Cf. Toledo, "Didi," 93–95.

75. For comparisons of Garrincha and Pelé see José Miguel Wisnik, *Veneno remédio: O futebol e o Brasil* (São Paulo: Companhia das Letras, 2008), 267–93; José Sérgio Leite Lopes, "'The People's Joy' Vanishes: Considerations on the Death of a Soccer Player," special issue, *Journal of Latin American Anthropology* 4, no. 2 and 5, no. 1 (2000): 78–105.

76. "Pernas que chutam direito de linhas tortas," *Última Hora,* 1 Aug. 1953; "Garrincha, o que chuta direito por pernas tortas," *Última Hora,* 15 Sep. 1955; "Garrincha: As pernas mais famosas da Suécia são de homem," *Manchete Esportiva,* 28 Jun. 1958, 2–3.

77. *Garrincha, alegria do povo;* Lopes, "'The People's Joy'"; Tiago Lisboa Bartholo and Antonio Jorge Gonçalves Soares, "Mané Garrincha como síntese da identidade do futebol brasileiro," *Movimento* 15, no. 1 (2009): 169–91.

78. Décio Pignatari, *Contracomunicação,* 3rd ed. (Cotia, São Paulo: Ateliê Editorial, 2004), 191.

79. "O encontro dos sonhos," *Placar,* 19 Nov. 1982, 42–47.

80. José Castello, *Pelé: Os dez corações do Rei* (Rio de Janeiro: Ediouro, 2004), 54; and on Pelé's NASL years, see *Once in a Lifetime: The Extraordinary Story of the New York Cosmos,* dir. Paul Crowder and John Dower (U.S.A., 2006).

81. Castro, *Estrela,* 316, 319, 327–36.

82. Castro, *Estrela,* esp. 234–54, 263, 273–77, 292–96, 298–301, 305–25, 370–72, 437–52, 454–58, 480–82, 486–87; Bartholo and Soares, "Mané Garrincha"; and Lopes, "'The People's Joy.'"

83. Lopes, "'The People's Joy,'" 81.

84. Gonçalo Ferreira da Silva, *Faleceu Mané Garrincha o fabricante de Joãos* (n.p., n.d.), 8; compare Barboza Leite, *Garrincha alegria do povo—ou a história do passarinho que jogava futebol* (Duque de Caxias: n.p., 1977); Raimundo Santa Helena, *Mané Garrincha* (Rio de Janeiro: n.p., 1983); and Paulo Teixeira de Souza, *Vida, paixão e morte de Mané Garrincha, a alegria do povo* (Rio de Janeiro: Europa Empresa Gráfica e Editora, 1983).

85. Lopes, "'The People's Joy,'" 87.

86. Castro, *Estrela,* 11, 16–20.

87. Lopes, "'The People's Joy,'" 94; Leite, *Garrincha,* 2.

88. Castro, *Estrela,* 27–33.

89. Ibid., 35, 44.

90. Ibid., 286.

91. Castro, *Estrela,* 51–59; Santos, *Minha bola,* 99–100.

92. "Até o Exercito rejeitou Garrincha," *Última Hora,* 23 Jul. 1953; "O Botafogo acabou com o jogo logo de saida vencendo facil," *Última Hora,* 27 Jul. 1953; "Garrincha, esperança do futebol brasileiro, ameaça eclipsar-se!," *Última Hora,* 3 Nov. 1955.

93. Mário [Rodrigues] Filho, "O nosso Sputnik," in *O sapo,* 234–36.

94. "Técnica dos brasileiros venceu fôrça física dos russos," *Correio da Manhã,* 17 Jun. 1958; "O C.D.B. futebol clube impressiona o mundo," *Jornal do Brasil,* 17 Jun. 1958; Nogueira, *Bola na rede,* 54; "Brasil tirou de letra o futebol científico russo," *Manchete Esportiva,* 21 Jun. 1958, 32; Vavá was also dubbed "Sputnik" on the cover of this issue.

95. "Sempre temi os artistas, e os brasileiros são artistas . . . ," *Manchete Esportiva,* 21 Jun. 1958, 50–54; "Katchalin elogiou Garrincha" and "Garrincha devolveu à Selecao as características do futebol brasileiro," *Correio da Manhã,* 18 Jun. 1958.

96. "Ninguém pode deter Garrincha," *Correio da Manhã,* 1 Jul. 1958.

97. Castro, *Estrela,* 155.

98. Nelson Rodrigues, "Meu personagem da semana," in *O berro impresso,* 412.

99. Galeano, *Soccer in Sun and Shadow,* trans. Mark Fried (London: Verso, 1998), 100; [Rodrigues] Filho, *Viagem,* 188–89; Aldemir Martins, George Torok, and Araújo Netto, *Brasil futebol rei* (Rio de Janeiro: Image, 1965), 103; Nogueira, *Bola na rede,* 59; Flávio Araújo, *O rádio, o futebol e a vida* (São Paulo: Editora SENAC São Paulo, 2001), 145.

100. Nelson Rodrigues, "Meu personagem da semana," *Manchete Esportiva,* 21 Jun. 1958, 8.

101. [Rodrigues] Filho, *Copa do Mundo, 62,* 179–82; Cabral and Ostermann, *O admirável,* 80.

102. Castro, *Estrela,* 122; and cf. [Rodrigues] Filho, "Garrincha," in *O sapo,* 211.

103. Poet Carlos Drummond de Andrade said he displayed an "astute simplicity"; "Seleção de ouro," in *Quando é dia de futebol* (Rio de Janeiro: Record, 2002), 52.

104. Castro, *Estrela,* 107; João Saldanha, *Os subterrâneos do futebol* (Rio de Janeiro: Tempo Brasileiro, 1963), 140–41.

105. Ivan Soter, *Quando a bola era redonda* (Rio de Janeiro: Folha Seca, 2008), 78–83; Santos, *Minha bola,* 101–3; Castro, *Estrela,* 244.

106. Moreyra, *Histórias,* 99–100; Castro, *Estrela,* 91.

107. Quoted in Nogueira, *Bola na rede,* 58.

108. Nelson Rodrigues, "O essencial é o supérfluo," in *A pátria,* 186–87; Armando Nogueira, "O anjo que dribla," in *O homem,* 73–75; Pompeu, *Canhoteiro,* 43.

109. Nelson Rodrigues, "Complexo de vira-latas," 52; Nelson Rodrigues, "Meu personagem da semana," *Manchete Esportiva,* 21 Jun. 1958, 8.

110. Saldanha, *Os subterrâneos,* 158–62; and compare "O C.D.B. futebol clube impressiona o mundo," *Jornal do Brasil,* 17 Jun. 1958.

111. [Rodrigues] Filho, "Palavras aos jogadores brasileiros," *Jornal dos Sports,* 30 Jun. 1958; and compare Nelson Rodrigues, "Vamos deixar o scratch ser campeão do mundo," *Jornal dos Sports,* 17 Jun. 1958; Bartholo and Soares, "Mané Garrincha," 185–86.

112. Nelson Rodrigues, "Vamos deixar o scratch ser campeão do mundo," *Jornal dos Sports,* 17 Jun. 1958.

113. [Rodrigues] Filho, "O maravilhoso Garrincha," *Jornal dos Sports,* 21 Jun. 1958.

114. Nogueira, *Bola na rede,* 58; [Rodrigues] Filho, "Garrincha," in *O sapo,* 210–13.

115. Casé, *O artilheiro,* 94–100, 120–21. When he lived with Elza in a chic apartment on the Lagoa in Rio, he sometimes fished there, looking like he had just arrived from the interior; Castro, *Estrela,* 371.

116. Quoted in André Iki Siqueira, *João Saldanha: Uma vida em jogo* (São Paulo: Companhia Editora Nacional, 2007), 186.

117. Wisnik, *Veneno,* 282–86; Lopes, "'The People's Joy,'" 94–95.

118. Admildo Chirol in *Na boca do túnel,* org. Milton Pedrosa (Rio de Janeiro: Livraria Editora Gol, 1968), 16.

119. Evaristo de Macedo Filho in Pedrosa, *Na boca,* 81.

120. Mário Jorge Lobo Zagallo and Italo Fratezzi in Pedrosa, *Na boca,* 101, 127.

121. For instance, Saldanha, *Os subterrâneos,* 161–62.

122. Pignatari, "Rivelino e o dragão," in *Contracomunicação,* 211.

123. Andrade, *Quando é dia,* 74, 99.

124. Saldanha, "Assim. . . . Entende?" in *Vida que segue: João Saldanha e as Copas de 1966 e 1970,* org. Raul Milliet (Rio de Janeiro: Nova Fronteira, 2006), 97–98; Roberto Assaf, *Bola de bola; Os técnicos, as táticas e as estratégias que fizeram história no futebol* (Rio de Janeiro: Relume Dumará, 2002), 87; Mário [Rodrigues] Filho, "O técnico do ano," *Manchete Esportiva,* 25 Jan. 1958, 443.

125. "No Brasil, o futebol é que faz o papel da ficção," in Nelson Rodrigues, *Brasil em campo,* ed. Sonia Rodrigues (Rio de Janeiro: Nova Fronteira, 2012), 14.

126. *Dino Sani (depoimento, 2011).*

127. On his calm demeanor, see "Pelé não é fábula de La Fontaine," *Manchete Esportiva,* 28 Jun. 1958, 40.

128. "Pelé fêz JK sorrir," *Manchete Esportiva,* 28 Jun. 1958, 62.

129. Angélica Basthi, *Pelé: Estrela negra em campos verdes* (Rio de Janeiro: Garamond / Fundação Biblioteca Nacional, 2008), 15; Castello, *Pelé,* 16.

130. Nascimento, *Pelé,* 45. "Pelé" came from the young Edson's mispronunciation of the name of the goalie, Bilé, on his father's team. Basthi, *Pelé,* 22–3; Nascimento, *Pelé,* 44.

131. "Retrato do Brasil-58: Um craque de bronze, conquistas de ouro," *Manchete Esportiva,* 12 Jul. 1958, 62; Pelé in *Pelé eterno.*

132. [Rodrigues] Filho, *Viagem,* 29.

133. Ibid., 31–36;

134. [Rodrigues] Filho, *Viagem,* 38; Lopes, "'The People's Joy,'" 99; *Pelé eterno.*

135. Didi in Vasconcellos, *Recados,* 181; Nogueira, *Bola na rede,* 36–37.

136. *Pelé eterno.*

137. [Rodrigues] Filho, *Viagem,* 66.

138. Odir Cunha, *Santos FC: 100 anos de futebol arte* (São Paulo: Magma, 2012); Assis Ângelo, *A presença do futebol na música popular brasileira* (São Paulo: O Autor, 2010), 44.

139. "Seleção: Muito fogo e pouca fumaça," *Folha da Noite,* 11 Sep. 1957.

140. Canôr Simões Coelho and Pedro Zamora, *O livro de Tostão* (Rio de Janeiro: Livraria Editora Gol, 1970), 25.

141. Nelson Rodrigues, "Cem por cento Dida," in *À sombra*, 68–70. Mário Filho detailed Dida's nerves and depression; [Rodrigues] Filho, *Viagem*, 177–80, 193–94, 197, 209–11, 216–22.

142. Nascimento, *Pelé*, 83–4; [Rodrigues] Filho, *Viagem*, 184.

143. Nelson Rodrigues, "A realeza de Pelé," in *À sombra*, 43.

144. [Rodrigues] Filho, *Viagem*, 222–23.

145. Albuquerque, *Eu e o futebol*, 105–6.

146. *Pelé eterno;* "Santos, de futebol bonito e arrasador, mostra o que vale," *Jornal do Brasil,* 8 Mar. 1961; "Remembering Pelé's gol de placa," 11 May 2011, accessed 4 Apr. 2013. www.fifa.com/classicfootball/news/newsid=1392726.html.

147. Wisnik, *Veneno*, 118–19.

148. Nelson Rodrigues, "O Pelé branco," in *À sombra*, 74–76; chap. 3.

149. *Antônio Wilson Honório (Coutinho)* (Rio de Janeiro: CPCOC / FGV, 2011); Carlos Fernando Schinner, *Coutinho: o gênio da área* (Santos: Realejo Edições, 2012), 135–38.

150. "Dois lances de Pelé decidiram a vitoria do Brasil sobre Gales," *Folha de São Paulo,* 17 May 1962; "Brasil, 2 a 0: Pelé abriu o 'ferrolho' mexicano," *Folha de São Paulo,* 31 May 1962; "Pelé for a da Copa até as quartas de final," *Jornal do Brasil,* 4 Jun. 1962; Basthi, *Pelé,* 89–92.

151. Cardoso and Rockmann, *O Marechal,* 270.

152. Geraldo Romualdo da Silva, "Time-base pode não parecer 'na cara' mas seu esqueleto veste côr grená," *Jornal dos Sports,* 27 Apr. 1966; Luiz Bayer, "Câmara," *Jornal dos Sports,* 29 Mar. 1966; Armando Nogueira, "Na grande área," *Jornal do Brasil,* 29 Mar. 1966; José Castelo, "Certeza de Gérson é time de bons que só precisa confiar em si," *Jornal dos Sports,* 23 May 1966; João Máximo, *João Saldanha* (Rio de Janeiro: Relume Dumará, 2005), 90–91.

153. "Formado o eixo 'Lambari-Londres,'" *O Globo,* 11 Apr., 1966; "Feola achou treino ruim e ameaça entrar em campo," *Jornal do Brasil,* 21 Apr. 1966; "Pontas sonham com a ponta sem temer vinda de Amarildo," *Jornal dos Sports,* 21 Apr. 1966; "Alegria de Garrincha foi o bom," *Jornal dos Sports,* 15 May 1966; Geraldo Romualdo da Silva, "Falta de afirmação faz escrete voltar aos dias incertos de 63," *Jornal dos Sports,* 1 Jun. 1966.

154. "A tranquilidade ainda nao alcançada," *Jornal do Brasil,* 2 Jul. 1966; "Brasil mostra melhor jôgo e vence Tchecos," *Jornal dos Sports,* 13 Jun. 1966; "Brasil vence Suécia acertando no 2o. tempo," *Jornal dos Sports,* 1 Jul. 1966.

155. "Acelerados os exames médicos para que todos sejam liberados na Semana Santa," *O Globo,* 4 Apr. 1966.

156. "Vavá," *O Globo,* 11 Apr. 1966.

157. "Brasil vence jôgo violento com Bulgária por 2 a 0," *Jornal do Brasil,* 13 Jul. 1966; Armando Nogueira, "Na grande área," *Jornal do Brasil,* 20 Jul. 1966.

158. Gilmar dos Santos Neves, "E a Inglaterra levou a melhor," *Fatos e fotos,* edição especial, *Copa 70,* 11 Jun. 1970, 84.

159. "Pelé ameaça deixar o futebol por causa da violência," *Jornal do Brasil,* 20 Jul. 1966; Nascimento, *Pelé,* 150–52.

160. "Brazil Cup" here includes the Taça Brasil and the Torneio Roberto Gomes Pedrosa—Taça de Prata (Robertão) knockout tournaments, which preceded the advent of a full national league in 1971. Cunha, *Santos,* 325.

161. Odir Cunha, *Donos da terra: A história do primeiro título mundial do Santos* (Santos: Realejo Edições, 2007), 75–76.

162. Schinner, *Coutinho,* 202–3; Cunha, *Santos,* 84–85.

163. Guterman, *O futebol,* 136–37; Nascimento, *Pelé,* 162–63.

164. Cunha, *Santos,* 328; Antonio Carlos Napoleão and Roberto Assaf, *Seleção Brasileira, 1914–2006* (Rio de Janeiro: Mauad X, 2006), 288; Saldanha, "Carta aberta ao futebol brasileiro," *Placar,* 27 Mar. 1970, 22–26.

165. For example, "Seleção prefere seguir viagem em ritmo de cautela," and Armando Nogueira, "Na grande área," *Jornal do Brasil,* 28 Jun. 1968.

166. Saldanha, "Futebol moderno," *Última Hora,* 10 Aug. 1966; Carlos Ferreira Vilarinho, *Quem derrubou João Saldanha: Põe em pratos limpos os detalhes da campanha de fritura e demissão do técnico que classificou a seleção brasileira para a Copa de 1970* (Rio de Janeiro: LivrosdeFutebol.com, 2010), 45–49.

167. Cardoso and Rockmann, *O Marechal,* 307–8.

168. Nelson Rodrigues, "Um escrete de feras," in *À sombra,* 142.

169. Santos, *Minha bola,* 126; Marco Antonio Santoro Salvador and Antonio Jorge Gonçalves Soares, *A memória da Copa de 70: Esquecimentos e lembranças do futebol na construção da identidade nacional* (Campinas: Autores Associados, 2009), 97.

170. Guterman, *O futebol,* 163.

171. Saldanha, *Vida que segue,* 75–77.

172. Máximo, *João Saldanha,* 95; Soter, *Quando a bola,* 119.

173. "O futebol criou coragem para a Copa," *Veja,* 12 Feb. 1969, 44–49; cf. "João não muda," *Veja,* 10 Sep. 1969, 48.

174. Máximo, *João Saldanha,* 96; Nelson Rodrigues, "João sem medo," in *À sombra,* 152–54.

175. Máximo, *João Saldanha,* 107; *Dário José dos Santos (depoimento, 2011)* (Rio de Janeiro: CPDOC / FGV, 2011).

176. The views of both Médici and Saldanha appear in Armando Nogueira, "Na grande área," *Jornal do Brasil,* 28 Feb. 1970, Vilarinho, *Quem derrubou,* 106.

177. "Feras cairam na armadilha: 2 a 0," *Jornal dos Sports,* 5 Mar. 1970; "A linha burra," *Jornal dos Sports,* 7 Mar. 1970; Saldanha, "O calção e a ceroula," *O Globo,* 13 Mar. 1970; "João diz que está tudo bem," *Jornal dos Sports,* 15 Mar. 1970; Armando Nogueira, "Na grande área," *Jornal do Brasil,* 15 Mar. 1970; Fernando Horácio, "A hora da verdade," *Jornal dos Sports,* 19 Mar. 1970.

178. Guterman, *O futebol,* 164–65; Siqueira, *João Saldanha,* 326–27; Vilarinho, *Quem derrubou,* 100–103; "Na volta, o mesmo Tostão?" *Veja,* 15 Oct. 1969, 62.

179. "Jogadores julgam a Seleção," *Jornal do Brasil,* 5 Mar. 1970.

180. "Pelé reage indignado com João Saldanha" and "Pelé: João me fêz jogar até doente," *Jornal dos Sports,* 19 Mar. 1970; Vilarinho, *Quem derrubou,* 136–40. For Saldanha's version, see his "Carta aberta ao futebol brasileiro," *Placar,* 27 Mar. 1970, 22–26, in which he refuses to blame Pelé, saying the player was "incapable of doing bad." Others speculated that he had made this comment as a political ploy; see Siqueira, *João Saldanha,* 346–47; Máximo, *João Saldanha,* 112–14.

181. The blame for Saldanha's fall remains a contentious issue. Some, as Armando Nogueira did at the time, argue that the coach more or less forced his own firing through his impolitic provocations and erratic acts. Others assert that he had been in a structurally impossible situation, so his removal was inevitable. Still others stress the machinations of Zagallo and others who wanted to replace him. Compare Máximo, *João Saldanha;* Siqueira, *João Saldanha;* and Vilarinho, *Quem derrubou* for thoughtful examples of these interpretations.

182. Cabral and Ostermann, *O admirável,* 111; "Carta aberta ao futebol brasileiro," *Placar,* 27 Mar. 1970, 22–26; "Por que eu saí," *O Globo,* 24 Mar. 1970.

183. Siqueira, *João Saldanha,* 372.

184. Salvador and Soares, *A memória,* 97.

185. "Zagalo assume Seleção e anuncia alterações," *Jornal do Brasil,* 19 Mar. 1970; "Zagalo muda as feras," *Jornal dos Sports,* 19 Mar. 1970; "Dirceu, Zé Carlos, Leão e Arílson: os cortados," *Jornal do Brasil,* 28 Mar. 1970.

186. "Lídio garante que Pelé tem condições para Copa," *Jornal do Brasil,* 19 Mar. 1970; "Junta médica vai examinar Seleção para Governo," *Jornal do Brasil,* 20 Mar. 1970; Siqueira, *João Saldanha,* 373; "Zagalo não fica preocupado com as modificações," *Jornal do Brasil,* 13 Apr. 1970.

187. Rivellino in Vasconcellos, *Recados,* 197; Cabral and Ostermann, *O admirável,* 115–16.

188. "Lentidão é tema para Copa," *Jornal dos Sports,* 16 Apr., 1970; Fernando Horácio, "Os gênios estão do nosso lado," *Jornal dos Sports,* 4 Jun. 1970.

189. "Brasil vence com arte mais pura da bola," *Jornal dos Sports,* 4 Jun. 1970; Zizinho, "Rei quase ganha estátua," *Jornal dos Sports,* 4 Jun. 1970.

190. Fernando Horácio, "Estamos no caminho certo," *Jornal dos Sports,* 8 Jun. 1970; Armando Nogueira, "Na grande área," *Jornal do Brasil,* 8 Jun. 1970; "A Inglaterra tremeu de medo," and "As feras amansam o leão da rainha" *Placar,* 12 Jun. 1970, 8–9, 26–27.

191. "França: 'Goleada foi aula maravilhosa,'" "Uruguai: 'Talento brasileiro salvou o futebol,'" and "Inglaterra: 'Quatro minutos de show,'" *Jornal dos Sports,* 23 Jun. 1970; "Imprensa do mundo destaca a superioridade do Brasil," *Jornal do Brasil,* 23 Jun. 1970; "Ele não existe," *Placar,* 12 Jun. 1970, 16.

192. "Os gênios estão do nosso lado," *Jornal dos Sports,* 4 Jun. 1970; "Brasil vence Peru na base de categoria," and Tostão, "Futebol alegre," *Jornal dos Sports,* 15 Jun. 1970; "Foi a vitória do time inimitável," *Jornal dos Sports,* 23 Jun. 1970.

193. "O Super-Rei," *Placar,* 12 Jun. 1970, 25.

194. Salvador and Soares, *A memória,* chaps. 6 and 9.

195. [Rodrigues] Filho, *O negro,* 329; Nelson Rodrigues, "O escrete do sonho," in *À sombra,* 160. Compare also Nelson Rodrigues, "Os 'entendidos' rosnam de frustração," "É hoje a batalha," and "As vacas premiadas somos nós" in *À sombra,* 148–57, Nogueira, *Bola na rede,* 28–30; Cabral and Ostermann, *O admirável,* 125; "Brasil, futebol e arte numa grande vitória," *Jornal do Brasil,* 5 Jun. 1970; "Na festa do povo a volta do futebol-arte," *Jornal dos Sports,* 4 Jun. 1970; Fernando Horácio, "A arte do jôgo e a fúria dos gols," *Jornal dos Sports,* 5 Jun. 1970.

196. Martins, Torok, and Araújo Netto, *Brasil futebol rei,* 79.

197. Lopes, "'The People's Joy,'" 99. This theme runs through [Rodrigues] Filho, *Viagem;* and Pelé's later autobiographies, Nascimento, *Pelé;* and Pelé with Robert L. Fish, *My Life and the Beautiful Game: The Autobiography of Pelé* (New York: Doubleday, 1977).

198. Pignatari, "Flama não se paga . . . ," in *Contracomunicação,* 189; Castello, *Pelé,* 37; *Pelé eterno.*

199. [Rodrigues] Filho, *Viagem,* 309–11; *Pelé eterno.*

200. Basthi, *Pelé,* 84–85; Nascimento, *Pelé,* 120–22; Benedito Ruy Barbosa and Edson Arantes do Nascimento, *Eu sou Pelé* (São Paulo: Paulo Azevedo, 1961).

201. Castello, *Pelé,* 55.

202. Basthi, *Pelé,* 78–79.

203. "Pelé casou!" and "Casamento do 'rei' Pelé foi singelo," *Folha de São Paulo,* 22 Feb. 1966; "Pelé e Rose em Munique," *Folha de São Paulo,* 23 Feb. 1966; Nascimento, *Pelé,* 141–42.

204. Basthi, *Pelé*, 79, 145–46.

205. Nascimento, *Pelé*, 143–44.

206. Nascimento, *Pelé*, 114.

207. See chap. 4 in this volume.

208. "Pelé marca gol mil, chora e pede ajuda para crianças," *Jornal do Brasil*, 20 Nov. 1969; Basthi, *Pelé*, 106–9; *Pelé eterno*.

209. Quoted in Garry Jenkins, *The Beautiful Team: In Search of Pelé and the 1970 Brazilians* (London: Pocket Books, 1999), 1; Wisnik, *Veneno*, 28; Flusser, *Fenomenologia do brasileiro: Em busca de um novo homem*, org. and trans. Gustavo Bernardo (Rio de Janeiro: UERJ, 1998), 100; compare Carlos Drummond de Andrade, "Em preto e branco," *Jornal do Brasil*, 16 Jun. 1970.

210. Vavá, "Pelé está adiantado 20 anos," *Jornal dos Sports*, 5 Jun. 1970.

211. Andrade, "O momento feliz" (20 Jun. 1970), in *Quando é dia*, 109–12.

212. Martins, Torok, and Araújo Netto, *Brasil futebol rei*, 15–18, 20, 24–25 (the quote appears on p. 25); Pedro Zamora, "De Friedenreich a Pelé," in Coelho and Zamora, *O livro de Tostão*, 21–28.

213. [Rodrigues] Filho, *Copa do Mundo, 62*, 335–36.

214. Cf. Wisnik, *Veneno*, 228–31.

CHAPTER 3

1. "A volta dos deuses do futebol," *Placar*, 3 Jul. 1970, 2–4; Ana Maria Bahiana, *Almanaque anos 70* (Rio de Janeiro: Ediouro, 2006), 156; Janet Lever, *Soccer Madness: Brazil's Passion for the World's Most Popular Sport* (Prospect Heights, IL: Waveland Press, 1995), 68.

2. "Chegada foi a maior festa de Brasília," and "Um milhão e meio de cariocas receberam campeões no maior carnaval da história," *Jornal do Brasil*, 24 Jun. 1970.

3. Lever, *Soccer Madness*, 69; Simoni Lahud Guedes, "Futebol e identidade nacional: Reflexões sobre o Brasil," in *História do esporte no Brasil: Do Império aos dias atuais*, ed. Mary Del Priore and Victor Andrade de Melo (São Paulo: Editora UNESP, 2009), 462–64.

4. Arno Vogel, "O momento feliz, reflexões sobre o futebol e o ethos nacional," in Roberto DaMatta et al., *Universo do futebol: Esporte e sociedade brasileira* (Rio de Janeiro: Pinakotheke, 1982), 112, 114.

5. Marco Antonio Santoro Salvador and Antonio Jorge Gonçalves Soares, *Memória da Copa de 1970* (Campinas: Autores Associados, 2009).

6. Ruy Carlos Ostermann, *Itinerário da derrota: Crônica de cinco Copas do Mundo sem Pelé* (Porto Alegre: Artes e Ofícios, 1992), 35.

7. *Folha de São Paulo*, 25 Apr. 1999; Gilson Gil, "O drama do 'futebol-arte': O debate sobre a seleção nos anos 70," *Revista Brasileira de Ciências Sociais* 25, no. 9 (Jun. 1994): 100–109; Claudemir José dos Santos, "Repensando o estilo à brasileira: Escolinhas de futebol e aprendizagem esportiva," in *Visão do jogo: Antropologia das práticas esportivas*, ed. Luiz Henrique de Toledo and Carlos Eduardo Costa (São Paulo: Editora Terceiro Nome, 2009), 220; *Folha de São Paulo*, 4 Apr. 1977. On *alegria* see Décio Pignatari, *Contracomunicação*, 3rd ed. (Cotia, São Paulo: Ateliê Editorial, 2004), 207–9; "Joguem com pés de craque, espírito de várzea," *A Gazeta Esportiva*, 7 Jun. 1978; and on *malandragem*, Antônio Jorge Gonçalves Soares, *Futebol, malandragem e identidade* (Vitória, Espírito Santo: SPDC / UFES, 1994).

8. Carlos Drummond de Andrade, "O momento feliz," *Jornal do Brasil,* 20 Jun. 1970.

9. *Jornal do Brasil,* 23 Jun. 1970, in *Memória,* Salvador and Soares, 20; Antonio Jorge Gonçalves Soares, Marco Antonio Santoro Salvador, and Tiago Lisboa Bartholo, "O 'futebol arte' e o 'planejamento México' na copa de 70: As memórias de Lamartine Pereira da Costa," *Movimento* (Porto Alegre) 10, no. 3 (2004): 116.

10. Ostermann, *Itinerário;* Tony Mason, *Passion of the People? Football in South America* (London: Verso, 1995), 77–95.

11. Sebastião C. Velasco e Cruz and Carlos Estevam Martins, "De Castello a Figueiredo: Uma incursão na pré-história da 'abertura,'" in *Sociedade e política no Brasil pós-64,* org. Bernardo Sorj and Maria Hermínia Tavares de Almeida, 2nd ed. (São Paulo: Brasiliense, 1984), 13–61.

12. On the 1964 coup d'état, see Thomas E. Skidmore, *The Politics of Military Rule in Brazil, 1964–1985* (New York: Oxford University Press, 1988), 3–17; on the ideas behind it, see Maria Helena Moreira Alves, *State and Opposition in Military Brazil* (Austin: University of Texas Press, 1990), 13–28; Shawn Smallman, *Fear and Memory in the Brazilian Army and Society, 1889–1954* (Chapel Hill: University of North Carolina Press, 2001), esp. 176–84. On the social and political movements of those years, see Cliff Welch, *The Seed Was Planted: The São Paulo Roots of Brazil's Rural Labor Movement, 1924–1964* (University Park: Pennsylvania State University Press, 1999); Dênis de Moraes, *A Esquerda e o Golpe de 64: Vinte e cinco anos depois, as forças populares repensam seus mitos, sonhos e ilusões* (Rio de Janeiro: Espaço e Tempo, 1989).

13. Skidmore, *The Politics of Military Rule,* 140–48.

14. Castelo Branco, *Mensagem ao Congresso Nacional,* 31 Mar. 1965 (Brasília: Departamento de Imprensa Nacional, 1965), 8; *Diário Oficial da União,* 9 and 11 Apr. 1964; Médici, *Mensagem ao Congresso Nacional,* 31 Mar. 1971 (Brasília: Departamento de Imprensa Nacional, 1971), 7; Skidmore, *The Politics of Military Rule,* 128; Elio Gaspari, *A ditadura escarnada* (São Paulo: Companhia das Letras, 2002) and *A ditadura envergonhada* (São Paulo: Companhia das Letras, 2002); and Carlos Fico, *Além do golpe: Versoes e controvérsias sobre 1964 e a Ditadura Militar* (Rio de Janeiro: Record, 2004).

15. Skidmore, *The Politics of Military Rule,* 117–35.

16. Daniel Aarão Reis, "Ditadura, anistia e reconciliação," *Estudos Históricos* 23, no. 45 (2010): 171–86.

17. Janaína Martins Cordeiro, "Anos de chumbo ou anos de oro? A memória social sobre o governo Médici," *Estudos Históricos* 22, no. 43 (2009): 85–110; Fabio Wanderley Reis, "O eleitorado, os partidos e o regime autoritário brasileiro," in *Sociedade e política,* org. Sorj and Almeida, 62–86. On press support see Ricardo Constante Martins, "Ditadura militar e propaganda política: A revista *Manchete* durante o governo Médici" (Master's thesis, Universidade Federal de São Carlos, 1999).

18. Ronaldo Costa Couto, *História indiscreta da ditadura e da abertura: Brasil: 1965–1985* (Rio de Janeiro: Record, 1999), 117. On regime propaganda, see Carlos Fico, *Reinventando o otimismo: Ditadura, propaganda e imaginário social no Brasil* (Rio de Janeiro: Fundação Getúlio Vargas Editora, 1997); and on the mixed nature of statist development, *Metas e bases para a ação de governo: Pronuncimentos do Exmo. Presidente da República e do Ministro do Planejamento e Coordenação Geral na Reunião Ministerial de 10./10/70* (Brasília, 1970); Peter Evans, *Dependent Development: The Alliance of Multinational, State, and Local Capital in Brazil* (Princeton: Princeton University Press, 1979).

19. Alencar Furtado, *Salgando a terra* (Rio de Janeiro: Paz e Terra, 1977); Skidmore, *The Politics of Military Rule,* 142–44.

20. Presidência da República, *Metas e bases para a ação de governo: Síntese* (Brasília, 1970) 6; and *II Plano Nacional de Desenvolvimento* (Brasilia, 1974), 61.

21. *O Cruzeiro,* 26 Jul. 1972, 102.

22. Nonetheless, the CBD received ten times more funding (in real terms) from its parent entity, the Ministry of Education and Culture, for the 1974 World Cup than it had for the 1966 World Cup. "Quadro relativo às prestações de contas das dotações do Ministério da Educação e Cultura, referente aos exercícios de 1957 a 1974," in A. Vivaldo de Azevedo, *João Havelange: Determinação e coragem* (São Paulo: Editar Publicações Técnicas, 1978), 114.

23. Nelson Rodrigues, "À sombra das grandes chuteiras," *O Globo,* 17 Jun. 1971; José Inácio Werneck, personal communication, Feb. 2011.

24. In Azevedo, *João Havelange,* 145.

25. José Paulo Florenzano, *A Democracia Corinthiana: Práticas de liberdade no futebol brasileiro* (São Paulo: FAPESP / EDUC, 2009), 61; Marcos Guterman, *O futebol explica o Brasil: Uma história da maior expressão popular do país* (São Paulo: Contexto, 2009), 161–62.

26. Hilário Franco Júnior, *A dança dos deuses: Futebol, sociedade, cultura* (São Paulo: Companhia das Letras, 2007), 144; Skidmore, *The Politics of Military Rule,* 111; Couto, *História indiscreta,* 115; Gilberto Agostino, *Vencer ou morrer: Futebol, geopolítica e identidade nacional* (Rio de Janeiro: FAPERJ / Mauad, 2002), 162.

27. Gil, "O drama"; Sérgio Settani Giglio, "Futebol-arte ou futebol-força? O estilo brasileiro em jogo," in *Futebol, cultura e sociedade,* org. Jocimar Daolio (Campinas: Autores Associados, 2005), 53–72; Soares, *Futebol, malandragem e identidade,* 105–10.

28. Ministério da Educação e Cultura, *Política nacional de educação física e desportos* (Rio de Janeiro: Departamento de Documentação e Divulgação, 1975), 16–17.

29. Marcelo Weishaupt Proni, *A metamorfose do futebol* (Campinas: Unicamp / Instituto de Economia, 2000), 122; José Miguel Wisnik, *Veneno remédio: O futebol e o Brasil* (São Paulo: Companhia das Letras, 2008), 321.

30. Havelange, "O CDB do nosso tempo," 10 Jan. 1975, in Azevedo, *João Havelange,* 78.

31. Fernando Gabeira, *O crepúsculo do macho,* 16th ed. (Rio de Janeiro: Codecri, 1981), 24; Franco Júnior, *A dança,* 144; Guterman, *O futebol,* 162–63; Dias Gomes, *Campeões do mundo* (São Paulo: Círculo do Livro, [1983]), 92.

32. "Curtição geral," *O Pasquim,* no. 54 (2–8 Jul. 1970); Eduardo Galeano, *Soccer in Sun and Shadow,* trans. Mark Fried (London: Verso, 1998), 137.

33. Salvador and Soares, *Memória da Copa de 1970.*

34. Lamartine Pereira da Costa, *Diagnóstico de educação física/desportos no Brasil* ([Rio de Janeiro]: Fundação Nacional de Matéria Escolar, 1971), 7.

35. On soccer as a "philosophical drama" more broadly, see esp. Christian Bromberger, *Le match de football: Ethnologie d'une passion partisane à Marseille, Naples et Turin* (Paris: Éditions de la Maison des sciences de l'homme, 1995).

36. Soares, *Futebol, malandragem e identidade;* Michael Hanchard, "Black Cinderella? Race and the Public Sphere in Brazil," in *Racial Politics in Contemporary Brazil,* ed. Hanchard (Durham: Duke University Press, 1999), 59–81.

37. Ostermann, *Itinerário,* 16.

38. Mason, *Passion of the People,* 92.

39. Pelé with Duarte and Bellos, *Pelé;* Guterman, *O futebol,* 188–89, 199–200; Angélica Basthi, *Pelé: Estrela negra em campos verdes* (Rio de Janeiro: Garamond / Fundação Biblioteca Nacional, 2008); *Once in a Lifetime: The Extraordinary Story of the New York Cosmos,* dir. Paul Crowder and John Dower, 2006.

40. Ostermann, *Itinerário*, 29–30.

41. *Placar*, 9 Mar. 1984.

42. Marcos Eduardo Neves, *Anjo ou demônio: A polêmica trajetória de Renato Gaúcho* (Rio de Janeiro: Gryphus, 2002).

43. Zico, *Zico conta sua história* (São Paulo: FTD, 1996); *Zico na rede,* dir. Paulo Roscio, Brazil, 2009.

44. *Placar*, 2 Jun. 1972, 5–6.

45. Proença, introduction to Sebastião Araújo, *O futebol e seus fundamentos: O futebol-força a serviço da arte* (Rio de Janeiro: Imago, 1976), 12; Proença, *Futebol e palavra* (Rio de Janeiro: Livraria José Olympio Editora, 1981), 135.

46. *Jornal dos Sports,* 22 Jul. 1971.

47. Guterman, *O futebol,* 182; Jacob Klintowitz, "A implantação de um modelo alienígena exótico e outras questões pertinentes: A Seleção Brasileira de Futebol—1978," *Encontros com a civilização brasileira* 5 (1978): 113–18.

48. Florenzano, *A Democracia,* 86.

49. Luiz Henrique de Toledo, *Lógicas no futebol* (São Paulo: Hucitec / Fapesp, 2002).

50. On the new "social use" of players' bodies, see Claudemir José dos Santos, "Repensando o estilo," 239.

51. Klintowitz, "A implantação," esp. 116–17.

52. Amarílio Ferreira Neto, *A pedagogia no exército e na escola: A educação física brasileira (1880–1950)* (Aracruz: Facha, 1999), 50–51. On the military's physical education system, see Decreto 23.532, *Coleção das Leis da República dos Estados Unidos do Brasil,* 1933, vol. 4 (Rio de Janeiro: Imprensa Nacional, 1934); Victor Andrade de Melo, "Escola Nacional de Educação Física e Desportos: uma possível história" (Master's thesis, Universidade Estadual de Campinas, 1996).

53. Ministério da Educação e Cultura, *Política nacional,* which reprinted Lei 6.251, 10 Aug. 1975 (discussed later in this chapter); Carlos Alberto Pinheiro, *Milhões no esporte do Brasil* (Rio de Janeiro: Image, 1974); interview with José Maurício Capinassu in Renato Soeiro and Elirez Bezerra da Silva, "Treinamento esportivo no Brasil, sua criação e evolução," *Congresso Brasileiro de História da Educação Física, Esporte, Lazer e Dança. As ciências sociais e a história da educação física, esporte, lazer e dança* (Ponta Grossa: Universidade Estadual de Ponta Grossa, 2002), DVD-ROM; Renato Souza Pinto Soeiro and Rafael Pinheiro, "Escola de Educação Física do Exército—EsEFEx," in *Atlas do Esporte no Brasil: Atlas do esporte, educação física e atividades físicas de saúde e lazer no Brasil,* org. Lamartine DaCosta (Rio de Janeiro: Shape Editora, 2005), 129.

54. Lamartine Pereira da Costa, *Sports Activities in Tropical Climates and an Experimental Solution: The Altitude Training* (Brasília: International Military Sports Council, 1966), and *Planejamento México* (Brasília: Ministério da Educação e Cultura, 1967).

55. The term runs through Costa, *Planejamento México,* in particular.

56. *Jornal do Brasil,* 22 Apr. 1983; Salvador and Soares, *Memoria,* 86–87; Franco Júnior, *A dança,* 142; Soares and Bartholo, "O 'futebol arte' e o 'planejamento México,'" 125. The trainers also believed that he did not understand what they were doing; João Máximo, *João Saldanha* (Rio de Janeiro: Relume, 2005), 104.

57. *Jornal do Brasil,* 10 Jun. 1970, 22.

58. "Heleno já quer Roberto," *A Gazeta Esportiva,* 8 Jun. 1978; Oldemário Touguinhó, *Jornal do Brasil,* 27–29 Jun. 1973.

59. Franco Júnior, *A dança,* 145.

60. Luiz Carlos Lisboa, org., *Reinaldo do Atlético Mineiro* (Rio de Janeiro: Editora Rio, 2003), 38; "Cláudio Coutinho (1939–1981)," *Veja,* 2 Dec. 1981, 127–28.

61. Interview with Lamartine Pereira da Costa, in Salvador and Soares, *Memória,* 93.

62. Florenzano, *A Democracia,* 61.

63. "Cláudio Coutinho (1939–1981)," *Veja,* 2 Dec. 1981, 127–28.

64. Florenzao, *A Democracia Corinthiana,* 104.

65. Soares and Bartholo, "O 'futebol arte' e o 'planejamento México,'" 123, 127; compare Soares, *Futebol, malandragem e identidade,* 101.

66. Interviews with former players Giancarlos and Cesar Sampaio, 27 May 2007.

67. *Jornal dos Sports,* 22 Jul. 1971.

68. "O futuro da Seleção na visão de Zagalo," *Jornal dos Sports,* 22 Jul. 1971.

69. Jorge Vasconcellos, org., *Recados da bola: Depoimentos de doze mestres do futebol brasileiro* (São Paulo: Cosac Naify, 2010), 198.

70. "Os pontas em seus lugares," *Jornal dos Sports,* 13 Jul. 1972; "Erros da estréia," *Veja,* 5 Jul. 1972, 76; "Os maxi prejuiças da Taça," *Veja,* 12 Jul. 1972, 53.

71. This paragraph draws on Jonathan Wilson, *Inverting the Pyramid: The History of Football Tactics,* esp. 50–51, 101–28, 257–62; Roberto Assaf, *Banho de bola: Os técnicos, as táticas e as estratégias que fizeram história no futebol* (Rio de Janeiro: Relume Dumará, 2002); and Thomaz Soares da Silva (Zizinho), *Verdades e mentiras no futebol* (Niterói: Imprensa Oficial, 2001). On the 4-2-4, see Rob Sweeney, "Brazil and the Rise of the Back Four: How Foreign Influences Led to the Back Four in Brazil," *The Blizzard* 2 (Sep. 2011), 104–12.

72. Galeano, *Soccer in Sun and Shadow,* 137.

73. On the politics of the 1972 Taça, see Agostino, *Vencer ou morrer,* 163, and interview with Juca Kfouri, *Caros Amigos* 1 (Apr. 1997); Adjovanes Thadeu Silva da Almeida, "O regime militar em festa: As comemorações do Sesquicentenário da Independência brasileira," in *A ditadura em debate: Estado e sociedade nos anos do autoritarismo,* org. Adriano de Freixo and Oswaldo Munteal Filho (Rio de Janeiro: Contraponto, 2005), 105–22.

74. "Erros da estréia," *Veja,* 5 Jul. 1972, 76; Achilles Chirol, "A honra de empatar com o Brasil," *Jornal dos Sports,* 29 Jun. 1972.

75. "Rivelino e/o Paulo César," *Placar,* 23 Jun. 1972, 18.

76. Otávio de Morais, "Que tal a taça?" *Jornal dos Sports,* 14 Jun. 1972; "Brasil foi mais time," *Jornal dos Sports,* 29 Jun. 1972.

77. Saldanha, "Jogo duro e cavado," *O Globo,* 10 Jul. 1972.

78. Morais, "Vitória para uma torcida madura," *Jornal dos Sports,* 10 Jul. 1972; Achilles Chirol, "Uma formula que o Brasil esgotou," *Jornal dos Sports,* 10 Jul. 1972.

79. "Zagalo: Os derrotistas não tiveram vez," *O Globo,* 10 Jul. 1972.

80. "O novo time e o novo Gérson," *Placar,* 2 Jun. 1972, 4.

81. The trip did allow trainers to meet with a noted Swedish expert on conditioning; column of Oldemário Touguinhó, *Jornal do Brasil,* 27 Jun. 1973.

82. "Meio-campo brasileiro comandou vitória sobre Argentina: 2 a 1," *O Globo,* 27 Jun. 1974.

83. David Winner, *Brilliant Orange: The Neurotic Genius of Dutch Football* (London: Bloomsbury, 2000).

84. Gil, "O drama," 105.

85. Celso Itiberê, "Temos esquema e talento," *O Globo,* 13 Jun. 1974.

86. "Em jogo, o ritual do futebol," *Veja,* 19 Jun. 1974, 70.

87. Saldanha, "Brasil antifutebol," *O Globo,* 19 Jun. 1974; Ênnio Sérvio, "Jogar para empatar," *Jornal dos Sports,* 10 Jun. 1974; "Gérson aponta erros do time e faz críticas a Paulo César," *O Globo,* 14 Jun. 1974.

88. Paulo Mendes Campos, *O gol é necessário: Crônicas esportivas,* 5th ed. (Rio de Janeiro: Civilização Brasileira, 2008), 61.

89. "Zagalo aceita derrota," *O Globo,* 4 Jul. 1974.

90. Saldanha, "A copa da retranca," *O Globo,* 27 Jun. 1974; "A Copa está provando que o meio-campo mudou," *Jornal do Brasil,* 24 Jun. 1974; José Paulo Florenzano, *Afonsinho e Edmundo: A rebeldia no futebol brasileiro* (São Paulo: Musa Editora, 1998), 116–17.

91. "Futebol europeu é superior ao nosso, dizem preparadores," *O Globo,* 19 Jun. 1974; "Preparadores querem provas do seu valor," *Jornal do Brasil,* 24 Jun. 1974.

92. Guterman, *O futebol,* 195.

93. "Givanildo pesa no balanço," *Placar,* 11 Jun. 1976, 4; "A teoria da competição," *Placar,* 7 Mar. 1978, 8.

94. "Onde dói?," *Veja,* 16 Feb. 1977, 65.

95. "Brandão, o que passou e o que vem agora," *Jornal dos Sports,* 11 Jun. 1976; Sérgio Noronha, "Derrubadores de sistemas," *O Globo,* 6 Jun. 1976; "Seleção rarefeita," *Placar* 11 Feb. 1977, 8–9; "E o Falcão, Seu Brandão?" *Placar,* 21 Jan. 1977, 5–8; "Talento. Assim a Seleção vai se salvando," *Jornal da Tarde,* 7 Feb. 1977; Antonio Maria Filho, "O triste carnaval do empate," *Jornal do Brasil,* 23 Feb. 1977.

96. Touguinhó, "O técnico das 18 contradições," *Jornal do Brasil,* 23 Feb. 1977; Guterman, *O futebol,* 196.

97. Antonio Maria Filho, "O triste carnaval do empate," *Jornal do Brasil,* 23 Feb. 1977.

98. "Havelange, CBD, o mundo," *Veja,* 14 Jun. 1972, 76–81.

99. Decreto-Lei 3.199, art. 3a and 44, 14 Apr. 1941, República dos Estados Unidos do Brasil, *Coleção das Leis de 1941, Atos do Poder Executivo,* vol. 3 (Rio de Janeiro: Imprensa Nacional, 1941), 47–54; Eduardo Dias Manhães, *Política de esportes no Brasil,* 2nd ed. (Rio de Janeiro: Paz e Terra, 2002), 80–85; Agostinho, *Vencer ou morrer,* 163.

100. Lei 6.251, 10 Aug. 1975, República Federativa do Brasil, *Coleção das leis de 1975: Atos do poder legislativo,* vol. 7 (Rio de Janeiro: Departamento de Imprensa Nacional, 1976), 133–44.

101. Joel Rufino dos Santos, *História política do futebol brasileiro* (São Paulo: Brasiliense, 1981), 82; Proni *A metamorfose,* 140–43.

102. "Flu luta pelo privilégio," *Placar,* 7 Nov. 1975, 59; "A arte de não cair no cabide," *Placar,* 22 Apr. 1977, 40–42.

103. "Heleno mostra o futuro do futebol brasileiro," *O Estado de São Paulo,* 23 Feb. 1975; cf. "Como na velha República," *Placar,* 3 May 1985, 11; Deliberação 3/68, "Determina a fiel observância das regras internacionais do futebol no tocante à Regra VII da International Board," 28 March 1968; and Deliberação no. 2/72, "Modifica o item 19 da Deliberação 2/65 que dispõe sobre competições internacionais de futebol," 11 Jan. 1972, in Conselho Nacional de Desportos, *Deliberações* (Rio de Janeiro: Grupo Tarefa, 1974), 232, 238–39.

104. Admildo Chirol, *Jornal do Brasil,* 10 Jun. 1970, 22; Lamartine Pereira da Costa, interview cited in Salvador and Soares, *Memória,* 80–81; *Jornal do Brasil,* 2 Nov. 1977; David Goldblatt, *The Ball is Round: A Global History of Soccer* (New York: Riverhead Books, 2008), 630–31.

105. Mauro Beting, *Bolas e bocas: Frases de craques e bagres do futebol* (São Paulo: Leiasempre, 2003), 129.

106. "O capitão de bom senso," *Placar,* 23 Jun. 1972, 24.

107. Ostermann, *Itinerário,* 57; José Inácio Werneck, personal communication, Feb. 2011.

108. "A teoria da competição," *Placar,* 7 Mar. 1978, 7; Zico, *Zico conta,* 64; Lisboa, *Reinaldo,* 38.

109. *Jornal do Brasil,* 27 May 1978, 25.

110. "Copa dos técnicos," *Jornal da Tarde,* 22 May 1978.

111. Klintowitz, "A implantação"; Florenzano, *A Democracia,* 156; "O técnico fala vários idiomas. Não fala futebol," *A Gazeta Esportiva,* 24 Jun. 1978.

112. "Ensaio geral," *Veja,* 8 Jun. 1977, 99.

113. José (Pepe) Macia, *Bombas de alegria: Meio século de histórias do canhão da vila* (Santos: Realejo Edições, 2006), 127.

114. "O que a Seleção pensa das táticas de Cláudio Coutinho," *Jornal da Tarde,* 6 Jun. 1977.

115. "Brasil arrasa Colombia, com Zico expulso," *Jornal dos Sports,* 10 Mar. 1977.

116. "O que a Seleçao pensa das táticas de Cláudio Coutinho," *Jornal da Tarde,* 6 Jun. 1977; "Eu, Falcão," *Placar,* 3 Apr. 1977, 7.

117. "Errando, sim, mas para acertar?," *Placar,* 11 Mar. 1977.

118. "Polivalência 'matou' Dirceu na Seleção," *A Gazeta Esportiva,* 21 Apr. 1978.

119. "Uma seleção sem saudossismo," *A Gazeta Esportiva,* 28 Apr. 1978.

120. "Começa a pintar a seleção do povo. Como em 70," *A Gazeta Esportiva,* 7 Apr. 1978; "Estamos perto do time do povo," *A Gazeta Esportiva,* 12 Jun. 1978.

121. "Coutinho fora," *Jornal da Tarde,* 15 Jul. 1977.

122. "Brasil no caminho do forte e do feio," *A Gazeta Esportiva,* 28 Apr. 1978.

123. "O Brasil jogou à européia" and "Neste empate, o Brasil perdeu muitos amigos," *A Gazeta Esportiva,* 21 Apr. 1978, 2–3; Jairo Regis, "Um futebol sem caráter," *Placar,* 28 Apr. 1978.

124. "Começa a pintar a seleção do povo. Como em 70," *A Gazeta Esportiva,* 7 Apr. 1978, 2; "Depois de Hamburgo, Seleção com jeito de campeã," *Placar,* 14 Apr. 1978, 4–5.

125. "Faltou polivalência," *A Gazeta Esportiva,* 2 Apr. 1978, 5; "Na derrota, a calma para reagir," *A Gazeta Esportiva,* 3 Apr. 1978; "Todos criticam: O povo, Zagalo, Zezé e os craques," *A Gazeta Esportiva,* 4 Apr. 1978, "Na Seleção Brasileiro, alguns bateristas estão tocando piano," *A Gazeta Esportiva,* 5 Apr. 1978.

126. "A culpa foi do Peru?" *Veja,* 28 Jun. 1978, 66; Paulo César O. Pinto, *Um idolo chamado Roberto Dinamite* (Rio de Janeiro: Editora Revan, 1987), 70.

127. "Os 22 dos últimos 20 anos," *A Gazeta Esportiva,* 6 Mar. 1978; "Uma seleção sem saudossismo," *A Gazeta Esportiva,* 28 Apr. 1978. "Alguem vai sobrar," *Placar,* 19 May 1978, 5–8.

128. "Os europeus e o 'novo' futebol brasileiro," *A Gazeta Esportiva,* 30 Apr. 1978.

129. "Coutinho testou 46 jogadores," *A Gazeta Esportiva,* 23 Jun. 1978; "Mil dias de campanha," *Placar,* 30 Jun. 1978, 27–31; Goldblatt, *The Ball is Round,* 630.

130. "Mil dias de campanha," *Placar,* 30 Jun. 1978, 30.

131. Grant Farred, *Long Distance Love: A Passion for Football* (Philadelphia: Temple University Press, 2008), 60–81.

132. "Peru Sem Vergonha," *Jornal dos Sports,* 22 Jun. 1978; "Um gosto de 'marmelada,'" *A Gazeta Esportiva,* 22 June 1978, 3; "Brasil, campeão, 8?" *Placar,* 30 Jun. 1978; Franco Júnior, *A dança,* 150; and for details of the favors that the Argentine military government did for Peru before the game, see Richard Giulianotti, *Football: A Sociology of the Global Game* (Cambridge: Polity Press, 1999), 102.

133. "A culpa foi do Peru?" *Veja,* 28 Jun. 1978, 67.

134. "No banco dos réus," *Veja,* 14 Jun. 1978, 76; Wisnik, *Veneno,* 329.

135. José Inácio Werneck, "Campo neutro," *Jornal do Brasil,* 20 Jun. 1978; "Brasil, apenas uma boa equipe," *Placar,* 30 Jun. 1978.

136. "Uma Copa sem astros," *Veja,* 21 Jun. 1978, 77. Joel Rufino dos Santos called Coutinho "captain Cyborg"; Santos, "Na CBD até o papagaio bate continência," *Encontros com a civilização brasileira* 5 (1978), 127. José Inácio Werneck found Coutinho's understanding of European tactics shockingly superficial, seeming to derive mainly from one book by English author Eric Batty. Personal communication, Feb. 2011.

137. "Polivalência é isso aí, Zé!" *A Gazeta Esportiva,* 6 Apr. 1978.

138. "Faltou polivalência," *A Gazeta Esportiva,* 2 Apr. 1978; "Garrincha: Polivalência sem gol nã presta," *A Gazeta Esportiva* 6 Jun. 1978.

139. "Brasil, pássario livre, foi presa na gaiola das táticas," *A Gazeta Esportiva,* 25 Jun. 1978.

140. "Técnico tem teorias inglesas, mas na prática está no ABC," *A Gazeta Esportiva,* 8 Jun. 1978, 19; "No banco dos réus," *Veja,* 14 Jun. 1978, 76; Ostermann, *Itinerário,* 62; "Fora! Basta! Chega!" *Placar,* 30 Jun. 1978.

141. "Brasil conseguiu na Copa exatamente o que mereceu," *Jornal do Brasil,* 26 Jun. 1978; "Seleção: Rica por fora, podre por dentro," *A Gazeta Esportiva,* 27 Jun. 1978.

142. "No banco dos réus," *Veja,* 14 Jun. 1978, 83.

143. Wisnik, *Veneno,* 328.

144. Proença, *Futebol e palavra,* 7; "Chega de polivalência: é na hora de voltar às nossas origens," *A Gazeta Esportiva,* 23 Jun. 1978; "Coutinho não sabe o mal que fez ao nosso futebol," *A Gazeta Esportiva,* 23 Jun. 1978; "Foi um jogo de duas caras," *A Gazeta Esportiva,* 25 Jun. 1978; "A Seleção, Coutinho e suas táticas. Ninguem aprova nada," *A Gazeta Esportiva,* 25 Jun. 1978; "Pausa para meditação," *A Gazeta Esportiva,* 26 Jun. 1978.

145. "Coutinho diz que só errou em 78 ao não escalar Zico de início," *Jornal do Brasil,* 4 Jan. 1981; "Coutinho explica. Explica?" *A Gazeta Esportiva,* 22 Jun. 1978; "Coutinho, feliz, espera aplausos!" *A Gazeta Esportiva,* 25 Jun. 1978.

146. Zico, *Zico conta,* 52.

147. "Brasil, campeão moral?" *Placar,* 30 Jun. 1978; Tostão, *Lembranças, opiniões, reflexões sobre futebol* (São Paulo: DBA, 1997), 109–11.

148. Klintowitz, "A implantação."

149. "Fora! Basta! Chega!" *Placar,* 30 Jun. 1977.

150. Toledo, *Lógicas,* 132.

151. Gil, "O drama," 107–8; "O futebol, segundo dois craques (e torcedores)," *O Globo,* 4 Jan. 1981; Tostão, *Lembranças,* 123.

152. "Copa de artificialismos," *A Gazeta Esportiva,* 4 Feb. 1978; "Solução é o futebol entregue ao futebol," *A Gazeta Esportiva,* 8 Aug. 1979.

153. "Um domingo no futebol do Brasil," reprinted in *Placar,* April 2000, 69–71; columns by Armando Nogueira in Proença, *Futebol e palavra,* 45–46.

154. "Esse garoto leva jeito," *Placar,* 26 Dec. 1976, 29–30.

155. Proença, *Futebol e palavra,* 134.

156. Beto Xavier, *Futebol no país da música* (São Paulo: Panda Books, 2009), esp. 184–89.

157. "O Brasil na Copa de 78," in Proença, *Futebol e palavra,* 20–21; Carlos Drummond de Andrade, "Brasil vitorioso não na Copa terá solução democrática,"[May 1978] in *Quando é dia de futebol* (Rio de Janeiro: Record, 2002), 149–50.

158. Manuel D'Almeida Filho, "O Brasil tricampeão," in Proença, *Futebol e palavra,* 19–20.

159. Florenzano, *A Democracia* and *Afonsinho e Edmundo.* Others, of course, did not resist *futebol-força* or the dictatorship.

160. Kleber Mazziero de Souza, *Divino: A vida e a arte de Ademir da Guia* (Rio de Janeiro: Gryphus, 2001), 160.

161. Souza, *Divino*, 188; "É Divino mesmo," *Placar*, 30 Jul. 1976, 6.

162. "Ademir da Guia: Divina perfeição," *Placar*, May 1992, 50.

163. *Um craque chamado Divino: Vida e obra de Ademir da Guia*, dir. Penna Filho (Brazil, 2007).

164. This paragraph is based on interviews in the film *Um craque chamado Divino*.

165. In Wisnik, *Veneno*, 324; Souza, *Divino*, 216; and cf. Nuno Ramos, *Ensaio geral: Projetos, roteiros, ensaios, memória* (São Paulo: Globo, 2007), 267; *Um craque chamado Divino*.

166. Souza, *Divino*, 169–70.

167. Juca Kfouri, "Qualquer hora era hora de ver o Divino jogar bola," in *Meninos eu vi . . .* (São Paulo: DBA Artes Gráficas, 2003), 22–23.

168. Souza, *Divino*, 193–95; Wisnik, *Veneno*, 325.

169. Paulo Cézar Lima Caju, *Dei a volta na vida* (São Paulo: A Girafa Editora, 2006).

170. *Futebol*, dir. Arthur Fontes and João Moreira Salles (Brazil, 1998), disc 3.

171. "Eu, o perseguido," *Placar*, 28 Apr. 1978.

172. João Saldanha, *Os subterrâneos do futebol* (Rio de Janeiro: Tempo Brasileiro, 1963); cf. José Dias, *Futebol de craques e dos cartolas pernas-de-pau* (Rio de Janeiro: Manad, 2000); Juca Kfouri, *Por que não desisto: Futebol, dinheiro e política* (Barueri, São Paulo: DISAL, 2009).

173. Caju, *Dei a volta*, 81.

174. Ibid., 70.

175. Ibid., 86.

176. Neves, *Anjo ou demônio*, 131.

177. Ostermann, *Itinerário da derrota*, 22

178. Cf. Florenzano, *Afonsinho*, 95–105; *Passe livre: Um documento vivo do futebol brasileiro*, dir. Oswaldo Caldeira (Brazil 1974).

179. "Rumo à Copa," *Veja*, 20 Jul. 1977, 83–84; "Um futebol sem caráter," *Placar*, 28 Apr. 1978; "A Seleção e a imprensa," *A Gazeta Esportiva*, 2 Mar. 1978; Caju, *Dei a volta*, 67.

180. "A Maravilha Negra," *Placar*, 29 Oct. 1976.

181. "Um novo grito de guerra no Rio: 'Mata!'" *Placar*, 14 May 1971, 2; Florenzano, *A Democracia*, 114; column by Oldemário Touguinhó, *Jornal do Brasil*, 27 Jun. 1973; "A Seleção e a imprensa," *A Gazeta Esportiva*, 2 Mar. 1978.

182. Saldanha, "Gato preto em campo de neve," in *Futebol e outras histórias* (Rio de Janeiro: Record, 1988), 189–90.

183. João Roberto Basílio, *Um escolhido: Autobiografia* (São Paulo: Editora Planeta do Brasil, 2008), 41; Florenzano, *Afonsinho*, 105.

184. *Futebol*, Fontes and Moreira Salles, disc 3.

185. Florenzao, *A Democracia*, 158; *Placar*, 4 Mar. 1977, 14; "Só falta uma volta," *Placar*, 18 Feb. 1977, 12–14; Felipe Dias Carrilho, *Futebol: Uma janela para o Brasil* (São Paulo: Nova Espiral, 2010), 100.

186. *Futebol*, Fontes and Moreira Salles, disc 3.

187. "Rivelino e/ou Paulo César," *Placar*, 23 Jun. 1972, 18, "O desiludido e agressivo Fã-Clube de Paulo César!" *A Gazeta Esportiva*, 25 Feb. 1978, 13; Caju, *Dei a volta*, 67.

188. *Placar*, 30 Apr. 1971, 16, cited in Florenzano, *Afonsinho*, 109; Caju, *Dei a volta*, 34, "P. César diz que até Alemanha usa habilidade," *Jornal do Brasil*, 14 Jul. 1980.

189. "Errando, sim, mas para acertar?" *Placar*, 11 Mar. 1977.

190. "Só falta uma volta," *Placar*, 18 Feb. 1977, 14; "Coutinho explica a fase de Romeu," *A Gazeta Esportiva*, 25 Feb. 1978.

191. "Coutinho convocou e explicou," *A Gazeta Esportiva*, 25 Feb. 1978.

192. Lisboa, *Reinaldo*, 52–64; "Reinaldo deve ir embora," *Placar*, 1 Nov. 1985, 30; "É hora de a torcida saber o que aconteceu comigo," *Placar*, 8 Sep. 1986, 38–41.

193. Lisboa, *Reinaldo*, 35; "Os mineiros, esses craques silenciosos," *Manchete Esportiva* 22 (14 Mar. 1978), 24; "Já temos centroavante," *Jornal da Tarde*, 18 May 1978; "Reinaldo volta a reinar," *Placar*, 9 Mar. 1984, 16; Ramos, *Ensaio geral*, 279–80.

194. Wisnik, *Veneno*, 327.

195. "É hora de a torcida saber o que aconteceu comigo," *Placar*, 8 Sep. 1986, 40; Wisnik, *Veneno*, 328.

196. "O homem da camisa 9," *Placar*, 20 Jan. 1978, 12; "Até o almirante acha que é o melhor do mundo," *Jornal da Tarde*, 18 May 1978.

197. *Movimento*, 6 Mar. 1978, 1, 9.

198. Florenzano, *A Democracia*, 121; Lisboa, *Reinaldo*, 41–42.

199. Florenzano, *A Democracia*, 122.

200. Carrilho, *Futebol*, 99. On Carlos and Smith's protest and its political context, see Amy Bass, *Not the Triumph but the Struggle: The 1968 Olympics and the Making of the Black Athlete* (Minneapolis: University of Minnesota Press, 2002).

201. Fassy, *Brasil: Tetra campeão mundial?* (Brasília: Horizonte, 1982), 53; cf. Oldemário Touguinhó and Marcus Veras, *As Copas que eu vi* (Rio de Janeiro: Relume Dumará, 1994), 87–93; Lisboa, *Reinaldo*, 64–71.

202. "O homem da camisa 9," *Placar*, 20 Jan. 1978, 12.

203. Ostermann, *Itinerário*, 57.

204. Lisboa, *Reinaldo*, 41, 38.

205. "Já temos centroavante," *Jornal da Tarde*, 18 May 1978.

206. Lisboa, *Reinaldo*, 56; "Brasil, apenas uma boa equipe," *Placar*, 30 Jun. 1978, 10.

207. José Silvério in *Telê Santana: Meio século de futebol-arte*, dir. Ana Carla Portella and Danielle Rosa (Brazil, 2009).

208. "Paulo Isidoro: 'Nós temos algo mais,'" *A Gazeta Esportiva*, 25 Jan. 1981, 8; compare João Saldanha, "Time pra cabeça," in *O trauma da bola: a Copa de 1982 por João Saldanha* (São Paulo: Cosac & Naify, 2002), 39–41.

CHAPTER 4

Epigraph: Nelson Rodrigues and Mário [Rodrigues] Filho, *Fla-Flu . . . e as multidões despertaram* (Rio de Janeiro, Editora Europa, 1987), 175.

1. "Defesa vazada," *Veja*, 28 Dec. 1983, 39.

2. Nordestino, *O Brasil entrega o ouro e ainda baixa as calças (o ex-país do futebol)* (São Paulo: n.p., [1984]).

3. Hilário Franco Júnior, *A dança dos deuses: Futebol, sociedade, cultura* (São Paulo: Companhia das Letras, 2007), 146.

4. Compare José Miguel Wisnik, *Veneno remédio: O futebol e o Brasil* (São Paulo: Companhia das Letras, 2008), 155–57.

5. Eduardo Monsanto, *1981: O ano rubro-negro* (São Paulo: Panda Books, 2010), 21.

6. Waldenyr Caldas, "O futebol no país do futebol," *Lua Nova* 3, no. 10 (1986): 24.

7. Paulo Roberto Falcão, *Histórias da bola* (Porto Alegre: L&PM, 1996), 85.

8. "Trinta anos depois, outra derrota amarga," *O Globo*, 16 Jun. 1980.

9. "Jogadores analisam os problemas do futebol brasileiro" and "P. César diz que até Alemanha usa habilidade,"*Jornal do Brasil* 14 Jul. 1980.

10. "Zenon: 'Agora o talento voltou a falar mais alto no Brasil,'" *A Gazeta Esportiva,* 2 Aug. 1979; Ricardo Benzaquen de Araújo, "Força estranha," *Ciência Hoje* 1, no. 1 (Jul./ Aug. 1982): 32–37.

11. Tostão, *A perfeição não existe: Crônicas* (São Paulo: Três Estrelas, 2012), 226; Armando Nogueira, *A ginga e o jogo* (Rio de Janeiro: Objetiva, 2003), 180–81.

12. *Relatório da Confederação Brasileira de Futebol 1981* (Rio de Janeiro: CBF, 1981), 13.

13. Alvaro Vicente Graça Truppel Pereira do Cabo, "Futebol e Carnaval: Uma mistura dos estereótipos cariocas," 21 Feb. 2012, accessed 21 Feb. 2012, www.ludopedio.com.br/rc /index.php/arquibancada/artigo/899.

14. Jal e Gual, *A história do futebol no Brasil através do cartum* (Rio de Janeiro: Bom Texto, 2004), 100.

15. José Miguel Wisnik, "The Riddle of Brazilian Soccer: Reflections on the Emancipatory Dimensions of Culture," *Review: Literature and Arts of the Americas* 39, no. 2 (2006): 198–209. Assertions of soccer's democratic power include Roberto DaMatta, "Esporte na sociedade: Um ensaio sobre o futebol brasileiro," in *Universo do futebol: Esporte e sociedade brasileira* (Rio de Janeiro: Edições Pinakotheke, 1982), 19–42; Araújo, "Força estranha," esp. 35; Betty Milan, *Brasil: O país da bola* (São Paulo: Biblioteca Eucatex de Cultura Brasileira, 1989), esp. 8–9; Philip Evanson, "Understanding the People: *Futebol,* Theater, Film, and Politics in Present-Day Brazil," *South Atlantic Quarterly* 81, no. 4 (1982): 399–412. On the sport's link to authoritarianism, see Roberto Ramos, *Futebol: Ideologia do poder* (Petrópolis: Vozes, 1984); Luiz Felipe Baêta Neves, *O paradoxo do coringa e o jogo do poder e saber* (Rio de Janeiro: Achiamé, 1979), 1–19; Janet Lever, *Soccer Madness: Brazil's Passion for the World's Most Popular Sport* (Prospect Heights, IL: Waveland Press, 1995); Robert M. Levine, "The Burden of Success: *Futebol* and Brazilian Society Through the 1970s," *Journal of Popular Culture* 14, no. 3 (1980): 61. Both sides make their case in Matthew G. Shirts, "Futebol: A mesa-redonda do I.E.B," in *Futebol e cultura: Coletânea de estudos,* ed. José Carlos Sebe Bom Meihy and José Sebastião Witter (São Paulo: Convênio IMESP/DAESP, 1982), 113–18.

16. "Falcão: 'Não posso mudar o Brasil,'" *A Gazeta Esportiva* 26 Jul. 1982.

17. Caldas, "O futebol," 30; Levine, "The Burden of Success," 61; Ruy Carlos Ostermann, "O universo de Gérson," in *Futebol e palavra,* org. Ivan Cavalcanti Proença (Rio de Janeiro: Livraria José Olympio Editora, 1981), 48–49; "Pelé Speaks," in *The Brazil Reader: History, Culture, Politics,* ed. Robert M. Levine and John J. Crocitti (Durham: Duke University Press, 1999), 254–57; "O que pensa o jogador brasileiro," *Placar,* 31 Dec. 1981, 46.

18. Sócrates and Ricardo Gozzi, *Democracia Corintiana: A utopia em jogo* (São Paulo: Boitempo, 2002), 20.

19. Décio Pignatari, *Podbre Brasil: Crônicas políticas* (Campinas: Pontes, 1988), 85.

20. Franklin Goldgrub, *Futebol, arte ou guerra? Elogio ao drible* (Rio de Janeiro: Imago Editora, 1990), 65.

21. *Heróis de uma nação: O maior time rubro-negro de todos os tempos!,* dir. Eduardo Leite and Marcelo Camargo (Brazil, 2007).

22. Sócrates and Gozzi, *Democracia,* 85.

23. "Uma goleada para ficar na história," *Jornal do Brasil,* 18 Apr. 1983.

24. "Flamengo dá de 5 na estréia de Carlos Alberto," "Zico dá exhibição de toques, dribles, gols," and "Carlos Alberto, carisma de um homem vitorioso," *Jornal do Brasil,* 18 Apr. 1983; "O massacre do grande capitão," *Placar,* 22 Apr. 1983, 6–10.

25. "O massacre do grande capitão," *Placar,* 22 Apr. 1983, 7.

26. Paulo Roberto Falcão, *O time que nunca perdeu,* 2nd ed. (Porto Alegre: AGE, 2010).

27. Flávio F. Moreira, *A venda de Zico—e Mengo bi-campeão* (n.p., n.d.), 4.

28. "Zico fica. Eis a fórmula," *Placar,* 3 Apr. 1981, 18.

29. "Mengo procura novo Zico," *Placar,* 27 Aug. 1982, 22–24; Zico, with Roberto Assaf and Roger Garcia, *Zico, 50 anos de futebol,* 2nd ed. (Rio de Janeiro: Editora Record, 2003), 122.

30. Santa Helena, *Flamengo campeão do mundo,* 2nd ed. (Rio de Janeiro: n.p., 1981).

31. Jorge Ben's 1969 hit song "País tropical" (Tropical Country) included the lyrics, "I live in a tropical country / . . . / I'm Flamengo and I have a *nega* [black woman] named Tereza." See also Marcel Pereira, *A nação: Como e por que o Flamengo se tornou o clube com a maior torcida do Brasil* (Rio de Janeiro: Maquinária, 2010), 97–98; Ruy Castro, *Flamengo: O vermelho e o negro* (Rio de Janeiro: Ediouro, 2004), 147–49.

32. "Gaúchos e cariocas," in Verissimo, *Outras do Analista de Bagé,* 41st ed. (Porto Alegre: L&PM, 1982), 43.

33. "Zico, um craque de Seleção," *Placar,* 24 Mar. 1978, 4–6.

34. *O Globo,* 9 Mar. 1976; Tostão, *A perfeição não existe: Crônicas de futebol* (São Paulo: Três Estrelas, 2012), 90.

35. "Zico, 17 anos de magia," *Placar,* 18 Mar. 1988, 32; Monsanto, *1981;* André Rocha and Mauro Beting, *1981: Como um craque idolatrado, um time fantástico e uma torcida inigualável fizeram o Flamengo ganhar tantos títulos e conquistar o mundo em um só ano* (Rio de Janeiro: Maquinária, 2011); and *Heróis de uma nação.*

36. Renato Maurício Prado in *Heróis de uma nação.*

37. Zico, *Zico, 50 anos,* 34–35.

38. Zico, *Zico conta sua história* (São Paulo: FTD, 1996), 10.

39. Zico, *Zico, 50 anos,* 37–38; Zico, *Zico conta,* 14–20.

40. Pereira, *A nação,* 118–19; Castro, *Flamengo,* 157; Roberto Assaf and Zico in *Heróis de uma nação.*

41. *Heróis de uma nação.*

42. Monsanto, *1981,* 181.

43. *Heróis de uma nação.* Zico urged his teammates to prepare for physical battle; "Zico quer Flamengo violento em Montevidéu," *Jornal do Brasil,* 21 Nov. 1981.

44. Monsanto, *1981,* 193.

45. "Flamengo promete garra e valentia," *Jornal do Brasil,* 22 Nov. 1981; "Uma campanha feita de técnica e disposição," and João Saldanha, "O Flamengo soube reagir," *Jornal do Brasil,* 24 Nov. 1981; "Agora, o mundo," *Placar,* 27 Nov. 1981, 3.

46. João Saldanha, "O anti-futebol do Flamengo," *Jornal do Brasil,* 21 Nov. 1981. Rather than "Mechanical Orange" as the Dutch were known, Flamengo was, in reference to its animal mascot, the "Mechanical Vulture"; Rocha and Beting, *1981,* 86.

47. Jonathan Wilson, *Inverting the Pyramid: The History of Football Tactics* (London: Orion, 2008), 263, 342; Rocha and Beting, *1981,* 86.

48. Saldanha, "A bola obedece," *Jornal do Brasil,* 15 Dec. 1981.

49. Luiz Carlos Ramos, *Vicente Matheus: Quem sai na chuva é pra se queimar* (São Paulo: Editora do Brasil, 2001), 102; compare "O gosto do poder," *Placar,* 1 Apr. 1977, 40–41.

50. Igor Ojeda and Tatiana Merlino, *A invasão corinthiana: O dia em que a Fiel tomou o Rio de Janeiro para ver seu time no maior estádio do mundo* (São Paulo: Livraria da Física, 2011); Plínio Labriola Negreiros, "A invasão corinthiana—Rio, 05 de dezembro de 1976," *Aurora* 9 (2010): 114–25.

51. *23 anos em 7 segundos: 1977—o fim do jejum Corinthiano,* dir. Di Moretti and Júlio Xavier (Brazil, 2009); João Roberto Basílio, *Um escolhido: Autobiografia* (São Paulo: Editora Planeta do Brasil, 2008).

52. Sérgio Scarpelli in *Ser campeão é detalhe: Democracia Corinthiana,* dir. Gustavo Forti Leitão and Caetano Biasi (Brazil, 2011); José Paulo Florenzano, *A Democracia Corinthiana: Práticas de liberdade no futebol brasileiro* (São Paulo: FAPESP / EDUC, 2009), 141, 168–70.

53. Matthew Shirts, "Sócrates, Corinthians, and Questions of Democracy and Citizenship," in *Sport and Society in Latin America: Diffusion, Dependency, and the Rise of Mass Culture,* ed. Joseph L. Arbena (New York: Greenwood Press, 1988), 98–99; and Casagrande in Juca Kfouri, *Corinthians: Paixão e glória* (São Paulo: DBA, [2006]), 95; Florenzano, *A Democracia,* 416–17.

54. Ramos, *Vicente Matheus,* 71–72.

55. "O gosto do poder," *Placar,* 1 Apr. 1977, 40; Sócrates and Gozzi, *Democracia,* 29.

56. Sócrates and Gozzi, *Democracia,* 42.

57. Sócrates and Gozzi, *Democracia,* 42–45, 52; Ramos, *Vicente Matheus,* 176–78.

58. Ramos, *Vicente Matheus,* 17–22; Sócrates and Gozzi, *Democracia,* 29; cf. Alex Bellos, *Futebol: Soccer, the Brazilian Way* (New York: Bloomsbury, 2002), 287–316.

59. Sócrates and Gozzi, *Democracia,* 46.

60. Interview in Jorge Vasconcellos, org., *Recados da bola: Depoimentos de doze mestres do futebol brasileiro* (São Paulo: Cosac Naify, 2010), 216.

61. Luis Tolosa Santos, "Futebol empresa e a 'Democracia Corinthiana': Uma administração que deu dribling na crise," (Master's thesis, Universidade Estadual de Campinas, 1990), 100.

62. Florenzano, *A Democracia,* 182.

63. *Ser campeão é detalhe.*

64. Santos, "Futebol empresa," 91.

65. Bellos, *Futebol,* 366; Santos, "Futebol empresa," 89; Luiz Henrique de Toledo, *Lógicas no futebol* (São Paulo: Hucitec / Fapesp, 2002), 114.

66. "A Travaglini bastam respeito e disciplina," *O Estado de São Paulo,* 23 Mar. 1980.

67. Florenzano, *A Democracia,* 182.

68. Santos, "Futebol empresa," 93.

69. Sócrates Vieira de Oliveira, "A democracia funciona," *Veja,* 16 Mar. 1983, 130; Zé Maria in *Folha de São Paulo,* 21 Feb. 1982; Florenzano, *A Democracia,* 186.

70. Sócrates and Gozzi, *Democracia,* 53.

71. Sócrates and Gozzi, *Democracia,* 63; "A noite em que Wladimir foi o dono da festa," *Folha de São Paulo,* 1 Mar. 1982; Florenzano, *A Democracia,* 202–3, 358.

72. "A democracia se consolida," *Placar,* 8 Apr. 1983, 15.

73. Santos, "Futebol empresa," 92.

74. "Dificuldades de uma democracia," *Placar,* 22 Apr. 1983, 8–9.

75. Vasconcellos, *Recados da bola,* 206.

76. Ibid., 208.

77. Ramos, *Vicente Matheus,* 146–48.

78. Interview with Zizinho, *O Pasquim* 13, n. 6/9 (1–7 Jul. 1982): 10.

79. Vasconcellos, *Recados da bola,* 208; "Sócrates, domínio de um líder," *A Gazeta Esportiva,* 9 May 1982.

80. "A magia de Sócrates," *Placar,* 20 Apr. 1984, 12.

81. André Baibich, "Nunca haverá igual—a trajetória do 'Doutor' Sócrates (1954–2011)," accessed 4 Dec. 2011, www.goal.com/br/news/619/especiais/2011/1/04/2787649/nunca-haverá-igual-a-trajetória-do-doutor-sócrates-1954-2011.

82. "Bebo, fumo e penso," *Placar*, 3 Mar. 1986, 31–33; "Os limites do prazer," *Placar*, 25 Mar. 1983, 51–53; Florenzano, *A Democracia*, 303.

83. "Jogadores estão se armando," *A Gazeta Esportiva*, 21 May 1982.

84. Florenzano, *A Democracia*, 271–72; "A Democracia em debates," *Placar*, 29 Apr. 1983, 16.

85. "A democracia se consolida," *Placar*, 8 Apr. 1983, 16; Toledo, *Lógicas*, 144–45.

86. Marcos Guterman, *O futebol explica o Brasil: Uma história da maior expressão popular do país* (São Paulo: Contexto, 2009), 206; and *Ser campeão é detalhe*.

87. "A democracia se consolida," *Placar*, 8 Apr. 1983, 16. In fact, clubs expanded supervision of their athletes; Francisco Xavier Freire Rodrigues, "Modernidade, disciplina e futebol: Uma análise sociológica da produção social do jogador de futebol no Brasil," *Sociologias* 6, no. 11 (2004): 279–81; Toledo, *Lógicas*, 131–36.

88. Sócrates, "A democracia funciona."

89. "Sócrates e o esquema," *A Gazeta Esportiva*, 14 Dec. 1982; Florenzano, *A Democracia*, 283–84.

90. Sócrates and Gozzi, *Democracia*, 57–58.

91. *Ser campeão é detalhe;* "Sócrates, o cérebro," *A Gazeta Esportiva*, 5 Jul. 1982.

92. "Vox Populi: Propaganda, não!" *Placar*, 3 Jun. 1977, 60; Guterman, *O futebol*, 207.

93. "CND autoriza Flamengo a usar propaganda no exterior" and "Mota quer contrato mais vantajoso ainda," *Jornal do Brasil*, 16 Dec. 1981.

94. "Verba da publicidade vai reforçar o time," *Folha de São Paulo*, 22 Jul. 1982.

95. Guterman, *O futebol*, 208.

96. Florenzano, *A Democracia*, 324–26; 356–57.

97. Sócrates and Gozzi, *Democracia*, 124–25.

98. "E, no Rio, Sócrates defende 'democracia,'" *O Estado de São Paulo*, 19 Apr. 1983; "Ô, ô, ô, queremos torcedor!" *Placar*, 24 Jul. 1981, 19–21; Carlos Augustus Jourand Correia, "As vozes do gramado: Relato de ex-atletas sobre a formação do Sindicato de Futebolistas Profissionais do Rio de Janeiro (1971–1982)," *Esporte e Sociedade* 5, no. 15 (2010): 1–20; Florenzano, *A Democracia*, 267.

99. "A Democracia em debate," *Placar*, 29 Apr. 1983, 16–18.

100. Zé Maria won a seat in the São Paulo City Council in the 1982 voting; Santos, "Futebol empresa," 102.

101. Santos, "Futebol empresa," 91.

102. Sócrates and Gozzi, *Democracia*, 138; Shirts, "Sócrates," 108; Guterman, *O futebol*, 216.

103. Vasconcellos, *Recados da bola*, 219.

104. Shirts, "Sócrates," 108.

105. Juca Kfouri, "Dificuldades de uma democracia," *Placar*, 22 Apr. 1983, 8–9; Bruno Chiarioni and Márcio Kroehn, *Onde o esporte se reinventa: Histórias e bastidores dos 40 anos de Placar* (São Paulo: Primavera Editorial, 2010), 106–7; Marilena Chauí, "Futebol, a difícil democracia," *Folha de São Paulo*, 18 Apr. 1983; Florenzano, *A Democracia*, 370–71, 375–76.

106. Juca Kfouri and Wladimir in *Ser campeão é detalhe;* Kfouri, "Dificuldades de uma democracia," *Placar*, 22 Apr. 1983, 8–9; Toledo, *Lógicas*, 165–74.

107. *A Gazeta Esportiva*, 1 Apr. 1983; Juca Kfouri, "Quem tem medo da Democracia Corinthiana?" *Placar*, 8 Apr. 1983, 3; Florenzano, *A Democracia*, 356.

108. "Um grande caso," *Veja*, 5 Jan. 1983, 24; "A democracia se consolida," *Placar*, 8 Apr. 1983, 16; Florenzano, *A Democracia*, 295–305.

109. Santos, "Futebol empresa," 97.

110. Kfouri, "Dificuldades de uma democracia," *Placar,* 22 Apr. 1983, 8–9.

111. Ibid., 8.

112. Sócrates and Gozzi, *Democracia,* 72.

113. Ibid., 82.

114. "Matheus: 'Corinthians precisa mais de mim, do que eu dele . . .'" *A Gazeta Esportiva,* 4 Jan. 1980; "Coríntians volta a viver momentos de crise" and "Valdemar Pires garante que não deixará o cargo," *Folha de São Paulo,* 29 Jul. 1982; Sócrates and Gozzi, *Democracia,* 101–2.

115. Sócrates and Gozzi, *Democracia,* 72.

116. "O indesejável goleiro Leão," *Placar,* 21 Jan. 1983, 36–37.

117. Sócrates and Gozzi, *Democracia,* 113.

118. Santos, "Futebol empresa," 97–98.

119. Sócrates and Gozzi, *Democracia,* 113; "Corinthians contra Leão. Crise no Parque," *O Estado de São Paulo,* 4 Feb. 1983; Wanderly Nogueira, "Leão: Seis aprovam," *A Gazeta Esportiva,* 14 Feb. 1983; Florenzano, *A Democracia,* 308–10; Santos, "Futebol empresa," 97–98.

120. Florenzano, *A Democracia,* 310–11; "Um astro ofuscado," *Placar,* 2 Mar. 1984, 30–31; "A Democracia posta à prova," *Placar,* 11 Feb. 1984, 40–41.

121. Sócrates and Gozzi, *Democracia,* 115.

122. Ibid., 114–15.

123. Florenzano, *A Democracia,* 391.

124. Ibid., 393–94.

125. Sócrates and Gozzi, *Democracia,* 116.

126. "O sonho não acabou," *Placar,* 11 Jun 1982, 42–43.

127. Florenzano, *A Democracia,* 278–81.

128. "A abertura corinthiana," *Placar,* 27 Nov. 1981, 61.

129. Florenzano, *A Democracia,* 467–68, 474–75.

130. "Waldemar derruba Casagrande e compra Lima," *Folha de São Paulo,* 11 Jun. 1984.

131. "O 1.º de abril dos velhos corinthianos," *Placar,* 12 April 1985, 38–40.

132. Sócrates in Kfouri, *Corinthians,* 23–30.

133. "A abertura colorada," *Placar,* 9 Mar. 1984, 40–41; Florenzano, *A Democracia,* 330–37; "O massacre do grande capitão," *Placar,* 22 Apr. 1983, 7.

134. Interview with Juca Kfouri, part 2, 21 Apr. 2011, Ludopédio, at www.ludopedio.com.br/rc/index.php/entrevistas/artigo/577.

135. Ricardo Benzaquem de Araújo, "Força estranha," *Ciência Hoje* 1, no. 1 (1982), 37; Lula in Santos, "Futebol empresa," 91; Shirts, "Sócrates."

136. Cf. Márcio Braga, "O esporte brasileiro já começa a mudar," *Placar,* 21 Oct. 1983, 33; Caldas, "O futebol," 26–27.

137. Marcelo Weishaupt Proni, *A metamorfose do futebol* (Campinas: Unicamp, 2000), 146–47.

138. José Dias, *Futebol de craques e dos cartolas pernas-de-pau: 50 anos de jornalismo esportivo* (Rio de Janeiro: Mauad, 2000), 65; "Futebol deve dar só alegrias," *Placar,* 28 Dec. 1979, 12–13, 16; "CBF, 22 minutos que mudaram o futebol," *A Gazeta Esportiva,* 19 Jan. 1980.

139. *Telê Santana: Meio século de futebol-arte,* dir. Ana Carla Portella and Danielle Rosa (Brazil, 2009).

140. André Ribeiro, *Fio de Esperança: biografia de Telê Santana* (Rio de Janeiro: Gryphus, 2000), 38, 80.

141. "A retranca de Zagalo desfigurou a Seleção," *Folha de São Paulo*, 9 Jun. 1982.

142. "Telê: Preferência nacional," *A Gazeta Esportiva*, 7 Feb. 1980; Franco Júnior, *A dança*, 152.

143. "Trinta anos depois, outra derrota amarga," *O Globo Esportivo*, 16, Jun. 1980.

144. "Seleção de Telê dá show e goleia Paraguai," *O Globo Esportivo*, 31 Oct. 1980.

145. "Futebol de campeões," *Veja*, 27 May 1981, 57.

146. Ribeiro, *Fio de esperança*, 122, 211.

147. "Razões de Telê," *A Gazeta Esportiva*, 15 May 1980, 16.

148. Werneck, "Campo néutro," and "Telê promete Seleção de guerreiros e operários," *Jornal do Brasil*, 11 Feb. 1980.

149. "Telê define a tática: Brasil jogará sem medo," *O Globo Esportivo*, 29 Dec. 1980.

150. "Telê sabe que seleção se forma com melhores," *A Gazeta Esportiva*, 9 May 1980.

151. "Os caminhos da seleção, segundo o seu técnico," *O Globo Esportivo*, 15 Jun. 1980; "Telê acha que vitória sairá pelas pontas," *Jornal do Brasil*, 18 May 1981; "Telê mantém esquema e insiste na seriedade," *Folha de São Paulo*, 25 Jun. 1982. "Jogo ensaiado de Telê não abre mão do improviso," *Veja*, 16 Jun. 1982, 58.

152. "Telê define a tática: Brasil jogará sem medo," *O Globo Esportivo*, 29 Dec. 1980; Cláudio Mello e Souza, "Os trabalhos que esperam por Telê," *O Globo Esportivo*, 4 Feb. 1980; Ribeiro, *Fio de Esperança*, 122; "Como seria a seleção de Telê Santana," *Veja*, 9 Jan. 1980, 52.

153. Wisnik, *Veneno*, 119–20, 327, 330–31; "Telê lança o carrossel brasileiro," *Folha de São Paulo*, 16 Jun. 1982; "Telê quer mais do carrossel," *Folha de São Paulo*, 19 Jun. 1982.

154. "Telê define a tática: Brasil jogará sem medo," *O Globo Esportivo*, 29 Dec. 1980.

155. *Telê Santana: Meio século.*

156. "Como seria a seleção de Telê Santana," *Veja*, 9 Jan. 1980, 52.

157. Franço Júnior, *A dança*, 152; Ribeiro, *Fio de Esperança*, 139.

158. *Telê Santana: Meio século.*

159. "Telê chega à Seleção com aplicação e disciplina que teve como jogador," *Jornal do Brasil*, 10 Feb. 1980.

160. "Agora sim, acabou um velho tabu," *Folha de São Paulo*, 21 Jun. 1982; "Medrado não assume 'revolução liberal,'" *Folha de São Paulo*, 22 Jun. 1982; Ribeiro, *Fio de Esperança*, 127; Oldemário Touguinhó and Marcus Veras, *As Copas que eu vi* (Rio de Janeiro: Relume Dumará, 1994), 82.

161. Wladimir Miranda, *O artilheiro indomável: As incríveis histórias de Serginho Chulapa* (São Paulo: Publisher Brasil, 2011), 18–22; "Virei bom exemplo," *Placar*, 3 April 1981, 20; "No divã do analista," *Placar*, 11 Sep. 1981, 26.

162. Miranda, *O artilheiro indomável*, 25–27.

163. "O jogo duro de Telê," *Veja*, 13 May 1981, 61; "Seleção se apresenta em ambiente tumultuado," "Serginho, um bom ator para uma triste comédia," and "Serginho é cortado e vaga fica com César," *Jornal do Brasil*, 5 May 1981. Miranda, *O artilheiro indomável*, 37–38; José Inácio Werneck, "Campo néutro," *Jornal do Brasil*, 6 May 1981; "Telê Santana critica a violência," *Folha de São Paulo*, 30 Jun. 1982; "Telê proíbe o time a reidar," *Folha de São Paulo*, 1 Jul. 1982.

164. Roberto C. V. Mack, *Futebol empresa: A nova dimensão para o futebol brasileiro* (Rio de Janeiro: Palestra Edições, 1980), 80–81, 87; Ruy Carlos Ostermann, *Itinerário da derrota: Crônica de cinco Copas do Mundo sem Pelé* (Porto Alegre: Artes e Ofícios, 1992), 78; "Sócrates pronto para a pancadaria," *Folha de São Paulo*, 1 Jun. 1982; "Violência já preocupa Giulite," *Folha de São Paulo*, 3 Jun. 1982; Fábio Matias Polli, *Futebol e cidadania: Um projeto para o Brasil* (Florianópolis: Papa-Livro, 1990), 25–33.

165. Marcos Eduardo Neves, *Anjo ou demônio: A polêmica trajetoria de Renato Gaúcho* (Rio de Janeiro: Gryphus, 2002), 148–49.

166. Neves, *Anjo ou demônio,* 164; "O atrevido Renato criou juízo," *Placar,* 21 May 1982, 20.

167. Saldanha, "Passeio húngaro," *Jornal do Brasil,* 17 Mar. 1986; "Renato, perigoso e sempre driblador," *Jornal do Brasil,* 5 Mar. 1986.

168. "Telê admite corte disciplinar," *Folha de São Paulo,* 3 May 1986; "Amizade sem limíte," *Placar,* 19 May 1982, 16–23; Neves, *Anjo ou demônio,* 176–79, 189–214.

169. Jô Soares, "Estou com Zé da Galera: Cadê os pontas, Telê?" *Placar,* 21 May 1982, 32; "Garrincha: 'Seleção tem que ter pontas,'" *A Gazeta Esportiva,* 15 May 1982; "Ponteiros: só fixos é que são problemas," *A Gazeta Esportiva,* 14 May 1982; "Renato reclama da falta de pontas e diz que time tive medo de atacar," *Folha de São Paulo,* 2 Jun. 1986.

170. *Jornal da Tarde,* 5 May 1986, quoted in Neves, *Anjo ou demônio,* 194; "Tita diz que pediria dispensa se fosse convocado para a ponta," *Jornal do Brasil,* 5 May 1981; Werneck, "Campo Neutro," *Jornal do Brasil,* 2 Jul. 1985. Carlos Caboclo and Renato Gaúcho in *Telê Santana: Meio século.*

171. "A geração de ouro na luta do tetra," *Placar,* 31 Dec. 1981, 81; "Caminhos da sorte e do azar," *Folha de São Paulo,* 14 Jun. 1982; Paulo César O. Pinto, *Um ídolo chamado Roberto Dinamite* (Rio de Janeiro: Revan, 1987), 113–15.

172. "Reinaldo é exigido para recuperar ritmo," *Jornal do Brasil,* 18 May 1981.

173. *Jornal da Tarde,* 31 Mar. 1980, in Ribeiro, *Fio de Esperança,* 168.

174. "Telê conta tudo: 'Aqui está meu time para a Copa,'" *Placar,* 13 Nov. 1981, 43.

175. Luiz Carlos Lisboa, org., *Reinaldo do Atlético Mineiro* (Rio de Janeiro: Editora Rio, 2003), 43. Like that other champion of *futebol-arte,* João Saldanha, Telê was homophobic; see "O Brasil não vai ganhar de ninguém," *Placar,* 4 Oct. 1985, 37; "Assim falou João Saldanha," in Saldanha, *O trauma da bola: A Copa de 82* (São Paulo: Cosac & Naify, 2002), 21–22.

176. "Reinaldo se defende," *Placar,* 27 Nov. 1981, 24; Lisboa, *Reinaldo,* 41–43; "Telê confirma a crítica a Reinaldo" and "Jogador protesta," *Jornal do Brasil,* 8 Jul. 1981.

177. José Inácio Werneck, "Campo néutro," *Jornal do Brasil,* 15 Dec. 1981.

178. Falcão, *Histórias,* 85.

179. "Futebol de campeões," *Veja,* 27 Mar. 1981, 57–58.

180. "Júnior: 'No nosso time, todos jogam," *A Gazeta Esportiva,* 27 Jun. 1982; Ostermann, *Itinerário,* 71; "Paulo Isidoro: 'Nós temos algo mais,'" *A Gazeta Esportiva,* 25 Jan. 1981.

181. Cabral, "No meio de campo," *O Globo Esportivo,* 22 Dec. 1980.

182. "É jogador demais," in Saldanha, *O trauma,* 54–55.

183. "Sócrates o cérebro," *A Gazeta Esportiva,* 5 Jul. 1982; "Pensamentos de Sócrates," *A Gazeta Esportiva,* 27 May 1982; "Sócrates, o domínio de um líder," *A Gazeta Esportiva,* 9 May 1982; "A Copa de Zico," *A Gazeta Esportiva,* 27 Jun. 1982; Wisnik, *Veneno,* 332.

184. "Paulo Isidoro: Sei que jogo uma grande cartada," *Jornal dos Sports,* 9 Jun. 1980; interview with Zizinho, *O Pasquim* 13, no. 679 (1–7 Jan. 1982): 9; interviews with Zizinho in Mario de Moraes, *Futebol é arte,* part 2 (Rio de Janeiro: FAPERJ, MIS Editorial, [2002]), 274–75, and Depoimentos para a posteridade, Museu da Imagem e do Som, Rio de Janeiro, 1985; "A dura lição do Brasil ao velho rival," *Veja,* 7 Jul. 1982, 46.

185. "Brasil repete 50, Uruguai é campeão," *Folha de São Paulo,* 11 Jan. 1981; "O povão e os catedráticos aplaudem o Brasil," *A Gazeta Esportiva,* 8 Jan. 1981; "Respeito é bom e o Brasil gosta," *Placar,* 9 Jan. 1981, 3–8; Paulo Planet Buarque, "Volta à humildade não nos fará mal," *A Gazeta Esportiva,* 11 Jan. 1981; Carlos Drummond de Andrade, "Balanço atrasado," *Jornal do Brasil,* 20 Jan. 1981.

186. Sérgio Cabral, "Foram 13 craques e um Telê," *O Globo Esportivo*, 8 Jan. 1981; João Saldanha, "O alegre futebol brasileiro," *Jornal do Brasil*, 8 Jan. 1981; "Futebol de campeões," *Veja*, 27 Mar. 1981, 56–58.

187. "Telê mantém o grupo para as eliminatórias," *Folha de São Paulo*, 12 Jan. 1981.

188. Alberto Helena Jr, "A vitória de um futebol impecável" and "3 a 1 na França. E um belo futebol, como nos velhos tempos," *Jornal da Tarde*, 15 Jun. 1981. On the criticism, see "Um jogo de advertência," in Saldanha, *O trauma*, 62–63.

189. "Opinião de Placar," *Placar*, 22 May 1981, 13; Porto, "Europeus, um desafio," *Jornal dos Sports*, 11 May 1981; "Europa baila conosco," *Placar*, 22 May 1981, 15.

190. "Zezé compara Seleção às de 58 e 70," *Folha de São Paulo*, 27 Jun. 1982; "Tudo lembra 1958, 62 e 70," *A Gazeta Esportiva*, 25 Jun. 1982.

191. "Seleção se despede com exibição. E 7 a 0 no Eire foi pouco," *Jornal do Brasil*, 28 May 1982; Osterman, *Itinerário*, 69–70.

192. "É preciso justificar em campo o favoritismo," *Folha de São Paulo*, 28 Jun. 1982.

193. Compare Osterman, *Itinerário*, 71–72; Touguinhó and Veras, *As Copas*, 104; Guterman, *O futebol*, 210.

194. Moreno, *A Copa que o Brasil deixou cair* (Fortaleza: Centro de Referência Cultural / Editora Henriqueta Galeno, 1982), 3.

195. *A Gazeta Esportiva*, 16 Jun. 1982, 6–7; João Saldanha, "Favoritismo aumentou," *Folha de São Paulo*, 18 Jun. 1982; "Brasil continua favorito," *Folha de São Paulo*, 30 Jun. 1982.

196. "O jogo fico fácil," in Saldanha, *O trauma*, 139.

197. "Último tango em ritmo de samba," *A Gazeta Esportiva*, 4 Jul. 1982; "Brasil deu lição no campeão," *A Gazeta Esportiva*, 3 and 4 Jul. 1982; "A dura lição do Brasil ao velho rival," *Veja*, 7 Jul. 1982, 46–49; "Nós nem chegamos a jogar tudo" and "'Voa, Argentina, voa', canta Júnior no vestiário," *Folha de São Paulo*, 3 Jul. 1982; "A dura lição do Brasil ao velho rival," *Veja*, 7 Jul. 1982, 49; "Brasil perto do título, e boa viagem, Argentina," *Jornal do Brasil*, 3 Jul. 1982.

198. Touguinhó and Veras, *As Copas*, 105; compare "Éder já virou ídolo na Espanha," *Folha de São Paulo*, 21 Jun. 1982.

199. "Os elogios ao futebol brasileiro," *Folha de São Paulo*, 16 Jun. 1982; "Brasil: 'Monstros do futebol,'" *A Gazeta Esportiva*, 20 Jun. 1982.

200. "Éder, o adorável irresponsável," *A Gazeta Esportiva*, 23 Jun. 1982.

201. "Um 'peladeiro' de ouro," *A Gazeta Esportiva*, Jun. 1982; "A festa bonita," in Saldanha, *O trauma*, 146–47; "Porque vencemos," *A Gazeta Esportiva*, 15 Jun. 1982; "A goleada do talento brasileiro," *Folha de São Paulo*, 19 Jun. 1982; "A goleada veio em ritmo de treino," *Folha de São Paulo*, 24 Jun. 1982.

202. Ostermann, *Itinerário*, 78.

203. Ostermann, *Itinerário*, 79; Wisnik, *Veneno*, 120, 339–41; cartoon by Glauco in *Folha de São Paulo*, 9 Jul. 1982.

204. "Italianos tentam encontrar uma solução para a crise," *Folha de São Paulo*, 27 Jun. 1982; Araújo Netto, "Itália, fria ou guerreira, eis a questão," *Jornal do Brasil*, 5 Jul. 1982; "Socorro, está chegando o grande Brasil, *Folha de São Paulo*, 5 Jul. 1982; "Misticismo e crise envolvem a Itália," *A Gazeta Esportiva*, 5 Jul. 1982.

205. "Falcão prevê dificuldades," *Folha de São Paulo*, 21 Jun. 1982; "Falcão, o 'rei de Roma,' que trabalha contra a Itália," *Folha de São Paulo*, 25 Jun. 1982; "Contragolpe não preocupa Oscar," *Folha de São Paulo*, 5 Jul. 1982.

206. Nuno Ramos, "Os suplicantes (aspectos trágicos do futebol)," in *Ensaio geral: Projetos, roteiros, ensaios, memória* (São Paulo: Globo, 2007), 252.

207. "Desta vez, nem 'campeões morais,'" *Folha de São Paulo*, 8 Jul. 1982; Flávio Costa, "Repetimos tudo, como em 50," *A Gazeta Esportiva*, 7 Jul. 1982; "Pálido, Giulite evita declarações" and "Para Júnior, só o destino poder explicar," *Folha de São Paulo*, 8 Jul. 1982; "Desastre," *Folha de São Paulo*, 6 Jul. 1982.

208. "A Itália mereceu," in Saldanha, *O trauma*, 165–66; Juca Kfouri, "Repito: A Azurra mereceu a vitória no Sarriá," in *Meninos eu vi . . .* (São Paulo: DBA Artes Gráficas, 2003), 60–61.

209. "Morte na praia," *Veja*, 14 Jul. 1982, 52; "Desastre," *Folha de São Paulo*, 6 Jul. 1982; "As imprevisíveis consequências do inesperado desastre brasileiro," *Folha de São Paulo*, 12 Jul. 1982; Touguinhó and Veras, *As Copas*, 107; João Saldanha, "Máscara de imbatível," *Folha de São Paulo*, 8 Jul. 1982; "A 'vendetta' contra o Brasil," *A Gazeta Esportiva*, 7 Jul. 1982; Moreno, *A Copa*, 6–9; Ostermann, *Itinerário*, 86; "Bearzot considera Brasil presunçoso e inocente," *Folha de São Paulo*, 6 Jul. 1982; "As verdades de Oscar sobre a Copa," *Folha de São Paulo*, 19 Jul. 1982.

210. "Itália não perdoa nossos erros" and "Desastre," *Folha de São Paulo*, 6 Jul. 1982; Gérson, "Entregamos o jogo," and Zagallo, "Muitos erros na defesa," *A Gazeta Esportiva*, 6 Jul. 1982; "'Perdemos porque fizemos menos gols', filosofa Telê," *Folha de São Paulo*, 8 Jul. 1982; "Paulo Emílio e as lições da Copa," *A Gazeta Esportiva*, 18 Jul. 1982.

211. "O sonho de Bearzot," *A Gazeta Esportiva*, 6 Jul. 1982.

212. Some blamed his stubbornness or poor lineup choices; João Saldanha, "O limite da estupidez," *Folha de São Paulo*, 6 Jul. 1982; interview with Zizinho, *O Pasquim* 13, no. 679 (1–7 Jan. 1982): 9; interview with Zizinho in Moraes, *Futebol é arte*, part 2, 274–75; "Pintinho diz que Telê é o culpado," *Folha de São Paulo*, 6 Jul. 1982; "A teimosia de Telê," *A Gazeta Esportiva*, 6 Jul. 1982.

213. Ostermann, *Itinerário*, 80; Serginho in *Telê Santana: Meio século*.

214. "Balanço da Copa," *A Gazeta Esportiva*, 13 Jul. 1982; Amaral, "Devíamos jogar feio," *A Gazeta Esportiva*, 7 Jul. 1982; "Só beleza não basta, é preciso defender," and the testimonies of coaches Mário Travaglini, Jorge Vieira, and José Poy, *Folha de São Paulo*, 18 Jul. 1982; Touguinhó and Veras, *As Copas*, 101–8.

215. Saldanha, "O limite da estupidez," *Folha de São Paulo*, 6 Jul. 1982.

216. "Brasil perdeu por amor ao futebol" and "Brasil se foi mas caiu de pé," *A Gazeta Esportiva*, 7 Jul. 1982.

217. *Jornal do Brasil*, 6 Jul. 1982; cf. Alberto Dines, "Telê, meu candidato para presidente," *Placar*, 16 Jul. 1982, 23.

218. *Telê Santana: Meio século*.

219. "Telê vai mesmo para o futebol árabe," *Folha de São Paulo*, 31 Jul. 1982; Ribeiro, *Fio de Esperança*, 227–30.

220. *O Estado de São Paulo*, 10 Jul. 1982, cited in Ribeiro, *Fio de Esperança*, 221.

221. Ribeiro, *Fio de Esperança*, 232.

222. Ibid., 242.

223. Ibid., 247.

224. "Seleção, escola que faltou a Bebeto," *Jornal do Brasil*, 21 Jun. 1985; "Estou pronto para lutar pelo tetra," *Placar*, 1 Nov. 1985, 41.

225. *Jornal da Tarde*, 22 Jan. 1986.

226. "Como quebramos a Bolívia em dois," *Placar*, 7 Jun. 1985, 12.

227. Sepalo Campelo, *A Copa 86 das oitavas ao final* (Niterói: n.p., 1986), 1; Maurício Cardoso, "Uma semana de alegria dupla," *Veja*, 11 Jun. 1986, 60–65; but cf. João Saldanha, "O Brasil não vai ganhar de ninguém," *Placar*, 4 Oct. 1985, 35; "Seleção perdida é reprovada de novo," *Jornal do Brasil*, 17 Mar. 1986.

228. "Maravalha!" and Kfouri, "Venha quem vier," *Placar,* 23 Jun. 1986, 16–29; "Nos pés de Careca, o melhor futebol do Brasil," *Veja,* 11 Jun. 1986, 62–63; "Josimar, tiro certeiro na estréia," *Folha de São Paulo,* 13 Jun. 1986; "Um herói brasileiro," *Placar,* 30 Jun. 1986, 30–36; Touguinhó and Veras, *As Copas,* 122–24.

229. "Zico renova esperança; agora, a Polônia" and "Cresce otimismo," *Folha de São Paulo,* 13 Jun. 1986; Ostermann, *Itinerário,* 104, 110.

230. Amaury Fassy, *Brasil: Tetra campeão mundial?* (Brasília: Horizonte, 1982), 72.

231. Juca Kfouri, "Geração sem glória," *Placar,* 30 Jun. 1986, 29.

232. Maurício Cardoso, "Uma nobre despedida," *Veja,* 25 Jun. 1986, 58–62.

233. Ostermann, *Itinerário,* 107, 112.

234. "Lazaroni confirmado como técnico da Seleção," *Jornal do Brasil,* 13 Jan. 1989.

235. "Telê é o técnico preferido dos cariocas e paulistanos; só 3% apóiam Lazaroni," *Folha de São Paulo,* 15 Jan. 1989; and on the politics of Lazaroni's rise, "Parreira apóia Teixeira para voltar ao comando da seleção," *Folha de São Paulo,* 3 Jan. 1989; "Jogo embalado," *Veja,* 11 Jan. 1989, 62; "Parreira critica Ricardo Teixeira," *Folha de São Paulo,* 14 Jan. 1989; "Ricardo Teixeira anuncia hoje os 23 selecionáveis; Lazaroni é o técnico," *Folha de São Paulo,* 16 Jan. 1989.

236. "Técnico copia a filosofia do 'sargento' Silva," *Folha de São Paulo,* 29 Jan. 1989; "Lazaroni precisa pagar aos árabes para assumir seleção," *Folha de São Paulo,* 14 Jan. 1989; "Os 1001 pepinos," *Placar,* 27 Jan. 1989, 14–15.

237. "Quem é Sebastião Lazaroni," *Folha de São Paulo,* 16 Jan. 1989.

238. "'Seleção das arábias' de Eurico Miranda tem 39 jogadores e dura apenas 15 dias" and "Relação só beneficia os empresários," *Folha de São Paulo,* 17 Jan. 1989; "Seleção falsa de Eurico valoriza o passe de Toninho em 1.000%," *Folha de São Paulo,* 4 Feb. 1989; "Bola dividida," *Veja,* 25 Jan. 1989, 73.

239. "Carlos Alberto Silva diz que CBF prefere 'cordeirinho' dirigindo seleção," *Folha de São Paulo,* 18 Jan. 1989.

240. "Lazaroni diz que esquema é ofensivo," *O Estado de São Paulo,* 15 Jul. 1989; "Lazarônico macarrônico: guia do dialeto falado à beira do gramado," *Istoé,* 6 Jun. 1990, 54; interview with Lazaroni in *Placar,* 18 Aug. 1989, 17; Roberto Benevides, "Gol de letra," *O Estado de São Paulo,* 14 Jul. 1989.

241. "Brasil vence Al-Ahli e Lazaroni faz críticas a Bebeto," *Folha de São Paulo,* 30 Mar. 1989; "Charles pede calma à torcida" and "Romário agora quer sair do time," *O Estado de São Paulo,* 5 Jul. 1989; "Quem é Sebastião Lazaroni," *Folha de São Paulo,* 16 Jan. 1989; "Romário faz sacrifício e reage," *O Estado de São Paulo,* 23 May 1990; "Romário pede um lugar" and "Bebeto também quer uma chance," *O Estado de São Paulo,* 13 Jun. 1990; "Lazaroni quer explorar os contra-ataques," *Jornal do Brasil,* 23 Jun. 1990.

242. "As pedras no caminho do Brasil," *Veja,* 20 Jun. 1990, 54.

243. "Lazarônico macarrônico: Guia do dialeto falado à beira do gramado," *Istoé,* 6 Jun. 1990, 54; interview with Lazaroni in *Placar,* 18 Aug. 1989, 17; "Tensão de decolagem," *Veja,* 6 Jun. 1990, 56.

244. "Seleção vence na estréia de Lazaroni," *Folha de São Paulo,* 16 Mar. 1989; "Minestrone à Lazaroni," *Istoé,* 6 Jun. 1990, 40–41; "Brasil procura a ressurreição," *O Estado de São Paulo,* 1 Jul. 1989; "Lazaroni pode perder o emprego" and "Seleção vence mas vive crise," *O Estado de São Paulo,* 2 Jul. 1989; "CBF poder trocar Lazaroni por Falcão," *O Estado de São Paulo,* 4 Jul. 1989; "Seleção joga futuro na Copa América," *O Estado de São Paulo,* 7 Jul. 1989; "Seleção é campeá e já tem time-base," *O Estado de São Paulo,* 18 Jul. 1989.

245. "Minestrone à Lazaroni," *Istoé,* 6 Jun. 1990, 41; Roberto Benevides, "E não é que o Dunga é mesmo o nosso Pelé?" *O Estado de São Paulo,* 6 Jun. 1990; "O guerreiro Dunga e seu

dia de glória," *O Estado de São Paulo*, 2 Jun. 1990; "Dunga tem sua vaga garantida," *O Estado de São Paulo*, 8 May 1990.

246. João Saldanha, "Um trabalho," *Jornal do Brasil*, 25 Jun. 1990; Juca Kfouri, "A ironia de uma derrota injusta," *Placar*, 29 Jun. 1990, 29; "Brilha, Seleção," *Placar*, 22 Jun. 1990, 10.

247. Nelson Motta, *Confissões de um torcedor: Quatro Copas e uma paixão* (Rio de Janeiro: Objetiva, 1998), 73.

248. Roberto Benevides, "Brasil, meu Brasil tão pouco brasileiro," *O Estado de São Paulo*, 23 Jun. 1990.

249. "Talento sepulta Era Dunga com 35 dias de vida," *Jornal do Brasil*, 25 Jun. 1990; Juca Kfouri, "Agora, nós somos a Itália," *Placar*, 22 Jun. 1990, 10; Flávio Araújo, *O rádio, o futebol e a vida* (São Paulo: Editora SENAC São Paulo, 2001), 226.

250. Roberto Benevides, "Gol de letra," *O Estado de São Paulo*, 11 Jul. 1989; Benevides, "Brasil, meu Brasil tão pouco brasileiro," *O Estado de São Paulo*, 23 Jun. 1990; Flávio Costa, "A Copa não é um laboratório," *O Estado de São Paulo*, 23 Jun. 1990.

251. For charges that Lazaroni's style was based in cowardice, see "Talento sepulta Era Dunga com 35 dias de vida," *Jornal do Brasil*, 25 Jun. 1990; Armando Nogueira, "Na grande área," *Jornal do Brasil*, 10 Jun. 1990.

252. Ari Borges, "Mataram a arte no futebol," *O Estado de São Paulo*, 12 Jun. 1990.

253. Manoel Santa Maria, *Futebol e economia: Fracassos da teoria* (Rio de Janeiro: author, 1990).

CHAPTER 5

Epigraph: Édison Gastaldo, *Pátria, chuteiras e propaganda: o brasileiro na publicidade da Copa do Mundo* (São Paulo: Annablume; São Leopoldo, RS: Unisinos, 2002), 58. The five stars would represent five World Cup triumphs.

1. Kariann Goldschmitt, "'Joga Bonito Pelo Mundo, Guerreiro': Music, Transmedia Advertising, and Brasilidade in the 2006 World Cup," *Popular Music and Society* 34, no. 4 (2011): 417–36.

2. Nogueira, "Na grande área," *Jornal do Brasil*, 30 Jul. 2002.

3. Roberto DaMatta, *A bola corre mais que os homens: Duas copas, treze crônicas e três ensaios sobre o futebol* (Rio de Janeiro: Rocco, 2006), 38; Frank J. Lechner, "Imagined Communities in the Global Game: Soccer and the Development of Dutch National Identity," in *Globalization and Sport,* ed. Richard Giulianotti and Roland Robertson (Oxford: Blackwell, 2007), esp. 112; Flávio Araújo, *O rádio, o futebol e a vida* (São Paulo: Editora SENAC São Paulo, 2001), 238–42.

4. Raffaele Poli, "The Denationalization of Sport: De-ethnization of the Nation and Identity Deterritorialization," *Sport in Society* 10, no. 4 (2007): 646–61.

5. Nelson Motta, *Confissões de um torcedor: Quatro Copas e uma paixão* (Rio de Janeiro: Objetiva, 1998), 137.

6. Alex Bellos, *Futebol: Soccer, the Brazilian Way* (New York: Bloomsbury, 2002), 5–25; José Miguel Wisnik, *Veneno remédio: O futebol e o Brasil* (São Paulo: Companhia das Letras, 2008), 364.

7. José Geraldo Couto, *Futebol brasileiro hoje* (São Paulo: Publifolha, 2009), 74.

8. David Harvey, *A Brief History of Neoliberalism* (Oxford: Oxford University Press, 2005), 20–63; Jean Baudrillard, *In the Shadow of the Silent Majorities, or, the End of the Social and*

Other Essays, trans. Paul Foss, John Johnston, and Paul Patton (New York: Semiotext(e), 1983); Theodore Levitt, "The Globalization of Markets," *Harvard Business Review* (1983): 92–102.

9. Fernando Collor, "Agenda para o Congresso: Uma proposta social-liberal (1)," *Jornal do Brasil,* 5 Jan. 1992.

10. Fernando Henrique Cardoso, "The Impact of Globalization on Developing Countries," in *Charting a New Course: The Politics of Globalization and Social Transformation* (Lanham, MD: Rowman & Littlefield, 2001), 257–70; Bryan McCann, *The Throes of Democracy: Brazil since 1989* (Halifax: Fernwood Publishing; London: Zed Books, 2008), 30–42; Tarcísio Costa, "Os anos noventa: O ocaso do político e a sacralização do mercado," in *Viagem incompleta. A experiência brasileira (1500–2000): A grande transação,* org. Carlos Guilherme Mota, 2nd ed. (São Paulo: Editora SENAC São Paulo, 2000), 247–82; Wendy Hunter, "The Partido dos Trabalhadores: Still a Party of the Left?" in *Democratic Brazil Revisited,* ed. Peter R. Kingstone and Timothy J. Power (Pittsburgh: University of Pittsburgh Press, 2008), 15–32.

11. Renato Ortiz, "Diversidade cultural e cosmopolitanismo," *Lua Nova* 47 (1999): 73–89; George Yúdice, *The Expediency of Culture: Uses of Culture in the Global Era* (Durham: Duke University Press, 2003), 109–32.

12. Richard Giulianotti and Roland Robertson, "Recovering the Social: Globalization, Football and Transnationalism," and David L. Andrews and George Ritzer, "The Grobal in the Sporting Glocal," both in *Globalization and Sport,* ed. Richard Giulianotti and Roland Robertson (Oxford: Blackwell, 2007), 58–78 and 28–45.

13. Renato Ortiz, "O advento da modernidade?" in *Posmodernidad en la periferia: Enfoques latinoamericanos de la nueva teoría cultural,* ed. Hermann Herlinghaus and Monika Walter (Berlin: Langer Verlag, 1994), 196.

14. "País do futebol e da raquete vive semana decisiva," *Folha de São Paulo,* 12 Nov. 2001; Luiz Henrique de Toledo, "Políticas da corporalidade: Socialidade torcedora entre 1990–2010," in *A torcida brasileira,* ed. Bernardo Buarque de Hollanda et al. (Rio de Janeiro: 7letras, 2012), 126–27; Bryan McCann, "Volleyball Nation: Brazilian Women's Vôlei," *Georgetown Journal of International Affairs,* 2 Jul. 2012.

15. Maurício Cardoso, "Um campeão sob medida," *Veja,* 18 Jul. 1994, 46–49.

16. "Parreira não vê lugar para Romário," *Jornal do Brasil,* 18 Dec. 1992; "Zagalo faz novas acusações," *Jornal do Brasil,* 19 Dec. 1992; "Romário e Ronaldinho, feitos um para o outro," *Placar,* Apr. 1997, 3.

17. "Para Zagalo, punição fez bem a Romário," *Folha de São Paulo,* 21 Sep. 1993; "Os uruguaios que se cuidem," *O Globo,* 8 Sep. 2003; Ronaldo Helal, "A construção de narrativas de idolatria no futebol brasileiro," *Alcéu* 4, no. 7 (2003): 27.

18. "O sonho de ser o dono da Copa," *Jornal do Brasil,* 21 Sep. 1993; "Jogador quis imitar Pelé," *Folha de São Paulo,* 20 Sep. 1993; Armando Nogueira, "Tesouros do Romário," *Jornal do Brasil,* 22 Sep. 1993.

19. "Os duendes de nossa alma," *Manchete,* 25 Sep. 1993, 15; Helal, "A construção," 26–33, and "Idolatria e malandragem: A cultura brasileira na biografia do Romário," in *Futbologías: Fútbol, identidad e violencia en América Latina,* ed. Pablo Alabarces (Buenos Aires: Clacso, 2003), 225–40.

20. José de Jesus Louzeiro in Marcus Vinicius Rezende de Morais, *Romário,* (Rio de Janeiro: Altadena, 2009), 25.

21. Edevair Faria in Morais, *Romário,* 31.

22. "Romario, Platini and 10 stars who emerged at the Olympics," Goal.com, 31 Jul. 2012, www.goal.com/en/news/1717/editorial/2012/07/31/3252864/romario-platini-10-stars-who-emerged-at-the-olympics; "A prata que teve gosto de lata," *Placar,* 7 Oct. 1988, 4–8.

23. "Com Bebeto no time e Romário no banco," *Placar,* 22 Jun. 1990, 21.

24. "Romário sozinho não vai ganhar a tetra," *Folha de São Paulo,* 20 Sep. 1993; "Romário 40 anos," *Placar,* Jan. 2006, 65; Filé in Moraes, *Romário,* 166–71; Jorge Caldeira, *Ronaldo: Glória e drama no futebol globalizado* (Rio de Janeiro: Lance! Editorial; São Paulo: Editora 34, 2002), 122.

25. "Malandro catalão," *Placar,* Mar. 1994, 11.

26. Ibid., 10–13.

27. He later played for brief spells in Spain, Qatar, the United States, and Australia.

28. "Vim para trabalhar," *Veja,* 25 Jan. 1995, 7; "Malandro catalão," *Placar,* Mar. 1994, 12.

29. "Romario onze Lieve heer van Eindhoven," accessed 13 Sep. 2012, www.youtube .com/watch?v=Jrv4luZvhJo&feature=relmfu.

30. "Malandro catalão," *Placar,* Mar. 1994, 10–13.

31. Simon Kuper, *Soccer Men* (New York: Nation Books, 2011), 85.

32. Arnaldo Ribeiro, "Craques da ponte aérea," *Placar,* 18 Jan. 2002.

33. "Romário maior que Pelé?" *Placar,* Apr. 2007, 57; "Terminologia no futebol," in Tostão, *A perfeição não existe: Crônicas de futebol* (Rio de Janeiro: Três Estrelas, 2012), 41; Antonio Lopes in Moraes, *Romário,* 98.

34. "Romario onze Lieve heer van Eindhoven."

35. "Vou fazer mil gols," *Veja,* 21 Jan. 2004, 9.

36. Jerônimo, Mário Tilico, Ênio Farias, and Valinhos in Moraes, *Romário,* 89–95; the quote is on page 90.

37. Wisnik, *Veneno,* 348.

38. "O fato é que não corremos nenhum risco nesta Copa," *Placar* no. 8, Jul. 1994, 26.

39. "A maior glória do século," *Placar,* no. 8, "A pátria de chuteiras," *Veja,* 13 Apr. 1994, 8; "O fato é que não corremos nenhum risco nesta Copa," *Placar,* no. 8, Jul. 1994, 27.

40. Fernando Calazans, *O nosso futebol* (Rio de Janeiro: Mauad, 1998), 67–68.

41. Noronha, "Crise de criação," *Jornal do Brasil,* 20 Dec. 1992; "Neto acha que falta talento," *Jornal do Brasil,* 16 Jul. 1991.

42. Matinas Suzuki Jr., "Nada muda, até os erros são os mesmos," *Folha de São Paulo,* 29 Jun. 1994.

43. Calazans, *O nosso futebol,* 70–71; "A noite de São Romário," *Manchete,* 25 Sep. 1993, 8; DaMatta, *A bola,* 50.

44. "A dura missão de Dunga: Domar o irreverente Romário," *O Globo,* 16 Jun. 1994; "Chama o Veio," *Placar,* Jun. 1997, 44.

45. "A pátria de chuteiras," *Veja,* 13 Apr. 1994, 7; "Romário, 40 anos," *Placar,* Jan. 2006, 65.

46. Santos in Moraes, *Romário,* 82.

47. Ostermann, *O nome do jogo* (Porto Alegre: Sagra Luzzatto / Palmarinca, 1998), 43; Flávio Araújo, *O radio,* 229.

48. "Copa breca escalada do futebol defensivo" and "Melhor defesa garante o título ao Brasil," *Folha de São Paulo,* 18 Jul. 1994.

49. "Artilheiro de palavra," *Placar,* no. 8, Jul. 1994, 13; cf. "Respeito é bom e a gente gosta," *Placar,* no. 2, Jun. 1994, 4–6.

50. Helal, "A construção."

51. "A maior glória do século," *Placar,* Dec. 1994, 9.

52. "Romario onze Lieve heer van Eindhoven."

53. Piloto, Zito, Luizinho, and Wilson Mussauer in Moraes, *Romário,* 62–63, 66–69, 84–86.

54. "Vim para trabalhar," *Veja,* 25 Jan. 1995, 8.

55. "Vim para trabalhar," *Veja,* 25 Jan. 1995, 8; "Romário quer ganhar Copa para entrar na história," *Folha de São Paulo,* 26 Jun. 1994; "Tráfico de influência," *Placar,* Dec. 2005, 68–73.

56. "Romário dedica o título a 'vascaíno no. 1,'" *Folha de São Paulo,* 19 Jan. 2001; Moraes, *Romário;* "Quatro anos atrás, Romário passou pelo mesmo problema," *O Estado de São Paulo,* 3 Jun. 2002; "Romário, 40 anos," *Placar,* Jan. 2006, 67; "Baxinharia," *Placar,* Dec. 2002, 30; "Conversa de surdos," *Placar,* Sep. 19–26, 2001, 16–19; Wisnik, *Veneno,* 347–48.

57. "A noite de São Romário" and "Os duendes de nossa alma," *Manchete,* 25 Sep. 1993, 8 and 15.

58. "A raposa em pele de porco-espinho," *Veja,* 18 Jul. 1994, 19; cf. "Do jeito que o povo gosta," *Placar,* Mar. 2000, 31.

59. "Vim para trabalhar," *Veja,* 25 Jan. 1995, 9.

60. "O adorado," *Jornal do Brasil,* 21 Jul. 1994; "Vim para trabalhar," *Veja,* 25 Jan. 1995, 8–9; "Vou fazer mil gols," *Veja,* 21 Jan. 2004, 9;

61. "A raposa em pele de porco-espinho," *Veja,* esp. Tetra 94, 18 Jul. 1994, 19; Helal, "Idolatria e malandragem," 228–29; "Artilheiro de palavra," *Placar,* no. 8, Jul. 1994, 13.

62. "Os primeiros planos para 94 incluem um serviço de espionagem feito pels próprios jogadores," *Manchete,* 25 Sep. 1993, 11.

63. "A raposa em pele de porco-espinho," *Veja,* esp. Tetra 94, 18 Jul. 1994, 19.

64. "Romário quer ganhar Copa para entrar na história," *Folha de São Paulo,* 26 June 1994; "O gênio da área: Romário diz que apenas começou a jogar," *O Globo,* 22 Jun. 1994; "Romário: 'Fico mais à vontade na hora de decidir,'" *O Globo,* 13 Jul. 1994.

65. "Os grandes eleitos do marketing," *Placar,* Apr. 1994, 26–27. The ads are available at www.youtube.com/watch?v=xGPE_8nCjHE&feature=relmfu and www.youtube.com/watch?v=H1jPcx24zJs; Paulo de Tarso, *Os cães ladram e a caravana passa* (Fortaleza: Edições Livro Técnico, n.d.), 2; Apolônio Alves, *A vitória do Brasil tetra campeão mundial de futebol na Copa 94* (Campina Grande, Paraíba: n.p., n.d.), 2; Banda Mel, "Homenagem a Romário," accessed 27 Aug. 2012, www.metacafe.com/watch/2106803/bandamel_m_sica_em_homenagem_rom_rio_1994_ao_vivo_live_show_rede_globo_de_tv/.

66. Capítulo IX, Artigos 48 and 50, Brazil, Decreto-Lei 3.199, 14 Apr. 1941, *Diário Oficial da União,* 17 Apr. 1941, 53; Caldeira, *Ronaldo,* 53–57, 124; Brazil, Lei n. 8.672, 6 Jul. 1993, available at www.camara.gov.br/internet/InfDoc/novoconteudo/legislacao/republica/Leisocerizadas/Leis1993v185n7.pdf; Fernando Marinho Mezzadri, "As possíveis interferências do estado na estrutura do futebol brasiliero," in *Futebol e globalização,* org. Luiz Ribeiro (Jundiaí, SP: Fontoura, 2007), 116–18; Marcelo Weishaupt Proni, *A metamorfose do futebol* (Campinas: Unicamp, 2000), 166–67; "Toninho Cecílio critica classe de jogadores: 'Categoria desunida,'" 24 Jul. 2012, accessed 14 Sep. 2012, http://globoesporte.globo.com/sp/vale-do-paraiba-regiao/noticia/2012/07/toninho-cecilio-critica-classe-dos-jogadores-categoria-desunida.html.

67. Part 2 of an interview with Juca Kfouri, 21 Apr. 2011, accessed 27 May 2011 at www.ludopedio.com.br/rc/index.php/entrevistas/artigo/S77.

68. "Não sou um robô," *Veja,* 5 Jan. 2000, 14; "Leve para voar," *Placar,* Mar. 2007, 53.

69. Interview with Ronaldo and Fabiano Farah, Executive Director of Grupo R9, 8 May 2007, accessed 27 May 2011 at http://leonardoweb.globo.com/noticias.asp?secao=leo&cod=256.

70. "O novo gênio da bola," *Veja,* 23 Oct. 1995, 113; "Não sou um robô," *Veja,* 5 Jan. 2000, 15.

71. Ken Foster, "Alternative Models for the Administration of Global Sport," in *The Global Politics of Sport: The Role of Global Institutions in Sport,* ed. Lincoln Allison (London: Routledge, 2005), 67; Richard Giulianotti, *Football: A Sociology of the Game* (Cambridge, UK: Polity Press, 1999), 89–90.

72. James Mosley, *Ronaldo: The Journey of a Genius* (Edinburgh: Mainstream, 2005), 226.

73. "Lágrimas no adeus: 'Perdi para meu corpo,'" Lancenet, accessed 26 Sep. 2012, www.lancenet.com.br/z_manchete_mobile/Lagrimas-Perdi-corpo_0_427157367.html; André Mendes Capraro, Everton Albuquerque Cavalcanti, and Doralice Lange de Souza, "'Cai o pano': Uma análise do encerramento da carreira de Ronaldo 'fenômeno' a partir de duas mídias digitais esportivas," *Movimento* 17, no. 3 (2011): 175–92.

74. Conrado Giulietti, "Fofômeno," ESPN Brazil, 10 Jan. 2012, accessed 12 Jan. 2012, http://espn.estadao.com.br/post/284730_fofomeno. See also the cover caption "Vale quanto pesa?" (Is he worth his weight?), *Placar,* Jan. 2009.

75. Capraro, Cavalcanti, and Souza, "'Cai o pano'"; Ronaldo turns to TV to help lose weight," ESPN.com, accessed 8 Oct. 2012, http://soccernet.espn.go.com/news/story/_/id/1168352/ronaldo-turns-to-tv-show-to-help-lose-weight?cc=5901.

76. Caldeira, *Ronaldo,* 47.

77. Caldeira, *Ronaldo,* 48–50; Mosley, *Ronaldo,* 25.

78. Mosley, *Ronaldo,* 28–29.

79. Caldeira, *Ronaldo,* 65–67.

80. "Duelo a três," *Placar,* Feb. 1994, 41.

81. "O tetra brasileiro está na boca do povo," *Placar,* Apr. 1993, esp. 42.

82. Caldeira, *Ronaldo,* 100–101.

83. "Técnicos escalam o Brasil para Copa 98," *Folha de São Paulo,* 18 Jul. 1994.

84. Caldeira, *Ronaldo,* 94, 98.

85. "Campeão do mundo," *Placar,* May 2003, 46; Caldeira, *Ronaldo,* 95–97.

86. Caldeira, *Ronaldo,* 131.

87. "Surge o fenômeno," *Placar,* May 2003, 48.

88. "O novo gênio da bola," *Veja,* 23 Oct. 1996, 109.

89. Compare Daniel Piza, *Ora bolas! da Copa de 98 ao Penta* (São Paulo: Editora Nova Alexandria, 2003), 100.

90. Caldeira, *Ronaldo,* 134; Mosley, *Ronaldo,* 62.

91. "O novo gênio da bola," *Veja,* 23 Oct. 1996, 109; Tostão, "As frases do craque," *Folha de São Paulo,* 7 Jul. 1999.

92. Mosley, *Ronaldo,* 63; Caldeira, *Ronaldo,* 134.

93. Caldeira, *Ronaldo,* 160.

94. "Futebol na raça," *Veja,* 7 Jan. 1998, 63.

95. "Chama o véio," *Placar,* Jun. 1997, 40–44; "A marca do Z," *Istoé,* 17 Jun. 1998, 130–31.

96. On Zagallo's superstitions, see for instance, "O apóstolo da sorte," *Veja,* esp. Tetra, 18 Jul. 1994, 51; Roberto Assaf, *Banho de bola: Os técnicos, as táticas e as estratégias que fizeram história no futebol* (Rio de Janeiro: Relume Dumará, 2002), 141–42.

97. "Ninguém tira o penta da gente," *Jornal do Brasil,* 12 Jul. 1998.

98. "A apenas dois passos da glória," *Veja,* 8 Jul. 1998, 86, cited in Marcelo Guterman, *O futebol explica o Brasil: Uma história da maior expressão popular do país* (São Paulo: Contexto, 2009), 251.

99. "Ronaldinho mostra recuperação," *Jornal do Brasil,* 14 Jun. 1998; Ostermann, *O nome,* 244; Caldeira, *Ronaldo,* 198–99; "Olha quem está jogando," *Placar,* Feb. 2001, 52.

100. "O verdadeiro Ronaldinho" and also "Brasil desencanta e dá goleada" and "A volta da confiança," *Jornal do Brasil,* 28 Jun. 1998.

101. Assaf, *Banho de bola,* 143.

102. "O dia de glória chegou," *Placar,* Jul. 1998, 36–38; "Brasil, vice, é campeão do século," *Jornal do Brasil,* 13 Jul. 1998; Gastaldo, *Pátria, chuteiras e propaganda,* 37–39.

103. "Derrota fria e irônica," *Jornal do Brasil,* 13 Jul. 1998.

104. Édison Gastaldo, "Accounting for Defeat: Sporting Speech and Communicative Resources in a World Cup Final Loss," *Vibrant: Virtual Brazilian Anthropology* 6, no. 2 (2009): 9–28; "O fim do sonho," *Placar,* Jul. 1998, 40; Piza, *Ora, bolas! Da Copa de 98 ao Penta* (São Paulo: Editora Nova Alexandria, 2003), 61–62; Wisnik, *Veneno,* 375.

105. "Pressão demais," *Veja,* 22 Jul. 1998, 88; Mosley, *Ronaldo,* 94–95.

106. "Pressão demais," *Veja,* 22 Jul. 1998, 88.

107. "O testemunho do capitão," *Placar,* Jun. 1999, 22.

108. The quotations here come from "Fim do mistério," *Placar,* Jun. 1999, 52–60. My version of events draws on that report, as well as "Pressão demais," *Veja,* 22 Jul. 1998, 88–95; Caldeira, *Ronaldo,* 202–21; Aldo Rebelo and Silvio Torres, *CBF Nike* (Rio de Janeiro: Casa Amarela, 2001), 124–29; Wisnik, *Veneno,* 370–71; "Indisposição geral," "Zagalo reconhece erro," and "Pressão demais," *Jornal do Brasil,* 15 Jul. 1998; "Edmundo descarrega a metralhadora" and "Lídio Toledo não descarta a epilepsia," *Jornal do Brasil,* 15 Jul. 1998.

109. "Fim do mistério," *Placar,* Jun. 1999, 60.

110. "Pressão demais," *Veja,* 22 Jul. 1998, 88–95. The theory that Ronaldo had suffered a panic attack was embraced by Dr. Lidio and team members at the time, though Roberto Carlos later denied it. See "A bomba que desculpa o 'Fenômeno,'" *Jornal do Brasil,* 13 Jul. 1998; "Indisposição geral," "Zagalo reconhece erro," and "Pressão demais," *Jornal do Brasil,* 15 Jul. 1998; "A verdade de Roberto," *Jornal do Brasil,* 16 Jul. 1998.

111. "Fim do mistério," *Placar,* Jun. 1999, 52–60.

112. "Brasil comove Ronaldinho," *Jornal do Brasil,* 15 Jul. 1998; Tostão, "Hora de cair na real," *Placar,* May 2000, 28; Ronaldo Helal, "Mídia, construção da derrota e o mito do herói," in *A Invenção do país do futebol: mídia, raça e idolatria,* ed. Helal and Hugo Lovisolo (Rio de Janeiro: Mauad, 2001), 149–62.

113. Piza, *Ora, bolas!* 61–62.

114. Interview with Filé in Moraes, *Romário,* 166–67; Piza, *Ora, bolas!* 72–73; Caldeira, *Ronaldo,* 121–23, 251; Mosley, *Ronaldo,* 119–20. On Toledo's influence over three decades, see "A eminência parda da Seleção," *Jornal do Brasil,* 3 Jun. 1998.

115. Caldeira, *Ronaldo,* 264–67; "Leve para voar," *Placar,* Mar. 2007, 49.

116. "Sete minutos," *Placar,* May 2003, 52; "Os treinos que ninguém viu," *Placar,* Feb. 2001, 56–57; Caldeira, *Ronaldo,* 273–75; Mosley, *Ronaldo,* 125–27; "Ronaldinho operado," *Jornal do Brasil,* 1 Dec. 1999; "Tem volta," *Placar,* May 2000, 40.

117. "Ronaldo se despede de 'ano sofrido,'" *Folha de São Paulo,* 19 Jul. 1999.

118. Tostão, "Hora de cair na real," *Placar,* May 2000, 34; "Tem volta," *Placar,* May 2000.

119. "Não sou robô," *Veja,* 5 Jan. 2000, 11.

120. "Você conhece. Você confia?" *Placar,* 6–12 Apr. 2001, 31–34; Helal, "Mídia, construção da derrota."

121. "Para Scolari, é grande o risco de não ir à Copa," *Folha de São Paulo,* 7 Sep. 2001.

122. "Scolari descarta Romário e já fala em semifinal," *Folha de São Paulo,* 15 Nov. 2001.

123. Ruy Carlos Ostermann, *Felipão: A alma do Penta* (Porto Alegre: Zero Hora Editora Jornalística, 2002), 16, 22–23; Tostão, "A vitória foi ótima, mas não apaga os erros," *Folha de São Paulo,* 15 Nov. 2001.

124. Ostermann, *Felipão*, 28–29.

125. "Seleção sabe que só o título pode garantir lugar na história," *O Globo*, 17 Jun. 2002.

126. Interview of Ronaldo Fenômeno and Fabiano Farah by Ronaldo Helal, 8 May 2007, accessed 20 Sep. 2012, http://leonardoweb.globo.com/noticias.asp?secao=leo&cod=288; Piza, *Ora bolas!* 165.

127. Antonio Jorge Soares, Ronaldo Helal, and Marco Antonio Santoro, "Futebol, imprensa e memória," *Revista Fronteiras* 6, no. 1 (2004): 70.

128. "Cobrados e rodados, Rivaldo e Ronaldo decidem na estréia," *Folha de São Paulo*, 4 Jun. 2002; "Ronaldo fica de molo para jogar semifinal," *Folha de São Paulo*, 22 Jun. 2002; "Médico dá prazo para seleção ter Ronaldo," *Folha de São Paulo*, 23 Jun. 2002; "Dia R," and Tostão, "Brasil é penta mundial," *Folha de São Paulo*, 1 Jul. 2002. Strong criticisms appeared in "Ronaldo tem pior atuação em Copas" and Juca Kfouri, "Dá nele, bola," *Folha de São Paulo*, 14 Jun. 2002.

129. "Ronaldo reescreveu a história. Como prometera" and "Ronaldo: Nascer e renascer de um craque," *O Estado de São Paulo*, 10 Aug. 2001; "Agora é no. 1," *Folha de São Paulo*, 18 Jun. 2002.

130. "Olha quem está jogando," *Placar*, Feb. 2002, 52.

131. "O milagre," *Placar*, May 2003, 54.

132. "O time do ano," *Placar*, Dec. 2002, 26.

133. Tostão, *A perfeição*, 72.

134. "Quadrado mágico ou trágico?" *Placar*, May 2006, 50–55.

135. "Quarteto de um mágico só," *O Estado de São Paulo*, 16 Jun. 2006. For general assessments of the team's performance, see Sérgio Augusto, "Só o sapo de Arrubinha nos derruba," *O Estado de São Paulo*, 11 Jun. 2006; Carlos Alberto Silva, "Faltou vergonha na cara!" *O Estado de São Paulo*, 1 Jul. 2006; Juca Kfouri, "Futebol de resultados," *O Estado de São Paulo*, 2 Jul. 2006; "Vergonha lá, orgulho aqui," *Placar*, Jul. 2006, 4; "O fiasco tem explicação?" *Placar*, Jul. 2006, 42–47.

136. "Parceria de Ronaldo e Corinthians abre caminho inédito para o futebol brasileiro," Machado Meyer Sendace Opice, 5 Apr. 2009, accessed 5 Oct. 2012, www.machadomeyer. com.br/noticias/parceria-de-ronaldo-e-corinthians-abre-caminho-inedito-para-o-futebol-brasileiro; "As cifras de um fenômeno," *Placar*, Jan. 2009, 35–36.

137. "Ronaldo in tranvestite scandal," accessed 15 Nov. 2012, http://news.bbc.co.uk/2 /hi/7374317.stm; "Uma escorregada fenomenal" and "Influente e comportado," *Veja*, 7 May 2008, 132–38; "Após bate-boca com travestis, Ronaldo vai para delegacia no Rio," Folha Online, 28 Apr., 2008, accessed 29 Oct. 2012, www1.folha.uol.com.br/folha/cotidiano /ult95u396571.shtml. On his commercial successes, see "Ronaldo: Simplesmente fenomenal!" 13 May 2009, accessed 5 Oct. 2012, http://gestaodoesporte.blogsport.com/2009/05/ronaldo-simplesmente-fenomenal.html; Gastaldo, *Pátria, chuteiras e propaganda*, 117.

138. "CBF confirma Ronaldo como membro do comitê organizador de 2014," ESPN Brasil, 1 Dec. 2011, accessed 2 Dec. 2011, www.espbr.com/noticias/cbf-confirma-ronaldo-membro-comite-organizador-2014; Juca Kfouri, "E Ricardo Teixeira vai submergir para sobreviver mais uma vez," 30 Nov. 2011, accessed 2 Dec. 2011, http://blogdojuca.uol.com. br/2011/11/e-ricardo-teixeira-vai-submergir-para-sobreviver-mais-uma-vez/; "Sob nova (?) direção," *Folha de São Paulo*, 13 Mar. 2012.

139. Daniela Pinheiro, "The President," *Revista Piauí* 58 (Jul. 2011), accessed 5 Oct. 2012 at http://revistapiaui.estadao.com.br/edicao-58-/the-faces-of-futebol/the-president.

140. Tostão, *A perfeição*, 44. David Goldblatt aptly terms these patterns "the inherent pathologies of the domestic game" in Brazil; *The Ball Is Round: A Global History of Soccer* (New York: Riverhead Books, 2008), 795.

141. Marcos Alvito, "Our Piece of the Pie: Brazilian Football and Globalization," *Soccer & Society* 8, no. 4 (Oct. 2007): 524–44; Ronaldo Helal, *Passes e impasses: Futebol e cultura de massa no Brasil* (Petrópolis: Vozes, 1997); Proni, *A metamorfose.*

142. Ernesto Rodrigues, *Jogo duro: A história de João Havelange* (Rio de Janeiro: Record, 2007), 369–70.

143. Rodrigues, *Jogo duro,* 371.

144. Mário [Rodrigues] Filho, *O negro no futebol brasileiro,* 4th ed. (Rio de Janeiro: Mauad / FAPERJ, 2003); João Saldanha, *Os subterrâneos do futebol* (Rio de Janeiro: Tempo Brasileiro, 1963), 209–15; Luiz Marcelo Vídero Vieira Santos, "A evolução da gestão no futebol brasileiro," Master's thesis (Fundação Getúlio Vargas, 2002), 29; Mezzadri, "As possíveis interferências," 113–15.

145. "Onde ARENA vai mal, mais um no nacional; onde vai bem, mais um também."

146. "Nabi na presidência desafia Club dos 13" and "Novo Brasileirão (se a CBF deixar)," *Jornal do Brasil,* 15 Jul. 1987; Juca Kfouri, "O país do quase no fundo do poço," *Placar,* 25 May 1987, 25; Helal, *Passes e impasses,* 86–91; Guterman, *O futebol,* 232–33; "Os caprichos do regulamento," *Placar* 21 Sep. 1987, 48; Mauro Beting, "Copa União 1987 e Clube dos 13—A Linha do Tempo e do Dinheiro," Lancenet, 25 Feb. 2011, accessed 31 Dec. 2012, http://blogs.lancenet.com.br/maurobeting/2011/02/25/copa-uniao-1987-e-clube-dos-13-a-linha-do-tempo-e-do-dinheiro/.

147. He used the term *articulação* to describe the battles that went into the selection of a World Cup host nation; "O dono da bola," *Veja,* 14 Nov. 2007, 15.

148. "Braga quer Eurico fora da diretoria," *Folha de São Paulo,* 16 Jan. 1989. On Miranda see esp. Bellos, *Futebol,* 287–316.

149. "Ricardo Teixeira anuncia hoje os 23 selecionáveis; Lazaroni é o técnico" and "Os homens do presidente," *Folha de São Paulo,* 16 Jan. 1989; Bellos, *Futebol,* 343.

150. Congress clamped down on these contributions after 2001.

151. Carlos Azevedo and Aldo Rebelo, "Corrupção no futebol brasileiro," *Motrivivência* 17 (Sep. 2001), 9, accessed 11 Nov. 2012, www.periodicos.ufsc.br/index.php/motrivivencia/article/view/5923.

152. "O eterno problema," *A Gazeta Esportiva,* 8 May 1980; José Dias, *Futebol de craques . . . e dos cartolas pernas-de-pau* (Rio de Janeiro: Mauad, 2000), 72, 90–93.

153. "Craques da muamba," *Veja,* 27 Jul. 1998, 26–31; "Alfândega da seleção vai ser feita hoje," *Folha de São Paulo,* 20 Jul. 1998; "Seleção volta sem pagar imposto" and "Planalto autoriza liberação de bagagens," *Folha de São Paulo,* 21 Jul. 1998; Gilberto Dimenstein, "Os heróis viraram sonegadores," *Folha de São Paulo,* 20 Jul. 1998; Pinheiro, "The President."

154. Traffic CEO José Hawilla later revealed the existence of a confidentiality clause in the original contract; "Jogada de milhões," *Veja,* 11 Aug. 1999, 15.

155. Azevedo and Rebelo, "Corrupção," 4; "Do luxo ao lixo," *Placar,* Jul. 2007, 58; "A era Teixeira," *Folha de São Paulo,* 26 May 2002; Bellos, *Futebol,* 343–44.

156. Bellos, *Futebol,* 348.

157. Pinheiro, "The President."

158. Juca Kfouri, *Por que não desisto: Futebol, dinheiro e política* (Barueri, São Paulo: DISAL, 2009), 63–64.

159. Santos, "A evolução," 46–49; Marcelo Weishaupt Proni, "Reflexões sobre o futebol empresa no Brasil," in *Futebol: Espetáculo do século,* org. Márcia Regina da Costa (São Paulo: Musa, 1999), 46–49; Proni, *A metamorfose,* 207–15.

160. Luiz Fernando Pozzi, "Futebol empresa," in Costa, *Futebol,* 61–69; Cesar Gordon and Ronaldo Helal, "The Crisis of Brazilian Football: Perspectives for the Twenty-First Century," *International Journal of the History of Sport* 18, no. 3 (2001): 139–58.

161. "Futebol do Brasil S.A.," *Veja*, 13 Sep. 1978, 110; "A difícil exportação do futebol decadente," *O Estado de São Paulo*, 17 Aug. 1980; "O país do (pobre) futebol," *Jornal da Tarde*, 24 Sep. 1990; Roberto C. V. Mack, *Futebol empresa: A nova dimensão para o futebol brasileiro* (Rio de Janeiro: Palestra Edições, 1980); Janet Lever, *Soccer Madness: Brazil's Passion for the World's Most Popular Sport* (Prospect Heights, IL: Waveland Press, 1995), 55–59.

162. Helal, *Passes e impasses*, 55–56; José Paulo Florenzano, *A Democracia Corinthiana: Práticas de liberdade no futebol brasileiro* (São Paulo: FAPESP / EDUC, 2009), 278–81.

163. For example, "HMTF ameaça barrar volta de Rincón ao Corinthians," *Folha de São Paulo*, 13 Feb. 2001.

164. Juca Kfouri, "Futebol em liquidação," in Costa, *Futebol*, 80–81.

165. Juca Kfouri, "A vez do 'esquema MSI'" in *Por que não desisto*, 77–78; Proni, *A metamorfose*, 221.

166. Artigo 26, lei 8.672 (Lei Zico), 6 Jul. 1993, *Coleção das Leis da República Federativa do Brasil*, vol. 85, no. 7 (Brasília: Imprensa Nacional, 1993), 1650; Helal, *Passes e impasses*, 113. On the struggles over the reform, see "Zico propõe modificação radical no futebol," *Jornal do Brasil*, 31 Oct. 1990; "Eleição na CBF é contestada em Brasília" and "Presidente da CBF tem imagem abalada após manobra da reeleição," *Folha de São Paulo*, 31 Jul. 1991; "Ricardo Teixeira: o cartola contra-craque," *Placar Urgente*, Oct. 1993, 1.

167. Eduardo Dias Manhães, *Política dos esportes no Brasil*, 2nd ed. (Rio de Janeiro: Paz e Terra, 2002), 116; "Manifesto dos Clubes da Primeira Divisão," 14 Sep. 1997, in Proni, *A metamorfose*, 198–99; Mezzadri, "As possíveis interferências," 125.

168. Lei 9.615, 24 Mar. 1998, *Coleção das Leis da República Federativa do Brasil*, vol. 90, no. 3 (Brasília: Imprensa Nacional, 1998), 1344–46.

169. "Reeleição na CBF gera ação anti-Lei Pelé," *Folha de São Paulo*, 1 Jul. 1999; "'Bancada da bola' renega rótulo, mas segue na ativa," *Folha de São Paulo*, 21 Jun. 2001, "Passe de mágica," *Placar*, 24–30 Aug. 2001, 41; Proni, *A metamorfose*, 202; Manhães, *Política dos esportes*, 117; Francisco Xavier Freire Rodrigues, "O fim do passe e a modernização conservadora no futebol brasileiro (2001–2006)" (PhD diss., Universidade Federal do Rio Grande do Sul, 2007), 214–15.

170. "Toda a história do caso Parmalat," *Placar*, Mar. 2000, 65.

171. Goldblatt, *The Ball is Round*, 793; Kfouri, *Por que não desisto*, 69–70. Multinationals committed their own misdeeds; several investments schemes seem to have functioned in part to launder money and evade taxes; see Kfouri, *Por que não desisto*, 71–72, 75–78.

172. Guterman, *O futebol*, 253; "O Leão no ataque," *Veja*, 3 Sep. 1997, 98–99; "O Leão está solto," *Placar*, Oct. 1997, 46–50; Bellos, *Futebol*, 320–23.

173. João Guilherme de Mattos Pimentel, "A relevância do profissionalismo no futebol e os impactos da credibilidade dos dirigentes na obtenção de patrocínio" (Master's thesis, Fundação Getúlio Vargas, 2011); Manoel Henrique de Amorim Filho, "A gestão de clubes de futebol—regulação, modernização e desafios para o esporte no Brasil," *Revista Interesse Nacional*, 16 Jul. 2012.

174. Azevedo and Rebelo, "Corrupção"; and Aldo Rebelo and Silvio Torres, *CBF Nike* (São Paulo: Casa Amarela, 2001); Senado Federal, *Relatório final da Comissão Parlamentar de Inquérito*, 5 vols. (Brasília, 2001).

175. Bellos, *Futebol*, 347; and on *cartolas'* resistance, see "Presidente da CBF esteve em CPIs do Futebol e do Nike," *Folha de São Paulo*, 6 Oct. 2005; "A CBF perde votação de goleada," *Veja*, 12 Dec. 2001; Azevedo and Rebelo, "Corrupção," 3.

176. "Senado aprova devassa em negócios de empresários," *Folha de São Paulo*, 8 Nov. 2001.

177. There were potential tax implications that followed from the location of the signing; Azevedo and Rebelo, "Corrupção," 5.

178. Azevedo and Rebelo, "Corrupção," esp. 6; Rebelo and Torres, *CBF Nike,* 18; Senado Federal, *Relatório,* vol. 1:12.

179. For salary statistics see Rebelo and Torres, *CBF Nike,* 33–34. On the legality of such remuneration, see Rebelo and Torres, *CBF Nike,* 34–35, 106–9; Senado Federal, *Relatório,* vol. 2:9–13.

180. Rebelo and Torres, *CBF Nike,* 30–31.

181. Azevedo and Rebelo, "Corrupção," 13–17. The six loans totaled US$39 million, with annual interest rates from 15% to 52%.

182. Uncertainty surrounded his sources of income and the purchase of his homes in Brazil and the United States; Rebelo and Torres, *CBF Nike,* 40, 144–45, 150–53.

183. Directors of the firm issued a letter to the CBF making clear that they had been hired to do an "operational audit"—quite a distinct service, they pointed out, and one that did not result in a report on the Confederation's overall finances. Senado Federal, *Relatório,* vol. 2:13–18.

184. Andrew Jennings, *Foul! The Secret World of FIFA: Bribes, Vote Rigging and Ticket Scandals* (London: HarperSport, 2006), 193.

185. These proposals, including a "Law of Social Reponsibility of Brazilian Soccer," appear in Senado Federal, *Relatório,* vol. 1:137, and *Proposições Legislativas* (anexo).

186. Teixeira had already mended relations with Zico when he named him technical director of the Seleção in 1998. Before butting heads over reform legislation, Teixeira had a major blowup with Pelé in 1993, when the ex-*craque* accused Teixeira of dismissing the bid that his young firm, Pelé Sports Marketing, had submitted for the transmission rights for the Brasileirão—rights that had instead gone to Traffic. Teixeira's father-in-law and protector, Havelange, barred Pelé from the much-publicized draw that established the groups for the 1994 World Cup. Pelé ended this feud around the end of the CPI Futebol, a gesture that many reformists took as a betrayal—or perhaps, as Rebelo suggested, a petty maneuver to shut down investigation into his marketing firm, which had begun in the Senate. "À sombra das chuteiras milionárias," *Veja,* 22 Dec. 1993; "Nas asas da bola," *Veja,* 28 Jan. 1998, 11; "A Era Teixeira," *Folha de São Paulo,* 26 May 2002; Ribeiro, *Os donos,* 275–76; Juca Kfouri, *Meninos eu vi . . .* (São Paulo: DBA Artes Gráficas, 2003), 98–99; Bellos, *Futebol,* 346–47.

187. "Contrato entre Nike e CBF sai ileso," *Folha de São Paulo,* 8 Nov. 2000; and see Tostão "Chega de arrogância," *Veja,* 2 Aug. 2000, 15; and "Depois da CPI," *Placar,* 14 Dec. 2001, 42–43; "AmBev vai pagar US$170 mi à seleção," *Folha de São Paulo,* 29 Mar. 2001; "Contrato 'muy amigo' da CBF," *Folha de São Paulo,* 8 Jun. 2001.

188. Jennings, *Foul!* 54–60; "Havelange e Teixeira são os nomes do suborno da ISL," *Carta Capital,* 25 Apr. 2012, accessed 26 Apr. 2012, http://cartacapital.com.br/havelange-e-teixeira-sao-os-nomes-do-suborno-da-isl/; "Justiça suíça confirma recebimento de propina por Havelange e Teixeira," *Carta Capital,* 11 Jul. 2012, accessed 8 Jan. 2013, www.cartacapital.com.br/sociedade/justica-suica-confirma-recebimento-de-propina-por-havelange-e-teixeira/; "Statement of the Chairman of the FIFA Adjudicatory Chamber, Hans-Joachim Eckert, on the examination of the ISL case," 29 Apr. 2013, accessed 30 Apr. 2013 at www.fifa.com/mm/document/affederation/footballgovernance/02/06/60/80/islreporteckert20.04.13e.pdf.

189. The Twitter campaign was called "Fora, Teixeira" (#ForaRicardoTeixeira), or "Teixeira Out." See "Movimento 'Fora, Teixeira' arma ação festiva no Twitter e já estuda ataque sobre Blatter," 16 Feb. 2012, accessed 10 Jan. 2013, http://esporte.uol.com.br/futebol/ultimas-noticias/2012/02/16/movimento-fora-teixeira-arma-acao-festiva-no-twitter-e-ja-foca-ataque-

sobre-blatter.htm. On Teixeira's position after his resignation, see Fábio Lucas Neves, "Eliminamos o câncer, mas nos esquecemos das sequelas," 13 Mar. 2012, accessed 13 Mar. 2012, http://terceirotempo.bol.uol.com.br/coluna_materia.php?id=1711; "O cartola e a arte," *O Estado de São Paulo*, 13 Mar. 2012, accessed 13 Mar. 2012, www.estadao.com.br/noticia_imp.php?req+impresso,o-cartola-e-a-arte-,847614,0.htm; Juca Kfouri, "Não há mal que sempre dure," 13 Mar. 2012, accessed 13 Mar. 2012, http://blogdojuca.uol.com.br/2012/03/nao-ha-mal-que-sempre-dure/ and "O dia seguinte," 13 Mar. 2012, accessed 13 Mar. 2012, http://blogdojuca.uol.com.br/2012/03/o-dia-seguinte-2/.

190. Bellos, *Futebol,* 345.

191. "Dívida dos clubes cresce em maior proporção que receitas," *Máquina do Esporte,* 4 Jan. 2013, accessed 6 Jan. 2013, www.maquinadoesporte.com.br/printnews.php?id=28032. On Marin, see Antero Greco, "O dono da bola sai. E que seja só o começo de mudanças," *O Estado de São Paulo,* 12 Mar. 2012; "Marin diz que Teixeira deixará de receber salários da CBF e minimiza oposição de Andrés," 12 Jan. 2013, accessed 13 Jan. 2013, http://terceirotempo.bol.uol.com.br/futebol/times/selecao/noticias/2013/01/marin-diz-que-teixeira-deixara-de-receber-salarios-da-cbf-e-minimiza-oposicao-de-andres-78025.html.

192. Verissimo, "O ocaso do driblador," in *Time dos sonhos: Paixão, poesia e futebol* (Rio de Janeiro: Objetiva, 2010), 103–4.

193. Luca Caioli, *O sorriso do futebol: Ronaldinho, o último romântico* (Sao Bernardo do Campo, SP: Mundo Editorial , 2006).

194. Caioli, *O sorriso,* 50–51; "A hora do gênio," *Istoé,* 7 Jun. 2006, 81, 83.

195. André Ribeiro and Vladir Lemos, *A magia da camisa 10* (Campinas: Editora Verus, 2006), 177

196. "A hora do gênio," *Istoé,* 7 Jun. 2006, 83 84.

197. "Decisão marca confronto de estilos distintos," *O Estado de São Paulo,* 30 Jun. 2002.

198. Daniel Piza, "O terceiro homem," *O Estado de São Paulo,* 22 Jun. 2002; "Ronaldinho: 'Não foi por acaso,' garante o dono do gol da classificação," *O Estado de São Paulo,* 22 Jun. 2002; "O Brasil que pedala—drible de Ronaldinho Gaúcho em Cole é a cara desta seleção," *Jornal do Brasil,* 24 Jun. 2002; "Último 'erre,' Ronaldinho brilha e apaga em 13 minutos," *Folha de São Paulo,* 22 Jun. 2002; Caioli, *O sorriso,* 102–3; *Todas as Copas: 1930 a 2006,* ed. Roberto Assaf and Jefferson Rodrigues (Rio de Janeiro: Areté Editorial, 2010), 269.

199. Interview with Fernandez in Caioli, *O sorriso,* 97.

200. "Mercado se agita por todos os cantos," *O Estado de São Paulo,* 21 Jun. 2002.

201. Caioli, *O sorriso,* 115–18.

202. Daniel Piza, "Focos amestrados," *O Estado de São Paulo,* 26 Jun. 2002.

203. Interview with Scolari in Caioli, *O sorriso,* 109.

204. "Quadrado mágico ou trágico?," *Placar,* May 2006, 50–57.

205. "Ronaldinho decepciona o mundo do futebol," *O Estado de São Paulo,* 2 Jul. 2006.

206. "Quarteto de um mágico só: Kaká," *O Estado de São Paulo,* Jun. 2006;

207. "Os Ronaldos decepcionam," *O Estado de São Paulo,* 14 Jun. 2006; "S.O.S. Ronaldinho," *Folha de São Paulo,* 7 Jun. 2006; "Na Copa, Ronaldinho vira só um meia," *Folha de São Paulo,* 27 Jun. 2006; "Longe do gol, Ronaldinho falha também no meio," *Folha de São Paulo,* 28 Jun. 2006; "Crime organizado," *Placar,* Jul. 2006, 46.

208. "Ronaldinho vive pior seca da história da 10 brasileira," *Folha de São Paulo,* 30 Jun. 2006; "Pesquisa Datafolha: Bem-me-quer, mal-me-quer," *Folha de São Paulo,* 30 Jun. 2006. The record exludes players sidelined by injury.

209. "Balada F.C.," *Placar,* May 2008, 47.

210. Tostão, "Retrato na parede," *Folha de São Paulo,* 10 Jun. 2012.

211. Wisnik, *Veneno,* 382; and compare Armando Nogueira, "A jóia do penta," in his *A ginga e o jogo,* 191–92.

212. Armando Nogueira, "A vez do drible," *Jornal do Brasil,* 23 Jun. 1998.

213. "A história secreta de Denílson," *Placar,* Oct. 1997, 68–71.

214. See, for instance, the account of his play against Scotland in "Agradável sufoco," *Istoé,* 17 Jun. 1998, 126–29.

215. Tostão, "Teoria sobre o craque," in *A perfeição,* 89.

216. "Robinho, o novo Denílson?" *Placar,* Apr. 2007, 60–66.

217. "Mãe de Robinho é libertada, e atacante está livre para decisão" and "Empresário ajuda a pagar resgate de R$500 mil," *Folha de São Paulo,* 18 Dec. 2004.

218. "Para sair, Robinho põe Santos no paredão," *Folha de São Paulo,* 5 Jul. 2005; "Santos aceita US$30 milhões, e Robinho vai para o Real Madrid," *Folha de São Paulo,* 30 Jul. 2005.

219. Goldblatt, *The Ball is Round,* 767; "Te cuida, Ronaldinho!," *Placar,* Sep. 2005, 56–57; "Vai para o trono ou não vai?," *Placar,* Oct. 2005, 40–42.

220. "Robinho vai para a Inglaterra, mas não para o Chelsea," *Folha de São Paulo,* 2 Sep. 2008; "Sem retorno," *Folha de São Paulo,* 1 Sep. 2010; "Os dilemas de Parreira," *Istoé,* 28 Jun. 2006, 78.

221. "Quadrado mágico ou trágico?" *Placar,* May 2006, 57; Tostão, "Parreira, coragem," *Folha de São Paulo,* 23 Jun. 2006.

222. "A 'era do coletivo,'" *Veja,* 9 Aug. 2006, 11–15; Galba Araújo, *Brasil da Era Dunga* (Rio de Janeiro: Livre Expressão, 2010).

223. "Todos os tropeços de Parreira," *Placar,* Jul. 2006, 42–47.

224. "Operação Ronaldinho," *Placar,* Feb. 2010, 33–39.

225. "O fantasma de Dunga," *Placar,* Feb. 2010; "Ronaldinho sonha com Copa de 2014," *Placar,* May 2010; Tim Vickery, "The Call of Ronaldinho," 8 Aug. 2011, accessed 19 Dec. 2012 at www.bbc.co.uk/blogs/timvickery/2011/08/world_cup_hosts_brazil_need_se.html.

226. Tostão, "Retrato na parede," *Folha de São Paulo,* 10 Jun. 2012.

227. Caioli, *O sorriso,* 80–82.

228. "Clube francês oficializa um acerto com 'petit Ronaldo,'" *Folha de São Paulo,* 18 Jan. 2001.

229. "Grêmio ganha a 1a. de Ronaldinho," *Folha de São Paulo,* 14 Feb. 2001; "FIFA libera Ronaldinho para jogar na Europa pelo PSG," *Folha de São Paulo,* 3 Aug. 2001; Caioli, *O sorriso,* 84–87.

230. "FIFA libera Ronaldinho para jogar na Europa pelo PSG," *Folha de São Paulo,* 3 Aug. 2001; Paulo Vinicius Coelho, *Bola fora: A história do êxodo do futebol brasileiro* (São Paulo: Panda Books, 2009), 128–29.

231. Pierre Lafranchi and Matthew Taylor, *Moving with the Ball: The Migration of Professional Footballers* (Oxford: Berg, 2001), 69–110; Tony Mason, *Passion of the People? Football in Latin America* (London: Verso, 1995), 50–59.

232. Gordon and Helal, "The Crisis," 150.

233. Lafranchi and Taylor, *Moving with the Ball,* 109; Claudia Silva Jacobs and Fernando Duarte, *Futebol exportação* (Rio de Janeiro: Editora Senac Rio, 2006), 49–62; Bellos, *Futebol,* 5–25; "Embaixadores da bola," *Placar,* Mar. 1994, 5–9. The 2011 figures come from "Brasil é o país que mais exporta jogadores, diz estudo," Globoesporte.com, 14 Dec. 2011, accessed 20 Jan. 2013, http://globoesporte.globo.com/futebol/noticia/2011/12/brasil-e-o-pais-que-mais-exporta-jogadores-diz-estudo.html.

234. On the Bosman "revolution," see Lafranchi and Taylor, *Moving with the Ball,* 213–29.

235. Coelho, *Bola fora,* 129.

236. "Figer confirma Uruguai como intermediário" and "STF proíbe CPI de usar dados de agentes," *Folha de São Paulo,* 14 Feb. 2001.

237. "Os 5 donos do jogo," *Placar,* Jul. 2011, 63–65; Coelho, *Bola fora,* 140–47; Kfouri, *Por que não desisto,* 75–76.

238. "Tevezmania," *Placar,* Sep. 2006, 50–55; "Turbulência corintiana 'contamina' o clássico," *Folha de São Paulo,* 14 Jun. 2007; "Carta de Kia racha mais o Corinthians," *Folha de São Paulo,* 23 Aug. 2006; Kfouri, *Por que não desisto,* 77–78.

239. Arlei Sander Damo, *Do dom à profissão: A formação de futebolistas no Brasil e na França* (São Paulo: Hucitec, 2005), 172–73.

240. Alvito, "Our Piece of the Pie," 535–36; Damo, *Do dom,* 137–44.

241. Cf. Wisnik's depiction of Ronaldinho as "postmodern," in *Veneno,* 381–83.

242. "Robinho e o paradoxo," in Verissimo, *Time dos sonhos,* 75–76.

243. Ibid.

CONCLUSION

Epigraph: Christopher Gaffney, "Mega-events and Socio-spatial Dynamics in Rio de Janeiro, 1919–2016," *Journal of Latin American Geography* 9, no. 1 (2010): 16–17.

1. Tim Vickery, "Burgeoning rivalry reveals philosophical differences," accessed 7 Jul. 2013, http://espnfc.com/blog/_/name/worldcupcentral/id/359?+5901; Juca Kfouri, "O campeão voltou!" and Tostão, "Melhor é impossível," *Folha de São Paulo,* 1 Jul. 2013.

2. "Notas de uma magra trincheira," *O Globo,* 25 Jun. 2013.

3. "'Epidemia' de manifestações tem quase 1 protesto por hora e atinge 353 cidades," *O Estado de São Paulo,* 29 Jun. 2013.

4. Christopher Gaffney, "A Calm Between Storms," 23 Jun. 2013, accessed 29 Jun. 2013, www.geostadia.com/2013/06/a-calm-between-storms.html?m=1 .

5. Antonio Prata, "Ninguém tá entendendo nada," *Folha de São Paulo,* 23 Jun. 2013.

6. "Milhares vão às ruas 'contra tudo'; grups atingem palácios," *Folha de São Paulo,* 18 Jun. 2013.

7. "Free Kicks and Kickbacks: The World Cup," *The Economist,* 3 Nov. 2007, 43.

8. Giampaolo Baiocchi and Ana Claudia Teixeira, "Pardon the Inconvenience, We Are Changing the Country," *Boston Review,* 26 Jun. 2013, accessed 9 Jul. 2013, www.bostonreview .net/blog/pardon-inconvenience-we-are-changing-country.

9. Signs reading simply "Vem pra rua" (Come to the street) were common, as were the trends #VempraRua, #ChangeBrazil, and #MudaBrasil on Twitter.

10. "Copa do Mundo de 2014 será no Brasil," *Folha de São Paulo,* 31 Oct. 2007; "Brasil só não vai abrigar a Copa de 2014 se não quiser," *Folha de São Paulo,* 8 Mar. 2003.

11. "Gente grande," *Folha de São Paulo,* 3 Oct. 2009.

12. Interview with Raquel Rolnik, "O espetáculo e o mito," *Página 22,* no. 55 (9 Aug. 2012), accessed 15 Apr. 2013, http://pagina22.com.br/index.php/2011/08/o-espetaculo-do-mito/.

13. Alan Tomlinson and Christopher Young, "Culture, Politics, and Spectacle in the Global Sports Event—An Introduction," in *National Identity and Global Sports Events: Culture, Politics, and Spectacle in the Olympics and the Football World Cup,* ed. Tomlinson and Young (Albany: State University of New York Press, 2006), 5. On denationalization see

Raffaele Poli, "The Denationalization of Sport: De-ethnicization of the Nation and Identity Deterritorialization," *Sport in Society* 10, no. 4 (2007): 6446–61.

14. Orlando Silva, "Futebol, um negócio que move paixões," *Cadernos FGV Projetos* 5, no. 13 (2010): 28.

15. Compare Claire and Keith Brewster, "Mexico City 1968: Sombreros and Skyscrapers," and David Rowe and Deborah Stevenson, "Sydney 2000: Sociality and Spatiality in Global Media Events," in Tomlinson and Young, *National Identity*, 99–116, 197–214.

16. India hosted the 2010 Commonwealth Games; China, the 2008 Summer Olympics; and South Africa, the 2010 World Cup. Russia will host the 2018 World Cup. Susan Brownell, *Beijing's Games: What the Olympics Mean to China* (Lanham, MD: Rowman & Littlefield, 2008); John Nauright, "Global Games: Culture, Political Economy and Sport in the Globalised World of the 21st Century," *Third World Quarterly* 25, no. 7 (2004): 1325–36; Scarlett Cornelissen, "The Geopolitics of Global Aspiration: Sport Mega-events and Emerging Powers," *The International Journal of the History of Sport* 27, nos. 16–18 (2010): 3008–25.

17. "Gente grande," *Folha de São Paulo,* 3 Oct. 2009.

18. Compare Joel Wolfe, *Autos and Progress: The Brazilian Search for Modernity* (New York: Oxford University Press, 2010).

19. Mustafã Contursi Goffar Majzoub, "O melhor tem de ser o maior," in *Futebol Top Brasil: O mais completo anuário do futebol brasileiro* (São Paulo: Sindicato do Futebol, 2005).

20. Roberto Andrés, "E o futebol, resiste?" 16 Nov. 2009, accessed 27 Aug. 2012, www .ludopedio.com.br/rc/index.php/arquibancada/artigo/141.

21. Gastaldo, "Os muito futebóis do Brasil," *Coletiva* 8 (2012), accessed 29 Sep. 2011, www.coletiva.org/english/index.php?option=com_k2&view=item&layout=item&id=98& Itemid=76&idrev=11.

22. José Paulo Florenzano, "Feras, mágicos e guerreiros: A hegemonia em jogo," *Aurora: Revista de Arte, Mídia e Política* 9 (2010): 108, 110–11.

23. Lyana Virgínia Thédiga de Miranda and Giovani de Lorenzi Pires, "Reconstruindo a imagem/identidade da seleção brasileira de futebol: A 'era pós-Dunga' na mídia," *Revista da ALESDE* 2, no. 1 (2012): 17–34.

24. "Entrevista exclusive—Cafu: "É preciso ganhar a Copa do Mundo para resgatar o brilho da Seleção Brasileira," Goal.com, 3 Jun. 2012, accessed 3 Jun. 2012, www.goal.com/br/news/619 /especiais/2012/06/03/3145007/entrevista-exclusiva-cafu-é-preciso-ganhar-a-copa-do-mundo; "Ademir da Guia: 'O importante é o título,'" 10 Aug. 2012, accessed 17 Oct. 2012, http://apublica. org/2012/08/ademir-da-guia-o-importante-e-titulo/.

25. "Craque nota 10?" *Placar,* Mar. 2011, 42–47.

26. "É treta, Mano!" *Placar,* Aug. 2011, 78–79; Benjamin Back, "Por que só no futebol a medalha de prata não vale nada?" 14 Aug. 2012, accessed 14 Aug. 2012, http://blogs.lancenet. com.br/benja/2012/08/14/mano-menezes-para-ou-continua; "Romário volta a fazer críticas ao trabalho de Mano Menezes," 20 Sep. 2012, accessed 21 Sep. 2012, www.lancenet.com.br /selecao/Romario-volta-criticas-Mano-Menezes_0_777522441.html.

27. "Mano diz que Barcelona tem muito a ensinar ao futebol brasileiro," *O Globo,* 18 Dec. 2011; André Baibich, "Por que os europeus estão na nossa frente?" 22 Dec. 2011, accessed 22 Dec. 2011, www.goal.com/br/news/3599/futebol-nacional/2011/12/22/2814809/por-que-os-europeus-estão-na-nossa-frente; Juca Kfouri, "Lições de bola (ainda o Barcelona . . .)," accessed 23 Dec. 2011, http://blogdojuca.uol.com.br/2011/12/licoes-de-bola-ainda-o-barcelona/.

28. Juca Kfouri, "Aguarde Guardiola," accessed 26 Nov. 2012, http://blogdojuca.uol .com.br/2012/11/aguarde-guardiola/; Roberto Vieira, "A seleção de Pep," 28 Apr. 2012, accessed 29 Apr. 2012, http://blogdojuca.uol.com.br/2012/04/a-selecao-de-pep/.

29. "Marin adota discurso emocionado e nacionalista para rejeitar Guardiola," 29 Nov. 2012, accessed 29 Nov. 2012, www.lancenet.com.br/selecao/Marin-emocionado-nacionalista-apresentar-Felipao_0_819518101.html.

30. "Ronaldo dispara: 'Talvez o pior momento do futebol do Brasil,'" 29 Nov. 2012, accessed 29 Nov. 2012, www.lancenet.com.br/futebo/Ronaldo-dispara-pior-futebol_0_819518106.html; "Jairzinho diz que futebol brasileiroa vive seu pior momento da história," 5 Feb. 2013, accessed 5 Mar. 2013, http://copadomundo.uol.com.br/noticias/redacao/2013/05/02jairzinho-diz-que-futebol-brasileiro-vive-seu-pior-momento-da-historia.htm; "Brazil legend Rivelino laments 'unstylish' Seleção," 28 Apr. 2013, accessed 28 Apr. 2013 at http://sambafoot.com/en /news/46233_brazil_legend_rivelino_laments_unstylish_selecao.html; "'Hoje o Brasil não tem time para 2014,' diz Carlos Alberto Torres," 23 Jan. 2012, accessed 24 Jan. 2012, http://sambafoot.com/pt/noticias/27884__hoje_o_brasil_nao_tem_time_para_2014___diz_carlos_alberto_torres.html.

31. "Real quer mais um do Santos: Neymar," *O Estado de São Paulo,* 28 Mar. 2006; Milton Neves, "Neymar, o raro," *Placar,* Jul. 2011, 39; "O próximo Rei," *Placar,* Jul. 2011, 41–47; "Pregado na cruz," *Placar,* Oct. 2012; Ronaldo Helal, "Neymar, Ronaldinho e o 'verdadeiro' futebol brasileiro," *O Globo,* 5 Aug. 2011.

32. Tostão, "Gente grande," *Folha de São Paulo,* 23 Jun. 2013; "'Não somos os melhores, mas podemos levar a Copa,' diz Parreira," *Folha de São Paulo,* 3 Jul. 2013.

33. The government set up a plan to increase the winning of medals by Brazilian Olympians; see "Governo contraria COB e traça metas," *Folha de São Paulo,* 18 Mar. 2008; Silvestre Cirilo dos Santos, Lamartine Pereira da Costa, and Carlos Henrique Virtuoso da Silva, "Rio 2016 e o Plano Brasil Medalhas: Seremos uma potência esportiva?" *Podium: Sport, Leisure, and Tourism Review* 1, no. 1 (2012): 64–86.

34. "Excesso de democracia no Brasil afeta organização da Copa, diz Valcke," 25 Apr. 2013, accessed 25 Apr. 2013, http://terceirotempo.bol.uol.com.br/noticia/excesso-de-democracia-no-brasil-afeta-organizacao-da-copa-diz-valcke-82881.

35. On the legislation, particularly the Lei Geral da Copa and the Ato Olímpico, see Heloisa Helena Baldy dos Reis, "Lei geral da copa, álcool e o processo de criação da legislação sobre violência," *Movimento* 18, no. 1 (2012): 69–99; Bárbara Schausteck de Almeida, Juliana Vlastuin, and Wanderley Marchi Júnior, "Proteção à marca versus liberdade de expressão? Discursos emergentes a partir dos megaeventos esportivos no Brasil," *Esporte e Sociedade* 6, no. 18 (2011), accessed 28 Nov. 2011, www.uff.br/esportesociedade/pdf/cs1801.pdf.

36. Gaffney, "Mega-events," 21; Thiago de Aragão Escher and Heloisa Helena Baldy dos Reis, "As relações entre futebol globalizado e nacionalismo: O exemplo da Copa do Mundo de 2006," *Revista Brasileira de Ciências do Esporte* 30, no. 1 (2008): 43.

37. "Mesmo atrasado, Brasil relaxa," *Placar,* Jul. 2010, 72–73; Edson Paulo Domingues, Admir Antonio Betarelli Junior, and Aline Souza Magalhaes, "Quanto vale o show? Impactos econômicos dos investimentos da Copa do Mundo 2014 no Brasil," *Estudos Econômicos* 41, no. 2 (2011): 409–39; Comissão de Turismo e Desporto da Câmara dos Deputados and Comissão de Desenvolvimento Regional e Turismo do Senado Federal, *Relatório do Fórum Legislativo nas Cidades-Sedes da Copa do Mundo de Futebol no Brasil* (Brasília, 2012); Michel Raspaud and Flávia da Cunha Bastos, "Torcedores de futebol: Violence and Public Policies in Brazil before the 2014 World Cup," *Sport in Society* 16, no. 2 (2013): 192–204.

38. "Romário: 'A Copa será no Brasil, mas não do Brasil,'" Lancenet.com, 13 Aug. 2011, accessed 13 Aug. 2011, www.lancenet.com.br/copa-do-mundo/Romario-Copa-sera-Brasil_0_534546719.html.

39. Rob Millington and Simon C. Darnell, "Constructing and Contesting the Olympics Online: The Internet, Rio 2016 and the Politics of Brazilian Development," *International Review for the Sociology of Sport* 9 (Sep. 2012): 10–14.

40. Martin Curi, Jorge Knijnik, and Gilmar Mascarenhas, "The Pan American Games in Rio de Janeiro 2007: Consequences of a Sport Mega-event on a BRIC Country," *International Review for the Sociology of Sport* 46, no. 2 (2011): 148–51.

41. Although they also denied everyday violence and other problems; "Pergunta sobre violência irrita Ricardo Teixeira," *Folha de São Paulo,* 31 Oct. 2007.

42. Raquel Rolnik, "Megaeventos esportivos e cidades: Impactos, violações e legados," *Coletiva* 8 (2012), accessed 29 Sep. 2012, www.coletiva.org/english/index.php?option=com_k2&view=item&layout=item&id=95&Itemid=76; Rolnik, "O espetáculo e o mito"; Lei 10.257, 10 Jul. 2001, Presidência da República, Casa Civil, Subchefia para Assuntos Jurídicos, accessed 16 Apr. 2013, www.planalto.gov.br/ccivil_03/leis/leis_2001/l10257.htm; Gaffney, "Mega-events"; *Domínio público,* dir. Raoni Vidal, accessed 23 Oct. 2012, http://vimeo.com/49419197.

43. "Copa 2014: Quem ganha esse jogo?" accessed 1 Jul. 2013, www.youtube.com/watch?feature=player_embedded&v=HmoLZBtqQ3c#at=38.

44. Ciro Barros, "As lições de 1950 para 2014," *Pública,* 16 Oct. 2012, accessed 7 Jan. 2013, www.apublica.org/2012/10/licoes-copa-1950-copa-do-mundo-2014-megaeventos/; Christopher Thomas Gaffney, *Temples of the Earthbound Gods: Stadiums in the Cultural Landscapes of Rio de Janeiro and Buenos Aires* (Austin: University of Texas Press, 2008), 68–76.

45. "Se não é necessário, demolir para quê?" *O Globo,* 12 Apr. 2013; "Ouçam o alerta da Aldeia Maracanã" *Publica,* 15 Jan. 2013, accessed 27 Jan. 2013, www.apublica.org/2013/01/oucam-alerta-da-aldeia-maracana; "Pais de alunos da escolar Municipal Friedenreich vão recorrer à Justiça contra mudança," *O Globo,* 11 Aug. 2012, accessed 25 May 2013, http://oglobo.globo.com/rio/pais-de-alunos-da-escola-municipal-friedenreich-vao-recorrer-justica-contra-mudanca-6678910.

46. Ruy Castro, "Beijos gelados," *Folha de São Paulo,* 10 Apr. 2013; *Domínio público.*

47. Brian Winter, "Brazil's Olympics will be fine. As for the World Cup . . ." 29 Aug. 2012, accessed 4 Sep. 2012, http://uk.reuters.com/article/2012/08/29/uk-brazil-olympics-odebrecht-idUKBRE875OZQ20120829.

48. "'Foi um teatro montado para entregar o Maracanã' diz manifestante," 9 Nov. 2012, accessed 24 Nov. 2012, http://apublica.org/2012/11/foi-um-teatro-montado-para-entregar-maracana-diz-manifestante/; Ciro Barros, "Maracanosso ou Maracadeles?" accessed 11 Sep. 2012, http://apublica.org/2012/06/maracanosso-ou-maracadeles/; "Dois consórcios disputam licitação para privatização do Maracanã," *O Globo,* 11 Apr. 2013; "Justiça cassa liminar e mantém licitação do Maracanã," Folha de São Paulo, 10 Apr. 2013. Ultimate ownership over the new Maracanã complex remained, however, far from clear. Rodrigo Constantino, "A estranha privatização do Maracanã e a justa revolta do Flamengo," 30 Aug. 2013, accessed 14 Oct.2013,http://veja.abril.com.br/blog/rodrigo-constantino/privatizacao/a-estranha-privatizacao-do-maracana-e-a-justa-revolta-do-flamengo/.

49. These phrases became common rallying cries at June 2013 protests. On FIFA's powers in Brazil, see John Sinnott, "A fair World Cup deal for Brazil?" 24 Jun. 2013, accessed 29 Jun. 2013 at www.cnn.com/2013/06/24/sport/football/brazil-protests-fifa-tax/index.html?iref=allsearch; Laurent Dubois, "Incitement," 23 Jun. 2013, accessed 23 Jun. 2013, http://sites.duke.edu/wcwp/2013/06/23/incitement/; Gregory Michener and Chris Gaffney, "Explaining Brazil's Vinegar Revolt," 27 Jun. 2013, accessed 29 Jun. 2013, http://m.aljazeera.com/story/20136241192884390.

50. Luiz Barreto, "Um balanço para o futuro," *Folha de São Paulo*, 3 Aug. 2010.

51. *The Brazilian Football Confederation's Bid to Host the 2014 World Cup*, accessed 11 Sep. 2012 at http://apublica.org/wp-content/uploads/2012/05/FIFA-1.Estado-Brasileiro-Garantias-Governamentais.pdf.

52. Rio de Janeiro 2016 Organizing Committee, *Candidature File for Rio de Janeiro to Host the 2016 Olympic and Paralympic Games*, vol. 1, accessed 17 Apr. 2013, www.rio2016.org.br/sites/default/files/parceiros/dossie_de_candidatura_v1.pdf; "Brazil's Gold: How Rio Won Its Olympic Bid," Knowledge@Wharton, 3 Mar. 2012, accessed 17 Apr. 2013, http://knowledge.wharton.upenn.edu/article.cfm?articleid=2446.

53. Escher and Reis, "As relações"; Simon C. Darnell, "Olympism in Action, Olympic Hosting and the Politics of 'Sport for Development and Peace': Investigating the Development Discourses of Rio 2016," *Sport in Society* 15, no. 6 (2012): 869–87.

54. Gaffney, *Temples*, 69–71; "Construção do Estádio Nacional," *Gazeta de Noticias*, 1 Apr. 1948.

55. Property destruction by fringe elements of the protesters and murders by police left some observers concerned that the country might head back into authoritarianism. Alberto Dines, "Democracia, a bandeira esquecida," *Correio Popular*, 20 Jul. 2013, accessed 22 Jul. 2013, www.observatoriodaimprensa.com.br/news/view/democracia_a_bandeira_esquecida; Claudio Bernabucci, "O Brasil, versão gramsciana," accessed 22 Jul. 2013, www.cartacapital.com.br/revista/757/o-brasil-versao-gramsciana-9310.html; Marianna Araujo and Vitor Castro, "Maré de terror," 1 Jul. 2013, accessed 2 Jul. 2013, www.apublica.org/2013/07/mare-de-terror-rio-de janeiro-favela-de-mar/.

WORKS CITED

BOOKS, ARTICLES, THESES

Abrahão, Bruno Otávio de Lacerda, and Antonio Jorge Soares. "A imprensa negra e o futebol em São Paulo no início do século XX." *Revista Brasileira de Educação Física e Esporte* 26, no. 1 (2012): 63–76.

———. "O que o brasileiro não esquece ncm a tiro é o chamado frango de Barbosa: Questões sobre o racismo no futebol brasileiro." *Movimento* 15, no. 2 (April/June 2009): 12–31.

Agostinho, Gilberto. "Nos e Ellos, Nosotros y Eles: Brasil X Argentina: Os inimigos fraternos." In *Memória social dos esportes: Futebol e política. A construção de uma identidade nacional*, organized by Francisco Carlos Teixeira da Silva and Ricardo Pinto dos Santos, 2:55–80. Rio de Janeiro: Mauad Editora / FAPERJ, 2006.

———. *Vencer ou morrer: Futebol, geopolítica e identidade nacional*. Rio de Janeiro: FAPERJ/Mauad, 2002.

Alberto, Paulina L. *Terms of Inclusion: Black Intellectuals in Twentieth-Century Brazil*. Chapel Hill: University of North Carolina Press, 2011.

Albuquerque, Almir (o Pernambuquinho). *Eu e o futebol*. São Paulo: Editora Abril, 1973.

Almeida, Adjovanes Thadeu Silva da. "O regime militar em festa: As comemorações do Sesquicentenário da Independência brasileira." In *A ditadura em debate: Estado e sociedade nos anos do autoritarismo*, organized by Adriano de Freixo and Oswaldo Munteal Filho, 105–22. Rio de Janeiro: Contraponto, 2005.

Almeida, Bárbara Schausteck de, Juliana Vlastuin, and Wanderley Marchi Júnior. "Proteção à marca versus liberdade de expressão? Discursos emergentes a partir dos megaeventos esportivos no Brasil." *Esporte e Sociedade* 6, no. 18 (September 2011): 1–21.

Alves, Maria Helena Moreira. *State and Opposition in Military Brazil*. Austin: University of Texas Press, 1990.

Alvito, Marcos. "Our Piece of the Pie: Brazil Football and Globalization." *Soccer & Society* 8, no. 4 (2007): 524–44.

Amorim Filho, Manuel Henrique de. "A gestão de clubes de futebol—regulação, modernização e desafios para o esporte no Brasil." *Revista Interesse Nacional*, 16 July 2012. Accessed 8 October 2012. http://interessenacional.uol.com.br/2012/07/a-gestao-de-clubes-de-futebol-regulacao-modernizacao-e-desafios-para-o-esporte-no-brasil/.

Andrade, Carlos Drummond de. *Quando é dia de futebol.* Rio de Janeiro: Editora Record, 2002.

Andrews, David L., and George Ritzer. "The Grobal in the Sporting Glocal." In *Globalization and Sport,* edited by Richard Giulianotti and Roland Robertson, 25–45. Oxford: Blackwell, 2007.

Ângelo, Assis. *A presença do futebol na música popular brasileira.* São Paulo: O Autor, 2010.

Antônio Wilson Honório (Coutinho). Rio de Janeiro: CPCOC / FGV, 2011.

Antunes, Fatima Martin Rodrigues Ferreira. *"Com brasileiro não há quem possa!": Futebol, identidade nacional em José Lins do Rego, Mário Filho e Nelson Rodrigues.* São Paulo: Editora UNESP, 2004.

———. "Futebol de fábrica em São Paulo." Master's thesis, Universidade de São Paulo, 1992.

———. "O futebol nas fábricas." *Revista USP: Dossiê futebol* (1994): 102–9.

Araújo, Flávio. *O radio, o futebol e a vida.* São Paulo: Editora SENAC São Paulo, 2001.

Araújo, Galba. *Brasil da Era Dunga.* Rio de Janeiro: Livre Expressão, 2010.

Araújo, José Renato de Campos. *Imigração e futebol: O caso Palestra Itália.* São Paulo: Editora Sumaré / FAPESP, 2000.

Araújo, Ricardo Benzaquen de. "Força estranha." *Ciência Hoje* 1, no. 1 (July / August 1982): 32–37.

Araújo, Sebastião. *O futebol e seus fundamentos: O futebol-força a serviço da arte.* Rio de Janeiro: Imago, 1976.

Arruda, Maria Arminda do Nascimento. "Dilemas do Brasil moderno: A questão racial na obra de Florestan Fernandes." In *Raça, ciência e sociedade,* organized by Marcos Chor Maio and Ricardo Ventura Santos, 195–217. Rio de Janeiro: FIOCRUZ / CCBB, 1996.

Aspis, Abrão. *Futebol brasileiro: Do início amador à paixão nacional.* Porto Alegre: Evangraf, 2006.

Assaf, Roberto. *Banho de bola: Os técnicos, as táticas e as estratégias que fizeram história no futebol.* Rio de Janeiro: Relume Dumará, 2002.

———. *História completa do Brasileirão—1971 / 2009.* São Paulo: Lance!, 2010.

Assunção, Matthias Röhrig. *Capoeira: The History of an Afro-Brazilian Martial Art.* London: Routledge, 2005.

Avelar, Idelber. "Mangue Beat Music and the Coding of Citizenship in Sound." In *Brazilian Popular Music and Citizenship,* edited by Idelber Avelar and Christopher Dunn, 313–29. Durham: Duke University Press, 2011.

Azevedo, A. Vivaldo de. *João Havelange: Determinação e coragem.* São Paulo: Editar Publicações Técnicas, 1978.

Bahiana, Ana Maria. *Almanaque anos 70.* Rio de Janeiro: Ediouro, 2006.

Barbosa, Benedito Ruy, and Pelé (Edson Arantes do Nascimento). *Eu sou Pelé.* São Paulo: Paulo Azevedo, 1961.

Barjud, Renan Almeida. "Raça em jogo: O negro no futebol campineiro no início do século xx." Trabalho de Conclusão de Curso, Universidade de Campinas, 2008.

Bartholo, Tiago Lisboa, and Antonio Jorge Gonçalves Soares. "Mané Garrincha como síntese da identidade do futebol brasileiro." *Movimento* 15, no.1 (2009): 169–91.

Bartholo, Tiago Lisboa et al. "A pátria de chuteiras está desaparecendo?" *Revista Brasileira de Ciências do Esporte* 32, no. 1 (September 2010): 9–23.

Basílio, João Roberto. *Um escolhido: Autobiografia.* São Paulo: Editora Planeta do Brasil, 2008.

Bass, Amy. *Not the Triumph but the Struggle: The 1968 Olympics and the Making of the Black Athlete.* Minneapolis: University of Minnesota Press, 2002.

Basthi, Angélica. *Pelé: Estrela negra em campos verdes*. Rio de Janeiro: Garamond / Fundação Biblioteca Nacional, 2008.

Baudrillard, Jean. *In the Shadow of the Silent Majorities, or, the End of the Social and Other Essays*. Translated by Paul Foss, John Johnston, and Paul Patton. New York: Semiotext(e), 1983.

Bellos, Alex. *Futebol: Soccer, the Brazilian Way*. New York: Bloomsbury, 2002.

Bocketti, Gregg P. "Italian Immigrants, Brazilian Football, and the Dilemma of National Identity." *Journal of Latin American Studies* 40 (2008): 275–302.

———. "Playing with National Identity: Brazil in International Football, 1900–1925." In *Negotiating Identities in Modern Latin America,* edited by Hendrik Kraay, 71–89. Calgary: University of Calgary Press, 2004.

Brewster, Claire, and Keith Brewster. "Mexico City 1968: Sombreros and Skyscrapers." In *National Identity and Global Sports Events: Culture, Politics, and Spectacle in the Olympics and the Football World Cup,* edited by Alan Tomlinson and Christopher Young, 99–116. Albany: State University of New York Press, 2006.

Bromberger, Christian. *Le match de football: Ethnologie d'une passion partisane à Marseille, Naples et Turin*. Paris: Éditions de la Maison des sciences de l'homme, 1995.

Brownell, Susan. *Beijing's Games: What the Olympics Mean to China*. Lanham, MD: Rowman & Littlefield, 2008.

Bueno, Eduardo, et al. *Futebol: A paixão do Brasil*. Porto Alegre: Buenas Idéias, 2009.

Butler, Kim B. *Freedoms Given, Freedoms Won: Afro-Brazilians in Post-Abolition São Paulo and Salvador*. New Brunswick: Rutgers University Press, 1998.

Cabo, Alvaro Vicente Graça Truppel Pereira do. "Futebol e Carnaval: Uma mistura dos estereótipos cariocas." Accessed 21 February 2012. www.ludopedio.com.br/rc/index .php/arquibancada/artigo/899.

Cabral, Cid Pinheiro, and Ruy Carlos Ostermann. *O admirável futebol brasileiro: A história da evolução e das grandes passagens do futebol brasileiro*. Porto Alegre: Edição de Gaúcha, n.d.

Caioli, Luca. *O sorriso do futebol: Ronaldinho, o último romántico*. São Bernardo do Campo, São Paulo: Mundo Editorial, 2006.

Caju, Paulo Cézar Lima. *Dei a volta na vida*. São Paulo: Editora Girafa, 2006.

Calazans, Fernando. *O nosso futebol*. Rio de Janeiro: Mauad, 1998.

Caldas, Waldenyr. "O futebol no país do futebol." *Lua Nova* 3, no. 10 (1986): 24–30.

———. *O pontapé inicial: Memória do futebol brasileiro (1894–1933)*. São Paulo: IBRASA, 1990.

Caldeira, Jorge. *A construção do samba*. São Paulo: Mameluco, 2007.

———. *Ronaldo: Glória e drama no futebol globalizado*. São Paulo: Editora 34, 2002.

Caldeira, Teresa Pires do Rio. *City of Walls: Crime, Segregation, and Citizenship in São Paulo*. Berkeley: University of California Press, 2000.

Campos, Paulo Mendes. *O gol é necessário: Crônicas esportivas*. Edited by Flávio Pinheiro. 5th ed. Rio de Janeiro: Civilização Brasileira, 2008.

Cândia, Ralph. *Comentários à lei do jogador do futebol*. São Paulo: Sugestões Literárias, 1978.

Candido, Antonio. *On Literature and Society*. Translated and edited by Howard S. Becker. Princeton: Princeton University Press, 1995.

Capraro, André Mendes, Everton Albuquerque Cavalcanti, and Doralice Lange de Souza. "'Cai e pano': Uma análise do encerramento da carrera de Ronaldo 'Fenômeno' a partir de duas mídias digitais esportivas." *Movimento* 17, no. 3 (2011): 175–92.

Cardoso, Fernando Henrique. *Charting a New Course: The Politics of Globalization and Social Transformation.* Edited by Mauricio A. Font. Lanham, MD: Rowman & Littlefield, 2001.

Cardoso, Tom, and Roberto Rockmann. *O marechal da vitória: Uma histora de rádio, TV e futebol.* São Paulo: A Girafa, 2005.

Carrano, Paulo Cesar R. "Ronaldinho: Ídolo esportivo ou mercadoria global?" In *Futebol: Paixão e política,* edited by Carrano, 95–110. Rio de Janeiro: DP&A, 2000.

Casé, Rafael. *O artilheiro que não sorria: Quarentinha, o maior goleador da história do Botafogo.* Rio de Janeiro: R. Casé, 2008.

Castello, José. *Pelé: Os dez corações do Rei.* São Paulo: Ediouro, 2004.

Castro, Márcio Sampaio de. *Bexiga: Um bairro afro-italiano.* São Paulo: Annablume, 2008.

Castro, Ruy. *Bossa Nova: The Story of the Brazilian Music that Seduced the World.* Translated by Lysa Salsbury. Chicago: A Cappella, 2000.

———. *Estrela solitária: Um brasileiro chamado Garrincha.* São Paulo: Companhia das Letras, 1995.

———. *Flamengo: O vermelho e o negro.* Rio de Janeiro: Ediouro, 2004.

———. *O anjo pornográfico: A vida de Nelson Rodrigues.* São Paulo: Companhia das Letras, 1992.

Caulfield, Sueann. *In Defense of Honor: Sexual Morality, Modernity, and Nation in Early Twentieth-Century Brazil.* Durham: Duke University Press, 2000.

Chiarioni, Bruno, and Márcio Kroehn. *Onde o esporte reinventa: Histórias e bastidores dos 40 anos de Placar.* São Paulo: Primavera Editorial, 2010.

Coelho, Canôr Simões, and Pedro Zamora. *O livro de Tostão.* [Rio de Janeiro]: Livraria e Editora Gol, 1970.

Coelho, Paulo Vinicius. *Bola fora: A história do êxodo do futebol brasileiro.* São Paulo: Panda Books, 2009.

Coimbra, Arthur Antunes [Zico]. *Zico conta sua história.* São Paulo: FTD, 1996.

Coimbra, Arthur Antunes [Zico], Roberto Assaf, and Roger Garcia. *Zico: 50 anos de futebol.* 2nd ed. Rio de Janeiro: Record, 2003.

Comitê Popular da Copa e Olimpíadas do Rio de Janeiro. "Megaeventos e abusos dos direitos humanos no Rio de Janeiro." Accessed 25 April 2012. www.ludopedio.com.br/rc/upload /files/223841_dossie_RJ.pdf.

Cooper, Frederick. *Colonialism in Question: Theory, Knowledge, History.* Berkeley: University of California Press, 2005.

Cooper, Kenneth H. *The Aerobics Way.* New York: Bantam, 1982.

Cordeiro, Janaína Martins. "Anos de chumbo ou anos de ouro?: A memória social sobre o governo Médici." *Estudos Históricos* 22, no. 43 (2009): 85–110.

Cornelissen, Scarlett. "The Geopolitics of Global Aspiration: Sport Mega-events and Emerging Powers." *International Journal of the History of Sport* 25, no. 16 (2010): 3008–25.

Correa, Floriano Peixoto. *Grandezas e miserias do nosso futebol.* Rio de Janeiro: Flores & Mano, 1933.

Correia, Carlus Augustus Jourand. "As vozes do gramado: Relato de ex-atletas sobre a formação do Sindicato de Futebolistas Profissionais do Rio de Janeiro (1971–1982)." *Esporte e Sociedade* 5, no. 15 (July / October 2010): 1–20.

Costa, Alexandre da. "O primeiro rei do futebol." *Revista de História,* 2 December 2011.

———. *O tigre do futebol: Uma viagem nos tempos de Arthur Friedenreich.* São Paulo: DBA Editora, 1999.

Costa, Emília Viotti da. *The Brazilian Empire: Myths and Histories.* 2nd ed. Chapel Hill: University of North Carolina Press, 1988.

Costa, Lamartine Pereira da, and Plinio Labriola. "Bodies from Brazil: Fascist Aesthetics in a South American Setting." *International Journal of the History of Sport* 16, no. 4 (1999): 163–80.

Costa, Márcia Regina da, org. *Futebol: Espetáculo do século.* São Paulo: Musa, 1999.

Costa, Maurício da Silva Drumond. *Nações em jogo: Esporte e propaganda política em Vargas e Perón.* Rio de Janeiro: Apícuri, 2008.

Costa, Tarcísio. "Os anos noventa: O ocaso do político e a sacralização do mercado." In *Viagem incompleta. A experiência brasileira (1500–2000): A grande transação,* edited by Carlos Guilherme Mota, 247 82. 2nd ed. São Paulo: Editora SENAC São Paulo, 2000.

Couto, José Geraldo. *Futebol brasileiro hoje.* São Paulo: Publifolha, 2009.

Couto, Ronaldo Costa. *História indiscreta da ditadura e da abertura: Brasil: 1965–1985.* Rio de Janeiro: Record, 1999.

Cruz, Sebastião C. Velasco e, and Carlos Estevam Martins. "De Castello a Figueiredo: Uma incursão na pré-história da 'abertura.'" In *Sociedade e política no Brasil pós-64,* organized by Bernardo Sorj and Maria HermíniaTavares de Almeida, 13–61. 2nd ed. São Paulo: Brasiliense, 1984.

Cunha, Odir. *Donos da terra: A história do primeiro título mundial do Santos.* Santos, São Paulo: Realejo Edições, 2007.

———. *Santos FC: 100 anos de futebol arte.* São Paulo: Magma, 2012.

Cunha, Olívia Maria Gomes da. "Black Movements and the 'Politics of Identity' in Brazil." In *Cultures of Politics, Politics of Cultures: Re Visioning Latin American Social Movements,* edited by Sonia E. Alvarez, Evelina Dagnino, and Arturo Escobar, 220–51. Boulder, CO: Westview, 1998.

Curi, Martin, Jorge Knijnik, and Gilmar Mascarenhas. "The Pan American Games in Rio de Janeiro 2007: Consequences of a Sport Megaevent on a BRIC Country." *International Review for the Sociology of Sport* 46, no. 2 (April 2011): 140–56.

DaMatta, Roberto. *A bola corre mais que os homens: Duas Copas, treze crônicas e três ensaios sobre o futebol.* Rio de Janeiro: Rocco, 2006.

———. "Antropologia do óbvio: Notas em torno do significado social do futebol brasileiro." *Revista USP. Dossiê futebol* (1994): 10–17.

———. *Carnavais, malandros e heróis: Para uma sociologia do dilemma brasileiro.* Rio de Janeiro: Zahar Editores, 1983.

———. "Esporte na sociedade: Um ensaio sobre o futebol brasileiro." In *Universo do futebol: Esporte e sociedade brasileira,* by Roberto DaMatta, Luiz Baêta Neves Flores, Simoni Lahud Guedes, and Arno Vogel, 19–42. Rio de Janeiro: Edições Pinakotheke, 1982.

———. *O que faz o brasil, Brasil?* Rio de Janeiro: Rocco, 1984.

DaMatta, Roberto, Luiz Baêta Neves Flores, Simoni Lahud Guedes, and Arno Vogel. *Universo do futebol: Esporte e sociedade brasileira.* Rio de Janeiro: Edições Pinakotheke, 1982.

Damo, Arlei Sander. "Ah! Eu Sou Gaúcho: O nacional e o regional no futebol brasileiro." *Estudos Históricos* 23 (1999): 87–117.

———. *Do dom à profissão: A formação de futebolistas no Brasil e na França.* São Paulo: Hucitec, 2005.

———. *Futebol e identidade social: Uma leitura antropólogica das rivalidades entre torcedores e clubes.* Porto Alegre: Editora da Universidade / UFRGS, 2002.

Dantas Junior, Hamilcar Silveira. "Esporte, cidade e modernidade: Aracaju." In *Os sports e as cidades brasileiras: Transição dos séculos XIX e XX,* organized by Victor Andrade de Melo, 241–64. Rio de Janeiro: Apicuri, 2010.

Dário José dos Santos (depoimento, 2011) (Rio de Janeiro: CPDOC / FGV, 2011).

Darnell, Simon C. "Olympism in Action, Olympic Hosting and the Politics of 'Sport for Development and Peace': Investigating the Development Discourses of Rio 2016." *Sport in Society* 15, no. 6 (2012): 869–87.

Darnell, Simon C., and Lyndsay M. C. Hayhurst. "Sport for Decolonization: Exploring a New Praxis of Sport for Development." *Progress in Development Studies* 11, no. 3 (2011): 183–96.

Del Priore, Mary, and Victor Andrade de Melo, eds. *História do esporte no Brasil: Do Império aos dias atuais.* São Paulo: Editora UNESP, 2009.

Dias, José. *Futebol de craques e dos cartolas pernas-de-pau.* Rio de Janeiro: Mauad, 2000.

Dino Sani (depoimento, 2011). Rio de Janeiro: CPDOC / FGV, 2011.

Djalma Santos (depoimento, 2011). Rio de Janeiro: CPDOC, 2011.

Domingues, Edson Paulo, Admir Antonio Betarelli Júnior, and Aline Souza Magalhães. "Quanto vale o show? Impactos econômicos dos investimentos da Copa do Mundo 2014 no Brasil." *Estudos Econômicos* 41, no. 2 (April / June 2011): 409–39.

Duarte, Gustavo, and Mario Alberto. *Charges do Lance!* São Paulo: Lance! Editorial, 2005.

Duarte, Orlando, and Mário Vilela. *São Paulo FC: O supercampeão.* São Paulo: Companhia Editora Nacional, 2011.

Dubois, Laurent. *Soccer Empire: The World Cup and the Future of France.* Berkeley: University of California Press, 2010.

Escher, Thiago de Aragão, and Heloisa Helena Baldy dos Reis. "As relações entre futebol globalizado e nacionalismo: O exemplo da Copa do Mundo de 2006." *Revista Brasileira de Ciências do Esporte* 30, no. 1 (2008): 41–55. Accessed 13 April 2013. www.ludopedio. com.br/rc/index.php/biblioteca/recurso/715.

Evans, Peter. *Dependent Development: The Alliance of Multinational, State, and Local Capital in Brazil.* Princeton: Princeton University Press, 1979.

Evanson, Philip. "Understanding the People: Futebol, Theater, Film, and Politics in Present-Day Brazil." *The South Atlantic Quarterly* 81, no. 4 (1982): 399–412.

Falcão, Paulo Roberto. *Brasil 82: O time que perdeu a Copa e conquistou o mundo.* Porto Alegre: AGE, 2012.

———. *Histórias da bola.* Porto Alegre: L&PM, 1996.

———. *O time que nunca perdeu.* 2nd ed. Porto Alegre: AGE, 2010.

Farred, Grant. *Long Distance Love: A Passion for Football.* Philadelphia: Temple University Press, 2008.

Fassy, Amaury. *Brasil: Tetra campeão mundial?* Brasília: Horizonte, 1982.

Fausto, Boris. *O crime do restaurante chinês: Carnaval, futebol e justiça na São Paulo dos anos 30.* São Paulo: Companhia das Letras, 2009.

Feijão, Rosane. *Moda e modernidade na belle époque carioca.* São Paulo: Estação das Letras e Cores, 2011.

Ferreira, Jorge. "O governo Goulart e o golpe civil-militar de 1964." In *O Brasil republicano.* Vol. 3, *O tempo do liberalismo excludente: da Proclamação da República à Revolução de 1930,* organized by Jorge Ferreira and Lucilia de Almeida Neves Delgado, 343–404. 4th ed. Rio de Janeiro: Civilização Brasileira, 2011.

Ferreira Neto, Amarílio. *A pedagogia no exército e na escola: A educação física brasileira (1880–1950).* Aracruz: Facha, 1999.

Fico, Carlos. *Além do golpe: Versões e controvérsias sobre 1964 e a Ditadura Militar.* Rio de Janeiro: Record, 2004.

———. *Reinventando o otimismo: Ditadura, propaganda e imaginário social no Brasil.* Rio de Janeiro: Fundação Getúlio Vargas Editora, 1997.

Florenzano, José Paulo. *A Democracia Corinthiana: Práticas de liberdade no futebol brasileiro.* São Paulo: FAPESP / EDUC, 2009.

———. *Afonsinho e Edmundo: A rebeldia no futebol brasileiro.* São Paulo: Musa Editora, 1998.

———. "Feras, mágicos e guerreiros: A hegemonia em jogo." *Aurora: Revista de Arte, Mídia e Política* 9 (2010): 103–13.

Flusser, Vilém. *Fenomenologia do brasileiro: Em busca de um novo homem.* Organized and translated by Gustavo Bernardo. Rio de Janeiro: UERJ, 1998.

Foster, Ken. "Alternative Models for the Administration of Global Sport." In *The Global Politics of Sport: The Role of Global Institutions in Sport,* edited by Lincoln Allison, 63–86. London: Routledge, 2003.

Foster, Kevin. "Dreaming of Pelé: Football and Society in England and Brazil in the 1950s and 1960s." *Football Studies* 6, no. 1 (2003): 70–86.

Franco Júnior, Hilário. *A dança dos deuses: Futebol, sociedade, cultura.* São Paulo: Companhia das Letras, 2007.

Franzini, Fábio. "A futura paixão nacional: Chega o futebol." In *História do esporte no Brasil: Do Império aos dias atuais,* edited by Mary Del Priore and Victor Andrade de Melo, 107–31. São Paulo: Editora UNESP, 2009.

———. "As raízes do país do futebol: Estudo sobre a relação entre o futebol e a nacionalidade brasileira (1919–1950)." Master's thesis, Universidade de São Paulo, 2000.

———. *Corações na ponta da chuteira: Capítulos iniciais da história do futebol brasileiro (1919–1938).* Rio de Janeiro: DP&A, 2003.

———. "Da expectative fremente à decepção amarga: O Brasil e a Copa do Mundo de 1950." *Revista de História* 163 (July / December 2010): 243–74.

———. "Esporte, cidade e modernidade: São Paulo." In *Os sports e as cidades brasileiras: Transição dos séculos XIX e XX.,* organized by Victor Andrade de Melo, 49–70. Rio de Janeiro: Apicuri, 2010.

Freire, Flora. "Copa do mundo motiva debate sobre legado nas cidades-sede." *Coletiva* 8 (April / May / June 2012). Accessed 25 September 2012. www.coletiva.org/site/index .php?option=com_k2&view=item&layout=item&id=109&Itemid=75&idrev=11.

Freitas, Adriana Oliveira de. "Abalou Bangu! A Fábrica Bangu e a república nascente (1889–1914)." Master's thesis, Universidade Federal do Espírito Santo, 2005.

Freitas Júnior, Miguel Archanjo. "No meio do caminho: Tensões presentes nas representações sobre o futebol e o ideal da modernidade brasileira na década de 1950." PhD diss., Universidade Federal do Paraná, 2009.

———. "Razão e paixão no futebol: Tentativas de implementação de um projeto modernizador." In *Futebol e globalização,* organized by Luiz Carlos Ribeiro, 213–33. Jundiaí, São Paulo: Fontoura, 2009.

Freyre, Gilberto. "A propósito de futebol brasileiro." *O Cruzeiro,* 18 June 1955.

———. "Ainda a propósito de futebol brasileiro." *O Cruzeiro,* 25 June 1955.

———. *Casa-grande e senzala.* 2nd ed. Rio de Janeiro: Schmidt, 1936.

———. "Foot-ball mulato." *Diario de Pernambuco,* 17 June 1938.

———. "Futebol desbrasileirado?" *Diário de Pernambuco,* 30 June 1974.

———. *Interpretação do Brasil: Aspectos da formação social brasileira como processo de amalgamento de raças e culturas.* Translated by Olívio Montenegro. Organized by Omar Ribeiro Thomaz. São Paulo: Companhia das Letras, 2001.

———. *Novo mundo nos trópicos.* 2nd ed. Rio de Janeiro: Topbooks, 2000.

———. "Prefácio à 1a. edição." In *O negro no futebol brasileiro,* by Mário [Rodrigues] Filho, 24–26. Rio de Janeiro: Mauad / FAPERJ, 2003.

Fry, Peter. "O que a Cinderela Negra tem a dizer sobre a 'política racial' no Brasil." *Revista USP* 28 (1995): 122–35.

———. "Politics, Nationality, and the Meanings of 'Race' in Brazil." *Daedalus* 129, no. 2 (Spring 2000): 83–118.

Furtado, Alencar. *Salgando a terra.* Rio de Janeiro: Paz e Terra, 1977.

Futebol Top Brasil: O mais complete anuário do futebol brasileiro. São Paulo: Sindicato do Futebol, 2005.

Gabeira, Fernando. *O crepúsculo do macho.* 16th ed. Rio de Janeiro: Codecri, 1981.

Gaffney, Christopher. "Mega-events and Socio-spatial Dynamics in Rio de Janeiro, 1919–2016." *Journal of Latin American Geography* 9, no. 1 (2010): 7–29.

———. *Temples of the Earthbound Gods: Stadiums in the Cultural Landscapes of Rio de Janeiro and Buenos Aires.* Austin: University of Texas Press, 2008.

Galeano, Eduardo. *Soccer in Sun and Shadow.* Translated by Mark Fried. London: Verso, 1998.

Garramuño, Florencia. *Primitive Modernities: Tango, Samba, and Nation.* Translated by Anna Kazumi Stahl. Stanford: Stanford University Press, 2011.

Gaspari, Elio. *A ditadura envergonhada.* São Paulo: Companhia das Letras, 2002.

———. *A ditadura escancarada.* São Paulo: Companhia das Letras, 2002.

Gastaldo, Édison. "Accounting for Defeat: Sporting Speech and Communicative Resources in a World Cup Final Loss." *Vibrant: Virtual Brazilian Anthropology* 6, no. 2 (July / December 2009): 9–28. www.vibrant.org.br/downloads/v6n2_gastaldo.pdf.

———. "Os muitos futebóis do Brasil." *Coletiva* 8 (April / May / June 2012). Accessed 25 September 2012. www.coletiva.org/site/index.php?option=com_k2&view=item&layout=item&id=98&Itemid=76&idrev=11.

———. *Pátria, chuteiras e propaganda: O brasileiro na publicidade da Copa do Mundo.* São Paulo: Annablume; São Leopoldo, Rio Grande do Sul: Ed. Unisinos, 2002.

Giacomini, Conrado. *São Paulo: Dentre os grandes, és o primeiro.* Rio de Janeiro: Ediouro, 2005.

Giglio, Sérgio Settani. "Análise da construção do ídolo a partir da trajetória de Ademir da Guia." *Oralidades: Revista de História Oral* 7 (January / June 2010): 101–124.

———. "Futebol: Mitos, ídolos e heróis." Master's thesis, Universidade Estadual de Campinas, 2007.

———. "Futebol-arte ou futebol-força?: O estilo brasileiro em jogo." In *Futebol, cultura e sociedade,* organized by Jocimar Daolio, 53–72. Campinas: Autores Associados, 2005.

Gil, Gilson. "O drama do 'futebol-arte': O debate sobre a seleção nos anos 70." *Revista Brasileira de Ciências Sociais* 25, no. 9 (June 1994): 100–109.

Giulianotti, Richard. *Football: A Sociology of the Global Game.* Cambridge: Polity Press, 1999.

Giulianotti, Richard, and Roland Robertson, eds. *Globalization and Sport.* Oxford: Blackwell, 2007.

———. "Recovering the Social: Globalization, Football and Transnationalism." In *Globalization and Sport,* edited by Richard Giulianotti and Roland Robertson, 58–78. Oxford: Blackwell, 2007.

Glanville, Brian. *The History of the World Cup*. London: Faber and Faber, 1984.

Goellner, Silvana Vilodre. "Imagens da mulher no esporte." In *História do esporte no Brasil: Do Império aos dias atuais,* edited by Mary Del Priore and Victor Andrade de Melo, 269–92. São Paulo: Editora UNESP, 2009.

Goellner, Silvana Vilodre, and Janice Zarpelon Mazzo. "Esporte, cidade e modernidade: Porto Alegre." In *Os sports e as cidades brasileiras: Transição dos séculos XIX e XX.,* organized by Victor Andrade de Melo, 169–92. Rio de Janeiro: Apicuri, 2010.

Goldblatt, David. *The Ball Is Round: A Global History of Soccer.* New York: Riverhead Books, 2008.

Goldgrub, Franklin. *Futebol, arte ou guerra?: Elogio ao drible.* Rio de Janeiro: Imago Editora, 1990.

Goldschmitt, Kariann. "'Joga Bonito Pelo Mundo, Guerreiro': Music, Transmedia Advertising, and Brasilidade in the 2006 World Cup." *Popular Music and Society* 34, no. 4 (2011): 417–36.

Gomes, [Alfredo] Dias. *Campeões do mundo.* São Paulo: Círculo do Livro, [1983].

Gomes, Flávio, and Petrônio Domingues, orgs. *Experiências da emancipação: Biografias, instituições e movimentos sociais no pós-abolição (1890–1980).* São Paulo: Selo Negro, 2011.

Gonçalves Júnior, René Duarte. "Friedenreich e a reinvenção de São Paulo: O futebol e a vitória na fundação da metropole." Master's thesis, Universidade de São Paulo, 2008.

Gordon, Cesar C., Jr. "'Eu já fui preto e sei o que é isso': História social dos negros no futebol brasileiro: segundo tempo." *Pesquisa de Campo: Revista do Núcleo de Sociologia do Futebol/UERJ* 3 / 4 (1996): 65–78.

———. "História social dos negros no futebol brasileiro: Primeiro tempo: 'Essa maravilhosa obra de arte fruto da mistura.'" *Pesquisa de Campo: Revista do Núcleo de Sociologia do Futebol/UERJ* 2 (1995): 71–90.

Gordon, Cesar, and Ronaldo Helal. "The Crisis of Brazilian Football: Perspectives for the Twenty-First Century." In *Sport in Latin American Society: Past and Present,* edited by J.A. Mangan and Lamartine P. DaCosta, 139–58. London: Frank Cass, 2002.

Graham, Richard. *Britain and the Onset of Modernization in Brazil, 1850–1914.* Cambridge: Cambridge University Press, 1972.

Guedes, Simoni Lahud. "Futebol e identidade nacional: Reflexões sobre o Brasil." In *História do esporte no Brasil: Do Império aos dias atuais,* edited by Mary Del Priore and Victor Andrade de Melo, 453–80. São Paulo: Editora UNESP, 2009.

———. "O Brasil nas Copas do Mundo: tempo 'suspenso' e história." *Aquinate* 3 (2006): 163–72.

———. *O Brasil no campo de futebol: Estudos antropólogicos sobre os significados do futebol brasileiro.* Niterói: EDUFF, 1998.

———. "O 'povo brasileiro' no campo de futebol." *A Margem* 1, no. 3 (1993): 5–16.

Gumbrecht, Hans Ulrich. *In Praise of Athletic Beauty.* Cambridge: Harvard University Press, 2006.

Gurgel, Anderson. *Futebol S / A: A economia em campo.* São Paulo: Saraiva, 2006.

Guterman, Marcos. *O futebol explica o Brasil: Uma história da maior expressão popular do país.* São Paulo: Contexto, 2009.

Halsenbalg, Carlos, and Nelson do Valle Silva. "Notes on Racial and Political Inequality in Brazil." In *Racial Politics in Contemporary Brazil,* edited by Michael Hanchard, 154–78. Durham: Duke University Press, 1999.

Hamburger, Esther. "Diluindo fronteiras: A televisão e as novelas no cotidiano." In *História da vida privada no Brasil*. Vol. 4, *Contrastes da intimidade contemporânea,* organized by Lilia Moritz Schwarcz, 439–87. São Paulo: Companhia das Letras, 1998.

Hamilton, Aidan. *Domingos da Guia: O Divino Mestre*. Rio de Janeiro: Gryphus, 2005.

———. *An Entirely Different Game: The British Influence on Brazilian Football*. Edinburgh: Mainstream Publishing, 1998.

Hanchard, Michael. "Black Cinderella? Race and the Public Sphere in Brazil." In *Racial Politics in Contemporary Brazil,* edited by Michael Hanchard, 59–81. Durham: Duke University Press, 1999.

———. *Orpheus and Power: The Movimento Negro of Rio de Janeiro and São Paulo, Brazil, 1945–1988*. Princeton: Princeton University Press, 1994.

———, ed. *Racial Politics in Contemporary Brazil*. Durham: Duke University Press, 1999.

Halsenbalg, Carlos, and Nelson do Valle Silva. "Notes on Racial and Political Inequality in Brazil." In *Racial Politics in Contemporary Brazil,* edited by Michael Hanchard, 154–78. Durham: Duke University Press, 1999.

Harvey, David. *A Brief History of Neoliberalism*. Oxford: Oxford University Press, 2005.

Helal, Ronaldo. "A construção de narrativas de idolatria no futebol brasileiro." *Alcéu* 4, no. 7 (July / December 2003): 19–36.

———. "Idolatria e malandragem: A cultura brasileira na biografia do Romário." In *Futbologías: fútbol, identidad e violencia en América Latina,* edited by Pablo Alabarces, 225–40. Buenos Aires: Clacso, 2003.

———. "Mitos e verdades do futebol (que nos ajudam a entender quem somos)." *Insight Inteligência* 52 (January / February / March 2011): 68–81.

———. *Passes e impasses: Futebol e cultura de massa no Brasil*. Petrópolis: Vozes, 1997.

Helal, Ronaldo, and Cesar Gordon Jr. "Sociologia, história e romance na construção da identidade nacional através do futebol." *Estudos Históricos* 13, no. 23 (1999): 147–65.

Helal, Ronaldo, and Antonio Jorge Soares. "The Crisis of Brazilian Football: Perspectives for the Twenty-First Century." In *Sport in Latin American Society: Past and Present,* edited by J. A. Mangan and Lamartine P. DaCosta, 139–58. London: Frank Cass, 2002.

———. "O declínio da pátria de chuteiras: Futebol e identidade nacional na Copa do Mundo de 2002." In *Anais XII COMPÓS—Associação dos Programas de Pós-Graduação em Comunicação Social,* 401–12. Recife: UFPE, 2003.

Helal, Ronaldo, Antonio Jorge Soares, and Hugo Lovisolo. *A invenção do país do futebol: Mídia, raça e idolatria*. Rio de Janeiro: Mauad, 2001.

Helal, Ronaldo, Hugo Lovisolo, and Antonio Jorge Soares, eds. *Futebol, jornalismo e ciências sociais: Interações*. Rio de Janeiro: EdUERJ, 2011.

Hollanda, Bernardo Borges Buarque de, João M. C. Malaia, Luiz Henrique de Toledo, and Victor Andrade de Melo. *A torcida brasileira*. Rio de Janeiro: 7letras, 2012.

Hollanda, Bernardo Borges Buarque de, and Victor Andrade de Melo, orgs. *O esporte na imprensa e a imprensa esportiva no Brasil*. Rio de Janeiro: 7letras, 2012.

Holston, James. *The Modernist City: An Anthropological Critique of Brasília*. Chicago: University of Chicago Press, 1989.

Hornby, Nick. *Fever Pitch*. New York: Riverhead Books, 1998.

Hunter, Wendy. "The Partido dos Trabalhadores: Still a Party of the Left?" In *Democratic Brazil Revisited,* edited by Peter R. Kingstone and Timothy J. Power, 15–32. Pittsburgh: University of Pittsburgh Press, 2008.

Ianni, Octávio. *A idéia do Brasil moderno*. São Paulo: Brasiliense, 2004 (orig. 1992).

Jacobs, Claudia Silva, and Fernando Duarte. *Futebol exportação*. Rio de Janeiro: Editora Senac Rio, 2006.

Jal e Gual. *A história do futebol no Brasil através do cartum*. Rio de Janeiro: Bom Texto, 2004.

James, C. L. R. *Beyond a Boundary*. Durham: Duke University Press, 1993.

Jenkins, Garry. *The Beautiful Team: In Search of Pelé and the 1970 Brazilians*. London: Pocket Books, 1999.

Jesus, Diego Santos Vieira de, and Valéria Lima Guimarães. "Muito além da festa: O VI sul-americano e as relações internacionais no centenário da independência do Brasil." In *1922: Celebrações esportivas do centenário*, edited by João Manuel Casquinha Malaia Santos and Victor Andrade de Melo, 37–57. Rio de Janeiro: 7letras / Faperj, 2012.

Jesus, Gilmar Mascarenhas de. "Construindo a cidade moderna: Introdução dos esportes na vida urbana do Rio de Janeiro." *Estudos Históricos* 13, no. 23 (1999): 17–39.

———. "Fútbol y modernidad en Brasil: La geografía historica de una novedad." *Lecturas: Educación Física y Deporte* 3, no. 10 (May 1998). Accessed 1 April 2012. www.efdeportes. com/efd10/geoe.htm.

———. "O futebol da *Canela Preta:* O negro e a modernidade em Porto Alegre." *Anos 90* 11 (July 1999): 144–52.

Jesus, Mauricio Neves de, with Arthur Muhlenberg and Lucas Dantas. *1981: O primeiro ano do resto de nossas vidas*. Rio de Janeiro: Livros de Futebol, 2011.

Kfouri, Juca. *Corinthians: paixão e glória*. São Paulo: DBA, [2006].

———. *Meninos eu vi . . .* São Paulo: DBA Artes Gráficas, 2003.

———. *Por que não desisto: Futebol, dinheiro e política*. Barueri, São Paulo: DISAL, 2009.

Kingstone, Peter R., and Timothy J. Power, eds. *Democratic Brazil Revisited*. Pittsburgh: University of Pittsburgh Press, 2008.

Klintowitz, Jacob. "A implantação de um modelo alienígena exótico e outras questões pertinentes: A Seleção Brasileira de Futebol—1978." *Encontros com a civilização brasileira* 5 (1978): 113–18.

Kowarick, Lúcio. *Trabalho e vadiagem: A origem do trabalho livre no Brasil*. São Paulo: Brasiliense, 1987.

Kuper, Simon. *Soccer Men: Profiles of the Rogues, Geniuses, and Neurotics Who Dominate the World's Most Popular Sport*. New York: Nation Books, 2011.

Kuper, Simon, and Stefan Szymanksi. "Felicidade. Por que sediar uma Copa do Mundo é bom para você?" *Coletiva* 8 (April / May / June 2012). Accessed 25 September 2012. www .coletiva.org/site/index.php?option=com_k2&view=item&layout=item&id=111&Itemi d=76&idrev=11.

———. *Soccernomics: Why England Loses, Why Germany and Brazil Win, and Why the U.S., Japan, Australia, Turkey—and Even Iraq—Are Destined to Become the Kings of the World's Most Popular Sport*. New York: Nation Books, 2009.

Leal, Murilo. *Reinvenção da classe trabalhadora (1953–1964)*. Campinas: Unicamp, 2011.

Lechner, Frank J. "Imagined Communities in the Global Game: Soccer and the Development of Dutch National Identity." In *Globalization and Sport*, edited by Richard Giulianotti and Roland Robertson, 107–21. Oxford: Blackwell, 2007.

Leite, Rinaldo Cesar Nascimento, Coriolano P. da Rocha Junior, and Henrique Sena dos Santos. "Esporte, cidade e modernidade: Salvador." In *Os sports e as cidades brasileiras: Transição dos séculos XIX e XX.*, organized by Victor Andrade de Melo, 213–40. Rio de Janeiro: Apicuri, 2010.

Lever, Janet. *Soccer Madness: Brazil's Passion for the World's Most Popular Sport*. Prospect Heights, IL: Waveland Press, 1995 (orig. 1983).

Levine, Robert M. "The Burden of Success: Futebol and Brazilian Society through the 1970s." *Journal of Popular Culture* 14, no. 3 (1980): 453–64.

———. "Elite Perceptions of the Povo." In *Modern Brazil: Elites and Masses in Historial Perspective,* edited by Michael L. Conniff and Frank D. McCann, 209–24. Lincoln: University of Nebraska Press, 1989.

———. "Sport and Society: The Case of Brazilian *Futebol.*" *Luso-Brazilian Review* 17, no. 2 (1980): 233–52.

Levine, Robert M., and John C. Crocitti, eds. *The Brazil Reader: History, Culture, Politics.* Durham: Duke University Press, 1999.

Levitt, Theodore. "The Globalization of Markets." *Harvard Business Review* (May / June 1983): 92–102.

Lisboa, Luiz Carlos, org. *Reinaldo do Atlético Mineiro.* Rio de Janeiro: Editora Rio, 2003.

Lopes, José Sergio Leite. "A vitória do futebol que incorporou a pelada: A invenção do jornalismo esportivo e a entrada dos negros no futebol brasileira." *Revista USP: Dossiê futebol* 22 (1994): 64–83.

———. "The Brazilian Style of Football and its Dilemmas." In *Football Cultures and Identities,* edited by Gary Armstrong and Richard Giulianotti, 86–95. London: Macmillan, 1999.

———. "Class, Ethnicity, and Color in the Making of Brazilian Football." *Daedalus* 129, no. 2 (2000): 239–70.

———. "Class, etnicidade e cor na formação do futebol brasileiro." In *Culturas de classe,* edited by Claudio H. M. Batalha, Fernando Teixeira da Silva, and Alexandre Fortes, 121–63. Campinas: Editora da UNICAMP, 2004.

———. "'The People's Joy' Vanishes: Considerations on the Death of a Soccer Player." Special issue, *Journal of Latin American Anthropology* 4, no. 2 and 5, no. 1 (2000): 78–105.

———. "Transformations in National Identity through Football in Brazil: Lessons from Two Historical Defeats." In *Football in the Americas: Fútbol, Futebol, Soccer,* edited by Rory M. Miller and Liz Crolley, 75–93. London: Institute for the Study of the Americas, 2007.

Lucena, Ricardo de F. *O esporte na cidade: O esforço civilizador brasileiro.* Campinas: Autores Associados, 2001.

Lyra Filho, João. *Cachimbo, pijama e chinelo: Memórias.* São Paulo: Editora Edaglit, 1963.

———. *Taça do mundo, 1954.* Rio de Janeiro: Irmãos Pongetti, 1954.

Machado, Felipe Morelli. "Bola na rede e o povo nas ruas! Estado Novo, imprensa esportiva e torcedores na Copa do Mundo de 1938: O futebol construindo a 'nação.'" *Recorde: Revista de História do Esporte* 4, no. 1 (June 2011). Accessed 20 September 2011. www.sport.ifcs.ufrj.br/recorde/pdf/recordeV4N1_2011_16.pdf.

Macia, José (Pepe). *Bombas de alegria: Meio século de histórias do canhão da vila.* Santos: Realejo Edições, 2006.

Mack, Roberto C. V. *Futebol empresa: A nova dimensão para o futebol brasileiro.* Rio de Janeiro: Palestra Edições, 1980.

Magazine, Roger. "'You Can Buy a Player's Legs, But Not His Heart': A Critique of Clientelism and Modernity among Soccer Fans in Mexico City." *Journal of Latin American Anthropology* 9, no. 1 (2004): 8–33.

Maio, Marcos Chor. "A questão racial no pensamento de Guerreiro Ramos." In *Raça, ciência e sociedade,* organized by Marcos Chor Maio and Ricardo Ventura Santos, 179–93. Rio de Janeiro: FIOCRUZ / CCBB, 1996.

Malaia, João M. C. "Torcer, torcedores, torcedoras, torcida (bras.): 1910–1950." In *A torcida brasileira,* by Bernardo Borges Buarque de Hollanda, João M. C. Malaia, Luiz Henrique de Toledo, and Victor Andrade de Melo, 53–85. Rio de Janeiro: 7letras, 2012.

Manhães, Eduardo. *João Sem Medo: Futebol-arte e identidade*. Campinas: Pontes Livros, 2004.

———. *Política de esportes no Brasil: Tendências*. 2nd ed. Rio de Janeiro: Paz e Terra, 2002.

Maranhão, Tiago. "Apollonians and Dionysians: The Role of Football in Gilberto Freyre's Vision of Brazilian People." *Soccer & Society* 8, no. 4 (2007): 510–23.

Maranhão, Tiago Fernandes, and Jorge Knijnik. "*Futebol mulato*: Racial constructs in Brazilian football." *Cosmopolitan Civil Societies Journal*, 3, no. 2 (2011): 55–71.

Markovits, Andrei S., and Lars Rensmann. *Gaming the World: How Sports are Reshaping Global Politics and Culture*. Princeton: Princeton University Press, 2010.

Marques, José Carlos. *O futebol em Nelson Rodrigues*. São Paulo: EDUC / FAPESP, 2000.

Martins, Aldemir, George Torok, and Araújo Netto. *Brasil futebol rei*. Rio de Janeiro: Image, 1965.

Mascarenhas, Gilmar. "Globalização e espetáculo: O Brasil dos megaeventos esportivos." In *História do esporte no Brasil: Do Império aos dias atuais*, edited by Mary Del Priore and Victor Andrade de Melo, 505–31. São Paulo: Editora UNESP, 2009.

Mason, Tony. *Passion of the People? Football in South America*. London: Verso, 1995.

Máximo, João. *Brasil: Um século de futebol: Arte e magia*. Rio de Janeiro: Aprazível Edições, 2005–06.

———. *João Saldanha: Sobre nuvens de fantasia*. Rio de Janeiro. Relume Dumará, 2005.

Mazzei, Leandro Carlos, and Flávia da Cunha Bastos, eds. *Gestão do esporte no Brasil: Desafios e perspectivas*. São Paulo: Ícone, 2012.

Mazzoni, Thomaz (Tomás). *Almanaque esportivo: 1939*. São Paulo: n.p., [1939].

———. *História do futebol no Brasil, 1894–1950*. Sao Paulo: Leia, 1950.

McCann, Bryan. *Hello, Hello Brazil: Popular Music in the Making of Modern Brazil*. Durham: Duke University Press, 2004.

———. *The Throes of Democracy: Brazil Since 1989*. Halifax: Fernwood Publishing; London: Zed Books, 2008.

———. "Volleyball Nation: Brazilian Women's Vôlei." *Georgetown Journal of International Affairs*, 2 July 2012.

Meihy, José Carlos Sebe Bom. "A National Festival." In *The Brazil Reader*, edited by Robert M. Levine and John C. Crocitti, 501–4. Durham: Duke University Press, 1999.

Meihy, José Carlos Sebe Bom, and José Sebastião Witter, eds. *Futebol e cultura: Coletânea de estudos*. São Paulo: Convênio IMESP / DAESP, 1982.

Melo, Victor Andrade de. *Cidade esportiva: Primórdios do esporte no Rio de Janeiro*. Rio de Janeiro: FAPERJ / Relume Dumará, 2001.

———, org. *Entre o requinte e o tribofe: Sports e sportsmen na literatura do século XIX—uma antologia*. Rio de Janeiro: 7letras, 2012.

———. "Escola Nacional de Educação Física e Desportos: Uma possível história." Master's thesis, Universidade de Campinas, 1996.

———. "Esporte, cidade e modernidade: Rio de Janeiro." In *Os sports e as cidades brasileiras: Transição dos séculos XIX e XX.*, organized by Victor Andrade de Melo, 19–48. Rio de Janeiro: Apicuri, 2010.

———, org. *Os sports e as cidades brasileiras: Transição dos séculos XIX e XX*. Rio de Janeiro: Apicuri, 2010.

———. "Sportsmen: Os primeiros momentos da configuração de um público esportivo no Brasil." In *A torcida brasileira*, by Bernardo Borges Buarque de Hollanda, João M. C. Malaia, Luiz Henrique de Toledo, and Victor Andrade de Melo, 21–52. Rio de Janeiro: 7letras, 2012.

Mezzadri, Fernando Marinho. "As possíveis interferências do estado na estrutura do futebol brasiliero." In *Futebol e globalização,* organized by Luiz Carlos Ribeiro, 107–28. Jundiaí, São Paulo: Fontoura, 2009.

Millan, Betty. *Brasil: O país da bola.* São Paulo: Best Editora, 1989.

Milliet, Raul, org. *Vida que segue: João Saldanha e as Copas de 1966 e 1970.* Rio de Janeiro: Nova Fronteira, 2006.

Millington, Rob, and Simon C. Darnell. "Constructing and Contesting the Olympics Online: The Internet, Rio 2016, and the Politics of Brazilian Development." *International Review for the Sociology of Sport,* 9 September 2012. Accessed 15 April 2013. http://irs .sagepub.com/content/early/2012/09/07/1012690212455374.

Miranda, Lyana Virgínia Thédiga de, and Giovani de Lorenzi Pires. "Reconstruindo a imagem/identidade da seleção brasileira de futebol: A 'era pós-Dunga' na mídia." *Revista de ALESDE* 2, no. 1 (April 2012): 17–34.

Miranda, Wladimir. *O artilheiro indomável: As incríveis histórias de Serginho Chulapa.* São Paulo: Publisher Brasil, 2011.

Monsanto, Eduardo. *1981: O ano rubro-negro.* São Paulo: Panda Books, 2011.

Monteiro, Rodrigo de Araujo. *Torcer, lutar, ao inimigo massacrar: Raça Rubro-Negro!* Rio de Janeiro: Editora FGV, 2003.

Moraes, Dênis de. *A esquerda e o golpe de 64: Vinte e cinco anos depois, as forças populares repensam seus mitos, sonhos e ilusões.* Rio de Janeiro: Espaço e Tempo, 1989.

Moraes, Hugo da Silva. "Jogadas insólitas: Amadorismo, profissionalismo e os jogadores de futebol do Rio de Janeiro (1922–1924)." *Esporte e Sociedade* 5, no. 16 (November 2010 / February 2011): 1–26.

Moraes, Marcus Vinícius Rezende de. *Romário.* Rio de Janeiro: Altadena, 2009.

Moraes, Mario de. *Futebol é arte.* Vol. 2. Rio de Janeiro: FAPERJ / MIS Editorial, 2002.

Moraes Neto, Geneton. *Dossiê 50: Os onze jogadores revelam os segredos da maior tragédia do futebol brasileiro.* Rio de Janeiro: Objetiva, 2000.

Morais, Jorge Ventura de and José Luiz Ratton Júnior. "Gilberto Freyre e o futebol: Entre processos sociais gerais e biografias individuais." *Revista de Ciências Sociais* (Fortaleza) 42, no. 1 (January / June 2011): 89–109.

Moreyra, Sandro. *Histórias de Sandro Moreyra.* Rio de Janeiro: Editora JB, 1985.

Mota, Carlos Guilherme. *Ideologia da cultura brasileira (1933–1974).* São Paulo: Editora Ática, 1985.

Motta, Nelson. *Confissões de um torcedor: Quatro Copas e uma paixão.* Rio de Janeiro: Objetiva, 1998.

Moura, Rodrigo Caldeira Bagni. "O futebol em Belo Horizonte nas décadas de 1920 e 1930: As partidas e diversões, os sururus e outras tramas." *Recorde: Revista de História do Esporte* 4, no. 1 (June 2011). Accessed 21 January 2013. www.sport.ifcs.ufrj.br/recorde/pdf/record-eV4N1_2011_11.pdf.

Muylaert, Roberto. *Barbosa: Um gol faz cinqüenta anos.* São Paulo: RMC Comunicação, 2000.

Napoleão, Antonio Carlos, and Roberto Assaf. *Seleção Brasileira, 1914–2006.* Rio de Janeiro: Mauad X, 2006.

Nascimento, Edson Arantes do (Pelé), with Robert L. Fish. *My Life and the Beautiful Game: The Autobiography of Pelé.* New York: Doubleday, 1977.

———, with Orlando Duarte and Alex Bellos. *Pelé: The Autobiography.* Trans. Daniel Hahn. London: Simon & Schuster, 2006.

———. "Pelé Speaks." In *The Brazil Reader,* edited by Robert M. Levine and John C. Crocitti, 254–57. Durham: Duke University Press, 1999.

Nauright, John. "Global Games: Culture, Political Economy and Sport in the Globalised World of the 21st Century." *Third World Quarterly* 25, no. 7 (2004): 1325–36.

Needell, Jeffrey. "Identity, Race, Gender, and Modernity in the Origins of Gilberto Freyre's *Oeuvre*." *American Historical Review* 100, no. 1 (February 1995): 51–77.

———. *A Tropical Belle Époque: Elite Culture and Society in Turn-of-the-Century Rio de Janeiro.* Cambridge: Cambridge University Press, 1987.

Negreiros, Plínio Labriola. "A cidade excludente e o clube do povo." *Revista de História* 163 (July / December 2010): 207–42.

———. "A invasão corinthiana—Rio, 05 de dezembro de 1976." *Aurora* 9 (2010): 114–25.

———. "A nação entra em campo: O futebol nos anos 30 e 40." PhD diss., Pontifícia Universidade Católica, São Paulo, 1998.

———. "Construindo a nação: Futebol nos anos 30 e 40." In *Futebol: Espetáculo do século,* organized by Márcia Regina da Costa, 214–39. São Paulo: Musa, 1999.

Neves, Luiz Felipe Baêta. *O paradoxo do coringa e o jogo do poder e saber.* Rio de Janeiro: Achiamé, 1979.

Neves, Marcos Eduardo. *Anjo ou demônio: A polêmica trajetória de Renato Gaúcho.* Rio de Janeiro: Gryphus, 2002.

Nogueira, Armando. *A ginga e o jogo.* Rio de Janeiro: Objetiva, 2003.

———. *Bola na rede.* 2nd ed. Rio de Janeiro: J. Olympio, 1974.

———. *Na grande área.* 2nd ed. Rio de Janeiro: Lance, 2008 [orig. 1966].

———. *O homem e a bola.* Rio de Janeiro: Globo, 1988 [orig. 1986].

Nogueira, Armando, and Araújo Neto. *Drama e glória dos bicampeões.* Rio de Janeiro: Editora do Autor, 1962.

Nogueira, Armando, Jô Soares, and Roberto Muylaert. *A copa que ninguém viu e a que não queremos lembrar.* São Paulo: Companhia das Letras, 1994.

Nogueira, Claudio. *Futebol Brasil memória: De Oscar Cox a Leônidas da Silva (1897-1937).* Rio de Janeiro: Editora Senac Rio, 2006.

Ojeda, Igor, and Tatiana Merlino. *A invasão corinthiana: O dia em que a Fiel tomou o Rio de Janeiro para ver seu time no maior estádio do mundo.* São Paulo: Livraria da Física, 2011.

Oliveira, Lúcia Lippi. *A questão nacional na Primeira República.* São Paulo: Brasiliense, 1990.

Oriard, Michael. *Reading Football: How the Popular Press Created an American Spectacle.* Chapel Hill: University of North Carolina Press, 1993.

Ortiz, Renato. "Diversidade cultural e cosmopolitanismo." *Lua Nova* 47 (August 1999): 73–89.

———. "O advento da modernidade?" In *Posmodernidad en la periferia: Enfoques latinoamericanos de la nueva teoría cultural,* edited by Hermann Herlinghaus and Monika Walter, 185–96. Berlin: Langer Verlag, 1994.

Ostermann, Ruy Carlos. *Felipão: A alma do Penta.* Porto Alegre: Zero Hora Editora Jornalística S.A., 2002.

———. *Itinerário da derrota: Crônica de cinco Copas do Mundo sem Pelé.* Porto Alegre: Artes e Ofícios, 1992.

——— , org. *Meia encarnada, dura de sangue: Literatura e esporte.* Porto Alegre: Artes e Ofícios, 2001.

———. *O nome do jogo.* Porto Alegre: Sagra Luzzatto / Palmarinca, 1998.

Pacheco, Leonardo Turchi. "Memórias da tragédia: Masculinidade e envelhecimento na Copa do Mundo de 1950." *Revista Brasileira de Ciências do Esporte* 32, no. 1 (September 2010): 25–40.

Patusca, Araken, with Marinho U. de Macedo. *Os reis do futebol.* São Paulo: n.p., 1945.

Pedrosa, Milton, org. *Gol de letra.* Rio de Janeiro: Gol, n.d.

———. *Na boca do túnel.* Rio de Janeiro: Livraria Editora Gol, 1968.

Peixoto, Afrânio. *Poeira de estrada: ensaios de crítica e de história.* 2nd ed. Rio de Janeiro: Francisco Alves, 1921.

Perdigão, Paulo. *Anatomia de uma derrota.* Porto Alegre: L&PM, 1986.

Pereira, Anthony W. "Public Security, Private Interests, and Police Reform in Brazil." In *Democratic Brazil Revisited,* edited by Peter R. Kingstone and Timothy J. Power, 185–208. Pittsburgh: University of Pittsburgh Press, 2008.

Pereira, Leonardo Affonso de Miranda. "Domingos do Brasil: Futebol, raça e nacionalidade na trajetória de um herói do Estado Novo." *Locus: Revista de História* 13, no. 2 (2007): 193–214.

———. *Footballmania: Uma história social do futebol no Rio de Janeiro, 1902–1938.* Rio de Janeiro: Nova Fronteira, 2000.

———. "O jogo dos sentidos: Os literários e a popularização do futebol no Rio de Janeiro." In *A história contada: Capítulos de história social da literature no Brasil,* edited by Sidney Chalhoub and Leonardo Affonso de M. Pereira, 195–231. Rio de Janeiro: Nova Fronteira, 1998.

———. "Pelos campos da nação: Um *goal-keeper* nos primeiro anos do futebol brasileiro." *Estudos Históricos* 19 (1997): 23–40.

Pereira, Marcel. *A nação: Como e por que o Flamengo se tornou o clube com a maior torcida do Brasil.* Rio de Janeiro: Maquinária, 2010.

Perrone, Charles A., and Christopher Dunn. "'Chiclete com Banana': Internationalization in Brazilian Popular Music." In *Brazilian Popular Music and Globalization,* edited by Perrone and Dunn, 1–38. New York: Routledge, 2001.

Philippou, Styliane. "Modernism and National Identity in Brazil, or How to Brew a Brazilian Stew." *National Identities* 7, no. 3 (Sept. 2005): 245–64.

Phillips, Brian. "Against Brazil." The Run of Play, 7 September 2009. Accessed 7 September 2009. www.runofplay.com/2009/09/07/against-brazil.

Pignatari, Décio. *Contracomunicação.* 3rd ed. Cotia, São Paulo: Ateliê Editorial, 2004.

———. *Podbre Brasil: Crônicas políticas.* Campinas: Pontes, 1988.

Pimentel, João Guilherme de Mattos. "A relevância do profissionalismo no futebol e os impactos da credibilidade dos dirigentes na obtenção de patrocínio." Master's thesis, Fundação Getúlio Vargas, 2011.

Pinheiro, Carlos Alberto. *Milhões no esporte do Brasil.* Rio de Janeiro: Image, 1974.

Pinheiro, Daniela. "The President." *Revista Piauí* 58 (July 2011). Accessed 5 October 2012. http://revistapiaui.estadao.com.br/edicao-58/the-faces-of-futebol/the-president.

Pinto, Paulo César O. *Um ídolo chamado Roberto Dinamite.* Rio de Janeiro: Editora Revan, 1987.

Piza, Daniel. *Dez anos que encolheram o mundo: 2001–2010.* São Paulo: Leya, 2011.

———. *Ora, bolas! Da Copa de 98 ao Penta.* São Paulo: Nova Alexandria, 2003.

Poli, Raffaele. "The Denationalization of Sport: De-ethnicization of the Nation and Identity Deterritorialization." *Sport in Society* 10, no. 4 (July 2007): 646–61.

———. "Understanding Globalization Through Football: The New International Division of Labour, Migratory Channels and Transnational Trade Circuits." *International Review for the Sociology of Sport* 45, no. 4 (July 2010): 491–506.

Polli, Fábio Matias. *Futebol e cidadania: Um projeto para o Brasil.* Florianópolis: Papa-Livro, 1996.

Pompeu, Renato. *Canhoteiro: O homem que driblou a glória.* Rio de Janeiro: Ediouro / Relume Dumará, 2003.

Porto, Roberto. *Botafogo: 101 anos de histórias, mitos e superstições.* Rio de Janeiro: Revan, 2005.

———. *Didi: Treino é treino, jogo é jogo.* Rio de Janeiro: Relume Dumará / Prefeitura, 2001.

Pozzi, Luiz Fernando. "Futebol empresa." In *Futebol: Espetáculo do século,* organized by Márcia Regina da Costa, 61–69. São Paulo: Musa, 1999.

Prado, Decio de Almeida. *Seres, coisas, lugares: Do teatro ao futebol.* São Paulo: Companhia das Letras, 1997.

Proença, Ivan Calvacanti. *Futebol e palavra.* Rio de Janeiro: Livraria José Olympio Editora, 1981.

Proni, Marcelo Weishaupt. *A metamorfose do futebol.* Campinas: Unicamp / Instituto de Economia, 2000.

———. "Reflexões sobre o futebol empresa no Brasil." In *Futebol: Espetáculo do século,* organized by Márcia Regina da Costa, 42–60. São Paulo: Musa, 1999.

Ramos, Luiz Carlos. *Vicente Matheus: Quem sai na chuva é pra se queimar.* São Paulo: Editora do Brasil, 2001.

Ramos, Nuno. *Ensaio geral: Projetos, roteiros, ensaios, memória.* São Paulo: Globo, 2007.

Ramos, Ricardo, ed. *A palavra é futebol.* Editora Scipione, 1990.

Ramos, Roberto. *Futebol: Ideologia do poder.* Petrópolis: Vozes, 1984.

Raspaud, Michel, and Flávia da Cunha Bastos. "Torcedores de futebol: Violence and Public Policies in Brazil Before the 2014 FIFA World Cup." *Sport in Society* 16, no. 2 (2013): 192–204.

Rebelo, Aldo, and Silvio Torres. *CBF Nike.* Rio de Janeiro: Casa Amarela, 2001.

Reis, Daniel Aarão. "Ditadura, anistia e reconciliação." *Estudos Históricos* 23, no. 45 (2010): 171–86.

Reis, Heloisa Helena Baldy dos. "Lei Geral da Copa, álcool e o processo de criação da legislação sobre violência." *Movimento* 18, no. 1 (2012): 69–99.

Ribeiro, André. *Diamante negro: Biografia de Leônidas da Silva.* 2nd ed. São Paulo: Companhia das Letras, 2010.

———. *Fio de esperança: Biografia de Telê Santana.* Rio de Janeiro: Gryphus, 2000.

———. *Os donos do espetáculo: Histórias da imprensa esportiva do Brasil.* São Paulo: Editora Terceiro Nome, 2007.

Ribeiro, André, and Vladir Lemos. *A magia da camisa 10.* Campinas: Verus Editora, 2006.

Ribeiro, Luiz Carlos, org. *Futebol e globalização.* Jundiaí, São Paulo: Fontoura, 2009.

Ribeiro, Péris. *Didi, o gênio da folha seca.* 2nd ed. Rio de Janeiro: Gryphus, 2009.

Ribeiro, Raphael Rajão. "Em busca de um campo: O futebol belo-horizontino e a transformação dos espaços na cidade (1904–1921)." In *Campo e cidade na modernidade brasileira: Literatura, vilas operárias, cultura alimentar, futebol, correspondência privada e cultura visual,* organized by Maria Eliza Linhares Borges, 97–125. Belo Horizonte: Argumentum, 2008.

Risério, Antonio. *A utopia brasileira e os movimentos negros.* São Paulo: Editora 34, 2007.

Rito, Lucia. *Zico: Paixão e glória de um ídolo.* 2nd ed. Rio de Janeiro: Relume Dumará / Prefeitura, 2000.

Rocha, André, and Mauro Beting. *1981: Como um craque idolatrado, um time fantástico e uma torcida inigualável fizeram o Flamengo ganhar tantos títulos e conquistar o mundo em um só ano.* Rio de Janeiro: Maquinária, 2011.

Rodrigues, Ernesto. *Jogo duro: A história de João Havelange*. Rio de Janeiro: Editora Record, 2007.

Rodrigues, Francisco Xavier Freire. "Modernidade, disciplina e futebol: Uma análise sociológica da produção social do jogador de futebol no Brasil." *Sociologias* 6, no. 11 (January / June 2004): 260–99.

———. "O fim do passe e a modernização conservadora no futebol brasileiro (2001–2006)." PhD diss., Universidade Federal do Rio Grande do Sul, 2007.

[Rodrigues] Filho, Mário. *Copa do Mundo, 1962*. Rio de Janeiro: Edições O Cruzeiro, 1962.

———. *O negro no futebol brasileiro*. 4th ed. Rio de Janeiro: Mauad / FAPERJ, 2003.

———. *O sapo de Arubinha: Os anos de sonho do futebol brasileiro*. Edited by Ruy Castro. São Paulo: Companhia das Letras, 1994.

———. *Viagem em torno de Pelé*. Porto Alegre: Editora do Autor, 1963.

Rodrigues, Nelson. *A pátria em chuteiras: Novas crônicas de futebol*. São Paulo: Companhia das Letras, 1994.

———. *À sombra das chuteiras imortais: Crônicas de futebol*. Edited by Ruy Castro. São Paulo: Companhia das Letras, 1993.

———. *Brasil em campo*. Edited by Sonia Rodrigues. Rio de Janeiro: Nova Fronteira, 2012.

———. *O berro impresso das manchetes*. Rio de Janeiro: Agir, 2007.

———. *O profeta tricolor: Cem anos de Fluminense*. Edited by Nelson Rodrigues Filho. São Paulo: Companhia das Letras, 2002.

Rodrigues, Nelson, and Mário [Rodrigues] Filho. *Fla-Flu . . . e as multidões despertaram!* Organized by Oscar Maron Filho and Renato Ferreira. Rio de Janeiro: Ed. Europa, 1987.

Rolnik, Raquel. "Megaeventos esportivos e cidades: Impactos, violações e legados." *Coletiva* 8 (April / May / June 2012). Accessed 25 September 2012. www.coletiva.org/site/index.php?option=com_k2&view=item&layout=item&id=95&Itemid=76&idrev=11.

Roman, Gustavo, and Renato Zanata. *Sarriá 82: O que faltou ao futebol-arte?* Rio de Janeiro: Maquinária, 2012.

Rosenfeld, Anatol. *Negro, macumba e futebol*. São Paulo: Editora Perspectiva, 1993.

Rowe, David, and Deborah Stevenson. "Sydney 2000: Sociality and Spatiality in Global Media Events." In *National Identity and Global Sports Events: Culture, Politics, and Spectacle in the Olympics and the Football World Cup*, edited by Alan Tomlinson and Christopher Young, 197–214. Albany: State University of New York Press, 2006.

Saldanha, João. *Futebol e outras histórias*. Rio de Janeiro: Record, 1988.

———. *Histórias do futebol*. 7th ed. Rio de Janeiro: Revan, 2001.

———. *O trauma da bola: A Copa de 82 por João Saldanha*. São Paulo: Cosac & Naify, 2002.

———. *Os subterrâneos do futebol*. Rio de Janeiro: Tempo Brasileiro, 1963.

Salun, Oscar Alfredo. "Palestra Itália e Corinthians: Roteiro de uma pesquisa em História Oral e futebol." *Oralidades: Revista de História Oral* 7 (January / June 2010): 89–100.

Salvador, Marco Antonio Santoro, and Antonio Jorge Gonçalves Soares. *Memória da Copa de 1970*. Campinas: Autores Associados, 2009.

Sander, Roberto. *Anos 40: Viagem à década sem Copa*. Rio de Janeiro: Bom Texto, 2004.

———. *Sul-Americano de 1919: Quando o Brasil descobriu o futebol*. Rio de Janeiro: Maquinária, 2009.

Sansone, Livio. *Blackness Without Ethnicity: Constructing Race in Brazil*. New York: Palgrave Macmillan, 2003.

Santos, Claudemir José dos. "Repensando o estilo à brasileira: Escolinhas de futebol e aprendizagem esportiva." In *Visão do jogo: Antropológica das práticas esportivas*, edited by

Luiz Henrique de Toledo and Carlos Eduardo Costa, 217–54. São Paulo: Editora Terceiro Nome, 2009.

Santos, Henrique Sena dos. "Notas sobre a popularização do futebol em Salvador, 1901–1912." *Esporte e Sociedade,* 5, no. 16 (November 2010 / February 2011). Accessed 29 September 2011. www.uff.br/esportesociedade/pdf/es1607.pdf.

Santos, João Manuel Casquinha Malaia. "'Diplomacia de pé': O Brasil e as competições esportivas sul-americanas de 1919 e 1922." *Tempo e Argumento* 3, no. 2 (July / December 2011): 43–76.

———. "Revolução Vascaína: A profissionalização do futebol e a inserção sócio-econômica de negros e portugueses na cidade do Rio de Janeiro (1915–1934)." PhD diss., Universidade de São Paulo, 2010.

Santos, João Manuel Casquinha Malaia, and Victor Andrade de Melo, orgs. *1922: Celebrações esportivas do centenário.* Rio de Janeiro: 7letras / Faperj, 2012.

Santos, Joel Rufino dos. *História política do futebol brasileira.* São Paulo: Brasiliense, 1981.

———. "No CBD até papagaio bate continência." *Encontros com a civilização brasileira* 5 (1978): 119–29.

Santos, Luiz Marcelo Vídero Vieira. "A evolução da gestão no futebol brasileiro." Master's thesis, Fundação Getúlio Vargas, 2002.

Santos, Luiz Tolosa. "Futebol empresa e a 'Democracia Corinthiana': Uma administração que deu dribling na crise." Master's thesis, Universidade de Campinas, 1990.

Santos, Newton César de Oliveira. *Brasil x Argentina: Histórias do maior clássico do futebol mundial (1908–2008).* São Paulo: Scortecci, 2009.

Santos, Nilton. *Minha bola, minha vida.* Rio de Janeiro: Gryphus, 2000.

Santos, Ricardo Pinto dos. "Comemorando o Brasil: que Brasil?" In *1922: Celebrações esportivas do centenário,* organized by João Manuel Casquinha Malaia Santos and Victor Andrade de Melo, 163–82. Rio de Janeiro: 7letras / Faperj, 2012.

———. "Tensões na consolidação do futebol nacional." In *História do esporte no Brasil: Do Império aos dias atuais,* edited by Mary Del Priore and Victor Andrade de Melo, 179–212. São Paulo: Editora UNESP, 2009.

———. "Uma breve história social do esporte no Rio de Janeiro." In *Memória social dos esportes: Futebol e política: A construção de uma identidade nacional,* organized by Francisco Carlos Teixeira da Silva and Ricardo Pinto dos Santos, 2:33–53. Rio de Janeiro: Mauad Editora / FAPERJ, 2006.

Santos, Silvestre Cirilo dos, Lamartine Pereira da Costa, and Carlos Henrique Virtuoso da Silva. "Rio 2016 e o Plano Brasil Medalhas: Seremos uma potência esportiva?" *Podium: Sport, Leisure, and Tourism Review* 1, no. 1 (January / June 2012): 64–82.

Santos Júnior, Nei Jorge dos. "Quando a fábrica cria o clube: O processo de organização do Bangu Athletic Club (1910)." *Recorde: Revista de História do Esporte* 6, no. 1 (January / June 2013): 1–19. Accessed 14 June 2013. www.sport.ifcs.ufrj.br/recorde/pdf/recordeV6N1 2013_15.pdf.

Santos Neto, José Moraes dos. *Visão do jogo: Primórdios do futebol no Brasil.* São Paulo: Cosac & Naify, 2002.

Schinner, Carlos Fernando. *Coutinho: O gênio da área.* Santos: Realejo Edições, 2012.

Schwarcz, Lilia Moritz. *O espetáculo das raças: Cientistas, instituições e questão racial no Brasil, 1870–1930.* São Paulo: Companhia das Letras, 1993.

Seigel, Micol. *Uneven Encounters: Making Race and Nation in Brazil and the United States.* Durham: Duke University Press, 2009.

Sevcenko, Nicolau. "A capital irradiante: Técnica, ritmos e ritos no Rio." In *História da vida privada no Brasil.* Vol. 3, *República: Da Belle Époque à era do radio,* organized by Sevcenko, 513–619. São Paulo: Companhia das Letras, 1998.

————. "Futebol, metrópoles e desatinos." *Revista USP: Dossiê futebol* (1994): 30–37.

————. *Orfeu extático na metrópole: São Paulo, sociedade e cultura nos frementes anos 20.* São Paulo: Companhia das Letras, 1992.

Sheriff, Robin E. *Dreaming Equality: Color, Race, and Racism in Urban Brazil.* New Brunswick: Rutgers University Press, 2001.

Shirts, Matthew. "Futebol: A mesa-redonda do I.E.B." In *Futebol e cultura: Coletânea de estudos,* edited by José Carlos Sebe Bom Meihy and José Sebastião Witter, 113–18. São Paulo: Convênio IMESP / DAESP, 1982.

————. "Socrates, Corinthians, and Questions of Democracy and Citizenship." In *Sport and Society in Latin America: Diffusion, Dependency, and the Rise of Mass Culture,* edited by Joseph L. Arbena, 97–109. New York: Greenwood Press, 1988.

Silva, Francisco Carlos Teixeira da. "Crise da ditadura militar e o processo de abertura política no Brasil, 1974–1985." In *O Brasil Republicano.* Vol. 4, *O tempo da ditadura: Regime military e movimentos sociais em fins do século XX,* edited by Jorge Ferreira and Lucilia de Almeida Neves Delgado, 243–82. Rio de Janeiro: Civilização Brasileira, 2003.

Silva, Francisco Carlos Teixeira da, and Ricardo Pinto dos Santos, orgs. *Memória social dos esportes: Futebol e política: A construção de uma identidade nacional.* Vol. 2. Rio de Janeiro: Mauad Editora / FAPERJ, 2006.

Silva, Marcelino Rodrigues da. *Mil e uma noites do futebol: O Brasil moderno de Mário Filho.* Belo Horizonte: Editora UFMG, 2006.

Silva, Thomas Soares da. *Mestre Ziza: Verdades e mentiras no futebol.* Niterói: Imprensa Oficial do Estado do Rio de Janeiro, 2001.

Siqueira, André Iki. *João Saldanha: Uma vida em jogo.* São Paulo: Companhia Editora Nacional, 2007.

Siqueira, Uassyr de. "Clubes recreativos: Organização para o lazer." In *Trabalhadores na cidade: Cotidiano e cultura no Rio de Janeiro e em São Paulo, séculos XIX e XX,* organized by Elciene Azevedo, Jefferson Cano, Maria Clementina Pereira Cunha, and Sidney Chalhoub, 271–312. Campinas: Editora da Unicamp 2009.

Skidmore, Thomas E. *Black Into White: Race and Nationality in Brazilian Thought.* Durham: Duke University Press, 1993 (orig. ed. 1974).

————. *Brazil: Five Centuries of Change.* 2nd ed. New York: Oxford University Press, 2010.

————. *Politics in Brazil, 1930–1964: An Experiment in Democracy.* New York: Oxford University Press, 1967.

————. *The Politics of Military Rule in Brazil, 1964–1985.* New York: Oxford University Press, 1988.

————. "Racial Ideas and Social Policy in Brazil, 1870–1940." In *The Idea of Race in Latin America,* edited by Richard Graham, 7–36. Austin: University of Texas Press, 1990.

Smallman, Shawn C. *Fear and Memory in the Brazilian Army and Society, 1889–1954.* Chapel Hill: University of North Carolina Press, 2002.

Soares, Antonio Jorge Gonçalves. *Futebol, malandragem e identidade.* Vitória, Espírito Santo: SPDC / UFES, 1994.

————. "O racismo no futebol do Rio de Janeiro nos anos 20: Uma história de identidades." *Revista Paulista de Educação Física* 13, no. 1 (1999): 119–29.

Soares, Antonio Jorge, and Ronaldo Helal. "Futebol: A construção histórica do estilo nacional." *Revista Brasileira de Ciências do Esporte* 25, no. 1 (2003): 129–43.

Soares, Antonio Jorge, Ronaldo Helal, and Marco Antonio Santoro. "Futebol, imprensa e mídia." *Revista Fronteiras* 6, no. 1 (2004): 61–78.

Soares, Antonio Jorge Gonçalves, Marco Antonio Santoro Salvador, and Tiago Lisboa Bartholo. "A imprensa e a memória do futebol brasileiro." *Revista Portuguesa de Ciências Desportivas* 7, no. 3 (2007): 368–76.

———. "O 'futebol arte' e o 'planejamento México' na copa de 70: As memórias de Lamartine Pereira da Costa." *Movimento* 10, no. 3 (2004): 113–30.

Sócrates and Ricardo Gozzi. *Democracia corintiana: A utopia em jogo*. São Paulo: Boitempo Editorial, 2002.

Soeiro, Renato, and Elirez Bezerra da Silva. "Treinamento esportivo no Brasil, sua criação e evolução." *Congresso Brasileiro de História da Educação Física, Esporte, Lazer e Dança. As ciências sociais e a história da educação física, esporte, lazer e dança*. Ponta Grossa: Universidade Estadual de Ponta Grossa, 2002. DVD-ROM.

Soeiro, Renato Souza Pinto. "A contribuição da Escola de Educação Física do Exército para o esporte nacional: 1933 a 2000." Master's thesis, Universidade Castelo Branco, 2003.

Soeiro, Renato Souza Pinto, and Rafael Pinheiro. "Escola de Educação Física do Exército—EsEFEx." In *Atlas do Esporte no Brasil: Atlas do esporte, educação física e atividades físicas de saúde e lazer no Brasil*, edited by Lamartine DaCosta, 129. Rio de Janeiro: Shape Editora, 2005.

Soter, Ivan. *Enciclopédia da Seleção: As Seleções Brasileiras de Futebol*. Rio de Janeiro: Folha Seca, 2002.

———. *Quando a bola era redonda*. Rio de Janeiro: Folha Seca, 2008.

Souza, Denaldo Alchorne de. *O Brasil entra em campo! Construções e reconstruções da identidade nacional (1930–1947)*. São Paulo: Annablume, 2008.

Souza, Jair de, Lucia Rito, and Sérgio Sá Leitão. *Futebol-arte: A cultura e o jeito brasileiro de jogar*. São Paulo: Empresa das Artes, 1998.

Souza, Kleber Mazzieio de. *Divino: A vida e a arte de Ademir da Guia*. Rio de Janeiro: Gryphus, 2001.

Souza, Marcos Alves de. "A 'nação em chuteiras': Raça e masculinidade no futebol brasileiro." Master's thesis, Universidade de Brasília, 1996.

Stam, Robert. *Tropical Multiculturalism: A Comparative History of Race in Brazilian Cinema and Culture*. Durham: Duke University Press, 1997.

Stepan, Alfred, ed. *Democratizing Brazil: Problems of Transition and Consolidation*. New York: Oxford University Press, 1989.

Stepan, Nancy Leys. *"The Hour of Eugenics": Race, Gender, and Nation in Latin America*. Ithaca: Cornell University Press, 1991.

Streapco, João Paulo França. "'Cego é aquele que só vê a bola': O futebol em São Paulo e a formação das principais equipes paulistas: S.C. Corinthians Paulista, S.E. Palmeiras e São Paulo F.C. (1894–1942)." Master's thesis, Universidade de São Paulo, 2010.

Sweeney, Rob. "Brazil and the Rise of the Back Four: How Foreign Influences Led to the Back Four in Brazil." *The Blizzard* 2 (2011): 104–12.

Taylor, Chris. *The Beautiful Game: A Journey Through Latin American Football*. London: Victor Gollancz, 1998.

Telles, Edward E. *Race in Another America: The Significance of Skin Color in Brazil*. Princeton: Princeton University Press, 2004.

Todas as Copas: 1930 a 2006. Rio de Janeiro: Areté, 2010.

Toledo, Luiz Henrique de. "Didi: A trajetória da folha-seca no futebol de marca brasileira." In *Memória afro-brasileira*. Vol. 2, *Artes do corpo*, edited by Vagner Gonçalves da Silva, 79–121. São Paulo: Selo Negro, 2004.

———. "Estilos de jogar, estilos de pensar: Esboço comparativo entre DaMatta e Archetti." In *Visão do jogo: Antropologia das práticas esportivas,* edited by Luiz Henrique de Toledo and Carlos Eduardo Costa, 255–65. São Paulo: Editora Terceiro Nome, 2009.

———. *Lógicas no futebol.* São Paulo: Hucitec / Fapesp, 2002.

———. *No país do futebol.* Rio de Janeiro: Jorge Zahar Editor, 2000.

———. "Políticas da corporalidade: Socialidade torcedora entre 1990–2010." In *A torcida brasileira,* by Bernardo Borges Buarque de Hollanda, João M. C. Malaia, Luiz Henrique de Toledo, and Victor Andrade de Melo, 122–58. Rio de Janeiro: 7letras, 2012.

———. "Ritual sem dono, evento sem nome. Os segredos da transformação da Copa do Mundo em um megaevento." *Coletiva* 8 (April / May / June 2012). Accessed 25 September 2012. www.coletiva.org/site/index.php?option=com_k2&view=item&layout=item&id =100&Itemid=76&idrev=11.

Toledo, Luiz Henrique de, and Carlos Eduardo Costa, eds. *Visão de jogo: Antropologia das práticas esportivas.* São Paulo: Editora Terceiro Nome, 2009.

Tomlinson, Alan, and Christopher Young. "Culture, Politics, and Spectacle in the Global Sports Event—An Introduction." In *National Identity and Global Sports Events,* edited by Tomlinson and Young, 1–14. Albany: State University of New York Press, 2006.

———. *National Identity and Global Sports Events: Culture, Politics, and Spectacle in the Olympics and the Football World Cup.* Albany: State University of New York Press, 2006.

Tonini, Marcel Diego. "Negros no futebol brasileiro: Olhares e experiências de dois treinadores." *Oralidades: Revista de História Oral* 7 (January / June 2010): 125–46.

Tostão. *A perfeição não existe: Crônicas de futebol.* São Paulo: Três Estrelas, 2012.

———. *Lembranças, opiniões, reflexões sobre futebol.* São Paulo: DBA Artes Gráficas, 1997.

Touguinhó, Oldemário, and Marcus Veras. *As Copas que eu vi.* Rio de Janeiro: Relume Dumará, 1994.

Ursi, José Melquíades. *Como nascem os craques da bola.* Lance Livre, 2006.

Valls, Eduardo. *1956: Uma epopéia gaúcha no México.* Porto Alegre: WS Editor, 2005.

Varnier, Thacia Ramos et al. "A emergência dos clubes esportivos em Vitória." *Esporte e Sociedade* 7, no. 20 (2012). Accessed 4 January 2013. www.uff.br/esportesociedade/pdf/es2005.pdf.

Vasconcellos, Jorge, org. *Recados da bola: Depoimentos de doze mestres do futebol brasileiro.* São Paulo: Cosac Naify, 2010.

Velloso, Monica Pimenta. *História e modernismo.* Belo Horizonte: Autêntica Editora, 2010.

———. "Os intelectuais e a política cultural do Estado Novo." In *O Brasil republicano.* Vol. 2, *O tempo do nacional-estatismo: do início da década de 1930 ao apogeu do Estado Novo,* edited by Jorge Ferreira and Lucilia de Almeida Neves Delgado, 145–79. 5th ed. Rio de Janeiro: Civilização Brasileira, 2012.

Ventura, Roberto. *Estilo tropical: História cultural e polêmicas literárias no Brasil, 1870–1914.* São Paulo: Companhia das Letras, 1991.

Verissimo, Luis Fernando. *A eterna privação do zagueiro absoluto: As melhores crônicas de futebol, cinema e literatura.* Rio de Janeiro: Editora Objetiva, 1999.

———. "Gaúchos e cariocas." In *Outras do Analista de Bagé,* 42–44. 41st ed. Porto Alegre: L&PM, 1982.

———. *Time dos sonhos: Paixão, poesia e futebol.* Rio de Janeiro: Objetiva, 2010.

Viana, Hermano. *The Mystery of Samba: Popular Music and National Identity in Brazil.* Edited and translated by John Charles Chasteen. Chapel Hill: University of North Carolina Press, 1999.

Vieira, Cláudio. *Maracanã: O templo dos deuses brasileiros.* Rio de Janeiro: Construtora Varca Scatena, 2000.

Vilarinho, Carlos Ferreira. *Quem derrubou João Saldanha: Põe em pratos limpos os detalhes da campanha de fritura e demissão do técnico que classificou a seleção brasileira para a Copa de 1970.* Rio de Janeiro: Livrosdefutebol.com, 2010.

Vogel, Arno. "O momento feliz, reflexões sobre o futebol e o ethos nacional." In *Universo do futebol: Esporte e sociedade brasileira,* by Roberto DaMatta, Luiz Baêta Neves Flores, Simoni Lahud Guedes, and Arno Vogel, 75–115. Rio de Janeiro: Edições Pinakotheke, 1982.

Welch, Cliff. *The Seed Was Planted: The São Paulo Roots of Brazil's Rural Labor Movement, 1924–1964.* University Park: Pennsylvania State University Press, 1999.

Williams, Daryle. *Culture Wars in Brazil: The First Vargas Regime, 1930–1945.* Durham: Duke University Press, 2001.

Wilson, Jonathan. *Inverting the Pyramid: The History of Football Tactics.* London: Orion, 2009.

Winner, David. *Brilliant Orange: The Neurotic Genius of Dutch Football.* London: Bloombsbury, 2000.

Wisnik, Guilherme. "Doomed to Modernity." In *Brazil's Modern Architecture,* edited by Elisabetta Andreoli and Adrian Forty, 22–55. London: Phaidon, 2004.

Wisnik, José Miguel. "The Riddle of Brazilian Soccer: Reflections on the Emancipatory Dimensions of Culture." *Review: Literature and Arts of the Americas* 39, no. 2 (2006): 198–206.

———. *Veneno remédio: O futebol e o Brasil.* São Paulo: Companhia das Letras, 2008.

Wolfe, Joel. *Autos and Progress: The Brazilian Search for Modernity.* New York: Oxford University Press, 2010.

Xavier, Beto. *Futebol no país da música.* São Paulo: Panda Books, 2009.

Yúdice, George. *The Expediency of Culture. Uses of Culture in the Global Age.* Durham: Duke University Press, 2003.

Zagalo, [Mário Lobo]. *As lições da Copa.* Rio de Janeiro: Bloch Edições, 1971.

LITERATURA DE CORDEL

Alves, Apolônio [dos Santos]. *A vitória do Brasil tetra campeão mundial de futebol na Copa 94.* Campina Grande, Paraíba: n.p., n.d.

Barros, Homero do Rêgo. *Boletim da Copa / 82.* Recife: n.p., 1982.

Campelo, Sepalo. *A Copa 86 das oitavas ao final.* Niterói: n.p., 1986.

Leite, Barboza. *Garrincha a alegria do povo—ou a história do passarinho que jogava futebol.* Duque de Caxias, Rio de Janeiro: author, 1977.

Moreira, Flávio F. *A venda de Zico—e Mengo bi-campeão.* N.p., n.d.

Moreno, Alvarus. *A Copa que o Brasil deixou cair.* Fortaleza: Centro de Referência Cultural / Editora Henriqueta Galeno, 1982.

Nordestino, Franklin Maxado. *O Brasil entrega o ouro e ainda baixa as calças (o ex-país do futebol).* São Paulo: n.p., [1984].

Ramos, João C. *Futebol, copa e Brasil.* Feira de Santana, Bahia: n.p., 1982.

Santa Helena, Raimundo. *Flamengo campeão do mundo.* 2nd ed. Rio de Janeiro: n.p., 1981.

———. *Mané Garrincha.* Rio de Janeiro: n.p., 1983.

Santa Maria, Manoel. *Futebol e economia fracassos da teoria.* Araruama, Rio de Janeiro: author, 1990.

Silva, Gonçalo Ferreira da. *Faleceu Mané Garrincha o fabricante de Joãos.* N.p., n.d.

Souza, Paulo Teixeira de. *Vida, paixão e morte de Mané Garrincha, a alegria do povo*. Rio de Janeiro: Europa Empresa Gráfica e Editora, 1983.

Tarso, Paulo de [Airton Fontanele]. *Os cães ladram e a caravana passa—o Brasil em todas as Copas*. Fortaleza: Edições Livro Técnico, n.d.

Victtor, J. *A discussão do Pó-de-Arroz com o Urubu*. Rio de Janeiro: Academia Brasileira de Literatura de Cordel, n.d.

PERIODICALS

A Batalha (1931–32, 1938–40).

A Gazeta (1938).

A Gazeta Esportiva (1945, 1977–85).

A Gazeta Esportiva Ilustrada (1962).

Correio da Manhã (1918, 1920–21, 1923, 1938, 1946, 1958–66, 1970).

Diário Pernambucano (1938, 1974).

Esporte Ilustrado (1949–50).

Fatos e fotos. Edição especial. Copa 70, 10, no. 488. 11 June 1970.

Folha da Manhã (1949–59).

Folha da Tarde (1949–59).

Folha de São Paulo (1960–2013).

Folha Seca (1958).

Gazeta de Notícias (1907, 1948, 1955).

Istoé (1990, 1998, 2006).

Jornal da Tarde (1977–86, 1990).

Jornal do Brasil (1911, 1933, 1950–present).

Jornal do Commercio (1916).

Jornal dos Sports (1931, 1933–34, 1938, 1945, 1949, 1957–59, 1965–81).

Manchete Esportiva (1957–58, 1978).

Movimento (1975–81).

O Cruzeiro (1955–72).

O Estado de São Paulo (1919, 1921, 1950, 1966–74, 1978–2013).

O Globo (1931, 1950, 1966–82, 1994–2013).

O Imparcial (1914–16, 1919–20, 1925).

O Paiz (1921).

O Pasquim (1973–84).

Placar (1970–2013).

Sports (1919).

Última Hora (1951–64).

Veja (1968–2011).

Vida Sportiva (1917–20).

WEBSITES

Agência Pública (www.apublica.org)

Blog do Juca (http://blogdojuca.uol.com.br)

Canal 100 (www.canal100.com.br)

Coletiva (www.coletiva.org)

Hunting White Elephants/Caçando Elefantes Brancos (www.geostadia.com)

Lancenet (www.lancenet.com.br)

Ludopédio (www.ludopedio.com.br)

Observatório da Imprensa (www.observatoriodaimprensa.com.br)

Sambafoot (www.sambafoot.com/pt/)

Soccer Politics / The Politics of Football (http://sites.duke.edu/wcwp/)

Terceiro Tempo (http://terceirotempo.bol.uol.com.br)

FILMS, VIDEOS

1958: O ano em que o mundo descobriu o Brasil. Directed by José Carlos Asbeg. Brazil, 2008. DVD.

23 anos em 7 segundos: 1977—o fim do jejum Corinthiano. Directed by Di Moretti and Júlio Xavier. Brazil, 2009. DVD.

Cidade de Deus. Directed by Fernando Meirelles. Brazil, 2002. DVD.

Copa 2014: Quem ganha esse jogo? Articulação Nacional da Copa. Accessed 1 July 2013. www .youtube.com/watch?feature=player_embedded&v=HmoLZBtqQ3c#at=38.

Domínio público. Directed by Raoni Vidal. Brazil, 2012. Accessed 23 October 2012. http:// vimeo.com/49419197.

FIFA World Cup. 4 vol. VHS.

Flamengo Hexa: 100 anos de futebol. Directed by Diogo Dahl. Brazil, 2011. DVD.

Futebol. Directed by Arthur Fontes and João Moreira Salles. 4 discs. Brazil, 1998. DVD.

Fútbol México 70. Directed by Alberto Isaac. Mexico, 2006. DVD.

Garrincha, alegria do povo. Directed by Joaquim Pedro de Andrade. Brazil, 1962. DVD.

Garrincha—Estrela solitária. Directed by Milton Alencar Jr. Brazil, 2005. DVD.

Giants of Brazil: Soccer World Cup History, 1950–1998. 2008. VHS.

Ginga—A alma do futebol brasileiro. Directed by Hank Levine, Marcelo Machado, and Tocha Alves. Brazil, 2005. DVD.

Heróis de uma nação: O maior time rubro-negro de todos os tempos! Directed by Eduardo Leite and Marcelo Camargo. Brazil, 2007. DVD.

History of Soccer: The Beautiful Game. 6 vols. U.K., 2003. DVD.

Isto é Pelé. Directed by Luís Carlos Barreto and Carlos Niemeyer. Brazil, 1974. VHS.

Once in a Lifetime: The Extraordinary Story of the New York Cosmos. Directed by Paul Crowder and John Dower. U.S.A., 2006. DVD.

Passe livre: Um documento vivo do futebol brasileiro. Directed by Oswaldo Caldeira. Brazil, 1974. DVD.

Pelé eterno. Directed by Anibal Massaini Neto. Brazil, 2004. DVD.

Santos, 100 anos de futebol arte. Directed by Lina Chamie. Brazil, 2012. DVD.

Ser campeão é detalhe. Directed by Gustavo Forti Leitão and Caetano Biasi. Brazil, 2011. www.sercampeaoedetalhe.com.br/extras.html.

Telê Santana: Meio século de futebol-arte. Directed by Ana Carla Portella and Danielle Rosa. Brazil, 2009. DVD.

Tostão, a fera de ouro. Directed by Paulo Laender and Ricardo Gomes Leite. Brazil, 1970. VHS.

Um craque chamado Divino: Vida e obra de Ademir da Guia. Directed by Penna Filho. Brazil, 2007. DVD.

Zico na rede. Directed by Paulo Roscio. Brazil, 2009. DVD.

GOVERNMENT DOCUMENTS

Brazil. Decreto 23.532, 19 October 1933. *Coleção das Leis da República dos Estados Unidos do Brasil, 1933.* Vol. 4. Rio de Janeiro: Imprensa Nacional, 1934.

———. Decreto-Lei 3.199, 14 April 1941. *Diário Oficial da União,* 17 April 1941.

———. Decreto-Lei no. 594, 27 May 1969. In República Federativa do Brasil. *Coleção das Leis de 1969.* Vol. 3, *Atos da Assembléia Legislativa. Atos do Executivo. 1969,* 64–65. [Rio de Janeiro]: Departamento da Imprensa, 1969.

———. Lei 6.251, 10 August 1975. *Diário Oficial da União,* 9 October 1975.

———. Lei 8.672, 6 July 1993. *Coleção das Leis da República Federativa do Brasil,* vol. 85, no. 7 (July 1993): 1640–61. Brasília: Imprensa Nacional, 1993.

———. Lei 9.615, 24 March 1998. *Coleção das Leis da República Federativa do Brasil,* vol. 90, no. 3 (March 1998): 1332–59. Brasília: Imprensa Nacional, 1998.

———. Lei 10.257, 10 July 2001. Presidência da República, Casa Civil, Subchefia para Assuntos Jurídicos. Accessed 16 April 2013, www.planalto.gov.br/ccivil_03/leis/leis_2001/l10257.htm.

———. Lei 12.035, 1 October 2009. Presidência da República, Casa Civil, Subchefia para Assuntos Jurídicos. Accessed 15 April 2013, www.planalto.gov.br/ccivil_03/_Ato2007–2010/2009/Lei/L12035.htm.

———. *Metas e bases para a ação de governo: Pronunciamentos do Exmo. Presidente da República e do Ministro do Planejamento e Coordenação Geral na Reunião Ministerial de 10./10/70.* Brasília: n.p., 1970.

Brazil. Congresso Nacional. Comissão de Turismo e Desporto da Câmara dos Deputados and Comissão de Desenvolvimento Regional e Turismo do Senado Federal. *Relatório do Fórum Legislativo nas Cidades-Sedes da Copa do Mundo de Futebol no Brasil.* Brasília, 2012.

Brazil. Senado Federal. *Relatório da Comissão Parlamentar de Inquérito referente ao relatório final da CPI: Futebol.* Brasília: [Congresso Nacional], 2001. www2.senado.gov.br/bdsf /item/id/82013.

Brazil. Conselho Nacional de Desportos. *Deliberações.* Rio de Janeiro: Ministério da Educação e Cultura, Grupo Tarefa, 1974.

Brazil. Ministério da Educação e Cultura. *Política nacional de educação física e desportos.* Rio de Janeiro: Departamento de Documentação e Divulgação, 1975.

Brazil. Presidência da República. *I Plano Nacional de Desenvolvimento.* Brasília, 1971.

———. *II Plano Nacional de Desenvolvimento.* Brasília, 1974.

———. Castello Branco, Humberto de Alencar. *Mensagem ao Congresso Nacional.* 31 March 1965. Brasília: Departamento de Imprensa Nacional, 1965.

———. Médici, Emílio Garrastazu. *Mensagem ao Congresso Nacional.* 31 March 1971. Brasília: Departamento de Imprensa Nacional, 1971.

———. *Metas e bases para a ação de governo: Síntese.* Brasília, 1970.

Cardoso, Fernando Henrique. "O impacto da globalização nos países em desenvolvimento: riscos e oportunidades." Speech at the Colégio de México, Mexico City, 20 February 1996. Accessed 20 July 2012.http://aacastro.tripod.com/globa3.htm.

Confederação Brasileira de Futebol. *The Brazilian Football Confederation's Bid to Host the 2014 World Cup.* Brasília, 2007. Accessed September 11, 2012. http://apublica.org/wp-content/uploads/2012/05/FIFA-1.Estado-Brasileiro-Garantias-Governamentais.pdf.

———. *Relatório.* 1979–85.

Costa, Lamartine Pereira da. *Diagnóstico de educação física/desportos no Brasil.* [Rio de Janeiro]: Fundação Nacional de Matéria Escolar, 1971.

———. *Planejamento México.* Brasília: Ministério da Educação e Cultura, 1967.

———. "Sports Activities in Tropical Climates and an Experimental Solution: The Altitude Training." Brasília: International Military Sports Council, 1966.

DaCosta, Lamartine, Dirce Corrêa, Elaine Rizzuti, Bernardo Villano, and Ana Miragaya, eds. *Legados de megaeventos esportivos.* Brasília: Ministério do Esporte, 2008.

República Federativa do Brasil. *Coleção das Leis de 1969.* Vol. 3, *Atos da Assembléia Legislativa. Atos do Executivo. 1969.* [Rio de Janeiro]: Departamento da Imprensa, 1969. Decreto-Lei no. 594, 27 May 1969, 64–65.

———. *Coleção das Leis de 1976.* Vol. 5, *Atos do Poder Legislativo. 1976.* [Rio de Janeiro]: Departamento da Imprensa, 1976. Lei no. 6.354, 2 September 176, 25–28.

INDEX

Brazilian players and other celebrities are listed under the name by which they are commonly known—often a first name or nickname—with full names following in parentheses. Italicized page numbers indicate illustrations.

Garrincha and, 71; Pelé and, 81; "rice powder" nickname, 28–29; Telê as coach at, 154

Flusser, Vilém, 91

folha seca (dry leaf) technique, 62–63, 66, 81, 202

Fonseca, Guilherme de Aquino, 19

Fontes, Lourival, 36

"football athletes," 102

"Foot-ball mulato" [Mulatto Soccer] (Freyre), 45–46

"Foreign Legion" attack, 66

Formiga (Francisco Ferreira de Aguiar), 120

Formula One racing, 167, 177

France, 16, 61, 77, 114, 157, 200; French team as "Brazilians of Europe," 161, 183; Ronaldinho in, 207; victory over Brazil in World Cup (1998), 197

frango ["chicken"] (goalkeeping blunder), 13

Freyre, Gilberto, 6, 14, 45–46, 50, 238n180; influence on Mário Filho, 48–49; on Leônidas, 46–47; "mulatto football" and, 54, 62

Friedenreich, Arthur, 10, 15–16, 18, 27; early career, 26, 28; El Tigre nickname, 15, 16, 28, 34; Pelé as successor of, 91; as provocative figure, 29–30; racial identity of, 28–29

Friedenreich, Oscar, 26, 29

Friends of Zidane, 176

Friese, Hermann, 26

Fuss-ball Porto Alegre club, 19

futebol (soccer): administration of, 10; ascension in Brazil, 3, 31–32; benefits ascribed to, 32; big soccer (*futebol grande*), 21, 26; commercialization of, 191; democracy and, 140; education and, 145; equipment, 21; globalization of, 167, 190–99, 209; golden age (1958–70), 7, 10, 53, 131, 165, 216; history of, 2, 5–9, 11, 225; individuality versus organization in, 210; as key part of national culture, 14; language of, 6; military dictatorship and, 97–98, 110; "new golden period," 84; race relations in, 55; scientific revolution in, 118–19, 130, 152; small soccer (*futebol pequeno*), 22; "soccer of results" (*futebol de resultados*), 168, 169, 205; social diversity and, 22; state support for, 35. See also *jogo bonito* (beautiful game); national style of play

futebol-arte (art soccer), 8, 10, 52, 54, 77, 95, 118; Afro-Brazilians identified with, 129; under attack, 101; democracy movement and, 140; Lima (Caju) and, 125; military regime and, 98; in Nike ads, 165; *povo* identified with, 98, 99; revival of, 131, 133–34, 152; Ronaldo and, 181; Saldanha and, 103; Telê as icon of, 154, 155, 158, 160; World Cup (1986) and, 161; Zico and, 134

futebol-empresa (enterprise soccer), 150, 195, 196, 210

futebol-força (strength soccer), 8, 77, 85, 95, 118, 256n159; Afro-Brazilian traits disparaged by, 99; comeback of, 129, 131, 162, 164; individual technique downplayed by, 98; under Lazaroni, 162, 164; Pelé's departure as opportunity for, 101; Ronaldo and, 181; scientism of, 130–31; in "service of art," 101; World Cup (1982) preparations and, 160. See also scientific revolution

futsal (indoor soccer), 165, 177, 178, 200

Galeano, Eduardo, 73, 106

Ganso, Paulo Henrique (Paulo Henrique Chagas de Lima), 217

Garcia, Celso, 137

Garramuño, Florencia, 5

Garrincha (Manuel Francisco dos Santos), 56, 75, 77, 82, 100, 111, 181; as "Brazilian Sputnik," 72; children fathered by, 68; Didi's relations with, 63–64; Gaúcho compared to, 155; as hero of golden age, 10; image of tropical-modern progress and, 7; injuries suffered in games, 61; life and death of, 67–77; Lima (Caju) compared to, 125; as *mestiço*, 55; origin of name, 53; point forward position of, 112; preparations for World Cup (1958) and, 57, 60; romances of, 69

Garrincha alegria do povo [Garrincha, Joy of the People] (film, 1962), 71

Gastaldo, Édison, 217

Gaúcho, Renato (Renato Portaluppi), 101, 123–24, 155

Geada, 59

Geisel, Ernesto, 127

gender, 14

General Motors, 194

Gento (Francisco Gento López), 66

Mazzola (José João Altafini), 65

Médici, Emílio Garrastazu, 86, 87, 93; dictatorial regime of, 96–97; as soccer fan, 97–98

Mendes, Jorge, 208

Mendes, Sérgio, 166

Mendonça, Marcos Carneiro de, 30–31

Menezes, Mano, 1, 8, 217, 218

meninos da Vila (kids from the Vila), 204

Messi, Lionel, 82

mestiços (mixed Amerindian-Europeans), 47, 55, 56, 92, 223; *brasilidade* (Brazilianness) and, 6–7; condescending depictions of, 99

Mexico, 87, 93, 122, 200

Mexico City, 100, 131

Michels, Rinus, 107

Milene (Milene Domingues; wife of Ronaldo), 187, 190

Military Center for Physical Education, 102

Miller, Charles, 16–19, 20, 231n24

Miranda, Eurico, 162, 192

miscegenation, 6, 45–46, 49

Moacir (Moacir Claudino Pinto), 64

modernity, Brazilian, 4, 8, 56, 108; African-descended identity and, 54; elite soccer and, 26; European models for, 102; sporting mega-events and, 216. *See also* tropical modernity

modernization, 9, 10, 98, 102, 117; globalization and, 199; military-sponsored, 160; professionalization of administration and, 195

"money men," 209

"mongrel complex" (*complexo de vira-latas*), 55–56, 68

Moreira, Ronaldo de Assis. *See* Ronaldinho (Ronaldinho Gaúcho)

Moreno, Alvarus, 158

Moreyra, Sandro, 73

Morumbi Stadium (São Paulo), 100

MPB [Música Popular Brasileira] (Brazilian Popular Music), 119

mulatismo (mulatto-ism), 7, 45–46, 47, 49, 50

mulattoes (mixed African-Europeans), 6–7, 33, 49, 92, 223; condescending depictions of, 99; elite fans of, 50

"mulatto football," 6, 11, 14, 54

mulherengo (womanizer), 69, 173

Muller (Luiz Antônio Corrêa da Costa), 169

Mundialito (1981), 157

music, popular, 118–19

Nair (Nair Marques; wife of Garrincha), 69, 72

Nascimento, Edson Arantes do. *See* Pelé

nationalism, 14, 31, 52, 215; loss to Italy and, 160; team "fighting spirit" and, 113; wild nationalism (*ufanismo*), 55

national style of play, 10, 16, 31, 46; art/strength debate and, 95; racialization of, 54; specifically Brazilian skills, 158

NationsBank, 195

Navegantes *bairro* (Porto Alegre), 24

Negro no futebol brasileiro, O [The Black Man in Brazilian Soccer] (Rodrigues Filho), 29, 47, 48, 88

Nelinho (Manoel Rezende de Matos Cabral), 101

neoliberalism, 167, 195

Netherlands, 107–8, 132, 139, 183, 208, 217

Neto, Gagliano, 37

New Zealand, 158

Neymar (Neymar da Silva Santos Júnior), 217, 218

Nike corporation, 175, 185–86, 193–94, 197, 200; "*Joga bonito*" (Play beautiful) marketing campaign, 165; Ronaldinho in commercials of, 206

Nobiling, Hans, 18

Nogueira, Armando, 95, 166, 239n2, 247n181

Nordestino, Franklin Maxado, 130

North American Soccer League (NASL), 68

Norway, 182

Novos Baianos, Os (music group), 119

Nunes, Heleno, admiral, 103, 110, 112, 114, 125, 126, 128

O'Higgins Trophy, 57

Olaria club, 169

Oliveira, Marinho Rodrigues, 122

Olivetto, Washington, 134

Olympics: Atlanta (summer 1996), 180; London (summer 2012), 223; Mexico City (summer 1968), Black Power salute at, 127; Rio de Janeiro (summer 2016), 214, 215, 221, 224; Seoul (summer 1988), 169

Olympique de Marseille (French club), 122

"Open Letter to Brazilian Soccer" (Saldanha), 87

Operários (Workers) FC, 23